SAILING AWAY FROM WINTER

SAILING AWAY FROM WINTER

SILVER DONALD CAMERON

[A DOUGLAS GIBSON BOOK]

100

McCLELLAND & STEWART

Library and Archives Canada Cataloguing in Publication

Cameron, Silver Donald, 1937–
   Sailing away from winter : a cruise from Nova Scotia to Florida and beyond / Silver Donald Cameron.

ISBN 13: 978-0-7710-1841-1
ISBN 10: 0-7710-1841-X

1. Cameron, Silver Donald, 1937- – Travel. 2. Simmins, Marjorie-Travel. 3. Magnus (Ketch). 4. Sailing – Atlantic Coast (U.S.). 5. Sailing-Nova Scotia – Atlantic Coast. 6. Atlantic Coast (U.S.) – Description and travel. 7. Atlantic Coast (N.S.) – Description and travel. I. Title.
GV815.C28 2006   910'.9163'4   C2005-905966-4

We acknowledge the financial support of the Government of Canada through the Book Publishing Industry Development Program and that of the Government of Ontario through the Ontario Media Development Corporation's Ontario Book Initiative. We further acknowledge the support of the Canada Council for the Arts and the Ontario Arts Council for our publishing program.

Typeset in Janson by M&S, Toronto
Printed and bound in Canada

A Douglas Gibson Book

This book is printed on acid-free paper that is 100% recycled, ancient-forest friendly (100% post-consumer recycled).

McClelland & Stewart Ltd.
75 Sherbourne Street
Toronto, Ontario
M5A 2P9
www.mcclelland.com
1 2 3 4 5   10 09 08 07 06

For Marjorie,
and in memory of Leo

CONTENTS

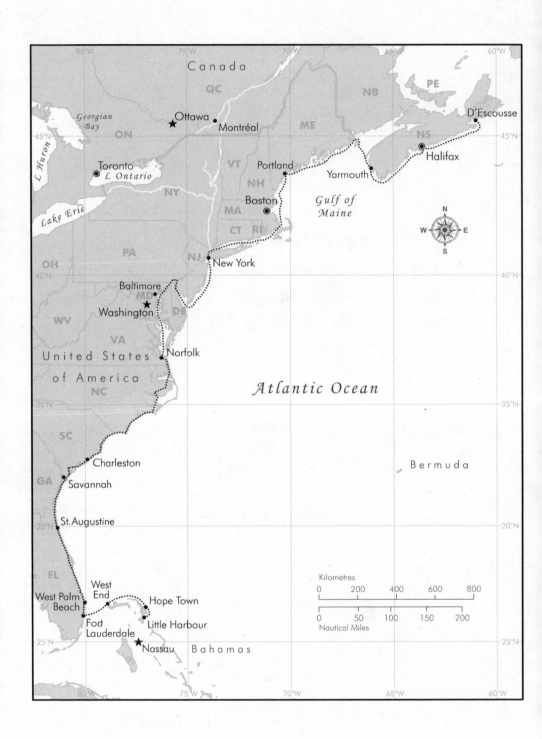

Canada

QC

Ottawa
Montréal

Georgian Bay

ON

NB

PE

D'Escousse

NS

L Huron

Toronto
L Ontario

Halifax

ME

45°N

Lake Erie

NY

VT

Portland

Yarmouth

NH

Boston

Gulf of Maine

N

W   E

S

MA

CT   RI

OH

PA

NJ

New York

40°N

Baltimore
MD

Washington

DE

WV

VA

Norfolk

United States
of America

NC

Atlantic Ocean

35°N

SC

Bermuda

GA

Charleston

Savannah

St. Augustine

20°N

FL

West
End

Hope Town

West Palm
Beach

Little Harbour

Fort
Lauderdale

Nassau

Bahamas

25°N

Kilometres
0   200   400   600   800

0   50   100   150   200
Nautical Miles

PART I

BASKETS OF DREAMS

A boat is a basket of dreams. When you acquire a boat – or, more accurately, when you are captured by a boat – dreams flower as inevitably as dandelions in the lawn.

Look deep inside the heart of that Sunday sailor in the little dinghy. Tomorrow he'll be a clerk in the drugstore again, but today – out here, with brilliant white canvas cutting curves in the deep blue sky above him, with the taste of salt spray on his lips – he's the master and commander of a ship.

He dreams of heroic ocean passages through roaring gales, exotic seabirds wheeling above the azure sea, foreign cities rising golden from the watery horizon. He imagines tropic anchorages rimmed with shocking white beaches, where the scents of frangipani and bougainvillea drift across the turquoise water. He sees himself walking through quaint villages where pink and green and yellow houses cluster around a bowl-shaped harbour, huddled under the palm trees.

Some people actually reach such anchorages, he thinks. They sail there in their own small ships. Why not me?

Count me in. I bought my first cruising sailboat in 1973, and I have dreamed those dreams ever since. I know where there really is an exquisite village of pink and green and yellow houses standing under the palm trees. A tall red-and-white candy-striped lighthouse towers above it. In front of the village lies a snug, almost-landlocked harbour. The village is two streets deep, with sand dunes standing at its back. Behind the dunes lies a long pink beach facing eastward across a coral reef to the open Atlantic.

That's Hope Town, in the Bahamas, at 26.32.49 North latitude, 76.57.59 West longitude. My home is at 45.35.29 North, 60.57.77 West, on the spruce-green harbour of D'Escousse, Nova Scotia. The course from home to Hope Town is 210 degrees true – roughly south-southwest. There's nothing much between the two villages except 1,377 miles of ocean.

But that's a long way in the open sea.

Especially for a married couple travelling with an elderly dog.

And directly against the Gulf Stream, the powerful ocean current that flows northeast all the way up the Atlantic coast of North America.

And with a skipper who is, er, far from young. People should tackle such adventures in their thirties or forties. But I have no choice. I can only do it now, in my late sixties.

But that's not a reason not to do it. And there *is* another way to get to Hope Town and the Bahamas. The Intracoastal Waterway.

"The Intracoastal Waterway?" said Marjorie, the light of my life. She was once a deckhand on a salmon fishing boat, and she later specialized in writing about the fisheries – but on the Pacific Coast, not the Atlantic. "The Bahamas?"

The Atlantic Intracoastal Waterway (ICW), I explained, is a winding, interconnected system of canals, inlets, bays, sounds, and rivers that provides a sheltered route from Norfolk, Virginia, down the U.S. coast to the Florida Keys. Cruising sailors sometimes call it "The Big Ditch." You can travel eleven hundred miles on the ICW and never enter the open sea. The route passes through some of the most beautiful and historic cities in the United States – Beaufort, Charleston, Savannah, St. Augustine. You slip along through the vast shallow sounds behind Cape Hatteras, through the Low Country of South Carolina, behind the Georgia Sea Islands, through the citrus groves of Florida's Indian River.

And the Bahamas – often confused with Bermuda or Barbados by the geographically challenged – are a six-hundred-mile spangle of tropical fragments lying in the aquamarine sea just east of Florida. Coral reefs and brilliant white beaches. Parrots and angelfish. Casinos and celebrities. Sunken treasure lost by the Spaniards and buried treasure interred by the pirates who once ruled the archipelago. Fishing villages and mysterious "blue holes" plunging deep into the earth. More than seven hundred islands, with a climate so steady and pleasant that it led someone to describe the Bahamas as "the isles of perpetual June."

That someone was George Washington, who could not tell a lie. If you can't trust George Washington, who in hell can you trust?

The westernmost islands of the Bahamas are just about fifty miles from Florida. At five knots, that's ten hours – a single day's run, in daylight. Piece of cake. Down the ICW, over to the Bahamas, spend the winter tanning ourselves under the palm trees. And I could write another sailing book about it. Maybe I could call it *The Big Ditch*. All my sailing books have had sub-titles: *Wind, Whales and Whisky: A Cape Breton Voyage. Sniffing the Coast: An Acadian Voyage. Schooner: An Offshore Voyage.*

This one could be *The Big Ditch: A Geriatric Voyage.*

"A thousand miles on this waterway," said Marjorie. "How long would it take?"

Averaging forty miles a day, just about a month.

"And it starts in Norfolk," said Marjorie. "But we're not in Norfolk. We're in Cape Breton Island. In Nova Scotia, sugar plum."

Details. A bagatelle. We'll just hop down the coast, thirty or forty miles a day, till we get to Norfolk.

"But those hops *are* in the open sea, aren't they?"

Well, yes.

"And it's a long way."

Well . . . yes. Another thousand miles at least. Well, more.

"How long would that take?"

There's a well-established pattern, I said. Nova Scotian boats usually leave in the summer and reach New York in September. They spend most of October in Chesapeake Bay waiting for the end of the hurricane season and head down the ICW around the first of November. You want to keep moving. If you're too slow, winter catches up with you and the trip becomes a chilly ordeal, not a pleasure cruise. You want to be in Florida by mid-December, and you cross to the Bahamas around Christmas or New Year's.

And then, in the spring, you turn around and go back.

"You're talking about a whole year," said Marjorie. "That's a long time."

"Not so long," I said. "It's a quarter of the time you took to get your university degree. And it ought to be an education in itself. Dolphins. Egrets. Coral reefs. Hibiscus. Alligators. Mangroves. Orchids. And think of the food. Grits and conch stews. Red snapper and dirty rice. All kinds of new food."

"Mmm," said Marjorie, who cares about food the way Audubon cared about birds. "But I worry about Leo."

Ah, yes. Leo the Wonder Whippet, Marjorie's constant companion for a dozen years and more. Our Brave and Faithful Dog. When I first met him, he was six and slender, and he ran like a bullet. Now he was an old fellow, though he still had the spirit of a gallant youth. He had arthritis, fatty deposits, congestive heart disease. He had sailed with us many times, but never for more than a week or two. And he had never relieved himself aboard. Not once.

"If we do forty-mile hops, we won't be at sea for more than about eight hours at a time," I said. "The BFD can last that long between pit stops. He lasts ten or twelve hours every night."

"It's not just pit stops," said Marjorie. "I don't want him to be miserable for months on end."

"But he'll be warm," I said. "And there won't be any snow. Remember last year?"

"Oh, yes," said Marjorie. The previous winter, Cape Breton had been buried in snow. The roads had become slit trenches through the snowbanks, and it had been impossible to walk the dog anywhere except in the trenches. Late in the season, thinking that much of the snow had melted, I had taken Leo on a shortcut across the backyard. I found myself up to my thighs in snow. When I looked down, I saw Leo – bundled in his fleecy coat, his eyes narrowed in the wind – *swimming* through the snow. His feet couldn't even reach the ground.

Why didn't you pick him up? Marjorie had cried. *Because I couldn't catch him!* I replied. *He could swim faster than I could wallow.*

"When we go south, there won't be any snow," I repeated. "And Leo will be with us twenty-four hours a day. That's what matters most to him."

"Rolling around in a berth, feeling seasick," said Marjorie. "I don't want to make him suffer in his last years."

"What about me, in my last years?" I said. "I have a couple of big things left on my life's agenda, and an extended cruise is one of them."

"Blackmail," said Marjorie. "And anyway, can we afford this trip?"

"No," I said. "But I've been saving for my old age since I was a callow stripling of forty. Well, this *is* my old age. If we have to dip into savings, so be it."

"We don't have to decide now," said Marjorie. "We can talk about it later."

A deft move. "Later," as any astute spouse knows, never comes. The resistant spouse can simply say "later" until the fever passes and the proposal fades away. And she knew I was frugal to a fault. I have survived for thirty years as a full-time freelance writer by not spending money, and by finding ways to get paid for doing the things I wanted to do anyway. I had developed a reflexive horror at the thought of dipping deeply into savings for any avoidable reason. To make the voyage, I would have to advocate a substantial excavation of the piggybank. The mind reeled. The spirit cringed. My ancestors rose up from their spirit world to remind me of the great Scottish proverb: "Money is flat, and is meant to be piled up."

In a form of marital judo, Marjorie had flipped me.

The Big Ditch, I thought. *The Voyage that Wouldn't Be.*

But you never know. There is a tide in the affairs of women, as Byron eloquently noted, and very often it's caused by scheming men. My greatest ally was the winter.

Between November and April, almost every Canadian dreams of palm-fringed beaches on tropic islands. Outside the window, snow whirls across the landscape in white tornadoes. Saltwater inlets, flowing rivers, and deep lakes all become gleaming sheets of ice. There are days when you can't leave the house. There are days when you can't *see* the house.

Marjorie detests winter. As the blizzards pounded Cape Breton, blowing the snow horizontally across the kitchen windows, I tuned in the weather channel and pointed out the agreeable temperatures in Florida, just across from the Bahamas. I started leaving books about the Bahamas lying on the coffee table. I began talking casually about the trip as though it were a firm plan, trying to create a tidal current running south.

"Pick up some extra suntan lotion for when we go south," I'd say.

"*When* we go south, Batman?" Marjorie would reply. "*If* we go south. You have a novel to write."

Sigh. I do want to write that novel, I truly do. My Artistic Conscience is not an irresistibly powerful one, but it regularly nags me to the point of heartburn. I haven't published a novel since 1980. I'm not getting younger. How long will I enjoy good health? Am I a novelist or not?

On the other hand, I tell my Artistic Conscience, one of the new novel's seven chapters is already written, and I could finish the book even if I had chronic onomatopoeia, malignant synecdoche, and incurable meiosis. But I couldn't go sailing in that condition. A fellow should sail while he can. It won't always be possible.

Donald, Donald, says the Artistic Conscience, you're hopeless. *Write* while you can. It won't always be possible. You're a booby, a tomnoddy, a whiffet. You deserve obscurity, frustration, and a nameless grave.

Shh! I said. And so we drifted along, the wind in my sails blowing southward, the Artistic Conscience conjuring up headwinds, Marjorie's doubts holding us hove-to.

In the summers, Marjorie and Leo and I cruised Cape Breton waters in *Silversark*, the twenty-seven-foot cutter I had built with my late wife, Lulu, helped by lots of friends. Because I never got along well with engines, *Silversark*'s only auxiliary power was a big set of oars. My fisherman bride was not impressed. She was accustomed to Cummins and Caterpillar diesels, not sheets of cloth hanging from sticks. She did not enjoy sitting still in a summer thunderstorm while the lightning shattered the sky. After sixteen years of lying motionless in the calms, I had come to agree with her. And I knew that a reliable engine would make a southern cruise possible. In 2001, I took a deep breath, raided the kitty, and installed a brand-new two-cylinder Yanmar in *Silversark*.

"Now," I said, "we can go south for the winter."

"We can talk about that later," said Marjorie.

Later, I thought. Seems to me I've heard that song before.

We drifted a few months longer, and then the phone rang. I heard the residual Scottish burr of my old friend Doug Gibson, then Maximum Leader of McClelland & Stewart, who modestly styled themselves "The Canadian Publishers."

"What are you writing that I can publish?" Gibson asked.

"A novel."

"Admirable," said Gibson. "But what about non-fiction?"

"Nothing."

"But surely you have a book you'd like to write."

I heard my Artistic Conscience chanting quietly in the background. I recognized the tune: "Cool Water."

> *Keep a-movin', Don . . .*
> *Dinna listen to him, Don . . .*

"Nope," I said.

"Come, come," said Gibson. "You must have *something* in the back of your mind."

"Well," I allowed, "I've just put an engine in our boat, and it *has* occurred to me to sail her south via the Intracoastal Waterway, spend the winter in the Bahamas, and write a book about that."

Aaaagh! cried the Artistic Conscience. *Dinna tell 'im that!*

"*Sailing Away from Winter!*" cried Gibson. "Great! Who's publishing this book?"

"It's not a book," I protested. "It's just a notion. A passing fancy. A foggy fantasy."

"I want you to do this trip," Gibson declared. "I'm going to make you an offer you can't refuse."

> *He's a de'il, no' a mon*, sang the Artistic Conscience,
> *And he spreads the burning sand wi' money . . .*

"I'll call you again within the week," Gibson said. "Ah, it's going to be a grand book."

The Artistic Conscience groaned. Wily old Gibson had us hooked. After a feeble resistance, I capitulated. The Artistic

Conscience huffed off, muttering about a sabbatical and a bottle of rum. I agreed to head south in July 2003, submitting a manuscript the following spring.

Defeated on the financial front, weakened by my assurances that Leo would love it, Marjorie struck a desperate blow.

"Sweetheart," she said, "*Silversark* is a wonderful boat, but she is, um, very small. She has five-foot-three-inch headroom and twenty square feet of living space. It would be like spending a year in a piano box."

A cogent point, alas. *Silversark* had a reliable engine, a double berth, good social space, a well-planned galley, and a comfortable cockpit. She drew only four feet of water, perfect for the shallow Intracoastal Waterway. She had two tables, on which two writers could set up their laptops separately. But she lacked headroom, a shower, refrigeration, and such electronic niceties as radar and autopilot.

"Dreamboat," I said, "are you telling me that we need another dreamboat?"

"No," said Marjorie. "Not unless you really do want to go south. But spending a year in a piano box is not a prospect I regard with relish."

Another boat. Ye gods.

But if I was ever to spend a winter in the Bahamas on my own boat, this might be my last opportunity. And, as the philosopher Travis McGee once noted, love is a condition in which the happiness of someone else becomes essential to your own. Making Marjorie miserable was no part of my plan.

If I chose a new boat, it would be a comfortable motor-sailer – a hybrid vessel with a powerful engine and an inside steering station. Only people who go to sea for pleasure would choose to steer from outside, in the wind and the wet. A motor-sailer can function as either a sailboat or a motorboat, depending on conditions. In the narrow waters of the ICW, we would motor a lot.

I searched the Internet. Yachtworld.com listed 51,580 yachts offered for sale by 1,499 brokers – and just 130 were motor-sailers or pilothouse sailboats between thirty-two and thirty-eight feet. Almost all were too big, too small, too awkward, or too expensive. They were located in Greece, Slovenia, Norway, Thailand, New England, and Ontario. In the heyday of fibreglass boatbuilding, motor-sailers were constructed mainly in northern Europe and the Pacific Northwest, and most of them were still there.

We weren't going to Europe to buy a boat – but British Columbia, happily, was a buyer's market. Fishing, lumbering, and mining had all tanked at once. A barbaric new government was slashing jobs and services. British Columbians were not dreaming of buying yachts. They were dreaming of solvency and survival.

The Web described several affordable pilothouse vessels in British Columbia, including a beautifully finished thirty-five-foot Endurance cutter named *Yucatan*. B.C. sailors would call her "skookum" – strongly built, powerful, substantial. She had everything we wanted. A salty B.C. friend scrutinized her and loved her. The broker answered endless questions satisfactorily. The shipping cost would be daunting, but we factored it into our offer. The owner accepted. Our credit union authorized a truly skookum loan. In late April 2002, we flew west.

Yucatan was splendid, but she had one astounding, utterly unexpected flaw. From the inside steering wheel, the helmsman could see the bow of the boat and little else. What's the point of "inside steering" if you can't actually steer from inside? We withdrew our offer.

A good sailor always has a Plan B. For two weeks we prowled the coast from Anacortes, Washington, to Halfmoon Bay, British Columbia. We did find vessels with usable pilothouses. But the enchanting Pacific Pilot was no larger than *Silversark*. The pilothouse of the New Bombay Clipper 31 seemed flimsy and the interior was inflexible. The elegant Truant 37 was too expensive. The Northsea 34 was workmanlike, spacious, and simple, and she sailed well. But her interior was finished with grey fuzzy stuff known as "mouse fur," and enormous clouds of smoke billowed from her exhaust.

We looked at centre-cockpit yachts with aft staterooms and fixed dodgers over the cockpit – the next best thing to a pilot-house. The Moody 36 was profoundly tired. The Seabird 37 had an ungainly forward cabin. The Finnsailer 29 was small, well designed, impeccably maintained. But with her stubby rig and shallow keel, she would sail like a forty-five-gallon drum.

We located a centre-cockpit Buccaneer 320 up the coast, built by Bayliner, the powerboat manufacturers. Not an inspiring pedigree. Her name was *Morning Wind*. Think about that. The Melancholy Slav who owned her would not fax us the particulars. We approached her with low expectations.

"This ees a trragedy," declared the Melancholy Slav, unlocking her. "My vife cannot sail, and I have eenjured my back. So my future ees not on the ocean. But I *luff* thees bot."

Well he might. *Morning Wind* was designed by the brilliant William Garden, and she had a more ingenious, livable interior than one would think possible in thirty-two-feet – two staterooms, two heads (each with a shower), a spacious lounge, a generous galley beside the engine room. She was well priced and well equipped.

True, she was high-sided and boxy. *Practical Sailor* once cruelly commented that these boats look like layer cakes on the water, and they are only tolerable sailers. But *Morning Wind*'s insurmountable problem was the Melancholy Slav himself. The boat had received two surveys, and he would not permit another. Nor would he arrange a sea trial.

"I have to save the name of my boat from smeer," he explained in an email. "Evil rumours will go around the coast if the boat keeps going up and down the ways without selling or out to sea for trials and don't sell."

"You see what's happening?" said Marjorie. "He *luffs* this boat. *He don't vant to sell it.* He'll put up one obstacle after another until we quit. So let's quit now."

We flew home to Nova Scotia.

"Morning wind and mouse fur," said Marjorie. "It's been an education."

Back home, we continued to trawl the Web and prowl the boat-yards. The LM 32 was lovely but pricey. The Colvic Victor was sold. The Gulfstar 36 and the steel-built Fisher knockoff had clumsy interiors. An acquaintance suggested I call King Nener, a retired airline pilot with a thirty-four-foot Dutch-built Rogger motor-sailer. Nener's health problems had kept *Seeboll* on the beach for three years, but he utterly refused to sell.

"I don't need the money," he said. "I'd only lose it on the stock market. Also, I subscribe to the belief that he who has the most toys when he dies wins!"

But he applauded my decision to buy a motor-sailer. *Seeboll*, he said, was sea-kindly and easy to handle. She had a hefty Perkins diesel. With a fair wind, her sails would shove her along at six knots. And in headwinds? Nener reminded me of the old saying that gentlemen do not beat to windward. A motor-sailer, it appeared, was an elderly gentleman's easygoing boat. Well, all right, I was apparently becoming an elderly gentleman. Still, I was not having much luck finding an elderly gentleman's boat. There just aren't many motor-sailers out there.

We found a Finnish-built Nauticat 33 lying neglected on Nova Scotia's South Shore, but – like *Morning Wind* – *Moomintroll* was only nominally for sale. Her owner, a retired businessman named Chops Viger, cheerfully conceded that he was poorly motivated. He had set his price. If I wanted to pay it, fine. If not, goodbye.

I began to see a pattern. Motor-sailer owners don't like to sell their boats, and they don't need to. They are independent spirits – pilots, professionals, entrepreneurs. They don't care if the high-testosterone crowd at the yacht club bar scorns their boats as not "real" sailboats. And they're not saving for the future. This *is* their future. They can afford to leave their boats on the beach for years, if need be. They love sailing, and they don't want motor-yachts, but they want more comfort than a traditional sail-boat provides. So they buy motor-sailers – and when they can't sail any more, they just furl the sails and motor.

And they're realists. They know their motor-sailers are their last boats. Selling will mark the end of one of the great joys of their lives. Their heads say "sell," but their hearts rebel.

What I was seeing was the love of boats and the sea, and the pain of leaving it behind. Wind in your face, the roar of the bow wave, a hammered silver sea. If you don't have to kiss it goodbye, why should you? I will be exactly the same when my turn comes. But it was not my turn yet, and I still wanted a motor-sailer.

In September, a curious boat named *Pumpkin* surfaced on the Web, a Viksund MS-33 centre-cockpit motor-sailer. I had never heard of a Viksund. But mid-September found me standing on a wharf near Detroit, cellphone to my ear.

"She's an exceedingly odd boat," I said.

"So she's off the list?" Marjorie asked glumly.

"Not yet," I said. "We'll talk again after I sail her tomorrow."

Pumpkin was built in Norway in 1973. She had all the essen-tials, and what she lacked could easily be added. She was heavily built, with deeply moulded non-skid decks, a husky rubber rub-rail, a stout canvas dodger, hand-rails everywhere. Her two short masts carried a low-aspect ketch rig. Her mizzen mast was mounted on the aft cockpit bulkhead, and her wheel on the forward one, leaving the spacious centre cockpit clear and open. She had a pointed canoe stern – a Scandinavian feature since the days of the Viking long-ships. Her only exterior wood was the bowsprit, the cabin doors, and the flagstaff. She only drew four feet of water, the same as *Silversark*. Perfect for the ICW.

But she was an exceedingly odd boat. Her inside steering was far up at the front of her cabin, behind a car-type windshield complete with wipers. Her working jib hung inside a canvas sausage, while a strangely shaped sail-bag in the rigging contained the genoa jib. Her trapezoidal portlights may once have been thought stylish. Her cockpit boasted two bar stools and a picnic table. Her after-deck was crammed with anchors, fenders, fishing-rod holders, man-overboard gear, and unused pin-rails.

Despite all the clutter, she looked solid, functional, and seakindly. Handsome, even, in a phlegmatic manner. Still, if your taste in vessels was formed by the lean, feather-lovely lines of Nova Scotia schooners, *Pumpkin* would take some getting used to.

But then, next morning, I went aboard with the owner.

I was stunned by her huge, airy interior. The salons of most sailboats are as dark as basement apartments, but the Viksund's big safety-glass windows flooded the accommodations with light. Two sets of upper and lower berths forward, and then a salon with nearly seven feet of headroom – plus a big galley with fridge and freezer, a spacious convertible dinette, a sizable head and hanging locker, and excellent visibility from her inside helm.

People could dance in the cockpit. Beneath it was a cavernous engine room with a little-used 35-hp Yanmar. Her roomy aft cabin provided a double berth and excellent access to her skookum steering gear. She was the only boat I had ever seen that seemed bigger inside than outside.

The more I looked at her, the more she looked like intelligence cast in fibreglas. And she carried a construction-quality certificate from Det Norske Veritas, the Scandinavian equivalent of Lloyd's of London.

The Yanmar purred as we motored into Lake St. Clair. The wind whistled, and the racing sailboats were reefed and heeling. With all sails set, *Pumpkin* surged along – rolling some, but scarcely heeling at all. She was more stately than sprightly, and her sails were old and baggy, but in a lusty breeze she sailed acceptably. And – even with the sails set – I could see perfectly from her inside steering station. She was not at all what I had in mind, and she needed a lot of upgrading. But she was ideal for our purposes – and she was very affordable. Back on the dock, I called home.

"Marjorie," I said, "we've found our boat."

Pumpkin arrived in Nova Scotia in early November – by truck. Two weeks later, Doug Gibson visited us, to discuss a different project that would delay *Sailing Away from Winter* until 2004.

I led Gibson to the boat-shop. He climbed up the ladder and boarded *Pumpkin*. He sat at the wheel and gazed through the windshield at the shop doors.

"Ahhh!" he said, smiling. It was all his fault, and he felt not a shred of remorse.

Rumrumrumrum ptoo!ptoo! rumrumrum ptoo! said the Yanmar, rumbling in the basement and spitting out water.

Cast off. Goodbye, goodbye!

Have a good trip! Don't worry about a thing!

And so we left, on July 21, 2004. We visited eighty-six ports. We passed through Nova Scotia, New Brunswick, Maine, New Hampshire, Massachusetts, Rhode Island, Connecticut, New York, New Jersey, Delaware, Maryland, Virginia, North Carolina, South Carolina, Georgia, Florida, and the Bahamas. Two provinces, fourteen states, three countries. My calculations indicate that I lifted the Brave and Faithful Dog on and off the boat 998 times, or possibly 1,003 times. We ran the engine for 622 hours, and travelled 3,087 miles. We did not use the sails very much.

We had mishaps and trials. We were cold, hot, bored, delighted, frightened, amused, and tired. The weather was cold, hot, boring, wet, dry, delightful, and frightening. We were flicked by the tails of four hurricanes. We ran aground and floated off, damaged the boat and repaired it, entertained guests, and were entertained ashore. The people we met were boring, delightful, adventurous, nutty, menacing, and amusing. We met divers, philosophers, airline pilots, insurance brokers, antique hippies, diplomats, veterinarians, publishers, sculptors, lawyers, belly dancers, cops, and tycoons.

We saw swamps, cities, hamlets, alligators, wild horses, pelicans, manatees, and other wildlife. People were fishing for cod, mackerel, menhaden, snook, shrimp, bonefish, lobster, and grouper. The dog lifted his leg on spruce, maple, myrtle, casuarina, palmetto, live oak, bougainvillea, and coconut palm.

We were away for 285 days. The boat wanted to stay down south for the summer, and we consented. Our overloaded car reached Nova Scotia on May 2, 2005. The skipper and the mate were lighter, browner, older, and younger. The BFD was so spry and eager that he seemed like a puppy, though he was approaching his fourteenth birthday and was still deaf, lumpy, arthritic, wheezing, and partly blind.

The End.

Now you know the narrative. Stick around and we'll get to the story.

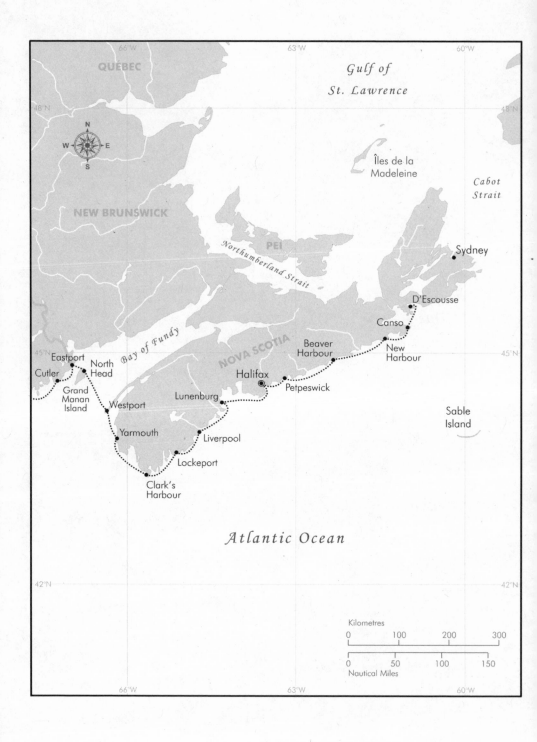

PART II

NEW SCOTLAND

From Isle Madame, where we live, you can see the flashing cherry on the top of a police car in Canso, on the mainland of Nova Scotia. Canso is on the *south* side of Chedabucto Bay.

Sailing for Canso, we were southbound, at last.

Edwin DeWolf crossed the bay with us – good old Edwin, a fine carpenter, an inspired fixer of almost anything, an irrepressibly cheerful companion. For thirty years we've worked together, played together, renovated houses, attended weddings and funerals, built boats and buildings. Every project I undertake relies heavily on his good sense, his inventiveness, and his big, open heart. His work was everywhere around us – the new countertop, the galley cabinets, the new locker lids. It was good to see him enjoying the boat as a boat, not a project in the shop.

We motored over to Canso on a monochrome morning – grey fog, grey sea, grey sky. Fragments of Isle Madame appeared, slipped away, emerged again. The wind was light, but *Magnus* rolled relentlessly in the leftover slop of an earlier wind. I had tied the dinghy on its side across the stern, and the rolling waves were tugging and tearing at it. Must do something about that.

Grey though it was, our fog-bound world was rich with life. Seals poked their heads up to look at us, and the sleek backs of porpoises rose and fell nearby. Gannets, petrels, gulls, and terns swung through the air and rode on the water.

"Look!" said Edwin, pointing. Tall spouts of mist rose and fell from the dull surface, perhaps a mile away. Whales, possibly a dozen of them, too far off to identify.

While Edwin and Marjorie handled the boat, I hunched in the skipper's chair below, poring over the electronic instruments, learning to read the radar, watching our progress on the computer screen, coming on deck from time to time to look around.

A black-and-white buoy emerged from the mist. The Canso fairway buoy? No, not yet. This one belonged to the buoyage system that guides supertankers and gypsum carriers up the Strait of Canso to the industrial terminals in Port Hawkesbury. The buoy fell into the mist astern. A few minutes later another one appeared. We altered course to the southward, and the low rocky shores around Canso gradually took shape. Throttling down, we slipped between the reefs and stony islets and made our way to the little marina.

Canso is unimpressive, its modest wooden houses flung down among the folds of the bedrock more or less at random, its waterfront dominated by commercial wharves and fish plants. History finds Canso and forgets it, and then finds it and forgets it again.

Cape Canso is the most easterly point on the mainland of North America, the place where the continent thrusts out a long rocky spine of land before foundering in the North Atlantic. When European fishermen arrived in the sixteenth century, they saw the Canso Peninsula as a big stony wharf jutting into an ocean of fish. Canso has been a major fishing port ever since. For most of that time, the fishery was a feudal undertaking, mercilessly exploiting fish, fishermen, and shore workers alike while piling up huge profits for its owners. I first came to Canso in

1972, to write a book about the bitter strike mounted by the town's fishermen simply for the right to form a union.[1] They lost the battle, but won the war; their chosen union was never certified, but a more docile union did gain recognition, and the fishery has been unionized ever since.

It was a pyrrhic victory. Industrial overfishing subsequently wiped out the fishery. The cod and haddock that once seemed inexhaustible are on the verge of extinction, and even once-despised species like pollock and redfish survive only in remnant populations. A bit of fishing still goes on, but the closure of the Atlantic ground fishery has flattened the town's economy.

Canso's location gave it a second industry; it was the North American terminus of the first transatlantic telegraph cables. But the undersea cable industry has also vanished, superseded by satellites and microwaves.

So Canso has been trying to reinvent itself. It holds an annual folk festival dedicated to the memory of Stan Rogers, Canada's national folksinging icon, whose family came from Canso and the nearby villages. Just thirty-two when he died in an airplane accident in 1983, he left a haunting body of work behind him.

A year earlier, on one of our sea trials, we had sailed over to Stanfest – but we skipped the music and stayed on the boat with Leo, who was having a very bad day. He was twelve years old, gimpy from arthritis and lumpy with fat deposits. He had congestive heart failure, and only a steady diet of medication prevented his lungs from filling with fluid. On that stifling, muggy day, he could hardly get his breath at all. He jumped restlessly about the boat, onto the dock, back onto the boat. He panted quickly, wheezing and rasping. His brave, observant eyes were bright with fear.

We gave him water, food, shade, quiet talk. We rigged a windsail to ventilate the boat. When he wanted to walk, we walked.

---

[1] Silver Donald Cameron, *The Education of Everett Richardson: The Nova Scotia Fishermen's Strike, 1971-72.* Toronto: McClelland & Stewart, 1977.

When he wanted to be still, we sat. And we talked about our own sadness. We could hardly bear the knowledge that our days with this eager, generous-hearted companion were inexorably drawing to an end.

"If we take him south," said Marjorie, "I'm afraid he won't come back." Her voice broke. "I don't want to bury him in some strange place, some place he's never known."

I nodded glumly. But you can't permit the fear of death to prevent you from living. And look: here was Leo a year later, back in Canso again, still with his old-dog infirmities, but looking and feeling better than he had in months.

In Canso, Edwin was only ten sea miles from home, but his wife, Joan, had driven a hundred miles around the bay to collect him. The four of us tidied the boat and had a drink, staving off the moment of farewell. When they drove away, Marjorie and I were truly on our own.

"*Magnus*?" called a voice from the next boat. "Silver Donald Cameron?"

I looked over. The elegant pilothouse sloop next to us was a Nautilus 36, a model I had seriously considered when we were looking for our new boat. The voice belonged to Dr. David Nettleship, a biologist I knew. He had followed the story of *Magnus*'s discovery and refit both in my Halifax newspaper columns and in *Good Old Boat* magazine, and he was madly curious to see her.

I was equally curious to see the Nautilus. Based in Halifax, she was skippered by Ron Hatcher and crewed by David Nettleship and Dave Wilson. The three had competed in the gruelling three-hundred-mile open-ocean race from Halifax to the French islands of St. Pierre and Miquelon. Their engine had died on the return trip, when they were motor-sailing against thirty-five-knot winds, so they had taken refuge in Canso and left the boat there for repairs. Now they were back to ferry her home. Like us, they were leaving in the morning, which was predicted to be grey and cold. Would they, I asked, operate the boat from the pilothouse?

No, they said. The inside helm wasn't really very useful. They'd sail the boat from the cockpit. Wouldn't I?

I hoped not. A midsummer day in Canso is like a raw autumn day elsewhere. To seaward, the continent slips grudgingly into the cold Labrador Current, its bedrock poking erratically through the surf for more than five miles in a tangle of brine-washed boulders and stubborn low islands bearing stubborn low spruce trees. These are the Canso Ledges, which also include numerous submerged "sunkers" – rocks that the racing tides may never uncover, which announce their presence only by foaming breakers whenever the sea is up. Shag Rock Breaker, Keeper Reef, The Old Man, The Washball, Gannet Ledges, The Roaring Bull.

Foggy and exposed, the Canso Ledges are exactly the type of place I had in mind when I insisted that our new boat should have an inside helm. A narrow waterway named Andrew Passage twists through the ledges, and I had never gone that way – on my only earlier passage through Canso, I had prudently sailed outside in the open sea – but this time I wanted to take the inside route, and I intended to steer from inside too.

Our neighbours left at 8:00 a.m., motoring around the rock breakwater and into the mist. They were steering from outside. It was July 25, for heaven's sake, and they were dressed in watch caps, rubber boots, and heavy orange anti-exposure coveralls. Their destination was Liscomb, sixty miles away. That was too far for us; we would be happy to reach one of the tiny fishing ports on the southwestern side of the Canso Peninsula.

We followed at ten, after I had adjusted the dinghy and done other minor chores. Andrew Passage was indeed an intricate and tortuous little strip of water, with breaking rocks and reefs all around. In the slate-grey wind-less morning, the Canso Ledges felt remote and wild, beyond the reach of settlement, even though the channel was marked by well-placed buoys and occasional fishing camps stood perched on the rocks. This ragged coast has always been a smuggler's dream, from the French and English colonists in the eighteenth century to the high-tech drug-runners of the present, so it was no surprise when a government plane buzzed low overhead.

. In a golf shirt and jeans, I sat in the skipper's chair behind the windshield. With the GPS, computer, and radar in front of me, I steered through the tight channel as easily and comfortably as if I had been driving down a winding roadway in a car.

We emerged from Andrew Passage, turned southwest, and ran down the coast past a dozen bays and a score of coves, marked by buoys and lighthouses and guarded by a spatter of rocky islands. Little Dover, Louse Harbour, Port Howe.

I last sailed the coastline west of Cape Canso in 1972. In those days, the shore was dotted with genuine fishing villages, and small boats put out every morning to pursue the cod and haddock that still schooled off the coast. These were the "inshore fishermen," the backbone of Atlantic Canada, the people whose presence gave the region its identity, its income and its politics, its songs and stories.

Thirty years ago, I had the company of small fishing boats all around me, nuzzled in beside the shore and creeping along the horizon. Now there were no boats out here at all. The only remaining inshore fishery was for lobster, whose heavily regulated stocks did seem to be holding their own. But the two-month lobster season in Guysborough County was over by the end of July, and the only boats out here now were pleasure boats like our own.

Rumrumrumrum ptoo!ptoo! rumrumrum ptoo! said the Yanmar down below, as we motored along the coast from Canso.

When we were upgrading *Pumpkin*, I thought of relocating the batteries into the bilge, to get the weight down. But – search as I might – I could find no hatch, no access of any kind. Should I saw a hole in the cabin floor? I needed advice. But who knew anything about a Viksund? Could there be an owners' association somewhere?

I did a Web search for "Viksund." Blink! Up came a site called *Viksund Båt AS – Berømt for trygghet til havs*. Easy for you to say, I thought. But it appeared to be the Viksund company's own website, and – by the look of the site – Viksund was still building boats. Maybe the company could put me in touch with other owners, or the designer. Maybe I could get a copy of the original owner's manual. I wrote an email. Back came a message:

> *The name of your boat is Viksund 31 Goldfish, a ketch rigged motor sailer. The boat was produced from 1971 to 1980. I do not know exact how many of these boat it was build but I presume about 200. Approx 25 of these was exported to the US. The design was the yard's own.*
>
> *There is no owners manual to this boat, we did not use this in those days.*
>
> *The hull for this type of boat was used as a motorsailer and as a fishing boat. In 1975 a Norwegian explorer (Ragnar Thorseth) sailed one of the boats from Norway to Iceland, Greenland, Labrador (Baffin Land) and to New York.*
>
> *With this boat you can go where ever you want to.*
>
> *Best Regard*
>
> *Rune Viksund.*

Rune Viksund was the owner, and the son of the founder. Established in 1966, Viksund was among the first fibreglass boatbuilders in Scandinavia. It builds boats in Norway, Sweden, and Sri Lanka. It has now produced six thousand boats, including fishing boats for Asia and Africa, power yachts for Europe, and rescue vessels for the Greenland coast guard. The reason I couldn't get into the bilge, Rune Viksund explained, was that the sealed floor was "meant as a double bottom." If a rock pierced the hull, the boat would not sink. Double bottoms are common on big ships, but I had never heard of one on a yacht.

The more we tore into *Pumpkin*, the more impressed we were. In addition to the double bottom, she had watertight bulkheads on either side of the engine room. All the lockers were glassed solidly to the hull, giving her many additional watertight compartments. She would be a very difficult boat to sink. And the fibreglass was massive, especially down at the bilge.

Rune Viksund remarked that Ragnar Thorseth had written a book about his voyage – in English. After much sleuthing and pleading, I got a copy of the book. Thorseth's *Cleng Peerson* was the fishing boat version, and his voyage had been truly remarkable. He spent days in howling gales off Greenland, and more days poking through drifting ice. At one point, Thorseth smashed an ice floe so hard that he dislodged the bulkheads and bent both barrels of a stowed shotgun – without seriously harming the hull. On another occasion, he ran his boat on the rocks far up an uninhabited river in Baffin Island. The nearest human beings were perhaps five hundred Arctic miles away. Gunning the engine, winching on anchor lines, Thorseth put an unbelievable strain on his boat – but she came off.

I had lucked out. *Pumpkin* was a hell of a boat, and by May 2003, she had been largely renewed. But she needed a distinctive and dignified name – something short and clear, easy to understand on a crackling marine radio. The new name also had to be unique, because she was being registered as a Canadian ship, and the Government of Canada would not accept any ship name that was already in use.

Perhaps we could find a noble name somewhere in her Viking heritage. Alas, most Norwegian names do not fall musically on the English ear. Dagmar, Hedwig, Yngeve, Freydis, Borghild. We looked at the names of the Norse gods. There must be plenty of ships named Thor. But what about the others? Odhinn, Freya, Tyr? Hmm . . . Heimdall? Frigga? Maybe not.

But seven kings of Norway and two kings of Sweden had been named Magnus, which descends from the Latin *magnus*, meaning "great." That's the root of such attractive English terms as *magnanimous*, *magnificent*, and *Magna Carta*. Two Norwegian kings seemed particularly admirable. Magnus I, or "Magnus the Good" (1024–47), fostered domestic peace and repealed the harsh laws of his predecessors. Magnus VI, or "Magnus the Law-mender" (1238–80), made peace with Scotland – and also revised the laws to embody the idea that crime is an offence against the state, not the individual, and therefore is not a matter for personal vengeance. That idea is really the foundation of modern civil society. Under Magnus VI, says our encyclopedia, "medieval Norway reached its greatest flowering and enjoyed peace and prosperity."

My kind of man. I even found a knot called the "magnus hitch," a variant of the rolling hitch. I eventually learned to tie it.

The Government of Canada approved the name. The Norwegian vessel from the United States had become the Canadian ship *Magnus*, registered in Halifax. But what about the sea gods? Traditionally, changing a ship's name is bad luck. Could some hallowed ritual repel the bad karma?

The question propelled our friend Peter Bonsey into a frenzy of research. He and Sylvia had sailed their boat, *Can Pyran*, to D'Escousse from England in 2002, and greatly enriched the village by their presence over the winter. They had already arranged for *Can Pyran* to be blessed by our priest, Father John J. Macdonald, suggesting that our ship also be included. Now Peter discovered an Interdenominational Denaming Ceremony devised by John Vigor, a well-known yachting writer.

The first requirement, says Vigor, is that the ship be cleansed of her old name. Every trace of the old name must be expunged – from the hull, logbook, lifebuoys, dinghy, everything. When no trace of "Pumpkin" remained, we called a group of friends together inside the shop. Father John J. stood with me on the bow of the vessel and spoke a Christian blessing. With great Vigor, I invoked the grace and favour of the ancient sea gods, Neptune and Aeolus. If we had known other gods, we would have called on them too. We wanted ecumenical and inclusive approval. *Magnus* was going on a long voyage.

I poured a tot of rum for Neptune, and spilled it on the bow. Then we shared the bottle with all hands. Our neighbour Greg Silver, a graphic designer, presented us with new vinyl nameplates. On launching day, the crane operator slipped two great straps under the boat and lifted her off her trailer. As she hung in the air, Marjorie picked up a bottle of champagne wrapped in masking tape.

"I christen this ship *Magnus*," she said. "May God bless her and all who sail in her."

She swung the bottle, and it bounced back, unbroken. She swung again. The bottle bounced again. She was horrified. A third failure would be very bad luck. She handed me the bottle. I aimed its thin side at a stainless-steel fitting on the bow, putting all my hopes and anxieties and frustrations into it. The bottle smashed into a million pieces, and champagne spurted across the wharf. The crane lifted the boat and set it gently in the water.

Reincarnation, I thought. Right before our eyes.

Magnus trundled on down the coast from Andrew Passage, past White Head, Raspberry Cove, Witch Cove, and the wide entrance to Tor Bay, where I once set a mournful scene in a novel.[2] I had

---

[2] Silver Donald Cameron, *Dragon Lady*. Toronto: McClelland & Stewart, 1980; Seal paperback, 1981.

hoped to reach Port Bickerton, fifteen miles farther on, but the grey ocean felt vast and lonely, and by 2:30 we were ready to end our first day alone. Off the entrance to New Harbour we turned in, steering for its fairway buoy. I looked at Marjorie and grinned.

"The course," I said, "is three-three-eight."

"You didn't look it up," said Marjorie.

"I don't have to," I smiled. "I remember it."

The memory was thirty-two years old. In 1972, I was sailing home to Isle Madame in my first cruising boat, a small wooden schooner named *Hirondelle*, built in Lunenburg. My very first cruise was a 250-mile trip from Lunenburg to Cape Breton. My crew and I had departed that morning from Isaac's Harbour, ten miles west. The morning was foggy, but the forecast said it would clear. It did not. In fact, it thickened. And it was windy. In most places, wind and fog don't occur together. In Nova Scotia, they do.

I steered the little schooner along behind a chain of offshore islands, my eye constantly flickering to my watch, my compass, and my chart, squinting to see the tips of the islands as we passed them in the fog. Lighthouse Point: check. Burke Point: check. We seemed to be doing about three knots, so Beach Point should appear in about twenty minutes. And yes, there it was.

The old make-and-break gas engine died, as it habitually did. We continued under sail, as we habitually did. After feeling our way along for a couple of hours, I calculated that we should be seeing the New Harbour fairway buoy. The fog was thicker than ever. By the time the buoy was eight minutes overdue, the skipper was visibly worried.

"What does it look like?" asked one of my companions.

"A steel skeleton tower about fifteen feet tall, floating on a steel disk," I muttered, glancing down at my chart.

"Like that?"

I looked up, startled. The shadowy outline of the buoy was dead ahead. If I hadn't veered, I'd have hit it.

Enough, I thought. We're turning in. I laid out the course with my parallel rules on the paper chart.

"Steer 338 degrees," I said. "Rigidly."

The schooner swung onto the new course, and we soon heard waves breaking on the shoreline – first to port, then to starboard, and finally dead ahead. Peering over the bow, we could see a faint line of white foam. We dropped the anchor in about eight feet of water. A fisherman spied us and towed us to the wharf. The navigation and steering had been almost too good. We had sailed all the way to the head of the harbour, steering right between a harbour buoy and the end of the wharf without seeing either one.

That night, a jolly group of fishermen gathered aboard the little schooner. In twenty minutes they had the engine running again, and the rest of the evening vanished in rum, storytelling, and song. New Harbour was a tiny place even then, but it had a lovely energy. It had its own small role in the world, and its capable, open-hearted people lived good quiet lives, with a fair degree of contentment.

That was thirty years ago. Now we were steering 338 degrees again, passing between the same buoy and breakwater, tying up to the same wharf. But New Harbour looked like a ghost town. A handful of fishing boats lay on their moorings, and a small cruising sailboat was tied to the dock. When we went for a walk, the village was so quiet as to be eerie – a dozen houses, nobody around, scarcely a dog barking. New Harbour felt like a place passed by and abandoned. I found myself humming Stan Rogers's "Make and Break Harbour," an elegiac song about this very shoreline:

> *In Make and Break Harbour, the boats are so few –*
> *Too many are pulled up and rotten.*
> *Most houses stand empty. Old nets, hung to dry,*
> *Are blown away, lost, and forgotten . . .*

New Harbour is a stark and beautiful spot, with sweeping views of the coast and the empty ocean – but when there are no fish, there's no reason to be here. In another thirty years, there may not be anyone living in New Harbour at all.

Rumrumrumrum ptoo!ptoo! rumrumrum ptoo! said the Yanmar, running down the coast past Country Harbour, Spanish Ship Bay, Ecum Secum, Necum Teuch. Grey seas, grey skies, calm weather. The boat was being steered by the autopilot, which is like an extra crew member. We made a lot of improvements to this boat . . .

Suddenly I'm back in the shop, and we're singing. *Remember that rainy evening I threw you out* . . . That's Edwin, on the shop floor, standing at the workbench, cutting the sliding doors for the new medicine cabinet in the head.

With nothin' but a fine-tooth comb . . . That's Bill, up in the main salon, kneeling on the seats in the dinette, installing two of the six new reading lights.

I know I'm to blame, well, ain't that a shame . . . That's me, up in the cockpit, trial-fitting the new exterior instrument panel. And now, all together:

BILL BAILEY, WON'T YOU PLEASE COME HOME?

Bobby Darin, 1960. We all remember. We all know the words. We are all old farts now. Bill and I are sixty-five, and Edwin, the young feller in the shop, is fifty-nine.

I am as happy building a boat or working on one as I am sailing one. A writer's life is lonely – hour after hour of sitting alone at a desk, staring out the window and wrestling with language. By suppertime, if the day has gone well, you've put some marks on four or five pieces of paper. It doesn't seem like much.

A boatbuilder's life, by contrast, is often sociable. You need other people to muscle timbers around, lift heavy weights, pass tubes and cables through inaccessible places. And you need to bring in people with specialized skills from time to time – like my brother-in-law, Terry Terrio, a fine welder, or Boyd Babin, our machinist. Or Claude Martell, who supplied and installed a whole suite of new Raymarine electronics – radar, GPS, speed and depth gauges, VHF radio and autopilot. Or Eddie and Brenda Rideout, who upgraded and replaced various cushions and mattresses.

And I am one of those lucky men who actually owns the workshop of his dreams. Many of the happiest hours of my life have been spent there. The shop is an arch-shaped building forty feet long, sixteen feet wide, seventeen feet high. It could serve very nicely as a small church. Red Green, eat your heart out.

"Don!" cries Bill. "Don't pick up that battery! Leave the heavy liftin' to the young feller!"

Bill Martin is a retired truck driver and all-round mechanic who lives with his wife in a tiny apartment in the senior citizens' residence next door to me. He is not happy there. Bill has been an active, hard-working man all his life, and the seniors' complex doesn't encourage its residents to do anything but watch TV. If you weren't old when you moved there, the place would soon make you old. There's no workshop, no recreation room, no library, no gym, no place to put in a garden.

But my shop is right across the road – and I use it intensely, but infrequently. So Bill does his own projects there, and also works on mine. Greg Silver also has a spacious shop, and Bill hangs out there too. He's a wonderfully good-humoured man, a great companion, and he knows a hell of a lot about engines, transmissions, and electricity. Bill is allergic to paint, but Edwin is a tolerable painter as well as a splendid carpenter and a remarkable problem-solver.

What I bring to the team is a knowledge of boats. For example, I know that people have drowned at anchor because they fell in the water and couldn't get back aboard – so I insisted on a swim platform at the stern, with a flip-down ladder. I knew that the locker tops under the seat cushions needed to be locked in place so they would stay put even if the boat were rolled over. I knew we needed a safety belt to keep the cook from falling backward away from the stove, and a crash bar to prevent the poor soul from falling forward into the soup.

Between the three of us, we had a pretty fair suite of skills. We even knew the same old songs.

> *There is a tavern in the town –*
> *In the town!*
> *And there my true love sits him down*
> *Sits him dowwnnn . . .*

Years before, Edwin had actually built the shop, with a little help from me. When it came time to shoehorn *Pumpkin* (not yet *Magnus*) into it – through doors that were six inches too narrow – Edwin figured out how to do it.

"We'll take off one of the doors and the piece of the wall it's hinged onto," he said. "We'll drop the whole thing down with a tackle and roll 'er aside on pipes. Then we'll roll 'er back when the boat's in, and stand 'er up again. Why won't that work?"

It would. It did. When Terry finished beefing up the trailer, the boat slipped in as slick as an eel in a bucket of liver.

Greg Silver has a name for this kind of thing: rustic engineering. Our rural neighbours are engineers by reflex. They know their environment intimately, and they know how to harness its forces. Lash two boats together at low tide and hitch your mooring line to a beam across them. The tide will lift the mooring off the bottom. Use the winter ice as a highway, or a working platform. That's how you get building materials to an island. I tied my boat once at a rugged private wharf – heavy pilings driven into the bottom, with a stout deck bolted to them. How were the pilings driven? The owner laughed. "With a backhoe, through the ice," he said.

Rustic Engineers use ancient and basic tools – wedges and levers to drive things apart, screw clamps and twisted ropes (known as "Spanish windlasses") to pull them together, rope and chain tackles and jacks and tripods to lift them up, rollers and skids to move them along.

There's always a way – and if the first way doesn't work, there's a second, and a third. If you don't know how to do it, your neighbour does. Someone in the village has the tools you need; just ask around. The greatest tool of all is the community itself, with its pool of knowledge and imagination. With that, you can certainly move boats. And wharves. And houses. And probably mountains as well.

When we levelled the boat inside the shop – *Put a jack under 'er! Pry up! Let 'er down easy on the blocks!* – many gallons of water seeped out around the bolts of the fitting that held the bottom of the rudder. Very alarming. Wherever water can leak out, it can leak in. Where was all that water coming from? Presumably from a leak around the bolts. So we removed all the bolts, squeezed goop into the holes, slathered goop around the bolts, and reinserted them. We pulled off the tattered-looking rudder too and sent it off to be rebuilt.

When we unloaded the boat, Marjorie and I found we had a new problem. Cavernous though it was, the shop was too small.

Pumpkin's previous owner, a doctor, was giving up boating altogether, and he had loaded all his boating and fishing equipment inside her. *Pumpkin* was utterly crammed with stuff. Seven anchors, seven boat-hooks, ten pumps, bags of sails, boxes of cutlery and dishes, foul-weather gear, life jackets, hip waders, fishing tackle, cushions, spotlights and flashlights, navigation books, miles of stiff old rope, extra blocks, hiking sticks, folding bicycles, wires and switches, rigging fittings, bolts and screws. The doctor had even donated his shaving kit, a hip flask of whisky, and his medical bag. How many boats come equipped with a stethoscope? It was like Christmas.

But *Pumpkin* herself filled most of the shop. With The Stuff out of the boat and sitting on the floor, the shop was an obstacle course.

"Well," I said, "we'll get another shed."

"Another?" said Marjorie. At one point I owned seven sheds, which she thought excessive. But we had sold several properties, and now I was down to three measly sheds. Clearly insufficient.

"Terrance Fortune is selling a shed. Big one, too, sixteen by twenty."

"How will you get it up by the shop?" asked Marjorie.

"Not a problem," I said. "Rustic engineering."

Under the direction of Claude Poirier, who runs the garage, and has the largest collection of sheds in the village, we jacked the new shed up on blocks, slipped the trunks of three saplings underneath it, and called Glenn Marchand, who owns a backhoe.

The backhoe is the Rustic Engineer's Ultimate Persuader. Backhoes are for digging, but they can also lift and hammer and carry and pull heavy weights. They can reach over fences, down into the water, and up into the trees. Standing in the bucket, a man can reach twenty feet into the air. Backhoes can hoist themselves over ditches on their booms and buckets without even using their wheels. I've seen them raise buildings, pull down chimneys, launch and retrieve big boats, transplant fair-sized trees, clear land, straighten bent metal, lift and lower masts.

Red Green would trade one of his fingers for a backhoe. Anyone would.

Glenn hooked his backhoe to the saplings under the new shed. The engine roared. The shed lurched forward. Glenn dragged the whole contraption down the main road and pushed it into place beside the shop. We levelled it up on concrete blocks.

"Where I come from," said Marjorie, shaking her head, "when a building is built, it stays put. Not here." But the old farts were already back at the shed, singing.

In Dublin's fair city
Where girls are so pretty

Edwin built a pedway – well, a shedway – connecting the shop to the shed, and then went away to renovate houses. Bill and I clambered up on the boat, removed the antiquated radio and navigation equipment, overhauled mysterious pumps, and replaced antique hoses. We removed the marine toilet, fibreglassed the intake and outlet holes in the hull, and installed a waterless composting toilet called an Air Head.

We removed a couple of old instrument sensors poking through the bilge near the engine and filled those holes too. Bill overhauled the interior lights and added seven new ones. He replaced all the twelve-volt wiring, discarding miles of brittle wire. I replaced all the shore-power wiring, added four new outlets, and rebuilt the two steering stations to accept the new Raymarine electronics instruments – VHF radio, depth and speed gauge, radar, GPS, and autopilot.

I ordered an electric anchor windlass. A geriatric sailor shouldn't be trying to pull up great lengths of anchor chain and a heavy anchor. I bought Spurs for the propeller, to cut off any old fishing lines and junk that got tangled up in it. We replaced the old hand-pump faucets, and we added a pressure water system. We installed a shower in the head, and a new pressure kerosene stove.

Oh, dear, what can the matter be?
Seven old ladies locked in a lavat'ry
They were there from Sunday to Saturday
Nobody knew they were there . . .

The spring came on. Launch day approached. We lured Edwin away from his renovations and back to the shop, and got him rebuilding the galley. Terry brought his arc-welder and transformed a jumble of stainless steel from Wilf's Salvage into a husky swim platform and boarding ladder. Marjorie painted the interior, recovered the seat backs, and laid a new carpet. We reinstalled the rudder, bolted down the windlass, and built storage space for a hundred metres of anchor chain. Sandy Macmillan, our sail-maker, converted our jib to roller-furling and provided a new tanbark mainsail and mizzen.

I wrote a lot of cheques.

As the countdown to launch day began, Jim Phillips arrived from Charlottetown to install our new diesel-fired Espar hot-water furnace. The new furnace would heat the two cabins independently, and would also heat the hot water. The system even included a heated towel-rail.

As the rest of us ran through our last-minute chores, Jim was all over the boat, connecting hoses and wires, cutting holes and installing fans and radiators. When he started the furnace up, it sounded like a jet engine inside the shop. The system was being balky, with pesky air bubbles repeatedly needing to be bled from the water lines. We strung a garden hose from a nearby house. As Jim filled and drained the hot-water lines, the bilges filled up with water.

Launch time. We took the front wall of the shop apart, jacked up the trailer, and took out the blocks that had supported the boat all winter. The boat tilted. Water poured out of the keel – from the very same bolts we had bedded so carefully in the autumn.

If water can pour out of the boat, water can pour in. My heart sank like a stone. If we put her in the water like this, she would leak like a colander.

We'll have to stop the launch. We would have to cut the keel open, find the leak, and fill the gap with resin. After that we would have to reglass the keel. It would take a vast amount of time – and money. We might not get the boat launched this summer.

"Wait, now," said Edwin. "What if we foamed it? If we squirt expanding foam in through the bolt-holes, it's going to push its

way back up where the water came down, and fill all the cracks.
Why won't that work?"

Worth trying. The crane was due on the wharf in two hours.
Edwin raced to the hardware store and bought half a dozen
aerosol cans of urethane foam. We plugged all the bolt-holes but
one, and injected the foam through the remaining bolt-hole.
Inside the boat, peering down at the keel, I saw air bubbling up
through the water – followed by plumes and curls of urethane
foam, driven into the boat through the bolt-hole. The gaps in
the fibreglass had extended right through the keel, but now the
foam had filled them.

We drove the bolts home and snugged them up. The launch
was on again. Marjorie was waiting at the wharf with a bottle of
champagne.

> *Farewell to Nova Scotia, the seabound coast,*
> *Let your mountains dark and dreary be,*
> *But when I am far away, on the briny ocean tossed,*
> *Will you ever heave a sigh and a wish for me?*

rumrumrum

We left early for the run down the coast to Beaver Harbour.
The forecast called for light winds and high clouds the next two
days. All down the Maritime and New England coastlines, the pre-
vailing summer wind is southwesterly, right on the nose. The quiet
weather gave us a chance to use the engine to put some sea miles
behind us. We had a long way to go, and the summer was passing.

This wasn't a pleasure cruise, not yet. It was more like a delivery trip.

But it was a pleasant run, all the same. The skies cleared and
the sun came out, and *Magnus* ambled along over the quiet sea.

In the late afternoon we turned in toward the land, motoring down an avenue between islands into Beaver Harbour.

In this whole spacious anchorage not a single public wharf survives, so we anchored overnight in a perfect little teacup of a cove. We rowed Leo ashore to a cobble beach, picking our way through the bleached driftwood while flocks of terns wheeled and screamed at our intrusion.

A simple meal. A glass of wine. A moment in the cockpit, under the stars. This was what cruising was supposed to be like.

Another run tomorrow.

When she was launched into salt water for the first time, *Magnus* was still a project, stripped and basic, lacking sails, anchors, and much else. She was still a project six days later, when a crowd of friends came aboard for an afternoon cruise in company with Greg Silver and Denise Saulnier on *Misty Cat*.

We started the engine and backed away from the wharf, motoring up Lennox Passage and nosing between the little islands near our home. We had special guests aboard that day – the musicians Scott Macmillan and Jennyfer Brickenden. Scott is a superb guitarist, a fine arranger and conductor, and a gifted composer whose *Celtic Mass for the Sea* had been performed just a year earlier at Carnegie Hall. Jennyfer's libretto for the *Celtic Mass* includes an ancient and ominous prayer:

> *That it may please Thee to give and preserve to our use the kindly fruits of the earth and restore and continue to us the blessings of the sea. Let not our faults or our frailty bring disaster upon us.*

Scott had brought his guitar along, and as we ploughed through the dark blue water, he played the Celtic jigs and reels of which he is one of the world's great masters – including a tune I had never heard before, a tune he was playing from a sheet of hand-written music.

"What's that one, Scott?" I asked.

Scott grinned and pointed at the title. "The Good Law Mender," it said.

"I wrote it this morning," said Scott. "It's a gift to this vessel and her owners."

At that moment, it seemed to me, *Magnus* – unfinished though she was – ceased to be a project. She was a ship, afloat in her proper element. She had her own life now, her own name, her own personality. She had her own destiny. She even had her own music.

rumrumrum

We left Beaver Harbour in the morning, heading for Petpeswick Inlet, a narrow fjord on the outskirts of Halifax. Another bright day, calm and lucid – a surprising interlude on a coast that is often storm-whipped and savage. Far offshore, white with white sails, like a ghost ship against the morning sky, a big ketch was gliding along parallel to us.

I found myself fretting about the dinghy, which in these quiet conditions was towing submissively behind us. That was all right for the moment, but towing a dinghy is literally a drag – and it can be a hazard. If it fills with water in boisterous conditions and can't be bailed, a dinghy can make the mother ship un-manageable. The only thing to do then is cut it away and let it go.

Yet the dinghy is essential. As cruising guru Tom Neale remarks, the dinghy is "the family car, the family pickup truck, the fuel tanker and water barge; it will probably be your towboat or tugboat, your fishing boat and your reef-diving boat; it will be your far-off and rough-terrain exploration four-wheeler. And that's just the beginning."

The big ketch seemed to be converging with us. Better keep an eye on her.

An oceangoing boat should really carry the dinghy aboard. Alas, though you can hoist a wooden or fibreglass dinghy aboard, it's not very good company. It covers your hatches, blocks your vision, attacks your shins, and snags your lines. So most people now use inflatables, as we had done the previous summer. But small inflatables are poor boats. Rowing one is like levering a doughnut through Jell-o, almost impossible in any wind. With an outboard, an inflatable moves like a doughnut driven by an eggbeater. Inflatables are desperately wet in a chop, and they are always vulnerable to abrasion, chafe, and puncture. You can't let them rub on things or drag them up a rocky beach. Even the nails of a dog can do them in.

In theory, you can deflate an inflatable and stow it tidily – but most sailors don't bother. So the inflatable proves to be just as much of a bulky nuisance as a hard dinghy, and much less of a boat.

The big ketch was definitely nearing our port side, much closer now.

Our solution to the dinghy dilemma was a Porta-Bote, a folding boat made of polypropylene. The Porta-Bote's two sides fold inward against the bottom, and the two halves fold together along the keel, making a surfboard-sized package of eight, ten, or twelve feet in length. Our eight-footer weighs forty-seven pounds. The boat is more than four feet wide, and very stable, though the flexible hull material dimples disconcertingly when you stand in it. The boats are guaranteed for ten years, and they are almost indestructible. With its drooping nose, the boat looks odd – but it tows well, rows well, motors well, and it carries a huge load.

The white ketch was quite close, and moving a bit faster than we were. Would she cross ahead of us? Why was she closing in on the coast? If she were bound for Halifax, surely she would stay out to sea.

We had intended to lash our Porta-Bote sideways across the swim platform without folding it, motor-cruiser style, as we had done with our inflatable the previous year. On the way across Chedabucto Bay, however, the Porta-Bote had scooped up gallons of water from every wave; in serious weather it would rip itself loose or make the mother ship uncontrollable.

The white ketch ducked to starboard, passing behind us, and then took up a parallel course between *Magnus* and the coast. I stuck my head on deck to make sure she was going well clear of us.

For now, unless we were going to lift the dinghy aboard, fold it up, and stow it against the lifelines every day – and I wasn't even sure it would stow there – we had no alternative but to tow it. There had to be a better way.

Suddenly the steady tone of the engine dropped abruptly, picked up again, then slowed down once more. Marjorie slapped her book shut, and we scrambled on deck. *Magnus* was just inside the high lump of Egg Island, still thirteen miles from Petpeswick. Glancing over the side, I saw a puff of white smoke. I shoved the throttle lever back and forth. The engine speeded up again, faltered briefly, picked up, and resumed its steady beat.

"What was that all about?" Marjorie asked.

"Dunno. Gremlins, maybe."

The VHF radio suddenly spoke out loudly.

"*Magnus, Magnus,* this is *Lioness*. Over."

I grabbed the microphone, called back, and looked around. We had veered off course, and had come much closer to the ketch.

"*Magnus,* what can we do to keep out of your way, over?"

"Sorry," I said. "We're heading for Petpeswick, but our engine was acting up. Over."

"I saw a little puff of white smoke from your exhaust. I'll go back up to six knots and steer back out to sea. Over."

"Thank you. Over."

I throttled back a little, and *Lioness* moved away.

"What was that white smoke?" asked Marjorie.

"Water in the fuel? I think that's what white smoke means."

"How would water get in the fuel?"

"Condensation, I suppose. Something more to check when we get to Halifax – if the engine doesn't quit outright in the meantime."

"Hard to believe we'd have come that close to the only other boat out here."

"Amazing," I said, shaking my head.

Listening intently to the drumming of the diesel under the cockpit, I went below to the skipper's chair. Marjorie took a last look around, came below, and picked up her book. Leo stretched out on the settee. *Magnus*, on autopilot, rumbled steadily down the coast.

Petpeswick Inlet winds into the low hills east of Halifax like a loosely thrown rope, its narrow channel hiding below deceptively broad waters. It seems more like a river than an inlet. Be careful, Phil had said, the marshes are just below the surface on either side.

Magnus nosed cautiously into the land, her engine just ticking over. I watched the depth sounder. Twelve feet. Ten. Off to starboard, a fishing wharf. Pleasure boats on moorings. Now a narrow stretch. Wet meadows of vivid green marsh grass. Muscular fishing boats at homemade docks. Then a wider expanse of water with a handsome little blue sloop on a mooring. Eight feet. A sharp bend to port, and there was Phil in his little outboard skiff, leading us into a basin so small that it doesn't even appear on the chart. We set the anchor, and he clambered aboard.

I have known Phil Thompson for thirty years, since I selected some of his poems for an anthology I was editing. I always wanted to visit the little fiefdom on Saltmarsh Island that he had inherited from his grandfather. And here we were.

Lean and brown, a tad older than fifty, Phil is a unique blend of artist, environmentalist, and alternate-energy technologist. He has lived and worked all over Canada, particularly in the North, but Saltmarsh Island is his world headquarters, the home terrain of his life. His family has been rooted in Petpeswick for generations. I remembered a snatch from one of his poems, about lobster fishing with his grandfather.

> We pushed the trap over the side
> where the biggest lobsters hide in Petpeswick.
>
> Then, because the wind was right
> we stood in the boat with jackets held open
> and sailed slowly back to the narrows
> like a two-masted schooner
> laughing as the sun sparkled off shells so brightly . . .

I unclipped the oars from *Magnus's* rigging. We boarded the Porta-Bote, and Phil climbed back into his skiff. We rowed ashore and took a tour of the tiny island. Leo nosed through the bushes, sniffing the new place.

"How does Leo like living on a boat?" Phil asked.

"He's been a star," said Marjorie. And he had been – going long hours without a chance to relieve himself ashore, waiting for his food until we were able to deal with the consequences, dozing here and there in the main cabin underway, exploring all new landfalls with eagerness and interest. Who knows? There might be something really interesting lying in the bushes. A discarded mackerel, perhaps a green-tinged bone.

Phil's house stands on the peak of the island's only hill, with a splendid view through the trees down to green marshes and sinuous mud-banked channels. It's a storey-and-a-half Cape Cod that might be more accurately described as a cottage – except that it's designed for year-round living.

Phil built the house himself, helped by his sons and friends. There are skylights instead of dormers, because dormers require the skills of a professional carpenter. The house has a chemical toilet, and its floors are well-worn unfinished plywood. A pretty rudimentary home, one might think.

But the building is a conservationist's demonstration project. It consumes less electricity than an electric hair dryer. On the south side, three big solar panels tilt toward the sun. From the north side comes the whir of a wind generator, mounted on a pole bolted to the house. Phil buys electricity from nobody.

The windows mostly face south, to gain the maximum benefit from the sun's heat. In the dead of winter, the meticulously insulated house is heated by three pilot lights on the gas appliances and by a three-hundred-watt heat dump that warms up when the wind generator is producing more power than the house can use. Those tiny heat sources create enough warmth to keep the temperature above freezing during Phil's frequent absences. When he's home, he burns wood he cuts on the island.

Interior items like the kitchen cupboards are, well, rudimentary. As a sometime realtor, Phil understands that nice cupboards in a kitchen are an important selling feature, but he isn't selling – and anyway, even the nicest cupboards are still only kitchen cupboards.

"I built this whole house for under $50,000 in the mid-1990s," Phil said. "The kitchen cupboards I wanted were going to cost $10,000. I thought that was insane. I bought a sailboat instead. Listen, I thought I'd make some spaghetti. That appeal to you?"

"Sure," I said. "Let me go get some wine."

"Good," Phil nodded. "I don't have any."

I rowed out to the boat. When I got back, Marjorie and Phil – who had never met before – were deep in conversation about writing, dogs, families, music, health, love and marriage. I don't think they noticed I was gone.

Over dinner, I steered the conversation back to the house, and to Phil's stripped-down lifestyle. It had occurred to me that the house was really a big square sailboat, permanently moored. The whole energy system – wind generators, deep-cycling golf-cart batteries, solar panels, minimal refrigeration – is exactly what many cruising sailors use.

"A lot of this is actually marine stuff," Phil nodded. "I wanted to show that it's possible to live off the electric grid fairly easily, using off-the-shelf components you can buy at a local hardware or marine store. The key is that you can't be wasteful. You have to keep the loads down."

You begin, he said, by scrapping anything that uses electric resistance heat – toasters, hair dryers, hot-water heaters. That leaves lighting, TV, water pump, stereo, laptop computer, cell-phone – devices that demand relatively little power. You heat with wood, using two or three cords annually, which the island provides. You cook with gas, and your gas stove also heats your water. In summer, you keep the beer cold in a thermoelectric cooler powered by a single solar panel. In a Nova Scotia winter, your whole world is a refrigerator.

Saltmarsh Island integrates the themes of Phil's life. He's been a senior civil servant in the Northwest Territories, a successful con-sultant and project manager, the winner of a Nova Scotia Energy Award for his hundreds of articles and radio talks on energy and conservation. But he's also a man of the arts, the author of two books of poems. Some have been set to music by classical com-posers. The environmentalist loves this setting, the poet loves this minimalist lifestyle, and the technologist makes it possible.

"I'm rich," Phil said. "I've got time, I've got choice. That's what 'rich' is."

He guided us with his flashlight as we picked our way down the needle-padded path in the darkness. The moon was out, and *Magnus* lay like a ghost ship on the silver water. We cradled Phil's gifts carefully – a Celtic stained-glass window hanging, a hand-painted ceramic tile that would protect our galley counter from hot pots, a borrowed book that would help me understand how we might harness the power of sun and wind to produce energy for the boat.

"Being rich means having time and having choice," I said the next morning, as Saltmarsh Island fell behind and we threaded our way back down the snaking channel to the sea.

"We all have choice, actually," said Marjorie. "But most of us don't know we have choices about things like electricity. And we don't know how many choices there are."

The sea and the sky were grey again as *Magnus* turned southwest past Chezzetcook and Shut-In Island. The fog seemed to thicken as we approached the busy traffic lanes off Halifax Harbour. The radar showed half-a-dozen moving blips. As our courses converged, the blips took shape in the mist as ethereal container ships, fishing boats, oil-supply vessels. One shape, grey on grey, glimpsed briefly in the mist, was a small naval vessel.

We passed Devil's Island and Thrum Cap, entering the main channel as we turned the corner inside McNabs Island. Mauger's Beach poked out toward the fairway in front of us – a long spit of land also known as Hangman's Beach because of the Royal Navy's ghoulish practice of hanging the tarred bodies of mutineers and deserters from gibbets at its tip as a warning to others.

The fog lifted slightly, revealing the villages clinging like lichen to the rocks of the western shore: Herring Cove, Ferguson's Cove, Purcell's Cove. Coming from seaward, we were approaching Halifax as it truly should be approached, as it had presented itself to generations of immigrants, merchants, admirals, tourists, pirates, peers, and poets. This is the way Trotsky and Churchill and Oscar Wilde came to Halifax, and this was Charles Dickens's last view of North America.

The Mi'kmaq called it Che-book-took, "the greatest harbour," and its magnificent harbour has made Halifax a world city, despite its modest size. The city is built on an egg-shaped peninsula, with the forested prow of Point Pleasant Park at its seaward tip. The commercial harbour lies beyond Point Pleasant, running inland past the downtowns of Halifax and Dartmouth to the broad circular expanse of Bedford Basin, where the convoys of two world wars assembled.

On the other side of Point Pleasant, the slender fjord known as the Northwest Arm gives the city a second harbour devoted to recreational uses. *Magnus* slipped quietly up the Arm, past the city's most expensive homes, each with its own dock. The Arm is peppered with moorings, and constantly traversed by rowing shells, sailing dinghies, outboard runabouts, ocean-racing sailboats, and plodding power cruisers. We belong to the Armdale Yacht Club, which occupies Melville Island, near the head of the waterway, and we had reserved a slip there. We tied up, signed in, and took stock.

Halifax is the centre of our little world. A compact city of 250,000 with a dense historic core, it is the capital of Nova Scotia, and the biggest city in Canada's whole Atlantic region. It is formed around its harbour, which reaches out and touches you at the most unexpected moments. You look through a slot between the office towers to see a lane of sparkling water – and then the water vanishes as the massive slab side of a container ship blocks the gap. You follow a trail through the Point Pleasant woods – recently savaged by Hurricane Juan – and suddenly you are at the footpath along the seawall, confronting a huge auto-carrier full of Toyotas and Nissans, inbound from the Orient. You leave a downtown restaurant late in the evening and find yourself in heavy fog. The waves slosh around the pilings, diesel engines mutter invisibly, bells and horns speak their warnings in the woolly night.

On such a night you suddenly remember that this sea touches Copenhagen and Bora Bora. This sea can take you anywhere. It marks and flavours this small capital, and makes it a city of the world.

Halifax has played a rich and bloody role in world history. Melville Island, for instance, where *Magnus* was tied, was once a military prison. Yachtsmen now store their sails and gear in cramped stone cells that once held French and American prisoners of war. A stone's throw away is Deadman's Island, the former prison graveyard. Bones occasionally emerge from its eroding cliffs, and nobody knows just how many people may be buried there, or who they are.

From the moment of its founding, Halifax was a military city, an administrative centre, a commercial centre, and a seaport. It still is. The city was founded by the British in 1749 to counter-balance the French fortress at Louisbourg, in Cape Breton, and to defend the thirteen English colonies to the south. Less than twenty years after Louisbourg was conquered, the ungrateful colonies to the south declared their independence. The fight against the rebels during both the Revolution and the War of 1812 was conducted largely by the British fleet based in Halifax.

> *And the rockets' red glare, the bombs bursting in air,*
> *Gave proof through the night that our flag was still there . . .*

Those rockets were fired at the siege of Baltimore in 1814 by a British force under Major General Robert Ross, who had sacked Washington and burned the White House three weeks earlier. Ross himself was killed at Baltimore. His body is buried in the Old Town Burying Ground, in downtown Halifax.

Three days after her arrival at Armdale, *Magnus* slipped her lines and motored out of the Arm and around Point Pleasant into the main harbour – "The Big Harbour" of *Theodore Tugboat*, the children's TV series. That day, the most striking feature of the harbour was not the container terminals and grain elevators, or the navy yard or the coast guard base. What dominated the harbour was the array of great sailing ships tied to its wharves – barques and barquentines, brigantines and topsail schooners.

They had come to this one-time British bastion to join in a glorious celebration of things French – the Congrès Mondial Acadien, the Acadian World Congress, the quadricentennial celebration of the survival of French Nova Scotia.

Exactly four hundred years earlier, in 1604, Samuel de Champlain established the first European settlement north of Florida, in the territory known as "Acadia," which included all the modern Maritime provinces and parts of New England. French settlers soon followed, and – though Acadia changed hands several times as France and England battled for control of North America – these "Acadians" prospered virtually unmolested until 1755.

By then Acadia had become the British colony of Nova Scotia, and the British governor insisted that the Acadians swear allegiance to the British crown. When they persistently refused, the governor rounded them up and deported them to the other British colonies, to France and to England. Their homes were torched, their livestock seized, and their farms distributed to British settlers. Le Grand Dérangement – the Deportation of the Acadians, as it was known in English – was an early essay in ethnic cleansing, and its echoes persist to this day.

A large number of the Acadians ended up in Louisiana, where their descendants became known as "Cajuns." But over the next few decades, thousands made their way back to Acadia. Their descendants included the LeBlancs, Boudreaus, Pettipas, Landrys, and Samsons, who are our neighbours in Isle Madame. By 2004, the Acadians were at last being recognized for who they were – the first Europeans to become rooted in America, the senior settlers of Canada, speaking a unique version of the French language preserved from the seventeenth century.

Now, four centuries after their ancestors arrived in Nova Scotia, the Acadians were having a party that would last all summer. A quarter of a million Acadian descendants were expected, of whom seventy thousand would attend the enormous family reunions in Acadian villages all over the Maritimes. The Acadian survival was being celebrated with numerous museum exhibits and publications, learned conferences at the French-language Université Ste. Anne, fêtes in a dozen centres, and a major cultural festival on the Halifax waterfront.

The Tall Ships had come to Halifax from Britain, Mexico, Romania, Poland, the United States, Germany, the Netherlands, and the Cayman Islands. Downtown Halifax was closed to automobiles. There would be fireworks, food, and music on the wharves. The Tall Ships would be open for visits by the public.

And the Nova Scotia Schooner Association would hold a schooner race.

Schooners are the signature vessels of Nova Scotia. Fast, nimble, and forgiving, they dominated the fishery almost as late as the Second World War. Small schooners – like my own little *Hirondelle* – fished near the shore; larger ones made extended fishing trips to the Grand Banks of Newfoundland. Because they preserved their catches in salt, they were known as "saltbankers." In the winter, the saltbankers often carried salt fish to the Caribbean, returning with salt, molasses, and rum.

In Nova Scotia, the pre-eminent fishing port was Lunenburg. Its New England counterpart was Gloucester, Massachusetts. The rivalry between the two ports eventually gave rise to the International Schooner Races. The first race, in 1920, was won by the Gloucester vessel *Esperanto*. Stung, the Lunenburgers commissioned a new vessel for the 1921 series. She was named *Bluenose*, and she won the title in her first season, defending it successfully until the schooner races ended in 1938. She became one of Canada's best-loved national symbols, and her image still adorns the Canadian dime.[3]

---

3 For the full story of *Bluenose* and her replica, see Silver Donald Cameron, *Schooner: Bluenose and Bluenose II*. Toronto: Seal Books, 1986. Revised and updated as *Once Upon a Schooner*. Halifax: Formac, 1992.

Bluenose finished her life as an interisland freighter in the Caribbean. She was wrecked on a Haitian reef in 1946. Fifteen years later, the Oland family, brewers of Schooner beer, commissioned a replica, built in the same yard from the same plans. *Bluenose II* was launched in 1964. When the Olands sold their brewery in 1971, they transferred the schooner to the Province of Nova Scotia for a dollar. She has been a government ship ever since, sailing the Great Lakes and both coasts of North America promoting Nova Scotia and running day cruises in Halifax Harbour during the tourist season.

When the Tall Ships visit Halifax, as they did both in 2000 and 2004, *Bluenose II* is the host vessel. She was berthed in her usual spot next to the cluster of eighteenth-century ironstone buildings known as Historic Properties. A bit farther down the harbour, near the Maritime Museum of the Atlantic, a dozen small schooners belonging to the Nova Scotia Schooner Association were rafted up inside an L-shaped wharf.

Magnus is a ketch, with her mainmast forward, the exact reverse of a schooner – but I had spent so much time with schooners and their owners that *Magnus* had been declared an honorary schooner for a day or two. The stout and stubby little ketch nosed in to the wharf, looking like a terrier among the greyhounds, and promptly got into trouble with the police.

"You can't tie up here," said the cop on the dock.

"I can," I said. "We're guests of the Schooner Association."

The cop said he knew nothing about that. That's true, I said. He called his superior. A woman hurried up. I recognized her: Mora Stevens, granddaughter of the late, legendary David Stevens, the old master shipwright of Second Peninsula, near Lunenburg.

"You can't tie up here," Mora said sternly. Then she looked again.

"Oh, Don! How are you?" She turned to the police officer. "It's all right. He's our guest."

"*Magnus* is a double-ender, right?" said the skipper of a nearby schooner. "We'll turn her around and sail her backward. Then she'll pass for a schooner all right."

We tied *Magnus* up, and I went off to crew with Tom Gallant – an Acadian – on his forty-seven-foot *Avenger*. Playwright, folksinger, actor, and scriptwriter, Tom is also an accomplished rigger and sailor, a diligent student of East Coast marine traditions. For nine years he commuted offshore between Nova Scotia and the Caribbean, sailing south via Bermuda each fall and north each spring.

He has been a cherished friend of mine for three decades and more. The very first time I brought Marjorie to Nova Scotia, Tom and his wife, Lissa, had us down to their little house near Lunenburg for dinner. When we arrived, Tom took one look at us, saw how much we mattered to each other, and opened his arms to Marjorie.

"Welcome to the family," he said.

Most sailboat races are intense competitions between highly tuned competitive machines built of exotic materials, trimmed down to minimum weight, and sailed by a crew of high-tech strategists, grim-faced sail trimmers, and flat-bellied "deck apes." Nova Scotia schooner races are not like that. The schooners compete with their full cruising gear – anchors and chain and bedding and tinned food. The crews consist of the owners and their families and any other friends and girlfriends and hangers-on who want to go sailing. Picnic baskets and cameras and coolers of beer are often involved.

This race was no exception. As we sailed off to the starting line, Tom called over to the skipper of *Comet II*, "Now remember, Alex, no fair *trying*."

This race, however, did have an extra competitive tang. Four of the competing schooners had been built by David Stevens – *Comet II*, *Dorothy Louise*, *Atlantica*, and Tom's *Avenger* – and the latter two were sister ships. David Stevens built *Avenger* in his shop in 1966, and the next year built *Atlantica* in the Atlantic Provinces Pavilion at Expo 67 in Montreal, with the world looking over his shoulder. *Atlantica*'s triangular Bermudan sails ran right to the masthead, while *Avenger* carried the traditional quadrilateral gaff sails. Both vessels had been recently rebuilt – *Atlantica* in a professional shop, at great expense, *Avenger* by Tom himself, aided by some of the old master craftsmen of Lunenburg. A year before, he had sailed down to the Caribbean for the first time in a decade. In the past year, Tom had sailed *Avenger* more than five thousand miles, and the almost-instinctive bond between the skipper and the ship was a beautiful thing to see.

The rest of the fleet didn't matter much to Tom. But he wanted to beat *Atlantica*.

The race started well, but the wind was light, and *Avenger* likes a breeze. Behind Georges Island, still inside the harbour, the wind faded almost completely. Even in these light airs, the larger boats pulled ahead of the smaller ones, the tight grouping at the starting line spreading out to become a string of schooners parading out of the harbour, a magnificent sight.

Atlantica trailed *Avenger* in the early going, and stayed behind as we left the harbour astern. The leader was *Comet II*, long and slender, built from an old design created by David Stevens's grandfather almost a century ago. Marjorie and I knew *Comet II* well. A few weeks earlier, she had been at our village wharf in Cape Breton.

The wind strengthened slightly as the fleet turned toward Herring Cove. Tom and his old friend Corky Wood exchanged the familiar lines of an old joke in a thick Lunenburg accent:

> *Wheah are we, Cappy?*
> *Well, Ah don't know, Corky.*
> *I think we're lost, Cappy.*
> *No, Corky, we're right heah!*

Avenger picked up a good gust of wind as we passed the Mars Rock buoy off Herring Cove, and made the final turn back toward the finish line in the harbour. Rolling her lee-rail down to the water, the big schooner surged toward Halifax. All her sails were set, even the fisherman staysail away up there between the two mast-heads, and she was literally hissing through the water.

"There you go, old girl," Tom muttered, reclining to leeward with his arm wrapped around the wheel. "That's the breeze we've been waiting for."

It was a beautiful moment, the long curves of the teak-planked deck sweeping up to the canted bowsprit, the sunlight gleaming off varnished wood, the graceful arc of the white sails brilliant against the sun.

But as *Avenger* moved across the harbour entrance, the wind fell light once again, and *Atlantica* slipped by. Tom made a couple of quick feints, trying to deke out her skipper and regain the lead, but he couldn't quite get past her. *Atlantica* crossed the finish line just ahead of *Avenger*, both placing well behind *Comet II*, the clear winner. While I had been sailing, Marjorie and Leo had stayed aboard *Magnus*. Just as the schooners crossed the finish line, her brother Geoffrey called from Calgary.

"How's it going?" he said.

"Geoffrey, this is unbelievable!" cried Marjorie. "I'm in Halifax Harbour, Tall Ships all over the place, Don's been out racing on a friend's schooner and they've just finished, there's a schooner coming in right here with a bagpiper playing on the deck, and –"

"I'm booking a ticket," said Geoffrey. "I've got ten days off. I'm coming down to go sailing with you."

The schooner with the bagpipes was *Comet II*, the winner owned by Alex Rhinelander and Catherine MacKinnon. Catherine plays a fiddle so sweet it would break your heart, and her brother Ian burst on the scene as part of a band called Rawlin's Cross, perhaps the only bagpiper, even in Nova Scotia, to play in night-clubs, and certainly the only one playing from the deck of a schooner. It had been a glorious afternoon. I felt like an acrobat tumbling in history – the eighteenth-century British forts looming on the skyline, the great ships with their spars towering above the city's wharves, and the quintessential Nova Scotian sailing vessels all around me, slicing through the waters of time and memory.

That evening Marjorie and Leo and I walked the waterfront, mingling with the happy crowd, going aboard the Polish barquentine *Iskra* with other old friends, and watching a spectacular fireworks display over the harbour. We got out the instruments and had a jam session, sitting in the cockpit of *Comet II*, rafted up with the other schooners. Marjorie and Tom played their guitars and Catherine her fiddle. Other players and by-standers came and went.

At one point Tom and I joined up to sing "The Governor's Blues," a grand rowdy song about sleazy politicians, which Tom wrote thirty years ago.

> *My daddy was a low-down pimp, and my momma was a red-light girl.*
> *My daddy had a sharkskin suit, and my momma had a golden curl.*
> *Everybody loved my momma. Nobody loved my dad.*
> *My momma used to work all night, and give Daddy ever'thing she had . . .*

We sang with gusto and joy, interpolating comments between the lines – *You don't tell me. Un-huh. What'd he say?* Marjorie played along, beaming at the two of us. You'd think, said Marjorie later, that you had done that song together a thousand times. Twice, I said. Maybe three times.

"Silver D, you're probably the only other person in the world that knows all the words to that," Tom laughed. "But I recorded it again on the new CD, did you know that? No? I'll give you a copy."[4]

Catherine MacKinnon picked up her fiddle and began another haunting slow air, plangent and sweet and melancholy. It felt like an ethereal exhalation from the most ancient parts of the soul. And the past was all around us – the Acadians, the forts, the salty old seaport, the historic ships both above the water and below it.

Sitting on the deck of a schooner, surrounded by my country's past and bathed in its music, poised to sail into an unknown future, I suddenly realized that I knew exactly who I was, and exactly where I was. And I liked it.

Geoffrey wasn't getting much sailing in.

Geoffrey is a professor of architectural history, a fine musician and writer, an ordained United Church minister, and a recent convert to sailing. Alas, the Tall Ships were gone when he arrived, and Halifax held us for several days of business and boat chores. So he and Marjorie played guitar and mandolin in the cockpit, and toured the art gallery and the historic buildings of Halifax.

We did set out for Lunenburg one misty morning – and our fancy electronics froze up before we even left the Northwest Arm. Our course lay along the rocky fringe of the open ocean, and though the forecast was acceptable, the visibility was poor, the wind was light, and a serviceman would be easier to find in Halifax. We turned back.

Back at the yacht club, the instruments worked perfectly. Of course. The gremlins always disappear at such moments. The car always runs perfectly when you take it to the mechanic. The washing machine only leaks when the repairman is not on the premises. *Magnus* is a Norwegian boat, I thought. Maybe

---

4 Tom Gallant, *Dance in My Body*, Atlantica Records, 2004.

she has Nordic trolls instead of gremlins. Little antic beings, lurking in the bilges, hell-bent on mischief.

If so, the trolls were in hiding. The smart instruments were all doing their respective digital things. We motored out to sea again on a day of gentle wind and high, thin overcast. We turned southwest around the wicked ledges of Sambro and made sail as we crossed the mouths of St. Margarets Bay and Mahone Bay. The flukey wind carried us halfway up Lunenburg Bay before dying completely. We puttered in past Battery Point and the silent fish plant, the colourful old town taking shape before us.

Lunenburg, Lunenburg. Do we love it or loathe it?

The town centre is a UNESCO World Heritage Site, a treasure-house of quirky and magnificent wooden buildings, some dating almost from the arrival of the original German settlers in 1753. Warehouses and shops, houses and churches, the ornate buildings rise up the hill in ranks from the waterfront – crimson and daffodil yellow, sage green and indigo, adorned with Victorian fretwork and shaped to Lunenburg's Teutonic architectural tastes. It is the prettiest town in the province – and probably the least welcoming.

We motored along the waterfront looking for a place to land and let the Ship's Dog relieve himself. The harbour was spiky with wharves, all deserted, all labelled PRIVATE – NO MOORING. We tied up temporarily at the Fisherman's Wharf – FISHERMEN ONLY – near the head of the harbour, a solid concrete structure with only a couple of boats tied to it. We heaved Leo ashore, along with a bag of garbage. While Marjorie and Geoffrey headed for the nearest green space with the BFD and the garbage, I fell into conversation with a fisherman. I silently dubbed him "Ernest Dogwater."

I was caught up in a swirl of memory. When I first saw my little schooner *Hirondelle*, she had been pulled up on the opposite shore. After I launched her, I tied her to the Foundry Wharf, right next door. And then Morris Allen – the famous Rigger Morris – rigged her for me.

"Ah, Mao-ris," said Dogwater. "Dead now, a' course. Didn't t'ink Mao-ris could evah die, he was dat pickled all d'time. I don't believe we have a rigger left in Lune-bug now – not a propah riggah, anyvways."

"What about Tom Gallant?" Tom had rigged several of the beautiful custom yachts built at Covey Island Boatworks in nearby Petite Rivière.

"Well, now," said Dogwater indignantly, "Tom Gallant may t'ink he's a riggah, but I don't t'ink he's any kind of a riggah. Oh, he can t'row in a splice or two, maybe, but dere's moa'n dat to bein' vwhat you'd rightly call a riggah."

Marjorie came back with Leo.

"Don," she said, "those garbage boxes are padlocked."

"Why, shu-ah," said Dogwater. "We got to padlock 'em. If you leave 'em open, dey fills up ovahnight, you. People puts *garbage* in 'em."

"Well yes," I said, "they're garbage boxes."

"But dey're for d' fishermen, and only for d'fishermen."

Somewhere I have a photograph of the playground swings at the magnificent rococo building that is the Lunenburg Academy, the town school. But school is out, so the chains on the swings are padlocked together. No Swinging After Hours.

"Any place in town to tie up?" I asked.

"No, dey ain't. But dey's moorings out in de ha'bour. You can take one o' dem and pay at de Yacht Shop."

We motored out into the harbour and picked up a mooring ball.

"What a town," I said to Geoffrey. "Morris Allen was an artist with cordage, and a more generous person you never met. But he liked a drink, and Lunenburg is still making him pay for it."

"You knew him?"

"I loved him." And I was back in the swirl of memory again.

Morris was a sunny, elfin man, tough and strong as shoe leather, and he lived with his beloved Bertha in a little house on the outskirts of town. His first wife wouldn't give him a divorce, so he and Bertha lived common-law – and Lunenburg was very arch and sniffy about that too. His workshop was a swaybacked shed smaller than a one-car garage. I sought him out when I was looking for someone to rig my schooner. Morris heard me out, and nodded vigorously.

"Sure, sure," he said. "Be no trouble to string a bit o' vwire over your little ship."

And so began a treasured friendship. Morris was a splendid storyteller, a fund of nautical knowledge, a generous host, a wicked harmonica player, and a genius with rope and wire. The work that came out of his tiny shop, redolent of Stockholm tar, was rooted in centuries of marine tradition. He was in his element swinging like a monkey far above the deck of a full-rigged ship.

Morris and a partner made all the rigging for HMS *Rose*, a full-scale replica of an eighteenth-century British naval vessel built for the U.S. Bicentennial and recently featured in the film *Master and Commander*.

"When vwe did it, the ship wasn't built yet," Morris said. "Every bit of d' rigging we did from the plans. And the crazy t'ing of it was, when we vwent to put it on the ship, everything fit! All except two little whisker stays on the bowsprit – those we had to do ovah."

Morris later made the beefy rigging for *Silversark*, the boat I launched twenty years ago, and that rigging adorns her still. When I had to have some new pieces made in the traditional manner, I asked Tom Gallant, and I believe Morris would have approved of the work Tom did – no matter what Dogwater might think.

Marjorie, Geoffrey, and I took the dinghy ashore, and enjoyed a fine dinner at an engaging little pub called The Knot. Afterward we wandered the streets of Lunenburg.

"I made a mistake," Marjorie confessed. "I should have used the washroom at the restaurant. Can we find one somewhere?"

"Sure," I said. But this was Lunenburg. At the Subway restaurant, she was told sternly that the Subway restroom was only for customers. But, said the cashier, there's a public washroom just at the end of the street. We walked down there and found the public washrooms. They were padlocked. No Peeing After Hours.

Tourists have replaced codfish as Lunenburg's main source of income, and the Lunenburg attitude toward both is similar: you depend on them, but you don't befriend them. Catch 'em, clean 'em, and ship 'em out.

We crossed the street to the Fisheries Museum of the Atlantic, where an increasingly agitated Marjorie finally found an available biffy – without even paying admission.

I waited in the hall, looking at an array of old portraits of deceased local worthies. One of them stopped me in my tracks. It was labelled "Harry W. Adams." Until that moment, I really had no notion that Harry W. Adams was a man. I always thought he was a schooner.

I first heard about the schooner *Harry W. Adams* from George Hebb, a nautical hippie of those same long-ago Lunenburg days, who had once casually remarked that a person could navigate a barrel to Bermuda. The idea had become an obsession, and George had actually built a thirteen-foot seagoing barrel for the purpose, though he never made the voyage. A Lunenburger by birth, but raised in Toronto, he had served part of his marine apprenticeship on the *Harry W. Adams*.

The *Harry W. Adams* was a noble Grand Banks schooner – 142 feet long and 27 feet wide, launched in 1937. She was the 180th schooner built at Lunenburg's Smith and Rhuland yard, the same yard that built both *Bluenose* and *Bluenose II*. The *Harry W. Adams* had a successful fishing career, but by the 1960s, she was unemployed, run down, and redundant. At that time, waterfront scavengers and hustlers were gathering up such schooners, converting them into primitive pleasure vessels, and selling them to romantic and rich Upper Canadians and Americans.

Enter a well-heeled Chicagoan whose family was falling apart. In one last desperate salvage effort, he bought the *Adams*, had her refitted, and hired a crew to deliver her to Chicago. George Hebb was a member of that crew.

Back home, the owner assembled his family and said something like this:

"This family is falling apart. I'm a philanderer, your mother's a lush, you kids squander your days doing dope and listening to weird music. You think your mother and I lead boring and meaningless lives. Maybe so. You also think we're stupid people who deserve no respect. Well, we'll see.

"I've bought a schooner, and we're going to sail it around the world. I know nothing about sailing a schooner. Neither do you. So we're starting even, and we'll see who's stupid and who's quick. I've hired a professional crew to bring the vessel to Chicago, and to sail with us as far as Bermuda. After that, we're on our own.

"This is my last decree as head of this family. When we get back, everyone's free to go their separate ways and do whatever they please. But I'm not going to see this family disintegrate without a struggle."

Meanwhile, the Lunenburg crew was en route to Chicago, cruising up the St. Lawrence and through the Great Lakes. On one memorable occasion, they were ghosting through a narrow Michigan waterway where bands of fog alternated with bands of clear sunlight. A young boy and his father were fishing from the shore.

An enormous oceangoing schooner suddenly glided out of the fog. George Hebb was aloft in the rigging, peering through the mist. He was leathery and brown, with long chestnut ringlets and a huge moustache. He wore ragged shorts, a red bandanna, and a big gold earring. As the ship pulled abreast of the boy and his father, George leaned far out toward them.

"Aaarr!" he snarled. "You swabs see a vessel pass this way – aaar! – with a black-bearded captain – aarr! – by the name of *Teach*?"

The boy squealed with terror and jumped into his quaking father's arms. The schooner vanished into the fog. When they told the story, who would believe them?

There were other yarns, plenty of them – like the time the *Adams* was all but sunk by the U.S. Navy off Bermuda, in an attempt to save her from foundering. And although the story has no doubt been enriched considerably in the telling and retelling, its essence is truthful, and it had a happy ending. The family did sail around the world, and during the voyage the parents rediscovered each other, while the kids turned into fine, responsible people. They arrived back in Chicago broke but happy. The last I heard of the schooner was around 1990, when she was said to be mouldering away at a dock somewhere in the southern United States.

It's a grand tale, but it says nothing about Harry W. Adams himself. Yet there he was, hanging on the wall of the Fisheries Museum, a rather stern-looking businessman of the early twentieth century. Who was he?

Next morning I asked museum director Ralph Getson. It turned out that Harry W. was the "Adams" of Adams and Knickle, the fish exporters whose big red buildings still adorn the Lunenburg waterfront. A wry and parsimonious member of Lunenburg's codfish aristocracy, he had commissioned the schooner that was named for him. Ralph also knew what had happened to the schooner. She was eventually scuttled in the Cape Fear River, in North Carolina, and he had aerial photos of her final repose. In the photos she looks like a small island, with trees growing from her hull.

Magnus would be in the Cape Fear River in November. Maybe, I thought, I'll go looking for the *Harry W. Adams* and pour a tot of rum on her ruins, a modest libation to the gods of grand ships and great stories.

I had only one real errand in Lunenburg. Our long-time sailmaker is Sandy MacMillan, the former Olympic sailor who runs the North Sails Loft in Lunenburg. He had been down to D'Escousse to install the new sails and try them out – and we had both been startled by *Magnus*'s very respectable performance as a pure sailing vessel.

"She's doing really well to windward," Sandy had marvelled. "She's not supposed to sail like this. I always suspected the Scandinavians knew things about motor-sailers that the rest of us never learned."

Sandy later made up a new mainsail-stowing system for *Magnus*. But it still needed a little piece to be measured in place and sewn to fit. Sandy was off racing in Mahone Bay – racing sailors, who buy a lot of sails, need to be coddled and fussed over – but if we could move the boat to the Fisheries Museum wharf, his colleague Cathy would take the measurements and sew the piece. Cathy came and went, and I was free for the day.

I called Tom Gallant. The schooners were racing again, this time from the Lunenburg Yacht Club on Herman's Island in Mahone Bay. Would Tom consider taking two more crewmen – me and Geoffrey? By all means.

We called a cab. As we drove over the causeway onto Herman's Island, I mentioned that the masts for my old schooner had come from "Billy Whynacht's vwoodlot" on Herman's Island. The driver asked about the schooner. I said it had been built by Frank Knickle in Blue Rocks, a tiny outport on Lunenburg Bay. Frank and I had walked through the woodlot and he had pointed out the trees to cut – "Dere's your fore-mast, you, and dat ovah dere, dat'll make your main boom." We cut the trees and hauled them out, peeled the bark off them, and dropped them in the boat.

"Ah, Fhrank," said the driver, shaking his head. "He evah tell you vwhat happened to him?"

"In 1941?" I said. "When the schooner left him?"

"Yea," said the driver. "Poor old Fhrank. He vwas a ha'd case, dat one."

I told Geoffrey the story later. In January 1941, Frank Knickle (pronounced "Kuh-nickel") was fishing near Sable Island, 165 miles offshore. The big schooner had a stack of dories nested on the deck, rowing boats eighteen or twenty feet long. As she sailed along, the schooner dropped the dories overboard, one after another, with two men in each boat. The men dropped heavy baited lines overboard, and then hauled them in, hour after hour, until they had filled the dory with codfish. At the end of the day, the schooner picked up the dories, lifting them aboard with heavy blocks and tackles, and then the fishermen cleaned, split, and salted the fish before grabbing a few hours' sleep. Before daylight they were ready to go again.

Dory-fishing, said one old Lunenburger, was "a disgustin' job. A fearful disgustin' job." When the fish were running, a doryman could work seventy-two hours straight. His earnings for a whole season might be $100.

On that midwinter day in 1941, a sudden storm came up. One by one, the fishing schooners picked up their dories and ran for shelter on the Nova Scotia coast. But the visibility had dropped quickly, and the schooner couldn't find Frank's dory. After searching for several hours, the skipper gave up and fled for Halifax; he knew he was leaving Frank and his dory-mate to their deaths, but he could no longer risk his ship and crew.

Frank's dory-mate was his brother-in-law, a man he'd known all his life, an old schoolmate. They rigged a little sail on the dory and ran her off before the gale. In the darkness, Frank could hear the great breaking seas foaming above him, and sometimes could get a glimpse of white from their crests as they roared down on the little dory.

After a couple of days, the gale blew itself out, and then the weather turned bitterly cold. The two men had no food and no water; they were reduced to eating raw codfish and drinking their own urine. They threw up, and the vomit froze hard on the bibs of their oilskin overalls. The winds came back and the seas filled the dory and they baled it out.

And through it all, Frank kept saying, "Bill, I t'ink vwe're gonna be picked up. Tomorrow vwe're gonna be picked up." And Bill would say, "Vwell, Frank, I hope you're right."

One black night, Bill complained bitterly about the cold. A sea struck the dory, and Frank felt rather than saw that Bill had fallen overboard. He reached out and hauled his dory-mate back aboard. Later in the night, Bill said, very quietly, "Frank, I'm feelin' a little bit vwarmer."

"Dat vwas when he was dyin', see?" Frank said to me. And sometime later Bill must have gone overboard again, because when daylight came Frank could see him "sittin' up on de ocean, frozen stiff, and I vwatched him dat way till he vwent out of sight, and dat vwas de last I ever saw him."

And now Frank was alone, and still he kept telling himself, *Frank, tomorrow you're gonna be picked up. Tomorrow, Frank, you're gonna be picked up.* On his eighth night at sea, a light appeared near the dory. He spoke, but there was no answer; he reached out but couldn't touch it. The light winked out, and then appeared again on the other side of the boat. Again he spoke and tried to touch it. The light went out, "and den it vwas da'hk, real da'hk." But the next morning, all but dead, he was picked up by a Massachusetts trawler.

He was in hospital for weeks, inside something that looked like a glass bell, slathered with medication that was "like cream'ry butter, only it vwasn't." His skin sloughed off, and regrew. Three times his fingernails fell off, and three times they grew back. Eventually he was shipped home to Lunenburg. When he felt well enough, he went down to the waterfront and asked his old skipper for a berth on his old ship. The skipper wept and refused to take him.

"I vwasn't sca'ed," Frank said. "It vwasn't my time for to go. And I knew it. It just vwasn't my time for to go."

I can see him yet, a short, solid man in bib overalls, red-and-blue doeskin shirt, and slouch cap. I can see his eyes watering as he remembered the story, and the way he thumped his fist on his chest when he told of his dory-mate's death, and said, "Vwhen I tell de story, it hurts me *here*."

Somewhere I have a tape of Frank telling this story, but I told it to Geoffrey as I am telling it now, from memory. It is burned into my brain, more vivid in my memory than many of the things that have actually happened to me.

This is the tradition that the small schooners honour. This is the diamond nugget of strength and nobility at the core of this mean, narrow-minded, and glorious little town. A town that can produce a Frank Knickle, a Morris Allen, a David Stevens, and others like them – such a town has something profoundly good at its heart, something as true and straight as a well-planed plank of oak. I don't have to like Lunenburg. But I'd be a fool if I didn't respect it.

And now we have paid the cabbie, and I am aboard *Avenger* again, and *Atlantica* is leading us once again.

> *Tired of seein' de transom of dat schoonah, Cappy, whyn't you just pass her?*
> *Tryin' t'do dat, Corky, but she don't vwant to let me by.*

Geoffrey is immersed in the moment – the sails, the hissing water, the canted deck, the wind lifting our hats. At last he is getting some real sailing. We pick our way along an intricate course through the scores of rocky, spruce-covered islands that speckle Mahone Bay – one island for every day of the year, or so they say. Dodging through narrow passages, ducking around shoals, slipping along beside the village of Indian Point, and back out into the open bay again. Geoffrey is beaming. But although *Avenger* slices beautifully through the water, *Atlantica* once again leads her across the line.

Tom and Catherine MacKinnon will be playing at the Yacht Club later in the evening, but I can't attend. I have a newspaper column to write. I strongly suggest that Marjorie and Geoffrey, who share a deep joy in music, should attend. I ask Geoffrey how he's enjoyed the day – and he surprises me by saying he found Tom a bit coarse. I suppose he is; that's part of Tom's persona, as it is part of mine. Tom and I are both pleased to be downwardly mobile middle-class kids, horrified at the idea of living "a normal life."

"But don't be misled," I caution Geoffrey. "Tom can be vain and cranky and self-centred, like most of us. But his reserves of spirit are truly awesome." And I tell him the story that Tom has since published in a powerful book called *A Hard Chance: Sailing into the Heart of Love.*[5]

In 1980, Tom met the two great loves of his life – *Avenger* and Melissa Groseclose, a free-spirited artist from Tennessee. Their courtship included a terrifying hundred-knot storm off the coast of Newfoundland. They married the next year, took a crew aboard, and sailed to Bermuda and the West Indies. Tom is a handsome man, and Lissa was stunning. Together they made a big bronzed beautiful couple. They commuted between the Caribbean and Nova Scotia for nine years.

Then a bus slammed into their van, giving Tom a concussion and broken bones – and leaving Lissa in a coma for six weeks, unable even to breathe on her own. She was not expected to live. But Tom and others stayed by her bedside and never quit trying to reach her. Six weeks after the accident, she opened one eye. And slowly she came back from the dead – learning, like a child, how to speak, to sit up, to stand, to walk.

---

5 Tom Gallant, *A Hard Chance: Sailing into the Heart of Love.* Halifax: Nimbus, 2005.

Eight months after the accident, Tom drove her home – and then devoted ten years of his life to caring for her. Some of Lissa's damage is permanent, but her recovery was astonishing, far beyond anything her doctors thought possible. All of which makes *A Hard Chance* that rarest of books, a thoroughly adult love story – a story about what we really give when we truly give our hearts, about the actual meaning of "for better, for worse."

"Wow," said Geoffrey when I had finished. "You'd never think it, sailing with him for a day."

"I've known him thirty-five years, and I had no idea he was capable of devotion like that," I said. "But he's a truly remarkable man."

After dinner, Marjorie and Geoffrey went off to the Yacht Club. Lissa was in the audience, and Geoffrey got to meet her. Tom was gentle and considerate with her, and gave an excellent show. Geoffrey came back in a reflective mood.

"Tom said at one point – very calmly – that the ocean can take you any time she feels like it, and there's really nothing you can do about it," said Geoffrey over a nightcap. "If you're a sailor, you just have to accept that."

"Tom says that fears about the future can destroy your happiness in the present moment," I said, "and the things you're worrying about probably won't happen anyway. I believe that, but I keep forgetting it."

"In that way, I think he's a bit like Christ," said Geoffrey thoughtfully. "He just simply isn't afraid. Most people are terribly afraid."

"Well, you're a certified clergyman," I said. "You're allowed to think things like that."

"That's one of Christ's most remarkable qualities," Geoffrey said. "He wasn't afraid. There aren't many people like that."

I nodded. I was remembering an Inuit shaman in one of Joseph Campbell's books who rather reluctantly talked about Sila, the greatest of all spirits, a spirit so mighty as to find expression not in words but in storms, snowfalls, and the tempests of the sea. Only on rare occasions does Sila speak to human beings – speaking gently, in a voice like a woman's.

And what Sila says is, *Be not afraid of the universe.*

"When you get into the LaHave River, tie up at the bakery," said Lorne Leahey, the skipper of the dainty little schooner *Amasonia*, with whom we'd been crossing paths all summer. Geoffrey and I were in the Yacht Shop, Lunenburg's tiny, tidy chandlery, paying our bill for the mooring.

Tie up at the what, Lorne? The bakery?

"Yep. Take it from me – tie up at the bakery," said Lorne. "Best place on the LaHave. I'll show you on the chart. In fact, I'll give you the chart. Send it back when you get a chance."

We motored out of Lunenburg Harbour and made sail again as we stood down the bay, trying out the new mainsail arrangement as we passed Feltzen South and Spindler Cove and turned southwest at The Ovens. Geoffrey stood on a stool beside the helm seat, watching the boat's progress on the electronic chart. During times of enforced idleness, waiting for the weather or the whims of the skipper, Geoffrey had been turning himself into a sailor. He would disappear into the aft cabin with W.S. Kals's *Practical Navigation* or Hervey Garrett Smith's *The Arts of the Sailor*, and then he'd emerge with a question.

"Show me how you convert true directions to magnetic?"

Sure. I just lay a straight-edge across the compass rose and read it off.

"Got a little twine I could use to practise whipping? Want me to put a whipping on the ends of the dock lines?"

You bet. (Those dock lines are still the only ones with tidy whippings on their ends.)

"When you're working with a paper chart, do you use parallel rules?"

No, I use a one-armed protractor. It doesn't slide across the chart and get away from me the way parallel rules do. I'll show you . . .

In principle, traditional coastal navigation is very simple – and it's fun. It's all about speed, time, and direction. If you know any two of these, you can figure out the other one. We were at Point A exactly two hours ago. We're now at Point B, ten nautical miles away. Very well: we've been sailing at five knots.

Or: we're leaving Point A, and sailing due west toward Point B. Since the boat does five knots, we should be in the vicinity of Point B in two hours.

It's not an exact science. Lifting and falling in the waves, a boat never sails an exact course. The person at the helm gets inattentive. The instrument that tells your speed and distance isn't perfectly accurate. The compass is rarely dead-on. The wind or the current may be running against you or carrying you sideways.

You allow for all these factors as best you can, never missing an opportunity to fix your position. But if you do your work carefully, you should get close enough to see or hear something that will confirm your position – a buoy, a radio tower, a lighthouse, a headland.

With electronic navigation, it's still about time, speed, and direction – but you can see your position on the computer screen. You know exactly where you are at all times. The GPS gives you your latitude and longitude anywhere on Earth. Set up Point B as a "waypoint," and the computer does the calculations. Course to steer: 290 degrees. Time to go: 3h 36m. If you wander far off course, the system will sound an alarm. You can even program the autopilot to take you right to your destination.

"Right," said Geoffrey. "But if the equipment breaks down, or you lose power –"

"Then you'd better know the old techniques. The ones you're learning."

So Geoffrey worked out our position as we left Lunenburg Bay and crossed the mouths of Rose Bay, Kings Bay, and Hartling Bay. We ducked inside West Ironbound Island and turned into the maze of islands where the LaHave River debouches into the sea. The estuary narrowed between Fort Point and Kraut Point, and above the narrows, directly opposite the town of Riverport, we saw a tall, narrow old building, with a wharf running out from it and a four-berth floating dock jutting out to the side. A bold sign faced the river, white against the brick-red shingles: LAHAVE BAKERY & OUTFITTERS. WELCOME.

Tied to the main wharf was a gleaming sixty-foot schooner. *Ninita*, designed by the famed Starling Burgess, had just been launched by Covey Island Boatworks. Her English owners – Lord and Lady Gollywobbler, we decided, naming them for the largest sail a schooner can carry – were in the midst of commissioning her. Her maiden voyage would be an Atlantic crossing, a daunting voyage on a big new boat.

With our modest little vessel snugged up to the floating dock, we went up to the bakery. The shop itself fronts on the highway – a dark, cool old room with vast glass windows and high ceilings, its display cases full of fresh bread, muffins, tarts, and cookies. The next room is a funky little luncheon café cluttered with antiques and bathed in delicious smells wafting upward from the basement kitchens.

But the building is not only a bakery. Directly behind the bakeshop, a craft co-operative sells the wares of eighteen local artists – weavers, painters, potters, glassworkers. At the shore end of the ground floor is a boatshop, where Kevin Wambach constructs exquisite small wooden craft. He built the elegant tender sitting in chocks on *Ninita*'s deck.

Directly above the bakery is a youth hostel, plus the bakery's own offices, filled with cages of songbirds. Farther back, the second floor contains showers, toilets, and a laundromat for visiting boaters, plus weaving studios in which a Halifax weaver does workshops. An Ontario publisher maintains a summertime office here as well. And on the third floor is the headquarters, factory, and corporate office of Homegrown Skateboards, where three or four young guys with baseball caps and body-piercings laminate skateboard decks.

"That business is owned by my son, Jesse," says Gael Watson, the bakery's proprietor.

The bakery building, it appears, is actually a layer-cake incubator mall.

The bakery business began when Gael's now-estranged husband, Mike, was laid off from his job working on OK Transport vessels, whose fleet was formerly based at the next wharf upriver. The OK Transport boats carried explosives for Canadian Industries Ltd. to Central America, Africa, and Europe – not the safest of jobs, but Mike loved it. During Mike's absences at sea, Gael established the bakery in the decrepit LaHave Outfitters building, which the couple had bought with friends. Antique and dilapidated, it had trees growing on its roofless third floor. That was twenty years and many dollars ago. The partners are long gone, and the restoration is not finished yet.

Bitten by the sea bug, Mike wanted to be a trader, using his own boat. In 1985, the couple bought a ninety-foot ex-scallop dragger and christened her *Selchie*. Baking, says Gael, "was the only thing I knew how to do that would make money." They installed a 500-hp generator, created a commercial bakery in what was once the officers' quarters, and cast off. For a decade of summers, the couple sailed their floating bakery from Nova Scotia's French Shore to Cape Breton, Newfoundland, and Prince Edward Island, becoming a minor legend in the process. When they separated, Mike took the ship – which was ultimately lost in the Caribbean – and Gael took the debts and the building. She's open seven days a week. With twenty staff here, and six in Mahone Bay, the bakery is a welcome source of employment for workers displaced from the vanished fishery.

"All my core bakers are former fish-plant employees," says Gael "They're used to long, awkward hours, standing on concrete floors. And they have a great work ethic."

"Don?" said a tentative voice. I turned around. A young woman in a bakery apron was smiling at me.

Nancy MacLean, from D'Escousse. The daughter of my neighbours Don and Rosemary. After living for six years in Singapore, Nancy had come home to Nova Scotia and taken a job at the bakery, along with her husband, Kee Peng. Her whole family is musical, and when Geoffrey and Marjorie went over to a picnic table with their instruments, Nancy joined right in. While they were playing, a silver Volkswagen Jetta pulled up – our D'Escousse neighbour Greg Silver, just passing through, pausing to drop off a jacket for Marjorie. Ah, but you're having a jam? He fetched his fiddle from the car.

There might have been a sadness in the music, for Geoffrey was leaving us here. While the music drifted out over the river, another car drove up: Ken MacInnis, his cousin-in-law, who would drive Geoffrey to the airport. When the two cars drove away, Nancy and Kee Peng went back to work, and – for the first time in three weeks – Marjorie and I were suddenly alone again.

Well, not quite. The BFD was lying in the grass under the table.

We stayed at the bakery for a second day while the remnants of Tropical Storm Bonnie swept by, giving us strong, gusty winds and brief but heavy showers of rain. Another storm, Hurricane Charley, was following right behind, but the forecast called for a day of light winds between the two. We made a break for Liverpool.

Liverpool is a charming town of three thousand, established in 1759 by seventy families from Connecticut. The local branch of the Nova Scotia Museum is housed in one of the province's oldest homes, built in 1766 for Simeon Perkins, a shrewd Yankee trader and merchant with interests extending from Labrador to the West Indies. Perkins was also a judge, a militia colonel, and a member of the Legislative Assembly, but he is best remembered for his voluminous and meticulous diary, which gives us a detailed account of daily life during one of Nova Scotia's most exciting historical periods.

I first came to Liverpool in 1968 to interview the novelist Thomas Raddall, some of whose novels drew heavily on the Perkins diaries. My favourite among Raddall's historical novels, *His Majesty's Yankees*, is set in Liverpool during the American Revolution. For Liverpool's Yankees – who had emigrated to Nova Scotia less than twenty years before – the conflict was not so much a revolution as a civil war, setting them against their own families across the Gulf of Maine and creating bitter divisions within Liverpool itself.

In that book, Raddall's heretical theme is that Nova Scotia remained loyal to the Crown not so much because Nova Scotians were dutiful and honourable subjects, but because they were living on a peninsula surrounded by the Royal Navy. Liverpool in particular swung firmly to the British side only after rebel privateers attempted to pillage the town, and were driven off by the local militia.

(One such privateer was a Scot named John Paul Jones, the one who said, "I hae no' yet begun tae fecht!" Among the places he sacked was "Isle de Madame where I made two raids, destroying the fisheries and burning all of the vessels that I could not carry away." In other words, he sank three fishing smacks and burned two sheds in Arichat. A string of such triumphs made him the father of the U.S. Navy.)

Liverpool's other famous artists are country singer Hank Snow – who has a museum in his honour – and photographer Sherman Hines, who has created a museum of photography in the Old Town Hall, with collections of works by photographers like Karsh, Steichen, Notman, the Nova Scotian marine photographer

Wallace MacAskill, and, of course, Hines himself. The museum also displays antique photographic equipment – cameras, tripods, magic lanterns, tintypes, daguerreotypes, stereotypes, prototypes, archetypes, and so on.

Hines is a prodigiously productive man who – I say it with more than a trace of envy – has published more than seventy books. As a matter of fact, I published one of his books myself: I wrote the text for *Outhouses of the West*.[6]

So it grieves me to admit that I didn't visit the museum.

Oh, I meant to. I set out to do it. I wanted to do it. But I didn't. I could make plausible excuses. I could point out that the museum is in the centre of town, a long walk from the Brooklyn Marina. I could claim that the museum wasn't open when I got there, for example, and who knows? That might even be true.

But the real explanation is to be found in Stephen Leacock's book *My Discovery of England*. In London, Leacock says, "after the fashion of every tourist, I wrote for myself a little list of things to do, and I always put the Tower of London on it. No doubt the reader knows the kind of little list I mean. It runs:

"1 Go to bank
  2 Buy a shirt
  3 National Picture Gallery
  4 Razor blades
  5 Tower of London
  6 Soap

"This itinerary, I regret to say, was never carried out in full. I was able at times both to go to the bank and buy a shirt in a single morning: at other times I was able to buy razor blades and almost

---

[6] Sherman Hines and Silver Donald Cameron, *Outhouses of the West*. Self-published, 1988. Reprinted Richmond Hill, ON: Firefly Books, 2000.

to find the National Picture Gallery." But Leacock never managed to see the Tower of London.

My list ran something like this:

1 Call John Steele at Covey Island Boatworks and ask him to recommend a marine electrician
2 Ask Randy Lohnes, the recommended electrician, to wire up the dedicated starting battery and install the galvanic isolator and repair pigtail for shore power cable
3 Drain Racor fuel filter and replace element
4 Museum of Photography
5 Pick up forwarded mail at post office
6 Visit Fort Point Lighthouse
7 Download email – use laptop on clubhouse phone after hours

The Fort Point Lighthouse (1855) marks the spot where Champlain landed in 1604, and contains an interpretive centre telling the story of Liverpool's very successful fleet of eighteenth-century privateers, the Nova Scotian counterparts of John Paul Jones. We didn't get there either.

But we did get the mail, and Randy did do the electrical work, and I did get the fuel filter cleaned out.

Hurricane Charley was no longer a hurricane when it roared through Liverpool during the night, but it was an impressive gale nevertheless. As the wind howled in the rigging, boaters clambered out on the floating dock in the darkness, checking their lines in the driving rain and wondering what they'd do if the heaving dock itself broke its mooring lines and went adrift.

But the lines held, and the gale blew itself out. We sailed for Lockeport, past places named by the French explorers of four centuries ago: Port L'Hebert, Sable River, Port Joli, and Port Mouton, which now rolls off the English tongue as "Port Matoon." Late that morning, *Magnus* was passing the undistinguished swelling in the sea known as Little Hope Island – which, said the local nineteenth-century historian James F. More, is "composed chiefly of sand, and is not much larger than a good-sized croquet ground."

Little Hope Island isn't important to anyone except – God knows why – to cartographers. You would think that a chart covering the southern tip of Nova Scotia would be called "Southern Nova Scotia" or "Lockeport to Yarmouth" or something similarly useful. But no. The chart we were sailing onto, which covers roughly one hundred miles of jagged coastline, was Chart 4230, "Little Hope Island to Cape St. Mary's."

What stranger, shaping a course for this coast, would think to look for a chart with a name like that? Or for "Taylors Head to Shut-In Island" or "Osborne Head to Betty Island" or "Red Point to Guyon Island." A sixty-five-mile stretch of coast on either side of Halifax is called "Egg Island to West Ironbound Island." Halifax is what you care about, but how would you know it was on that chart?

No doubt the question unmasks me as an irremediable land-lubber. Cape St. Mary's is a conspicuous feature from seaward; Little Hope Island is a flat and featureless lump, but with a lighthouse it would have been as notable a sea-mark as anything else around. These features denote the coast as a sailor sees it. For all I know, the first chart of the area may have been drawn by the great navigator Captain Cook, who charted much of the coast of Atlantic Canada in the eighteenth century. Lockeport and Yarmouth didn't amount to much then. But they do now, and it may be time to update the chart titles.

I was also curious about the island's name. Little Hope Island. What was little – the island, or the hope? The latter, it seemed; a good many ships were wrecked on the island. (Even more depressing is Lesser Hope Rock, in closer to the shore.) In 1866, the first lighthouse was erected on Little Hope. It was eventually replaced by a substantial concrete structure. In December 2003, just eight months before *Magnus* passed it, the concrete lighthouse was demolished by a winter storm.

How on Earth did our grandfathers ever build these light-houses on these tiny, wave-swept bumps in the ocean? Gull Rock Light, in the entrance to Lockeport Harbour, sits on a smooth slab of stone just a few feet above the waterline. A square, squat building, it could easily pass for a medieval castle. With a few archers and some tubs of boiling oil on the roof, it would be almost impossibly secure from attack.

> *Looks like John Paul Jones! Headin' this way!*
> *Heh, heh, heh. Heat up d'oil, b'ys.*

Lockeport has always been a fishing town, and still is – though, like every other fishing town, it's been hard hit by the groundfish closure. It now relies on offshore lobstering. We motored in and tied up at the local marina, which consists of two finger piers. It was Sunday, and nobody on any of the three or four cruising boats at the dock seemed to know who actually ran the place.

We walked around the quiet town, a little grid of streets on an island connected to the mainland by a causeway. Within a block of the marina we found the bank, laundromat, hardware store, a couple of restaurants, and a great general store and deli. The town had many fine old homes and an atmosphere of order and stability, though the boarded-up buildings gave it a certain aura of sadness and decline.

At the head of the wharf was a tiny, clean restaurant, to which we repaired for fish and chips, always a safe choice in Nova Scotia. Our waitress was a tall, slim, young dark-haired woman.

In the morning a gang of fish-plant workers clustered around the plant gates, smoking and laughing. A couple of them wandered out on a nearby wharf. I needed some diesel: who owned the marina?

"Fella at the hardware store," one said. So I went to the hardware store.

"No, it's the fella at the restaurant." So I went to the restaurant.

"I can pump some diesel for you," said the man in the restaurant, "but the owner isn't in yet."

We filled the tank. And then at last I found the owner – who proved to be the tall, slim, young dark-haired woman who had been our waitress the night before.

We left Lockeport on a wind-less morning, motoring out into a pearly day where the sea, the sky, and the fog all blended together, boats and buoys and islands floating in formless space.

I sat at the helm, while the radar searched the horizon and the laptop computer talked to the GPS, which in turn talked to half-a-dozen satellites overhead, constantly recalculating the ship's position and relaying it to the computer, which in turn showed a little green boat moving steadily across the chart on the monitor. Along the side of the screen, constantly changing numbers gave latitude and longitude, speed over the ground, the distance to the destination, the time it would take to get there, the direction we were steering, and the actual track we were making over the ground.

Unbelievable. Two decades earlier, electronic charts had been literally a dream, and one of the leading dreamers was Mike Eaton, a quiet, enthusiastic ex-Royal Navy officer. I met him in 1992 at the Bedford Institute of Oceanography in Dartmouth, Nova Scotia. An alert, wiry man with wispy white hair, Eaton was regarded by his colleagues in the Canadian Hydrographic Service as the father of electronic charts in Canada, and perhaps in the world.

In a prophetic paper twenty-five years ago, Eaton painted a picture of a future ship entering the oil terminal at Placentia Bay, Newfoundland, with the skipper at a computer console using an electronic chart. The chart would allow the skipper to zoom in and out on Come-by-Chance Harbour, superimposing fishing areas in green and traffic control zones in purple, calculating the shortest safe course, and overlaying the radar display on the chart to see his distance from the fishing fleet and the shore.

Thus equipped and informed, a skipper could sail through narrow passages to the dock in zero visibility, using little more than a video screen and a joystick. With such an electronic chart, Eaton said, "he can walk it in just like in a video game."

But how would one actually create an electronic chart?

The cheapest and easiest method is by scanning a paper chart into the computer. The result is a genuine chart, but a static one, really just an electronic picture of the original paper document. But Mike Eaton and his colleagues in Dartmouth and around the world were boldly imagining an "intelligent" chart – a chart that would "know" that zooming-in meant the navigator wanted more detail. It would provide layers of information (or remove it) on command: soundings, landmarks, wharf locations, tidal changes, currents, seabed contours, weather information, and so on.

Eaton's imaginary "electronic chart" was actually a powerful information system – an Electronic Chart Display and Information System (ECDIS) – consisting of a constantly changing database hiding in layers under the surface of something that only looked like a traditional chart. The structure of such a system, Eaton explained, is not that of a chart at all. It's "really an entirely different animal."

An ECDIS system would start with regular chart information – but far more information than could ever be crammed onto a single sheet of paper. All that information would be carefully fed into the database by chartmakers and programmers. The chart information would be enriched by a constant stream of data from half-a-dozen secondary technologies: GPS satellites, radar, gyrocompass, anemometer, depth sounder, atomic clock, whatever. The intelligent chart would assimilate all this information and show it as a simple, familiar graphic image: a ship moving across a chart.

By the early 1990s, ECDIS was being tested on coast guard ships, U.S. naval vessels, and Canadian ferries. I saw one on the bridge of the *Princess of Acadia*, the Digby–Saint John ferry. It was the most advanced system on Earth, and I thought it was magic. Someday, I thought, this will be available on yachts. But not in my lifetime.

Yet there I was, sitting at *Magnus's* inside wheel, with my laptop computer in front of me. On the screen was a raster chart – a familiar nautical chart, showing deep water in white, shallow water in blue, landmasses in buff. Charts are elegant, classical artifacts, graphic one-page representations of buoys, water depths, heights of land, lighthouses, bluffs, church spires, water towers, and anything else that might help the mariner fix his position. But the chart on the computer also showed my ship, with a green arrow poking forward from the bow in the direction we were heading. To set a course for a particular harbour, I simply click on the chart to designate the harbour's entrance buoy as a "way-point." A dashed line would shoot forward from the ship to the buoy. That dashed line would be my course. To put the ship on course for the buoy, I would simply steer to align the green arrow from the boat with the dashed line.

It might be pitch dark outside, impenetrable fog, pouring rain. No matter. Thanks to dozens of satellites streaking overhead, any skipper can now know exactly where he is – and if he gets into trouble, the flick of a switch on the VHF radio will broadcast a distress signal identifying his vessel and giving her exact position.

Today's navigators owe a huge debt to thousands of hydrographers, cartographers, and programmers whose names we will never know. But I do know one of them: Mike Eaton, who in 2005 received the Order of Canada for doing a very good thing with his life.

Despite the electronic miracles, of course, the habits of thirty years persist. Whenever the fog allows, you take note of light-houses, buoys, and prominent headlands, constantly confirming your position. Yes, that's the lighthouse at The Salvages, another medieval keep like Gull Rock – squat, square, and on a ledge almost awash. When a huge dome appears on the horizon, you pore over the chart and the pilot book to see what it is. Aha! A radar installation on the low-lying plain of Baccaro Point, dwarf-ing the nearby lighthouse.

Suddenly the fog comes in thick and dank and cold. We turn on the automatic foghorn in the loud-hailer, almost the only piece of original equipment that remains with the boat. While the horn blows a blast every minute, I stay glued to the radar.

A year ago, I could make no more sense of the radar screen than I could of a Rorschach inkblot, but I have learned a little since then. The radar picks up a blip directly ahead – something in the water but not big enough to be a vessel. The minutes pass, and the blip comes closer and closer. Eventually, dead ahead, a fisher-man's high-flyer emerges from the fog, a tall pole on a buoy, with a radar reflector on top of it. Miraculous. The radar has insisted that something smaller than a vessel is there, and there it is.

The fog stays with us while we grope toward the N2 buoy that marks Cape Sable, the second most southerly point in Canada. It thins as we make our way up the west side of Cape Sable Island and clears completely for our entrance into Clark's Harbour.

Cla'ks Ha'bah – Clark's Harbour to you – is still a flat-out fishing community with a busy commercial wharf and no facilities for yachts at all. Its wharves are lined with fat, ugly, rule-beating boats. Their length, prescribed by regulation, may not exceed forty-four feet – but these obese, overpowered boats are almost twenty-five feet wide, with square, open sterns. You could play hockey in the cockpits. They're named for the fishermen's wives and kids. *Larry and Sisters, Reuben and Sisters, Scottland and Matthew, Tyson & Kandice, Kelly 'n' Kids, Jolene and Colby.* Apparently nobody in the family can be left out.

Okay, Colby, okay! I'll put your name on the friggin' boat too! Now stop flingin' macaroni at your mother!

Clark's Harbour, like the other ports farther along the Sou'West Shore, relies on the fecund fishing grounds on Georges Bank. This area also has the mildest weather in the province, which means it has the longest fishing season. The lobster fishery is robust, and the fishermen are still allowed to take groundfish, like cod and haddock. When Marjorie and I walked down to the end of the wharf, we saw fish swirling inside cages – small codfish, captured live, to be delivered alive to Chinese restaurants in New York.

A deserted boardwalk ran along the shore, attached to a park and a tourist bureau, but not many tourists or cruisers find their way to Clark's Harbour, and the town doesn't need to care much about them. Fishing is what matters. The port authority had a harbourmaster who was supposed to collect fees from visiting vessels, but his office was never open, and when I asked the fishermen about paying for dockage, they just grinned and shrugged. Thirty years ago, most small Nova Scotian ports were like this, completely focused on fishing, easygoing and friendly, almost surprised when visitors showed up. People on the wharf were casually curious – Where y' from? Where y' headed? What kinda boat y'got there? – but tourists were really no more important to them than migrating butterflies.

Tail wagging, Leo nosed up to a tall woman in jeans, carrying a camera. Her name was Shelly Nickerson, and she was taking scenic photos for the local tourist bureau. She was driving on to West Head, another small artificial harbour a couple of miles away, where the local coast guard lifeboat was based. Could I come along? I could.

We drove past half-a-dozen active boatbuilding shops – the Cape Island boat, the workhorse of the Nova Scotia fishery, was created here, and the industry is still going strong, though a fishing boat today costs upward of $400,000. The former "coxswain" – the captain – of the coast guard lifeboat was Ronnie Newell, whom I'd known slightly, and who turned out to be Shelly's cousin. We stopped at his house, but he wasn't home. Shelly dropped me off at the lifeboat base near the West Head wharf.

I was looking for advice. Beyond Clark's Harbour, *Magnus* would be increasingly subjected to the Bay of Fundy tides, the highest in the world. The volume of water that sweeps in and out of Fundy twice a day is greater than the volume of all the world's rivers combined, and when these mighty currents pour through narrow passages and over underwater obstacles they can produce ferocious rips and eddies – standing waves and overfalls that can be downright dangerous to a small boat. This is no place for a stranger to go blundering about in ignorance. But nobody knows the local waters – anywhere – better than the coast guard lifeboat crews.

The lifeboat service is an example of the federal government doing something spectacularly right, and it started right here in Clark's Harbour. Forty years ago, a fierce gale roared over the local fishing fleet. Most fishermen made it to shelter, but one boat capsized close to shore. The crew was left clinging to the keel of the overturned boat, near enough to shore that their friends and neighbours on the beach could see their struggles – but nobody had a boat powerful enough and stout enough to go out and take them off. As the whole town watched in horror, the men were blown offshore to their deaths.

It should not be possible for men to drown within sight of potential rescuers. Clark's Harbour petitioned the government for a small, powerful rescue vessel specifically to protect the extensive fishing fleet of southern Nova Scotia. The coast guard agreed, and eventually set up a chain of eighteen lifeboat stations along both coasts and throughout the Great Lakes. The first was established at Clark's Harbour, in 1966.

These "Waveney-class" vessels were incredible boats. Designed in the United States, they were eventually used in Britain, Australia, Portugal, Norway, Italy, Iran, and elsewhere. They were forty-four feet long, with twin 200+=hp diesel engines. Their hulls were steel, their superstructures aluminum, and they were designed to flip upright instantly if capsized – as several were. They were rough, tough, noisy little boats; the crews communicated using headsets, and reported that going to sea in a Waveney was like going to sea in an oil drum full of diesel engines.

The crews were just as tough. The coast guard manned the boats with local fishermen, who would be rescuing their friends and families, and who knew the local waters intimately. The lifeboats routinely towed in disabled yachts and fishing boats from forty and fifty miles offshore, dragged them off the rocks, plucked the crews off sinking vessels. They even towed small freighters.

They went out in any kind of weather. The Groundhog Day gale of February 2, 1976, developed winds of 100 miles per hour, gusting to 116, with a twelve-foot storm surge. Raging waves were dragging whole houses right off the shore. The Westport lifeboat was out that day, looking for a vessel in distress, when the skipper, Henry Porter, came through a sea and saw a house floating dead ahead. There was nothing he could do but open the throttle and drive right through it. Shingles flew, and the house exploded. Aside from some metal dings and scraped paint, the boat was fine.

The forty-four-footers have been retired now, replaced by bigger, faster boats. The duty skipper who greeted me at the Clark's Harbour base was Brian Goulden, a tall, lean man who was one of only three active veterans of the original Waveney lifeboats.

"We were cowboys, and the government didn't know we existed," he grinned. "We put those boats through some awful stuff. We'd run them right up on the rocks deliberately, to provide a stable working platform. And then you just put them in reverse and scraped back off. I think Henry Porter in Westport went through something like fourteen propellers.

"And our boss, Captain Don Williams – he'd just shrug off the damage. 'That's what we're in business for,' he'd say.

"These new boats are Cadillacs. Come on down to the wharf, I'll show you."

The new boats are impressive – faster, far more comfortable, and with a much greater operating range. But they have their defects too. Built to a British design, they were not intended for work in really cold water, and in midwinter the intakes for the engine cooling water clog up with slush. Visibility is poor, except dead ahead. And these boats have aluminum hulls, which are much more delicate. You don't run them up on the rocks on purpose.

In fact, the whole service has become notably more governmental in flavour. The skippers are now captains, not coxswains, and have to have tickets. They're also supposed to conform to safety standards that make sense for most vessels, but not for lifeboats. For example, the first duty of the skipper is not to endanger the vessel or the crew – but that's exactly what effective lifeboat crews have to do.

"You know, Brian," I said, looking at the instruments in the wheelhouse, "*Magnus* actually has most of the same electronics aboard. Smaller scale, but the same instruments."

Brian nodded.

"Most yachts do today, and that makes a big difference. It used to be that in the summer, about half our distress calls were from yachts, but we don't get very many now."

"Tell me about routes to Yarmouth," I said. "It looks as though there's an inside route right through the Tusket Islands."

"Schooner Passage," nodded Brian. "Don't go there. It doesn't save you much distance, and it's treacherous. Go inside Seal Island and Mud Island, outside Outer Bald Tusket, inside Green Island. Choose your tide right, and you'll get an extra two or three knots from the current. Here, I'll show you on the chart."

I thanked him, and went outside to take some photos. All of a sudden Brian and three crewmen came running by, jumping aboard the lifeboat, starting the engine, casting off lines.

"Youngster driftin' out to sea on an air mattress," called Brian. "Lockeport. See you!"

And the stout red vessel was gone, the water frothing in her wake as Brian steered out around the rock breakwater and opened up the throttle.

Late evening, and the concrete wharf is again swathed in thick fog, amber under the lamp standards. Leo and I amble along on our last outing. A pickup truck rolls slowly down the wharf, turns around, pulls up beside us. A young couple, with a toddler.

"Kinda boat y'got theah?" the young man asks. "Wheah y' headin?" Yarmouth, I tell him, and yes, I say, we're planning on catching the morning tide.

"Ay-uh," he says, looking around at the fog. "Hope it fines up for yuh."

It did "fine up" in the morning, and *Magnus* picked her way carefully along the coast in sunlight, though the light wind once again opposed us. I looked warily at the lump of Seal Island on the horizon. As the most southerly point in Nova Scotia, Seal Island is an important turning-point, and its proximity to Fundy gives it a lethal combination of four-knot currents and dense fogs. It has been the site of 180 documented shipwrecks, and probably a similar number of forgotten ones. I was grateful to be well away from it, navigating in sunlight with modern electronics.

As *Magnus* motored along, other boats appeared, all heading our way – a big sloop out near Seal Island, a couple of smaller ones emerging from some little anchorage in the Tuskets. More islands appeared on the horizon: Gannet Dry Ledge, Green Island.

Somewhere on the low-lying coast lay the entrance to the Chebogue River, where we had a mooring if we wanted to use it.

The mooring belonged to Dave Fraser, the coast guard engineer in Clark's Harbour, who had visited *Magnus* the previous afternoon. The youngster on the air mattress had been recovered before the lifeboat arrived, and the crew was back in port.

I was changing the engine oil and the fuel filters when Dave arrived, and I asked him if he could see any water in the filter. No, he said, but the filter is pretty dirty. He thought we should dismount the whole filter, disassemble it, and clean it. We did that – or rather he did, while I helped and asked questions. Marjorie made a cold plate, and Dave stayed to eat with us. He was glad of the diversion, he said. Lifeboat duty consists of brief spurts of excitement interspersed with long periods of boredom.

Thinking of Dave's mooring, I scanned the low coastline again. The entrance to the Chebogue wouldn't be apparent until you were practically in the river, and in any case we wanted to make Yarmouth today. We would press on. Up ahead I could see a broad field of breakers in an otherwise minimal sea.

"Marjorie," I said, "here comes our first tide rip."

She scrambled up to look, and gave a little cry of dismay. The tide rip looked like rapids in a river – a field of standing waves, four or five feet high, constantly breaking and reforming in the same location, shaped by the tide as it poured across an underwater ledge. Soon we were into it, the boat pitching and ducking its head, water sloshing over the foredeck and washing across the windshield.

"How much longer?" Marjorie asked.

"Not long," I said. "I can see the end of it. But this is a calm day, and the tide is with us. Can you imagine what this would be like in a howling gale with a big tide? It doesn't bear thinking about."

From a cruising sailor's viewpoint, Yarmouth is the most welcoming town in Nova Scotia.

We make our way slowly up the historic waterfront, once the home of an astonishing fleet of sailing ships. The waterfront is still a busy place – this is the leading port in southern Nova Scotia, with direct freight and ferry service to Portland and Bar Harbor, Maine. Among the vessels looming over us is the huge, mean-looking twin-hulled ferry, the *Cat*, which travels at fifty-five miles per hour and crosses to Bar Harbor in less than three hours.

A young woman welcomes us to Killam's Wharf, a set of floating docks that belong to the town. The docks are next to a brick-paved square with flower beds, grass, a bandstand. Showers, laundry, power, and water are on the site, and the first night's berthage is free. Cruising boats are all around us, anchored off the wharf, tied up alongside. One short block up the hill is a pleasant, human-scale Main Street, with all the facilities a Main Street should have. Machine shops, chart agents, and other marine suppliers are all around us. Rudder's Restaurant and brew pub is next door.

I look out at the harbour, where boats fly the flags of Quebec, Massachusetts, New Brunswick. But something is wrong here. Normally an anchored boat points its bow into the wind, and the flags fly out astern. But these flags are flying backward. I almost feel dizzy. How can this be? Have the laws of physics been repealed? Then I realize that the falling tide is flowing out of the harbour, but the wind is flowing into it. The tide controls the boats, but the wind controls the flags.

We walk the dog, go to Rudder's. Over a splendid seafood dinner, we discuss our next move.

Normally, Nova Scotian boats sail directly from Yarmouth to Bar Harbor, in the track of the *Cat*. The trip is about a hundred miles, and takes about twenty-four hours. That route is a little north of west, and boats bound south often prefer a more southerly course toward Gloucester or Cape Cod. That's more than two hundred miles of ocean sailing; Cape Cod is closer to three hundred miles. Not a practical plan for Marjorie and her two old dogs.

"Tell me again how we'll do it?" Marjorie asked.

"We'll go to Westport," I said. "That's about thirty miles. From there it's fifty miles across to Jonesport, Maine, which seems to be a port of entry – a long run between pit stops for Leo, but it's possible. Alternatively, we'll go from Westport to Grand Manan Island, up the bay, and then it's a short hop to Eastport, Maine, which certainly is a port of entry."

"It's a long way round, isn't it?"

"Yes, but it's the only way I can see to avoid an overnight passage. I'll call U.S. Customs tomorrow."

Next day, I called the 1-800 number for U.S. Customs.

That number is not accessible from your area code.

Why am I not surprised? These 1-800 numbers have become a curse. If the 1-800 number doesn't work – and it often doesn't – you're stuck. You don't have a real number.

Three "Waterway Guides" provide guidance to sailors for the whole east coast of the United States. The *Northern Waterway Guide* covers Delaware Bay to the Canadian border and gives a real number for the North Atlantic Customs Management Center in Boston. I dialled and got passed along to a knowledgable-sounding man. Could we enter the United States at Jonesport, possibly on the coming Sunday?

No. Jonesport isn't a staffed port. The boat can enter there, but not the people.

Hard to separate them.

The people aboard need to fill in Form I-68 in the presence of an officer, so you have to go to a staffed port. The idea is that an Immigration officer should see you at least once in a season.

Okay, we'll go to a staffed port. What are the choices?

In eastern Maine? Eastport, Lubec, and Bar Harbor.

Eastport, then. Probably on Sunday.

Well, Eastport is staffed only from 8:00 to 4:00, Monday through Saturday. Lubec is at the bridge to Campobello Island, so it's staffed twenty-four hours a day. Sunday, you'd have to go to Lubec.

Thank you.

Sigh. Lubec is on Lubec Narrows, through which the tide swirls at up to eight knots. Against a current like that, *Magnus* would sail backward. With such a current behind her, she would careen through a narrow waterway, only half under control, at the breakneck speed of fourteen knots. Not a good idea. But we could sail north around Campobello Island to reach Eastport from the rear, so to speak, and then motor over to Lubec – though we might still wind up swirling around in fierce currents.

The phone rang again. It was a customs officer from Lubec.

Was it you that was asking about entering at Lubec?

It was.

If I were you, I'd enter at Eastport. Currents are pretty strong here, and there's no real good place to tie up.

But Eastport isn't open Sundays.

Who told you that?

Your colleague in Boston.

Eastport's open every day, up to about 6:30. Has to be – they meet the ferry from Deer Isle, New Brunswick, and it runs every day.

The boys in Boston, he assured me, were talking through their brass hats. (Mainers often discern this habit in Bostonians.) Eastport was open Sundays. Come on over.

I walked down the street to the Canada Customs office in Yarmouth. Did we need an outbound clearance for the United States? Wouldn't be a bad idea, said the officers, and filled one out. Back at the boat, Marjorie and I reviewed the documents. Clearance, check. Passports, check. Health and rabies certificates for the BFD, check. Ship's registration papers, check. Lots of ID.

Anything else? If the boat were searched, was there anything in the lockers to alarm even the most paranoid customs officer? Anything that looked like it might belong to a drug smuggler, a money-launderer, a socialist, a subversive, an illegal immigrant, a terrorist, an atheist, a pervert? No?

Good to go. So we went.

Digby Neck and its adjoining islands thrust south from Nova Scotia like a witch's bony forefinger, dividing St. Mary's Bay from the Bay of Fundy. At the first joint is Petit Passage, and beyond that is Long Island. At the second joint is Grand Passage, and the fingertip is Brier Island. Westport is on Brier Island, and the Fundy tides boil fiercely past its waterfront on Grand Passage.

Because we wanted to reach Westport at slack water, we stayed in Yarmouth till the noon hour. As we cleared the harbour mouth, Marjorie looked astern.

"Don!" she cried. "The *Cat!*"

The ferry was right behind us, towering above us. I spun the wheel to starboard, out of her path, and kept right on turning to take her wake head-on. *Magnus* bounced through the waves and eased back on her course. Aboard the giant ferry, a man recognized *Magnus*, squinted through a camera, and pressed the shutter. He was Rudy Haase, a retired boatyard owner who had twice done the trip we were embarked upon, more than half a century earlier. In his photo, *Magnus* looks like a bathtub toy.

Although we'd started late, we were soon in danger of reaching Westport too early. I called the Westport Coast Guard crew, who confirmed that the tide was still swirling in Grand Passage. The day was tranquil and sunny, with only a light wind blowing from the north. We shut down the engine and idled along under sail. A couple of draggers were towing nearby, and the coast lay off in the distance like a steely smudge with occasional white spots marking the big churches in the Acadian villages. It was like sailing in an oil painting, a timeless, serene tableau.

From time to time, I chatted with the Westport Coast Guard on the radio. An hour before slack water, a speedboat put out from

Westport. As it approached, it resolved itself into an inflatable coast guard launch with a tall, greying man at the wheel. His name was Neil Green, and he had come to pilot us in.

Like Clark's Harbour, Westport is a fishing community rarely visited by yachts, and it was a disappointment. The harbour was small, crowded, and dirty, with a scum of floating garbage bobbing in a corner of the wharf. The best berth available was on the outside of four husky fishing boats, and no sooner were our lines ashore than the wharfinger was aboard demanding a twenty-dollar fee to tie up.

For what? we wondered. No electrical power, no water, and a steeplechase over fish-holds and gunwales to get ashore. A miserable policy of privatization has off-loaded former government wharves onto communities across the region, and all of them are strapped for funds, understood. But we didn't get much for our money in Westport.

Brier Island bills itself as Nova Scotia's eco-tourism destination, and with some justice – it offers excellent hiking and whale-watching, and its location on the Atlantic Flyway makes it an exceptional place for birding. Westport was also the hometown of Joshua Slocum, the first man to sail alone around the world. Slocum stopped here for a few days during his epic voyage in the 1890s, but his family home was one of those washed away in the Groundhog Day gale, and his only memorial in Brier Island seems to be a stone cairn erected by the Slocum Society, an international cruising organization. Overall, Westport presented itself as a drab, beaten-looking little place, and when the fog came rolling back it was downright bleak.

Seeking a lift from the rising tide, we left late for Grand Manan Island, motoring through dense fog all the way. We sat side by side in the wheelhouse, our foghorn braying regularly, watching the radar and the GPS. *Magnus* chugged steadily forward, the engine muttering, the boat rocking rhythmically from side to side. Motoring in fog feels like floating in space or walking on a tread-mill. The boat rocks and rumbles, suspended in the greyness, going nowhere.

The boost from the tide never materialized, and we gradu-ally realized that we would not make Grand Manan before dark. The daylight slowly faded. In the thick murk of darkness and fog, all we could see was the red-and-green loom of our running lights diffused in the sodden air, and the soft glow of the instru-ments. We couldn't see a thing, but the electronic chart told us exactly where we were.

"I don't like this," Marjorie muttered nervously.

"Six minutes to the harbour buoy at North Head, Grand Manan," I said. "And nothing on the radar except the shoreline."

"This is spooky," said Marjorie. "I don't like not being able to see anything."

"I don't like it much either, but everything's fine," I said. "Think of what it was like years ago, with no instruments except a compass."

"What's that?" exclaimed Marjorie.

A pulsing red glow up ahead – the flashing light of the buoy. We changed course for the little harbour behind the stone break-waters, now only half a mile away. The charcoal night was still and quiet. I pulled back on the throttle, and *Magnus* nosed slowly into the gloom. The ghostly shape of a breakwater appeared. I throttled back to a dead idle. The instruments were reporting us to be right at the harbour entrance. We went on deck.

"Fishing boat! Over there!" said Marjorie, pointing to star-board. "Close!" I spun the wheel. We idled alongside. She caught hold of the fishing boat's foredeck. Stern line in hand, I grabbed the side deck. The deck rolled over in my hand; what I had grabbed was only a small log, rough with bark. I lunged for a pipe sticking up in its cockpit. It fell over; it was only the handle of a sledgehammer. I scrambled onto the fishing boat, groped around until I found an eyebolt, then went forward to tie the bow line.

In the darkness, Marjorie passed Leo over to me, and the three of us worked our way up the narrow side deck and then across a second fishboat that lay between us and the floating dock. The shore towered high above us, and the ramp looked almost vertical. We had seen thirteen-foot tides in Yarmouth, fifteen-foot tides in Westport, and in both those places I had pushed on Leo's rump to help him up the steep wooden ramps. But the tidal range in Grand Manan is the height of a two-storey house, and the surface of the long ramp leading up to the shore was made of sharp-toothed aluminum.

Worried about the metal cutting Leo's paws, I carried him up the ramp. We walked around the parking lot at the head of the wharf, looking down on the bowl of the harbour, with its ghostly lines of boats clustered inside the massive stone breakwater.

Back aboard, with Leo settled for the night, Marjorie poured us each a tot of rum.

"I'm still shaky," she said. "I didn't enjoy that run at all. And I'm absolutely bagged."

"It wasn't much fun," I agreed. "But it's always surprising, you know, how you just keep on keeping on, and eventually it's over. And I've never sailed a boat so well equipped for this kind of thing."

"We've been running for five days out of the last seven," Marjorie said. "It's still summer. Let's explore. Let's take a day off and see Grand Manan."

"Absolutely. Let's be tourists."

Grand Manan is a world of its own – fifteen miles in length, seven miles in width, population 2,650, the largest island in an archipelago in the mouth of the Bay of Fundy. If you project the Maine–New Brunswick border into the sea, you hit Grand Manan.

I had been to the island eleven years earlier with a group of naturalists. It was an odd experience. I was apprehensive about close encounters with earnest granola-crunching tree-huggers; I was, after all, an unreformed curmudgeon who liked to smoke tobacco, drink alcohol, fondle sweaty bodies, and eat dead animals. En route, listening to the radio, I was unsettled to hear a CBC commentator talking about the rise of insect-rights groups. The concept of insect rights has a certain miserable logic, I admit. All life is part of the world's life, insects included. Still, some consciousness-raising will be needed. When I speak feelingly about the sanctity of life, I do not have black flies and mosquitoes in mind. Dear God. Insect rights? What kind of week would this be?

Indeed, one naturalist did express moral angst about the cruelty of removing earwigs from her canoe – rather than killing them or even dumping them, she had learned to take them paddling with her – but overall it had been a fascinating week, finding harebells and bunchberries on the clifftops, watching periwinkles and monkfish in the tidal pools, and examining carnivorous plants – sundew and pitcher plants – in the bogs. We had seen five species of whale in a single afternoon, including the gravely endangered Atlantic right whale, which has been hunted almost to extinction.

Grand Manan is also a prime location for viewing birds such as plovers, herons, sandpipers, guillemots, bald eagles, geese, ducks, and even peregrine falcons, as well as the common species of gulls, terns, and cormorants. It's one of the rare places where a birder on the land can observe pelagic birds, which live almost entirely at sea: petrels, phalaropes, and shearwaters.

These are miraculous birds. The sooty shearwater, for instance, breeds in New Zealand, the Falklands, and Cape Horn, while the greater shearwater nests in the isolated Tristan da Cunha group in the middle of the South Atlantic. The delicate-looking Arctic tern, not much bigger than a robin, breeds from Massachusetts to the Arctic – but it spends the winter in southern Africa and the Antarctic.

About 275 bird species have been recorded on the island, and half the main floor of the island's fine little museum is given over to a magnificent collection of bird specimens. These are the legacy of a Grand Manan fisherman named Allan Moses, who became an internationally recognized pioneer ornithologist.

In the morning, Marjorie and I took Leo for a walk. North Head is a pleasing village, and in the dying days of August it was absolutely at its best. The day was baking hot, and the tide was low again. Standing at the head of the ramp, we saw a virtual anthology of boats in the harbour – the ubiquitous fibreglass Cape Island fishing boats, of course, but also steel draggers, West Coast–style purse seiners, open weir-seiners, tuna boats with observation towers, and graceful double-ended herring carriers of sixty to eighty-five feet in length, built of wood and derived from now-vanished sailing vessels. A few sailboats and small dories were mixed in among the workboats, and a beautiful sightseeing schooner lay off on a mooring. A number of scows were moored nearby – work platforms for the numerous fish farms, many equipped with pile-drivers.

Birds overhead, and the sea glittering off into the distance. A treed road that rose and fell over the low bluffs. Small, sturdy houses and inviting little inns. Gift shops, galleries, a farmers' market, a well-stocked department store masquerading as a hardware. We walked as far as the North Head Bakery, an "artisanal" bakery where we treated ourselves to sweet pastries and a cappuccino.

At a gift shop we asked if there might be a local driver who would take two people and a Brave and Faithful Dog for a tour. Leighton Spicer, they said.

A rangy man with a minivan, Leighton is a native of the island and knows it intimately. He picked us up at the wharf, where we were looking at a visiting sailboat that had tied up in a very bad place, a spot where the boat would be far out of the water at low tide. All the loungers on the wharf were shaking their heads. We shook our heads with the best of them, but the skipper seemed remarkably unconcerned.

Leighton Spicer drove us all around the island. We visited the three lighthouses that guard the three corners of the island: Southwest Head, Swallowtail, The Whistle. Grand Manan's villages, clustered on the low, ragged east coast, owe their existence to the fact that Fundy's tumultuous waters are an unparalleled nursery for marine life. Grand Manan is surrounded by scallops, lobster, tuna, cod, haddock, pollock, hake, mackerel and herring, herring, herring.

The herring are mainly caught in weirs, which are visible all around the shores of the island. An invention of the Passamaquoddy Indians, weirs are heart-shaped structures of net fastened to stakes driven into the sea floor, with a straight fence of netting leading from the shore into the dimple of the heart. The fence directs schools of herring into the weir, where they swim around in circles until the fishermen sweep them up in a seine net and pump them into a herring carrier. The herring scales are stripped off in the process and sold separately to produce "pearl essence," which puts the iridescent gloss in lipstick, eyeshadow, and metallic paints. One Grand Manan father allegedly forbade his daughter to wear makeup because he thought it barbaric for women to go around with herring scales smeared on their faces.

Small herring are sold as sardines, and packed by Connors Brothers in a processing plant at Seal Cove. Traditionally, huge quantities of the larger herring were smoked – soaked in brine, then hung on sticks in a barnlike building with wood fires smouldering on the floor. Four to six weeks later they were removed, decapitated, deboned, packed in ten-pound boxes, and sold to New England and the Caribbean. Smoked herring are delicious, though salty, but the demand for them has faded badly, and the island's many commercial smokehouses now stand idle, though islanders still smoke a few herring for themselves.

Although Grand Manan's east coast is low, its west coast is a forbidding rampart of basalt columns rising as much as four hundred feet from the sea. This solid wall is broken only once, by a deep gorge behind a cobble beach that demarks the jade-green waters of a hauntingly beautiful lagoon. This is Dark Harbour, or *Dahk Hahbah*, as it is pronounced locally.

Dark Harbour has no permanent settlement; it is the preserve of dulsers and drinkers. In 1993, the island had seventeen churches, one for every 155 people – Baptists, Wesleyans, Pentecostals, Jehovah's Witnesses, and a few Anglicans and Catholics. Even the Moonies had a presence on the island, though only as proprietors of a lobster pound. In one village store I found twenty editions of the Bible along with many commentaries, not to mention nylon Bible cases at $27.95. (In fairness, I also found a whole rack of New Age and environmental music.)

In a place with so many churches, the outlook for Christian charity cannot be good. So the lower-caste drinkers slaked their sinful thirsts at Dark Harbour, where, on my previous visit, a genial inebriate had offered me a choice of refreshments from his well-stocked bar at ten in the morning. For him, the night was not yet over.

This time, Leighton, Marjorie and I received no such offers, and we found Dark Harbour a relatively industrious-looking place, with boats coming and going, and a fleet of brightly painted dories hauled up along the shore.

The boats belonged to dulse harvesters. Dulse is a burgundy-coloured edible seaweed beloved of people all around the Bay of Fundy. It grows in the intertidal zone, and during the summer dulse-harvesters sally forth at low tide to pluck it by hand from the rocks. You see it lying in "drying fields" all over Grand Manan. It can be popped into soups or salads, fried, dried, or ground up and used as a condiment. A friend of mine in Parrsboro claims it tastes best when crisped on a woodstove and washed down with beer.

Like caviar, dulse is an acquired taste. Its texture and flavour was described by one visitor as "salted garbage bag," but it contains fifty-two trace minerals and now sells internationally to health-food stores. And the very best dulse in the world, connoisseurs insist, the Dom Perignon of dulse, comes from Dark Harbour.

We filled up a couple of water containers at Leighton's home, and he dropped us back at the wharf. The poorly moored sailboat was now truly high and dry; from the floating dock, we looked up six or eight feet to the bottom of the keel. But the laugh was on us. It seemed that the boat's propeller shaft had come uncoupled from the engine and had slipped backward, hanging up against the rudder and sticking out under the bottom of the boat. When the tide had gone out, the skipper had simply walked under the boat, pushed the shaft back into place, and bolted it home. The Fundy tides had saved him from a haul-out that might have cost him several hundred dollars.

The use of the tides, he told us, was the secret to sailing in the Bay of Fundy. Heading south, we should leave early and motor right along on the morning tide. The summer southwesterly breeze, which blows in your face, generally comes up in the afternoon. Above all, don't fight the tides. Ride them whenever you can.

Good counsel, but not always easy for a stranger to follow. If the tide is low at 6:00 a.m., it will oppose you all morning, and the wind will be against you in the afternoon. Which do you choose?

In the end, we decided simply to get up in the morning and go, unless both wind and tide were opposing us. We rose the next morning at daybreak, and motored out of North Head into the misted rising sun. The weather was calm and still, the eastern sky coloured like bruises and peaches. Swallowtail Light was still flashing on its rocky promontory, and a circle of crooked herring weir pilings stood leaning in toward one another like a prayer circle.

We rounded the north end of the island and steered for the coast of Maine. I ran the yellow Q flag up the mast: the quarantine flag, flown by vessels arriving from foreign parts. We checked our customs preparations again: boat ready, papers in order, U.S. courtesy flag ready to fly. Teeth brushed, hair combed, shoes shined, pinko-commie-anarchist tendencies stowed in cold storage.

The day remained smudgy, with occasional patches of real fog. Schools of fish fed on the surface, and we heard the breath of whales but never saw them. Passing south of The Wolves, we found the lighthouse on East Quoddy Head at the northern tip of Campobello Island and turned south into Head Harbour Passage.

The tide funnels strongly through this passage, and *Magnus* was soon swinging and twisting in the currents and eddies. Just ahead and a bit to starboard lay Western Passage and The Old Sow, the largest whirlpool in the western hemisphere – so named, some say, for the piglike grunting it emits when the tides are running strongly and the 250-foot whirlpool is churning furiously. "I didn't mind so much gettin' caught in it," one fisherman is said to have remarked. "What I resented was havin' to row uphill to get out."

We angled across the international boundary in the middle of Friar Roads, and made our way to the concrete commercial wharf of Eastport. Inside the wharf was a small basin, full of fishing boats, along with the occasional yacht and a U.S. Coast Guard inflatable launch. A fisherman waved us to a berth alongside a lobster boat.

We tied up, and I phoned Eastport Customs. No answer, so I left a message. Leo was eager to go ashore, but the rule is that only the master of an inbound ship may go ashore, and only to contact customs. Would a customs officer object if he met an uncleared foreign dog relieving himself at the roadside? Unlikely – but the United States is a tad touchy about its borders these days.

So we waited. And waited. I called again: still no answer. But Lubec had said Eastport was open. I called Lubec. Wait, they said, we'll call Eastport on the radio. We waited.

"*Magnus!*" A pleasant-looking gent of middle years in a U.S. Customs uniform was calling from the dock. His name was Barry Thompson.

"Hi!" I called. "You want to come aboard?"

"No, no," he said. "Just come up to the office and we'll clear you in."

We walked up to the office, an imposing stone building at the head of the wharf. I presented our papers, and Thompson filled in forms by hand, and on the computer that glowed incongruously in the dark basement of the old building. Two couples sauntered in.

"Just a moment," said Thompson to me. He turned to the newcomers. "Help you?"

"Just want to clear in," said one of the men.

"Purpose of your visit?"

"Lunch. Then we'll head back."

"All right," said Thompson. He noted their cruising licence, sent them off, and turned to me. "People come and go across this border all the time. You get to know them. You get farther south, you'll find they don't know what to do with you. But here it's routine." He handed back my papers along with a cruising licence. "Check in with customs again when you get farther south. Portland or Boston."

"That's it?"

"That's it. Enjoy your time in the United States."

I walked back down to the boat and showed the licence to Marjorie.

"We're in," I said. "Pass Leo over to me. Let's go look at America."

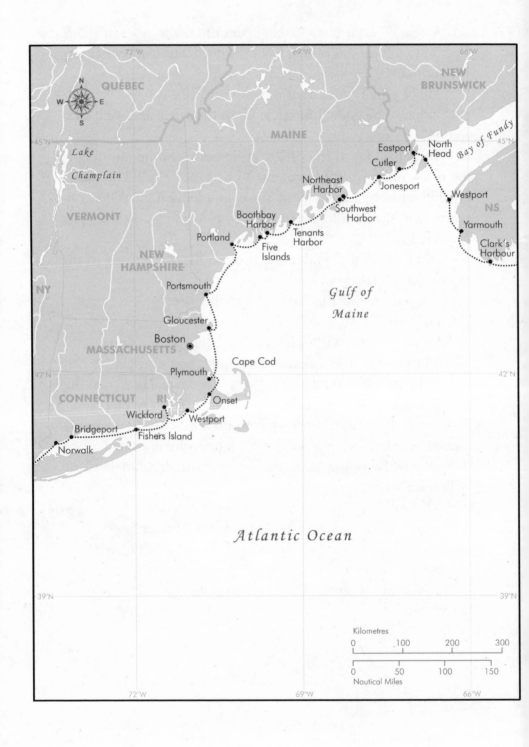

PART III

NEW ENGLAND

Eastport feels like the town at the end of the road because that's what it is – "the most easterly city in the United States," located on an island at the end of a chain of islands. "City" is wishful thinking; the population is about two thousand. The huge concrete wharf serves bulk carriers that sometimes pick up logs, granite, and paper products, and a sizable excursion schooner is moored alongside it, but mostly it serves as a breakwater for small craft and a recreational promenade for the town.

We met two new species of wildlife on the Eastport wharf: the American Coastal Line-Dipper and the Automatic Talker. Line-Dippers may be found on piers, breakwaters, bridges, and boats all the way from Maine to Miami, patiently casting their fishing lines out into the water but rarely catching a fish. At first light, when I carried Leo up the steep ramp to the wharf for his morning constitutional, the Line-Dippers were already on station, methodically whipping their rods back and forth. When the BFD and I – sometimes with Marjorie – took a turn on the wharf before bedtime, the Line-Dippers were still there, fishing late into the night, illuminated by streetlights as they patiently pitched their lines into the blackness.

The Line-Dippers and the strollers support not one but two fast-food joints on the wharf itself, a shanty near the shore and a trailer – Nutty Norm's – out on the dock itself. Leo and I once found ourselves passing near Nutty Norm's back door just when the proprietor was emerging.

"Hello," I said.

"I just changed my oil," said the proprietor, presumably Nutty Norm himself. "That's really important, you know. You should do it all the time. Most people don't do it often enough. Here, come and see." He tugged me into his trailer to look at his impeccable stainless vats, filled with golden clear cooking oil. While I stood there and the dog pulled at his leash, Nutty Norm explained how often cooking oil should be changed, and why. He excoriated the slovenly habits of most fast-food restaurants, expressed his solicitous feelings for his customers, and delivered a general disquisition on quality control in chip-wagon cuisine.

He was, I realized, an Automatic Talker. Automatic writers are people who can write without thinking, tapping into a flow of text from their own subconscious or someone else's, maybe even Someone Else's, depending on your beliefs. When they pick up a pen, the text flows out. Automatic Talkers are similar. When they open their mouths, the talk spills forth – an endless flow of it. What they say is completely disconnected to anything going on around them. Their talk is an audible segment of an internal conversation running on endlessly within them, an internal river of silent but unremitting speech.

Nutty Norm – a thoroughly amiable man (with admirable standards of quality) – was not the only Automatic Talker in Eastport. We walked down Water Street, whose three commercial blocks constitute a National Historic Waterfront District, anchored by the grey stone pile of the Customs House at one end and the library three blocks away. It's a pleasant district, although – like most gentrified waterfronts – it is lined with vewy pwetty shops that make it easy to buy porcelain figurines, scented soap, or tea cosies, but not milk or shingle nails or bond paper.

I had a story to file, so we went into a café to ask about finding Internet access. The proprietor, who might have been Norm's sister, launched into a dissertation on the implications of converting her business to an Internet café, the learning curve she would face, the question of whether the additional income would warrant the additional cost, the importance of travellers to the town, the role of cruising yachts in the tourism mix, and much more.

Another Automatic Talker. But she had no idea where we could connect to the Internet. Perhaps the library.

We walked on to the Peavey Memorial Library, a dignified red-brick structure trimmed in white and framed by trees. It looks like a postcard of New England. Yes indeed, Internet access was available, but only on the library's own computers. No, I couldn't bring my laptop up and plug it in.

I wandered into the circular reading room, all wood and windows, with a section that read, MAINE AUTHORS. I expected the usual local-interest books by little old ladies with three names – *Cowbell Poems* by Hermione Whiffenpoof Featherduster, *Pioneer Days on the Appendectomy River* by Ernestine Euphemia Foulbottom – but I was about to be chastened. The authors of Maine are heavy-hitters: Stephen King, E.B. White, Sarah Orne Jewett, Linda Greenlaw, E.A. Robinson, Artemus Ward.

The Peavey Library also houses an 1814 letter from Admiral Sir Thomas Hardy – the same Hardy from whom the dying Lord Nelson requested a kiss. Hardy's letter demands the surrender of Eastport, and requires the citizens of Eastport to swear allegiance to the British throne. If not, the cannons of his fleet will save the town for Britain by levelling it. Eastport became British in an eyeblink.

Overall, this part of Maine is not fertile soil for Yankee pride. It was seized by the British during the Revolution and again during the War of 1812. The Brits collected customs duties in Maine ports for several years, and Lord Dalhousie, the governor of Nova Scotia, eventually used the proceeds to establish Dalhousie University, in Halifax. In fact, what some U.S. commentators call "the worst U.S. naval disaster prior to that of Pearl Harbor" took place just a few miles down the coast, near Castine. The British seized the area in 1779, and Massachusetts sent a substantial expedition to recover it. When British reinforcements arrived, the nineteen U.S. vessels fled up the Penobscot River, where all were scuttled or burned by their own crews. One of the U.S. soldiers sent scrambling through the woods was Lieutenant Colonel Paul Revere.

It would have been nice to see Admiral Hardy's letter, but of course we didn't: we had no time. We were looking for Internet access, which we ultimately found at the office of a good-natured realtor.

Eastport is shielded from the Bay of Fundy by Campobello Island, once the summer home of Franklin Roosevelt. Campobello is Canadian, but it can be reached by land only over a bridge across the Lubec Narrows from Maine. We could get around Campobello by retracing our course back into Canada and out around the northern tip of the island – or we could save eight miles or more by going under the bridge and through the swift tidal currents of the Narrows.

The U.S. Coast Guard maintains an inflatable rescue launch at Eastport, and I asked one of its crewmen about going through the Narrows. He shook his head. He couldn't really give advice, but he could confirm that the Narrows was a tricky passage. So we took the long way around, motoring back into Head Harbour Passage in the sunny morning. The last of the flood tide was swirling around the boat in glassy gyres. *Magnus* forged ahead, making 5.5 knots through the water, but only 2.7 knots over the ground.

Out in the bay we rode the falling tide down the coast, rolling out the jib and motor-sailing down the seaward side of Campobello to Quoddy Head, where we altered course for Cutler. We had seen occasional lobster buoys, but as we turned in for Cutler we found them everywhere. Even the entrance channel was cluttered with buoys. We slowed right down, creeping under the hill known as the Eastern Knubble, sliding around the corner into the little harbour.

Cutler was enchanting, a cleft in the rocky shore that tapered into a small river running back into spruce-clad hills. A scattering of houses lay along the bluff, and a couple of high, spindly wharves thrust out into the harbour. The tide was low, and the only access to the wharves was straight up their vertical ladders. A lobster fisherman was just making fast to a mooring.

"Any visitor moorings?" I called.

"Take that one," he pointed. Among the close-set moorings, I backed up, idled forward, spun the wheel this way and that. Handling a motorboat is not like driving a car. A boat is a toy of wind and tide; in addition, the rotation of the propeller throws the stern one way when the boat is moving forward, the other way when it goes astern. To make matters worse, most boats won't back up straight, and turn tighter in one direction than the other. And when you approach a mooring ball, you can't see it because it disappears behind the bow.

But Marjorie snagged the weed-coated mooring line with the boathook, and we hauled it aboard. *Eleanor Kathleen*, said the stencilled letters on the mooring ball, with a phone number. But the cellphone had No Service, and we never found a payphone ashore. *Eleanor Kathleen*, whoever you are, we owe you one. We rowed Leo ashore at a dark little beach tucked between the rocks and walked along the road to the wharves, past immaculate wooden houses with well-tended gardens and trim patches of lawn.

Three more sailboats came in behind us, anchoring a little farther out in the harbour. Cruising in the Maritimes, I thought, we anchor all the time. Why were we not anchoring too? Why were we using wharves and moorings? These strong tidal currents concerned me, yes, and I was glad to be sure we wouldn't drag the anchor in the night. But –?

The dog, I thought. I was getting pretty good at heaving him over the stern rail, down to the swim platform and into the dinghy, and then rowing him ashore. But the closer we were to the shore, the better – and if I could simply lift him onto a wharf, that was best of all. The needs of the BFD were clearly a major factor in shaping the cruise.

I rowed the BFD ashore again in the morning, and then we left, weaving through the lobster buoys, heading for Jonesport. We set the jib and mizzen, and *Magnus* leaned over slightly, slipping down the coast at six knots. The features on this shore bore all kinds of strange and wonderful names: Scabby Ledge and the Scabby Islands, The Old Man, Misery Ledge, Fairy Head, Starboard Island, the Double Head Shot Islands. We skirted the edge of a vast tidal eddy, where dolphins and seals were playing and feeding, scrutinized and nagged by a huge flock of gulls and other seabirds. Oddly enough, we never saw a big whale.

Magnus was down by the bow and listing to starboard again, which she always seemed prone to do. I could never quite figure out why. I had shifted some pigs of lead ballast from under the main settee to the aft cabin, trying to bring her bow up, and I found myself wondering what else I could do, what other heavy items could be shifted from starboard to port. More hard work, heaving and hauling blocks of lead. I found myself remembering Captain Fred Wolf, the Lunenburg compass adjuster who swung the compass on my little schooner, all those years ago. He and his wife had recently sailed to Europe and back on a twenty-one-foot sloop. Had he enjoyed it?

"Oh, yes," he said.

Would he do it again?

"Oh, no."

Why not?

"Travelling by small boat," he said, "is the most expensive possible way to travel third-class."

He had a point. Marjorie had already remarked – rather forcefully – that she couldn't live permanently on a boat. I was beginning to doubt whether I could either. There is no time off; you are constantly on the alert, monitoring the course, watching for buoys, listening to the engine, checking for traffic. Components of the boat are always moving – fraying, chafing, wearing, rattling, binding – which produces a never-ending list of maintenance chores. And there is always room for improvement – a line that can be led more conveniently, better stowage, more hand-rails, whatever. The work never ends. And we allegedly do it for pleasure.

Sailing Away from Winter: How I Gave Up Cruising and Found Golf.

And nothing beats cruising for keeping a person humble. I was getting better at handling *Magnus* under power, but I was still very cautious, uncertain how the boat would behave in varying conditions. I had screwed up before, and I knew I would screw up again.

But at least I was not alone. In Eastport, when we were having dinner at a restaurant high above the harbour, I watched a lean, elegant ketch make its approach to a small wharf. I smiled with joy as the skipper made a complete mess of the job, stopping too early and failing to get a line ashore, then going around for another try, coming in too fast and sheering away while people on the wharf frantically tried to hold on to the docklines, then blowing sideways away from the dock. It was tremendously sat-isfying to watch, almost as entertaining as the Three Stooges.

The previous year, I had provided similar entertainment myself. In Merigomish, Nova Scotia, I ran *Magnus* aground in the mud and hauled her off with an anchor. Then a passing power-boater led us to the Pictou Yacht Club guest mooring in Blackhall Gut, where we slept very peacefully. As we left the next morning, Marjorie cast off the mooring line and dropped it overboard. I put *Magnus* in gear – and immediately heard the clunk-clunk-clunk of the mooring ball banging under the boat. I had wrapped the heavy mooring line around our propeller. It took me three hours – and five dives – to unwrap it.

"I did not like it," said Marjorie, "when the only part of you I could see above the water was the soles of your little feet."

I didn't like it much either. I later told the story to an expe-rienced Pictou sailor, "Trap" Stright.

"What galls me, Trap," I said, "is that I knew better than that."

"Sure you did," nodded Trap. "So did I, when I did it. We all knew better. What's that got to do with it?"

We crossed the mouth of Englishman Bay and headed into Moosabec Reach, the riverine strip of protected water that leads to Jonesport. The lobster buoys grew thicker and thicker, lying sideways in the current with little V ripples flowing around them. In Maine, traps are often double-buoyed in "toggles," so that even if the lower buoy is pulled completely underwater by the stream-ing tides, the upper one will still float.

Steering a slalom course through the buoys, we passed a blocky schooner with three stubby masts anchored in Moosabec Reach and made our way into Jonesport. We took a slow look at the fleet of anchored boats, an almost even mix of work boats and pleasure craft, and slid up to a floating dock attached to the state pier. Leo towed Marjorie up the steep ramp to find a patch of green. Moments later, a sunny-faced man in a battered Boston Whaler puttered up beside us.

"Welcome to East Jonesport!" he said. "Heading south?"

His name was Sune Loreen, and he owned the well-regarded Jonesport Shipyard up at the head of the cove. He had moorings available – floating docks anchored in the harbour, able to accommodate a boat on each side – with showers and a laundromat at the shipyard itself.

"We just had another boat here from Cape Breton," he said. "They had been up the Saint John River in New Brunswick, and they just left yesterday. Name of the boat was –"

"*Seaduction*?" I said. "From Port Hawkesbury? Jim and Carol Organ?"

"That's right. You know them?"

"Very well. I've been hoping to catch up with them."

"Well, you just missed them. Look, see that mooring . . ."

Jim Organ is a cheerful Newfoundland-born millwright, Carol Ann a techno-savvy teacher. They had made this same southern trip two years before, and I had followed their progress through Carol Ann's photos and comments posted on the Web. Their advice was responsible for many of the upgrades on *Magnus*. We had hoped to sail in company with them at least part of the way south. Well, if they stayed a few extra days in some port farther south, we might catch them yet. But we were surprised at how disappointed we were to have missed them.[7]

In truth, we were beginning to feel lonely. We had met interesting people and made new friends as we went along, but we had not seen a familiar face since the LaHave River. After living

---

7 As a boy, Jim sailed on a Newfoundland schooner with his grandfather, but he only returned to sailing in 1984, when he built the winning vessel for *The Great Paper Boat Race of the World* – a paper replica of a Viking longship, with a crew of six oarsmen. The story is told in my book *Wind, Whales and Whisky: A Cape Breton Voyage*. Toronto: Macmillan Canada, 1991.

for thirty years in a Cape Breton village, in a small province, and in the little world of Canadian writing and publishing, I was accustomed to swimming in a sea of long-term relationships, no more aware that I was doing so than a fish is aware of the water. And I missed it.

Cruising books often talk about the quick intensity of cruising friendships – the instant "best friends" you meet along the way, travel with for a few days or weeks, and meet again years later in some unexpected place. People who have made snowbird expeditions like ours often remark that little flotillas of southbound cruisers spontaneously coalesce, move on together for some period of time, and then dissolve. But we had fallen behind the southbound boats we had met – in Liverpool and Yarmouth – because of our roundabout route; the others had gone offshore across the Gulf of Maine.

I identified another species in Jonesport. The Maine Bigwhisker seems to flourish all through Downeast Maine. Backwoods hippies of indeterminate age left over from the 1960s or maybe from the nineteenth century, Maine Bigwhiskers wear workboots, twill pants, and plaid shirts, and have long, spadelike beards that begin just south of their eyes and terminate just north of their navels. They resemble a crowd of sombre Red Greens but with longer beards. When Maine Bigwhiskers speak, which they do infrequently, their mottled beards brush the top four buttons of their shirts. They indicate assent by nodding slowly and saying, "Ayyuh." Their thoughts and errands are mysterious, but they too swim in their villages like fish in the water, and I found them curiously reassuring.

In the shipyard laundromat I met a tired-looking woman in her forties, waiting for a load of washing to dry. Her name was Jo Anne McKay, and she was from the eighty-eight-foot, three-masted "galleon" we had seen in Moosabec Reach. *RawFaith* was designed and built by her husband, George, and their three sons, inspired by the plight of their disabled daughter. It was intended to be the only wheelchair-accessible tall ship in the United States, and its mission was to make the experience of sailing available to the disabled.

RawFaith had taken four years to build and rig. She was still unfinished inside, and she had no engine. Despite these details, the family was preparing to sail south within the following few weeks and intended to spend the winter in Florida. Jo Anne later asked Marjorie for any simple but nourishing recipes. Jo Anne was doing all the cooking, all the cleaning up, and all the laundry on *RawFaith*. When Marjorie said that didn't seem fair, the lady looked wistful. *RawFaith* had drained the family's coffers, and we saw handbills in several places soliciting donations from the faithful to sustain the venture. Townspeople seemed skeptical, though they had been supportive; the ship's sails, for instance, were sewn in the basement of a local church.

In the end, *RawFaith* did sail from Jonesport a few weeks later, but her steering gear and one of her masts were broken in a gale, and the coast guard towed her into Rockland, one hundred and twenty miles south, where a coast guard "captain of the port" order directed her to stay until she had passed an inspection. She was expected to stay at least for the winter.

We passed *RawFaith* again the next morning. The evening forecast had been for southerly winds of five to ten knots, which would mean a day of motoring into a light chop, but we awoke to thick fog. Well, perhaps it would clear. I dumped our extra five-gallon jug of diesel into the tank and took Leo ashore in the dinghy while Marjorie cleared the boat for departure and made coffee and sandwiches.

By seven, the fog was thinning, but the forecast was now for southwest winds of ten to twenty knots – moderately strong winds, right on the nose. But I was anxious to get south ahead of the advancing winter, hoping to stay in comfortable autumn weather all the way to Florida. In *Steered by the Falling Stars*, Dan Spurr vividly describes the consequences of delay. He and his wife passed through the Cape Cod Canal on September 22, and sailed in heavy mittens, insulated boots, and parkas all the way down the ICW. They had bitter winds in Chesapeake Bay, ice on the decks in the Carolinas. They were still shivering in northern Florida.

Well, the Cape Cod Canal was still a long way ahead of us, and it was now the first week of September. The mornings were already getting chilly. So we cast off at seven-thirty, motoring back out into Moosabec Reach and heading for the Beals Island highway bridge – the first bridge we had ever gone under, with thirty-nine feet of clearance at high tide. Our masthead is thirty-seven feet off the water, and a radio aerial reaches up another two feet. With the tide halfway down and falling, I calculated that we had several feet to spare – but it did not look that way from the deck. It was a relief to emerge unscathed on the other side.

"Don," said Marjorie quietly, "look at that." While I had been looking up, she had been looking forward – and what she had seen was an apparently unbroken carpet of lobster traps from one shore of the waterway to the other, and forward as far as the eye could see. Incredibly, the buoys were closer together than anything we'd seen yet.

Twirling the steering wheel furiously, I picked a way through the buoys. We left Moosabec Reach through a tiny passage between the rocks, crossed a bit of open water, and threaded our way through Tibbetts Narrows. Heading out to sea past the abandoned lighthouse at Nash Island, we picked up a spike on the horizon – the Petit Manan lighthouse, marking the point where we would turn down the coast.

The wind had risen steadily. Although the sounder was reporting depths of up to 250 feet, the lobster buoys were still thick. Punching into a three- or four-foot chop, *Magnus* was throwing water back on the windshield, making it difficult to see the buoys. And it seemed there was something wrong with the radar, which had suddenly stopped transmitting. Then the autopilot didn't seem to be following the course. Next I heard the warbling of the cellphone, which was plugged in and charging. But the inverter seemed to be cutting in and out. The computer chirped, telling me it was running not on the ship's batteries, but on its own internal battery. I looked at the GPS. We were moving, but the display wasn't changing. The GPS was frozen.

This coast is more ragged even than the eastern shore of Nova Scotia, I thought – a maze of rocky ledges, granite islands, lurking shoals, and narrow guts with the tide racing through them. Thousands of lobster buoys, all eager to tangle your propeller. Dense fogs that come and go in minutes. Are we going to get through this obstacle course against a strong wind and steep seas, with a dying electrical system and no technological aids?

"Marjorie," I said, "we're turning back. Call Sune's shipyard and see if there's any place near here that we could find a marine electrician."

But the VHF radio wasn't working. Marjorie picked up the cellphone and reached Patricia Loreen, Sune's wife. By now I was sweating and anxious, trying to find my way through a cluster of islands, rocks, and ledges, working back toward Jonesport. Patricia wanted to know where we were exactly.

"*I don't know*," I snapped. "Just coming up to Shipstern Island, I think."

"She doesn't think there's an electrician this side of Jonesport."

"Okay. Then tell her we're coming back."

And at that moment, the cellphone died.

We made our way back to Jonesport the old way, by dead reckoning, setting compass courses and picking our way from buoy to buoy. The wind kept rising. By the time we reached Jonesport, it was screeching. And now I made a horrible error.

To control a sailing vessel when you're docking in a strong wind, you head into the breeze and let the wind slow you down. In a motorboat, in a strong wind, you should do the same thing. But I was still unfamiliar with motorboat techniques, and I forgot that. Instead I came downwind to the floating dock. *Magnus* was moving far too fast. I threw the engine in reverse and gunned it. Even with the engine at full throttle, I couldn't slow her down.

Up on the foredeck, holding a dockline, Marjorie stared wildly at the onrushing dock. She heard the engine roaring and thought, My husband has gone mad. He's out to destroy the boat. I'll be catapulted right off the bow. She threw herself headlong on the foredeck and hung on grimly as *Magnus* slammed obliquely into the floating dock. With a sickening thump, the boat bounced off into the harbour.

The Three Stooges flashed before my eyes. I circled around, headed into the wind, and landed the boat easily. But *Magnus* had a terrible scar on the port bow. When I took a closer look, I saw that a protruding bolt had made a long, narrow gouge in her hull.

We went back out to the mooring, shut off all the electrics, and ran the engine for a couple of hours. When we tried the electrics again, everything worked fine. We called Sune and arranged for a local fisherman with some electrical know-how to come out in the morning.

I climbed in the dinghy and inspected the damage. It was worse than I thought – a deep gouge about three feet long, with a four-inch section where the bolt had punched right through the hull. It was a major setback. We'd have to haul the boat, grind down the damaged area to a feather edge, build up a patch with a dozen layers of glass cloth, fair it and smooth it and paint it. In the end it would be as good as new – but how long would it take, and what would it cost?

I went to bed in a black depression, and woke up feeling worse.

"This was supposed to be fun," I told Marjorie. "But it's just bloody hard work, frightening, and miserable. Fuel problems. Electronic problems. Diabolical tides and contrary winds. Now we have a hole in the boat. We're not sailing gracefully along in the sunlight, we're freezing to death motoring through the fog.

Now I have to get the boat patched up and figure out why our electronics have gone wrong.

"Who needs this? It was my dream, not yours. The hell with it. We could be home in two weeks. Let's go."

"No," said Marjorie.

"No?" I was utterly astounded. She hadn't much wanted to do the trip in the first place, and she had been alternately bored, restless, worried, lonely, and uncomfortable. I thought that quitting would be my decision – and if I decided to go home, she'd happily agree.

"No?" I said again.

"No," said Marjorie. "Look, it doesn't make any difference what you say or what anyone else says – if we quit, I'll wear it. Everyone knows you're the sailing nut, so if we turned around, who was responsible? It won't matter how much you protest. They'll just say, Sure, he's being chivalrous about it, but we know what really happened. She made him quit.

"There's no way I'll set myself up for that kind of public humiliation. And you need to do the trip too, for your own mysterious reasons. We're going on. Don't even talk about it any more. We're going on."

I was thunderstruck. This woman is full of surprises, I thought. She's a marvel. She's a lion. She's astute as hell – and she really knows her husband.

But I wanted to quit. I recognized my own feelings, and they were the same feelings I'd had at other major turning-points: If this is the way it's going to be, who needs it? We all make dumb decisions. There's no shame in recognizing them. Changing your mind is often the truly sane thing to do, and I had done my share of it.

Sailing Away from Winter: Cap'n Crunch's Concluding Cruise.

But my scrappy little beloved was also right. She would indeed be saddled with the blame, no matter what I said. She was right about me too. I needed this trip to settle something in myself. I had always felt that my cruises were too short, that I could maybe live on a boat, that boats were meant to take you to distant places. Now we were putting all those ideas to the test.

Yes, I thought, I need to settle some of these issues. I can't go along thinking that if only things were different, I could be basking in the Bahamas on my own boat. Maybe what I'll learn is that I certainly could do that, but it's not worth the wear and tear on body, soul, and bank account. Maybe I'll learn that cruising means leaving books unwritten and relationships neglected – and that's too high a price to pay.

But I need to do it, and see if I like it – and if I don't, I'd better adjust my self-concept to accord with reality. In three years I'll be seventy, for God's sake. It's time I knew who I really am.

Okay. Unless something further went wrong, we'd go on. And if we had to spend a week in Jonesport and freeze our patooties in the Carolinas, so be it.

A small boat pulled up beside the mooring. Brad Peabody came aboard, a quiet, methodical man. He took a look at our electrical system and shook his head.

"You got enough electrical stuff in here for a hundred-footer," he said. "But let's see. The system was running all right before yesterday? Yes? Okay, if the instruments aren't getting enough power, why not?" He ran some tests. He thought the alternator was small, but it was producing enough power, and the batteries appeared to be charged.

"I think it's the battery switch," he said. "Probably a corroded terminal in there, or something. It's sealed, you can't open it up, but if it was my boat, I'd change that switch. I'll drive you to the hardware store."

We got into his boat to look at the gash. Brad craned over the side and ran a finger along the gouge. My heart sank again.

A hole right through the boat. How many days, how many thousands of dollars –?

"Hull'n'Deck," said Brad. "It's a sort of a fibreglass putty. Just trowel it in, and it sets up hard's a rock. We'll pick some up."

We changed the battery switch, and Brad left. I went to see Sune. I was not completely convinced that the switch was the problem – or the only problem, at any rate. Could he recommend a trained marine electrician somewhere in Mount Desert Island? And what did he think of Hull'n'Deck?

"There's a good electrician named Bill Tefft in Southwest Harbor," Sune said. "I'll get you his number. And Hull'n'Deck is an excellent product. Do you want me to come out and have a look?"

"I'd love it."

Out at the mooring, Sune peered at the gash. Was there any way I could get at the gash from inside the boat? No: the whole area was covered with an interior liner.

"Well, you can do it from outside," said Sune. "It's not a difficult repair. When you get someplace you're going to stay a while, get a professional to do a permanent repair – he'll make it stronger than new. For now, Hull'n'Deck will do fine. Make sure you work it well into the hole so you make a bit of a lip inside to hold it from popping out. Then just sand it, fair with fairing compound, sand again, and paint it. I'll give you the paint and the fairing compound. Do you want to work from my skiff?"

No, my little Porta-Bote would do fine. And so, as the evening fell, I put on my Tyvek coveralls and hung over the bow of the dinghy, trowelling polyester goop into the gash and smoothing it with a putty knife while battalions of mosquitoes feasted on my forehead. My advisers were correct: it was righteous stuff, and it quickly set up rock-hard.

I went back in to take Leo ashore, and pay Sune for the mooring.

"Have a good trip," said Sune. "You've got a good forecast for tomorrow."

"Thanks," I said. "This episode hasn't exactly left me brimming with confidence."

An expression of surprise crossed Sune's broad, open face.

"I think you've done everything right," he said. "You turned back when it made sense to turn back, you've sought out the best advice you could get, and made the best repairs you could make. The only way you're ever going to know if the electrical system's fixed is to try it – and you've got the name of someone good to call if it doesn't. How could you have done it better?"

"Well, not crack into the wharf in the first place."

"Accidents happen," Sune said. "Everybody makes mistakes. The test is how well you deal with them. And you've dealt with them really well."

What a lovely thing to say. And what a helpful one too.

We set off in the morning sunlight, and had a pleasant and absolutely uneventful passage to Mount Desert Island.

Six-thirty in the morning on September 7, in Northeast Harbor, a posh village on a keyhole of water in the hills of Mount Desert Island. A crisp, sunny late-summer morning, the sky clear, the sun just rising, the whole world rinsed in heavy dew. Leo the Wonder Whippet and I have just come ashore at the dinghy dock for his morning walk. This cruise has given new life to him. At home, he sometimes had to be lifted up into the car; now he leaps on and off the boat – and in and out of the dinghy – as if he were a puppy, not a thirteen-year-old with an enlarged heart and a touch of arthritis.

Sailors sometimes talk about "dog-leg courses." We have settled into sailing dog-bladder courses, travelling no farther than Leo can manage between shore visits. Our dog-bladder route to this town from Yarmouth has taken us twelve days. The *Cat* does it in two hours. And we can only anchor in places where we can comfortably get the dog ashore; otherwise, we need a dock.

At sea Leo snoozes in the V-berth or in the dinette. When it's rough, he snuggles close to the person who's off-watch. But when we tie up, he is prancing with eagerness to get ashore. Transporting him to a patch of grass also ranks among the first tasks of the morning, and the last of the evening. So here I am, idling around the waterfront with a plastic bag in my pocket.

There is not much action this morning at the harbourmaster's office or the Chamber of Commerce building where sailors shave and shower. The free Island Explorer buses, sponsored by L.L.Bean, nose into every corner of this big, beautiful island, but they are not yet running. The only thing moving is the exhaust from a yellow schoolbus, idling at the head of a nearby wharf. It is waiting for a little ferry full of students coming in from the outlying Cranberry Isles.

Northeast Harbor marks the first time we have felt that our voyage has really taken us somewhere different. When we called on the radio to arrange a mooring, the harbourmaster sent a launch out to guide us in. At moorings all around us, splendid glistening yachts gazed at their own varnished reflections in the still water; elegant homes peeped out tactfully between the trees. Everything around us had that perfectly simple, well-proportioned, unpretentious quality that can only be achieved by spending lots of money.

Well, no wonder. Mount Desert Island has been the summer home of a great deal of old money ever since Gilded Age "rusticators" with names like Vanderbilt and Pulitzer built their enormous "cottages" here in the late nineteenth century. Many of the great cottages burned in a disastrous fire that swept the island in 1947, but enough remain to give the island a distinct savour of discreet opulence.

In Downeast Maine, boats were – and commonly still are – tools for working people. Mount Desert, by contrast, is famous for yachts, and the island boasts some of the finest and most famous yards in the United States – notably Hinckley Yachts, who have been building superlative vessels here since 1928, and Morris Yachts, established in 1972 by Tom Morris, whose family had owned a vacation home in the area since 1886. The boats built here are clean, conservative, seaworthy, magnificently finished – and priced accordingly. A twenty-year-old Morris just twenty-eight feet long carries an asking price of U.S. $100,000.

The Island Explorer buses are dog-friendly (and bike-friendly and wheelchair-friendly), and so the three of us later took the bus into Bar Harbor, where we wandered the streets, browsed in the shops, and ate a takeout lunch in the central square of this tastefully touristy little town. In this case, though, the pleasure was as much in the bus trip as in the destination. More than thirty thousand acres of Mount Desert Island belong to Acadia National Park, and as the bus looped around the island and crossed through the mountains, it stopped at tea shops and trailheads – the park includes more than one hundred and twenty miles of hiking trails – as well as at various villages and settlements. More than two million people visit the park every year, and it seems a model of understated organization. The park rangers, for example, not only lead interpretive hikes and cruises, but also present evening programs on history, geology, wildlife, and ecology. You can take trolley tours, bus tours, and horsedrawn carriage tours – over roads built by John D. Rockefeller, Jr. – and if you want, you can bring your own horse to a horse camp.

Back at the boat, I got in the dinghy and scrubbed the brown beard off *Magnus*'s waterline, then called Bill Tefft. We still didn't seem to have the power we expected; though we shut most of our devices down overnight, the batteries were too flat in the morning to start the furnace, for instance.

A Boston Whaler soon came skimming up the harbour, driven by a man literally tall, dark, and handsome. "Wow. A Tom Selleck clone," whispered Marjorie, a little too mistily. Bill Tefft looked over our electrical system and opined that the batteries might be incorrectly wired – but if we wanted the whole system checked over, he'd prefer that we bring *Magnus* to Southwest Harbor, a couple of miles away, where he had his shop. We could use his mooring.

Southwest Harbor is bigger, more exposed, and more industrial than Northeast Harbor – an active fishing port, with a large coast guard station, the Hinckley yard, and various smaller repair shops around the shore. Bill's shop was flanked by a seafood-market-cum-restaurant and Downeast Diesel, the local Yanmar dealer.

Over the next four days, Bill checked over the whole system, while the components of the system took turns failing. It appeared we'd blown the alternator – but then it started working. Then the fridge refused to restart after being shut down. And every time, the basic problem was dead batteries. Somehow, we just weren't generating enough power.

It's a small alternator and a fairly small bank of batteries, said Bill, and I think your equipment is just demanding too much power from the two of them. Could we increase the size of the alternator, as various people had suggested? No, said John Spafford, the Yanmar dealer, because the V-belt wouldn't handle the extra load. In fact, the engine had been snapping V-belts every fifty hours. I showed John a broken V-belt. Yeah, he said, heat. That overloaded alternator is wearing down the belts. Do you ever smell rubber in the engine room? Yeah? And is there a lot of black rubber dust in the engine room? That's why.

Bill had some suggestions. Reduce the electrical demand by frequently shutting off the fridge, which was the big power-sponge; with our heavily insulated icebox the food would stay cold a long time anyway. Charge the phones from the twelve-volt system and leave the inverter off except when it's actually needed. Buy a spare alternator from John, who had an extra one, never used, at less than half-price. Accept that you're going to have to run the engine several hours a day with light loads to keep the batteries up. That's not good for a diesel, but it seemed unavoidable.

And if it were his boat, said Bill, he would install a Link 10 solid-state battery monitor, which not only tells you how fully the batteries are charged, but also shows you in real time how much electricity you're using or generating. Then you'll be able to tell when you should shut off the fridge, and when you need to charge the batteries.

I took the dinghy across the harbour to West Marine to buy a battery monitor. They had none in stock, but they could get one in a couple of days. I ordered it. On a notice board at a nearby marina I saw an ad for a lightly used Honda generator. After consulting Bill, I bought it. At anchor, we could run the generator instead of the diesel and save the wear on the main engine.

"You know," I said to Marjorie, "we've made this damn boat too complicated. Furnace. Freezer. Pressure water. Hot showers. It's nice to have these conveniences – when they work – but they're costing us a lot of time and money."

"No," said Marjorie. "We're not just aboard for a few days or a couple of weeks. This boat is our home for almost a year. I want to be able to freeze food, and I want to be warm in the morning. Did you order the whatchamadoo from Doo Bop?"

"The wha – do you mean, did I order the battery monitor from West Marine?"

"That too."

I cracked up.

Frustrated though I was by our cranky electrics, I still found Marjorie's expectations perfectly reasonable. For better and for worse, this is not the 1890s, when Joshua Slocum went sailing. And the electrical situation still didn't entirely make sense to me. After all, the system had worked all the way down from Nova Scotia. What had weakened it? Or had we just been lucky?

In the meantime, Bill Tefft was treating us like old friends. We stayed on his mooring, used the shower in his office building, caught up on our email over his phone line. We borrowed his car to shop and do our laundry in a squalid laundromat, which absorbed $3.50 in quarters per load, and sported a sign on the dryer saying, *CAUTION: don't use high heat on delicate clothing such as lace underwear and bras. may cause fire and melt your undergarments.* A delicious thought. Our mail had been sent to Belfast, an hour's drive away – but now we were not going to Belfast. When we were done in Southwest Harbor, we were going south, south, south. We borrowed Bill's car to pick up the mail. Driving a car again was an enormous novelty, and the drive to Belfast was like a tiny vacation from the boat and its problems.

Bill was an excellent electrician, much in demand, with an incisive and well-filled mind. He had worked for both Hinckley and Morris, and still did contract work for both. He had done pre-med at university, slipped sideways into zoology, and was steering toward marine biology when President Carter cut the grant program he had been counting on. At thirty-five, he had gone back to college to do a degree in fine arts, specializing in photography, which he loved. But boat electrics were his bread and butter.

He had served in the navy during the reign of George Bush, Sr., and he couldn't stand the Bushes, noting that the Bush family compound is in Maine, at Kennebunkport, and that Mainers knew the family well enough to dislike them intensely. He recalled George Senior declaring that Americans would have to lower their expectations and consumption. But didn't Bush himself "drive a Cigarette boat that eats gallons per minute? Well, that's different – I didn't mean Americans shouldn't recreate, they have to recreate, I recreate like anyone else. Aagh."

He was not alone; in early September, Bush Junior was leading in the polls, but the bumper stickers around town were solidly anti-Bush.

REGIME CHANGE BEGINS AT HOME! MORE TREES, LESS BUSH. RE-DEFEAT BUSH 2004.

Bill liked working on boats like ours, helping people who were actually doing something with their boats. At Hinckley, he had worked on some wonderful boats that were little more than ornaments. One family owned a summer home nearby, a sprawl-ing waterfront mansion that they occupied during one month in the summer. They also had a luxurious Hinckley, worth nearly a million dollars, and every spring the Hinckley yard varnished its brightwork, waxed its hull, rigged it, and moved it to a mooring in front of the owners' home. The owners arrived and looked at the boat for a month, and then went away, whereupon the boat went back into storage.

"They never used it?" I said.

"They might have taken it out for an afternoon under power, up in some sheltered place like Somes Sound," Bill said. "But no more than that. The sails were never unfurled."

We did useful things with our time – read, wrote, played a little music, filled the water tank, submitted an early newspaper column. The clean autumn days rolled smoothly past. Tied to the town dock, right beside Bill's shop, we met the ultimate Coastal Line-Dipper – a short, gruff man named Neil, probably in his early sixties, who appeared on the dock soon after dawn and often stayed till dusk, casting his line in the water and pulling in small fish, which he kept alive in a floating pen. A couple of times a week, he would sell the fish for bait and start all over again. His home was an antiquated bilious-green van that looked as though it had been painted with a broom, which he kept in Bill Tefft's parking lot. In the winter he worked at the Maine ski hills. Almost time to go there, he told me, the evenings were getting chilly.

Tell me about it, I thought. Marjorie had picked up a rasp-berry-coloured fleece sweater.

We also filled the diesel tank – a startling experience, since I managed to get 52.5 gallons into a 50-gallon tank. Whoops: I must have been thinking in Imperial gallons, which are 20 per cent larger than U.S. gallons. So we had been within a hair of running out of fuel. Remember that for future reference, I told myself. Be conservative: fill early.

On Friday, the battery monitor arrived. On Saturday, I worked with Bill all day to install it, making sure that every electrical device in the boat went to a common ground, allowing the monitor to determine how much power was being consumed moment by moment. At the end of the day, Bill calibrated the instrument, and the three of us celebrated with a beer, while the little round dial flashed amperage and voltage readings from the battery.

"I don't imagine your wife's very pleased with us," said Marjorie. "Taking up your whole Saturday."

Bill laughed.

"We talked about that," he said. "I said, Remember the other night, when we were going to go to bed early with a bottle of wine and some candles and have a sensual time of it. But you got a call that four Shelties had eaten sixteen pounds of joint compound – how likely is that? – and you had to go. I understand that; you're a veterinarian.

"Don and Marjorie have an emergency on their hands, they didn't plan on all this, and it's the time of year when my business is winding down. All winter I'm going to be home, not making any money, and we're not going to be very happy about that. So give me a break. Working with animals is what you do; working on boats is what I do."

He finished off his beer.

"I'll be down in the morning before you go, with the bill," he said. "Why don't you charge the batteries with the generator, and we'll check over the readings on the monitor in the morning?"

I ran the generator for a couple of hours. The next morning the batteries didn't have enough power to start the furnace. The monitor confirmed it: the little red readout was flashing LO LO LO.

"What?" cried Bill. "How can that be?" He thought for a moment. "We did check the batteries, didn't we? Let's check 'em again."

We did, carefully. Three batteries were marginal, and one was poor.

"Let's get new ones," said Marjorie. "There's no point doing all this if the batteries are no good."

"Yeah," I said gloomily. "But it's Sunday. We'll be here another day, and the nights are getting cold. Christ, Bill, I like Maine – but we came here to visit, not to settle."

Bill laughed delightedly.

"Maybe I can do something." An hour later he was back with four new batteries.

"Got 'em from Morris Yachts," he said. "I'll settle up with them in the morning. Let's get 'em in."

An hour later, the new batteries were in place, and everything seemed to be working perfectly.

"I think you're good to go," said Bill. "If you have any trouble, call me. You could stop in Bass Harbor and just take a mooring. They all belong to Hinckley or Morris, and the season's over. Nobody's going to bother you."

We thanked him warmly – by now he really *was* an old friend – and headed out to sea. Two hours later we were on a rolling mooring in Bass Harbor. Tomorrow we would try to put some miles behind us. We didn't know it then, but for the rest of the trip, we would run all the equipment as much as we pleased – and we would never have serious electrical problems again.

The next day's run was magnificent. The coastline here consists of deep bays separated by clusters of islands with narrow "thorofares" between the islands. At daybreak we slipped out of Bass Harbor across Blue Hill Bay and threaded our way through Casco Passage. The breeze was stirring as we crossed Jericho Bay and entered the Deer Island Thorofare, passing the pretty little town of Stonington. Linda Greenlaw, the swordfish captain from *The Perfect Storm*, lives on nearby Isle au Haut. We wanted to visit her island, but winter was chasing us. We crossed Isle au Haut Bay without stopping and entered the twisting Fox Island Thorofare, tying up briefly at the deserted yacht club in North Haven, where we took Leo for a walk.

Maine, they say, is the wealthiest state in the Union during the summer, and the poorest at other times. By mid-September villages like North Haven look as though they've been hit by a neutron bomb, which vaporized the people but left the buildings intact. As we left, a huge four-masted schooner slipped past the anchored boats in the narrow thorofare, a ghost skirting a ghost town.

Out into Penobscot Bay itself now, in a lusty, cheerful breeze, crossing paths with a long, sleek racing sloop with dun-coloured Kevlar sails, a lot of money tacking up the bay. Then into Muscle Ridge Channel with the wind fading away, picking our way through the lobster buoys to the perfect cup-shaped refuge of Tenants Harbor.

White and grey houses were perched around the rim of the little basin, the anchored boats basking in their own golden reflections, the smooth black curves of a traditional day-sailer's hull set off by her glowing varnished mast. The coast of Maine known to us all from films and novels, the exquisitely composed atmosphere of long-established family summers sustained by – cough – adequate finances. We dinghied to the public dock. Leo jumped ashore and went trotting up the long gangway. Near the head of the wharf stood the white East Winds Inn, a classic summer hotel. Marjorie and I sipped gin-and-tonics on the wide veranda, the dog lying quietly at our feet. People dressed with casual elegance drifted into the dining room behind us. A little red-sailed Drascombe Lugger beat up to her mooring. It was like having a drink inside a postcard.

An unspeakably foul reek greeted us when we returned to the dinghy. We choked, our eyes watered, our stomachs heaved. The stench came from a well-rotted grey herring carcass lying in the stern of the skiff. I quickly scooped it overboard while

Marjorie held Leo clear of it, but the grey slime and filthy stink persisted. Back at the boat, I scrubbed and rinsed vigorously, but despite detergent, soap, bleach, and vinegar, the awful smell lingered for days.

"My God," said Marjorie, a handkerchief to her nose, "do you think a gull dropped it there?"

"What else?" But later, browsing some of the discussions on a cruising website, I read a comment about nearby Cape Porpoise. "The Maine Coastal Cruising Guide says the cove is used mostly by lobstermen, the entrance is narrow and loaded with lobster pots and not to be surprised if you get a dead fish on your deck if you try to use the dock."

Maybe Tenants Harbor dislikes pampered yachtsmen – or maybe the rusticators and the fishermen aren't quite so compatible after all.

Boothbay Harbor was the motherlode of pampered yachtsmen, but a cheerful fisherman hailed us as we were dropping the mizzen and led us to Brown's Wharf in the inner harbour. The guidebook had made Brown's Wharf sound charming, and it was – flowerpots on the pilings, hotel and restaurant at the pierhead, wireless Internet service – but it was also twice as pricey as any marina we'd seen. We took a mooring instead, and dinghied across the harbour to walk the streets and look for a few food items.

We found a convenience store and asked the clerk where the nearest full-service food store might be. In Hanford, she said. A nearby town, I assumed. What about fresh fruit and vegetables? She shrugged. We wandered out to the pleasant square fronting on the town wharf and asked a woman at a whalewatching booth.

"What did you want?" she asked.

"Well, fresh cucumbers, for instance."

She pulled out a plastic bag under the counter and handed us two cucumbers.

"Fresh from my garden. Would you like some tomatoes too?"

"Absolutely."

Ask and you shall receive. Later, of course, we realized that "Hanford" was actually Hannaford, the supermarket chain. Why do food stores shun the word *food* in their names? In the States, you go to Winn-Dixie, Piggly Wiggly, Hannaford, or Publix. In Canada, Sobeys or Loblaws, the Superstore or Safeway. In England, Sainsbury's or Tesco. Some marketing smarty should establish a chain named The Great Big Food Store.

We motored out of Boothbay Harbor at 7:15. Two good running days behind us, and Portland ahead of us. Another running day after Portland, perhaps two, and we would be out of Maine. The state was spectacularly beautiful, the villages charming, the people engaging – but the nip of autumn was in the air, and it was time to be gone. South, south, south!

Once again the forecast called for light adverse winds, and *Magnus* set off bucking modest seas. Lobster boats were coming and going, and the mat of buoys continued right down the coast. Steering carefully through a field of them, Marjorie remarked that they have magnets in them that draw your boat down on them. Ah, you think, I'll clear that green-and-purple one easily, but as you come nearer – even on autopilot – the boat seems to edge closer and closer to the buoy until you have to wrench the wheel over to avoid it. The lobstermen themselves go roaring lightheartedly through the buoys – but they all have wire cages around their props. If I were going to cruise here regularly, I'd have one too.

At the mouth of Booth Bay, we turned south at The Cuckolds, and the gentle southerly wind turned into a whistling south-westerly, right on the nose. The boat pitched and rolled, corkscrewing through the seas. The dog was sliding around on the seats. I was clinging to the wheel. The hell with Portland. The hell with this.

"Is there some place we can turn in?" Marjorie asked, as if reading my thoughts.

"See what you can find," I said, passing her the guidebook and the chart. "We're in the mouth of Sheepscot Bay."

"There's a little place called Five Islands," she said after a moment. "Secure protection, fuel, a great seafood outlet, and a rustic view. Anchoring is not advised, but the yacht club has guest moorings."

We nosed in along the shore, rounded a point, and there it was – a miniature village on a cleft in the bedrock. Lobster boats, dinghies, and day-sailers bobbed at their moorings. Across from the village proper, a cluster of elegant homes stood on two tiny islands, connected by catwalks and bridges. An apparent community hall stood on pilings between the islets.

We picked up a yacht club mooring, and I dinghied ashore to pay for it. The young man at the Sheepscot Bay Boat Company shrugged.

"Season's over," he said. "Everybody from the yacht club's gone home. Don't worry about it."

The eighteen houses on the islets turned out to be a private summer compound, and the yacht club was an offshoot. The glassed-in hall was a communal dining room. Some of the houses don't have kitchens at all. Such arrangements don't come cheap; a new septic system was recently delivered by helicopter.

Like the other communities we'd seen, Five Islands closes down with an audible click after Labour Day. But we went for a long walk in the hot afternoon, and at the top of a hill we found a little food market under a sign that read, FIVE ISLANDS FARM. In front of the building were rioting flowers, cobalt-blue ceramic basins, concrete birdbaths adorned with embedded glass chips. Sun umbrellas protected tables loaded with fresh fruits and vegetables. Inside we found shelves of preserves, gourmet foods from near and far, wooden barrels filled with bottles of wine.

Marjorie lit up with joy. She bought potatoes and Vidalia onions, sweet corn, broccoli, McIntosh apples, mesclun salad mix, all fresh, all local. She bought local Brie, Italian salami, cassis jam, and a loaf of Italian bread. She bought three bottles of wine, organic local beef, Maine sea salt, and – of all things – "white fig preserves" imported from southwest France. The whole order cost less than a single restaurant meal. We trudged back to the boat for a memorable lunch.

Late that afternoon, an elegant dark-blue Morris sloop picked up a mooring. While Leo and I were ashore, her master rowed in, wondering who to pay for the mooring. Nobody cares, I told him. Tom was from Portland, so I asked about places to moor in town. Most of the marinas and yacht clubs were in South Portland, on the opposite side of the harbour, he said, but if we wanted to visit downtown Portland, the best bet was Portland Yacht Services. Others, like DeMillo's – which also includes a seafood restaurant on a former ferryboat – would probably be crowded and expensive.

That evening, I heard a knock on our hull. Tom was alongside in his dinghy.

"Look," he said, "I don't know why I didn't think of this – but we have a slip right in downtown Portland, right next to DeMillo's, and we won't be using it tomorrow. Just tie up there."

And so the next evening we sat in the cockpit, enjoying the Friday-night bustle of the Old Port district, relishing a superlative salad and savouring the unique, caramel-like taste of the white fig preserves. Raising our glasses of award-winning wine, we toasted the generosity of Mainers.

Portland was our first real city since Halifax, and we walked its compact, lively downtown with great enjoyment. For decades, Portland was a backwater, which preserved it from the improvements that disfigured so many other cities during the 1960s and

1970s, and its low-rise red-brick downtown has now been restored with grace and imagination. Old brick buildings, Internet cafés, gift shops, and marine stores jostled with Irish pubs and new condos right alongside a working waterfront with fishermen's wharves, shipping piers, yachts, and excursion boats.

Downtown Portland has numerous whimsies, like a mailbox that looks like a huge fire hydrant, a gift to Portland from its sister city of Shinagawa, Japan. Tucked in the bushes of a mini-park is a gaily coloured ceramic lighthouse. A similar one stands on the Long Wharf, just outside DeMillo's restaurant.

Judging by the bumper stickers, Democrats here were just as enraged by Bush as their cousins down east: I'M LOOKING FOR A FLORIST TO SEND TWO BUSHES TO IRAQ, read one. NEVER ELECT A SON OF A BUSH, read another. A photo of a commanderly looking Bush was labelled UNITED WE FALL. And, in the middle of the cleverness, a stark statement direct from the American conscience: THERE IS NO FLAG LARGE ENOUGH TO COVER THE SHAME OF KILLING INNOCENT PEOPLE. The bitter opposition to Bush, though, didn't translate into obvious enthusiasm for John Kerry. Kerry would not likely win the election, but Bush might lose it.

Back on the boat, we had another glorious lunch with Five Islands produce – tomatoes and cucumbers dressed with olive oil and white balsamic vinegar, Brie, salami, Italian bread, white-fig preserves.

"Did you phone the marine creature here?" asked Marjorie.

"Did I – oh. You mean, did I call DeMillo's, to ask if we can use their laundry and their showers?"

"That's the one."

Uh-huh.

I could have thrown a tennis ball to DeMillo's wharf, but to reach its facilities, we had to tote the laundry the full length of both wharves. A jagged slab of concrete, covered with graffiti, stood on its edge on the Long Wharf. It was a section of the Berlin

Sailing from D'Escousse, July 21, 2004 (JOE TERRIO)

The best place to
tie up on the
LaHave River

Off the Nova Scotia
coast, the old sea dog
scans the horizon

Dories on the beach at Dark Harbour, Grand Manan Island

Beaching the boat at low tide, North Head, Grand Manan Island

Marjorie plays the guitar at Southwest Harbor, Maine

A tern schooner tacks through Fox Island Thorofare,
North Haven, Maine

Evening calm at
Tenants Harbor, Maine

Autumn harvest at a
roadside stand, Five
Islands, Maine

A fishing vessel heads to sea in Gloucester, Massachusetts

An unimpressed Leo inspects Plymouth Rock

Hard aground in Norwalk, Connecticut, *Magnus* heels far
to starboard

Towers and turbulence: running down New York's East River

Sailing by the Statue of Liberty

Wall, displayed in Portland to remind Americans of their heritage of liberty.

As we read the inscription, a grey-haired man in his sixties approached us.

"I am from Berlin," he said. "Do you remember the Berlin airlift?"

"Yes," I said, "I'm old enough to remember that."

"We were schtarving!" he said. "Cut off from West Germany, no food, nossing. And se Rossians all around us. We didn't know what was going to happen to us. Then the airlift started, and we had food again – milk, eggs, soup. All powdered, of course, but it was *good*!

"I was only a boy zen, but I thought, Someday I go to America, and say thank you to America. For all that food. For coming when we were schtarving. And now here I am in America, and I say thank you."

Marjorie and I looked at each other.

"I'm very glad to hear that," I said. "And very impressed that you came so far, after all these years, to say that."

"I hope you enjoy your visit," said Marjorie.

"Oh, yes!" said the man, smiling broadly. "I enjoy it very much. It is a wonderful country!"

"It is," I agreed. "It's a wonderful country."

We smiled and almost bowed, and then we parted.

"No point telling him we're Canadians," said Marjorie.

"No," I said. "It would only have spoiled the moment for him."

"Maybe we were the right people to hear it too," said Marjorie. "It *is* a wonderful country."

I was glad she felt that, because she had been very doubtful about travelling in the States.

Do Americans have any concept of the appalling disservice that their popular culture does to their country? American film and television in particular present the United States as either vapid and sentimental or as lawless, violent, and dangerous.

Well, racism persists, and thugs do roam the mean streets, exercising their constitutional right to bear arms. But the Americans who don't appear on TV are the dedicated workers against racism and sexism and poverty, or the ones who have transformed cities like Portland. Prime-time TV doesn't feature the poets, the scientists, the philanthropists, the devoted teachers and naturalists. It ignores the friendly and generous people we had met all the way down the coast of Maine.

The man from Berlin was not deceived by the fact that America broadcasts its worst face to the world. He knew that America is a multicoloured fabric made up of many yarns and strands, with an authentic goodness deep in the weave of it.

Thank you, he said. It's a wonderful country, he said. And it is.

On the other hand, dealing with U.S. Customs continued to echo Abbot and Costello. Who's on first, what is on second, I don't know is on third. Who? He's on first.

In Eastport, Barry Thompson said, "Call in when you get to Bar Harbor." He gave me a 1-800 number. In Bar Harbor, the number was "not valid for the area." I went to the Southwest Harbor Coast Guard base and asked for a number. They gave me the same 1-800 number. I told them it didn't work. They gave me a number in Portland. The Portland guy gave me a number for Bar Harbor. An answering machine in Bar Harbor gave me a number in Bangor. The Bangor guy said, "You're all clear here. Call in again when you get to Portland or Boston."

In Portland, I called Portland. When did you arrive? asked the Portland guy. Day before yesterday, I said. You were supposed to call in immediately, he said, and you're subject to severe penalties if you don't. And we do impose those penalties. This failure has been entered in the computer as a warning.

Wait, I said, the Bar Harbor guy who was actually in Bangor said Portland *or* Boston. Yeah, said Portland, but that means wherever you stop next. Boston if you didn't stop in Portland, but you did. What's your next port of call? Portsmouth, I hope, I said. Well, Portsmouth is another customs district, so call the 1-800 number and report in immediately when you get there.

Can I get a list of the customs districts? No. And the 1-800 number doesn't work. It does work, he said, I get lots of calls through that number.

I hung up and tried the 1-800 number again. It still didn't work. Not valid for the area.

Wait a minute. "The area." That 1-800 number – created for the convenience of foreign yachtsmen, of course – is probably valid only for phones with U.S. area codes. I went to a pay phone and called the 1-800 number. It worked. Where was the central office located? Orlando. Did they have a regular phone line in Orlando, not toll-free? They did. I tried it on my Canadian cell-phone. It worked.

And did Orlando have a list of customs districts? No. Look, said Orlando, the safest thing for you to do is to call us every time you make a new port, and we'll patch you through to the local office wherever you are.

So that became the docking drill. Docklines double and single, let the dog have a tinkle, give the customs a dingle, then with neighbours you mingle with your drinks and your Pringles.

Who's on first? said Costello. Yes, said Abbot.

It was pouring rain the morning we planned to leave for Portsmouth. The early forecast called for gentle northerly winds of five to ten knots, but as we prepared to cast off, a blast of wind swept through the moored boats, making whitecaps on the harbour. Turning on the radio, we learned that the forecast now called for northeasterly winds twenty to twenty-five, with gusts to thirty and lots more rain – the outer fringe of the disintegrating Hurricane Ivan, in fact. The hell with that. We'd stay put.

But Portland is not a good harbour in northeasterly winds, and Tom would need his berth. We moved over to Southport Marine, a full-service marina located on a well-protected cove in South Portland. I had been studying the techniques for manoeuvring a power boat, and sighed with relief when I managed to turn *Magnus* twice within the narrow marina channels and place her more or less where I wanted her, snugging her up nose to nose with a big catamaran named *Adagio*.

Adagio's skipper was a genial, leathery fellow named Jim Schulz. He and his wife, Sandy, were moving aboard permanently. They had already sold their house and furnishings, and were just selling their car. They planned to migrate north and south with the seasons. Sadly, their sixteen-year-old Bichon Frise would not be going along. She was blind, and she also had an inoperable tumour and canine Alzheimer's. She rarely knew who she was or where she was, and she couldn't even negotiate a curb on her own.

"She was a great companion for fifteen years," Jim said sadly, "but in the last year she went south very fast." She would be going for her last trip to the vet the very next day – and when she did, Jim was devastated. Marjorie and I looked at Leo. Leo wagged his tail.

When the rain eased, we walked to the nearby shopping plaza to pick up a few groceries and a couple of things at the hardware store. We found a Tim Hortons doughnut shop, which instantly made us homesick. Tim Hortons is eastern Canada's favourite hangout; every little Maritime town seems to have two or three, and the chain runs TV ads showing the gratitude of Canadians abroad for air-mailed tins of Tim Hortons coffee. We went in for a coffee, hoping to alleviate our homesickness – and strangely enough we did, though we were amused to see a Stars and Stripes sticker on the door of the kitchen.

"Do you think we'll ever catch up with Carol and Jim?" Marjorie asked.

"I doubt it. They're just too far ahead." I had recently heard from them; they were in Newport, Rhode Island, having made a glorious downwind charge non-stop from Portland right around Cape Ann, across Massachusetts Bay, and through the Cape Cod Canal.

We were not desperately lonely, and we were happy to be making new friends like the Schulzes. But we certainly missed the comforting presence of old friends – and it was slowly dawning on us that we were not truly "cruising" the U.S. coast, lingering and savouring the places we visited. We were doing a delivery trip, at least as far as the Chesapeake. On a delivery trip, you get up in the morning and get moving, unless you're prevented by the weather, the wind, or the condition of the crew or the boat. You don't stop in lovely little places like North Haven; you just have lunch and carry on. You want your six knots, so you don't sail in light winds; you motor.

I was increasingly worried that we were moving south too slowly, though I kept reminding myself that we did have some slack time built into the schedule; we had planned to loiter in Chesapeake Bay for a month. Even if we arrived in the Chesapeake two weeks late, we should still be able to leave Norfolk by November 1. And though there was a distinctly autumnal bite in the Maine air, Carol and Jim were enjoying eighty-five-degree weather in Rhode Island.

The forecast for the next day was fifteen knots from the north and declining – a wind that should chase us cheerfully down to New Hampshire. I wondered how far south the infernal lobster traps would continue to infest the waterways. Sandy Schulz called Maine "the confetti coast," because the trap buoys were as thick as confetti dumped in the water. Somewhere I had heard that there were a million lobster traps in Maine, and it seemed we had seen most of them.

Time to get going. Time to escape from Maine.

Twenty-four hours later, after a fine day of running, we were bemused to find ourselves moored in Maine.

We left Portland early, motoring down the coast in the hazy sunlight. We passed by Saco, Cape Porpoise, and Kennebunkport, where George W. Bush had just visited the family summer estate. In the late afternoon, we made our way into the Piscataqua River, bound for the Portsmouth Yacht Club just below the city. New Hampshire at last.

The Piscataqua is known for fierce currents and turbulent wakes, and we saw both as we rode up the river on a flooding tide of more than three knots. Vessels of all sizes created a veritable boil of wakes, making big yachts at moorings roll and toss wildly. Even the fuel docks at the yacht club pitched and heaved as *Magnus* drew alongside. *Magnus* rolls easily too, and the motion of the two together was spectacular.

"Well," said the young dockmaster, "you might find it quieter across the river. In Pepperrell Cove. We have moorings over there too."

Pepperrell Cove is in *Maine*. Ye gods.

And the cove is named for Sir William Pepperrell, a figure familiar to me from Nova Scotian history. Pepperrell was the general in command of the New England army that captured the "impregnable" fortress of Louisbourg in 1745. It was a portentous expedition – the first time the American colonies had ever joined together for any major undertaking. Just thirty-one years later, they would unite again in the War of Independence (as Americans call it) or the American Revolution (as Canadians call it). Some of the same men would fight in both conflicts – a Massachusetts gunner named Seth Pomeroy, for instance, who kept a diary and fought both at Louisbourg and Bunker Hill.

The proto-American army was really a militia, a citizen army, and its officers were leaders in their own local communities – "men of consequence in rustic neighbourhoods," if I recall Francis Parkman's droll description correctly. The officers raised their own forces from their own districts. Their style of command was novel and well suited to the troops they commanded. Pepperrell, for instance, was noted for his light hand on the reins, his concern not with textbook methods and rigid discipline, but with initiative and results. His citizen soldiers were volunteers, and they could not be commanded with the expectation of absolute obedience, like European regular troops. They were well motivated too, since Louisbourg was a constant threat to New England commerce, and a nest of Papist heresy to boot.

They captured the fortress by attacking it from behind, from Gabarus Bay, dragging their cannons and supplies, slashing a path through the bogs and scrubby woods. Such an unorthodox strategy had never occurred to the fortress's French military architects, who had always expected an assault from the sea. Their feat proved that colonial citizens could defeat a European army on their own territory, using their own woodsmen's methods. They held Louisbourg for three years, losing about as many men to disease and dissipation as they had lost in battle.

And then the English revealed their contempt for this achievement, and for American opinion generally, when they calmly returned Louisbourg to France. The Americans were understandably enraged, and their rage fuelled the fire that would burst into outright rebellion a generation later.

I have never been sure who to cheer for in the Louisbourg conflict – the French proto-Cape Bretoners or the democratic vanguard from New England. Indeed, I admire many people on both sides – including Pepperrell, evidently an exceptionally sane and capable man. He was knighted for his achievements at Louisbourg, and streets have been named for him in both Halifax and Cape Breton. He presumably lived out the rest of his life among the green and rocky scenery I was viewing from *Magnus*'s foredeck.

As we dinghied ashore, we passed a motor launch named *Sir William Pepperrell*. We picked up some wine and groceries at Frisbee's Supermarket, said to be the oldest family-owned business in America, founded in 1828 and operated today by the sixth generation of the family. Frisbee's is a great store, selling not only groceries and wine, but also *The Woodenboat* magazine, T-shirts, souvenirs, CDs, and fresh meat (sliced up, we learned, by a butcher from Ontario). When it was founded, there might have been men living in the village who had served with Pepperrell.

Pepperrell had captured us too. We had walked in New Hampshire – but we had not escaped from Maine. *Magnus* heaved and wallowed until bedtime, lay fairly still for five or six hours, then resumed heaving and wallowing at 4:00 a.m., when the fishermen started leaving the harbour. Even when the water looked absolutely calm, *Magnus* rolled and rolled.

Before we could leave, I had to take Leo ashore – and in all this rolling it was no mean trick to get the dinghy attached to the boat, and the dog transferred to the dinghy. The sun had just risen, and in the yellow light of the morning I saw a massive bulk carrier entering the river, with the words CANADA STEAMSHIP LINES in huge letters on her side. Canada Steamships belonged to Canada's prime minister, Paul Martin, who navigated it through some tricky tax dodges, registered its ships abroad, and manned them with Third World crews. He allegedly turned the company over to his children, but I suspect the company president would accept phone calls from the prime minister.

Nice to have a little reminder of home, I thought, watching as two big barn-red tugboats latched onto the ship and moved it on up the river. Standing on the shore, I saw that the little flotilla was making a heavy wake. Oh God.

I watched helplessly, unable even to warn Marjorie as *Magnus* began to roll dramatically back and forth. When Leo and I got back to the boat, we found her in the cockpit nursing a sore hand and swearing lustily. She had been making the coffee, and had stepped up to the cockpit to watch for the dinghy. When the wake hit, she could only clutch a grab-rail and hang on for dear life, watching helplessly as the coffee pot and the water pitcher slid back and forth across the table. Once, twice, three times – and then crash! down on the cabin carpet they went, spilling coffee, water, and grounds everywhere. No morning coffee, and a soggy mess to clean up. She was so angry that she punched a bulkhead and hurt her hand.

Portsmouth is said to be a charming city, but we left without seeing it – and also without regret.

Twenty miles of motoring in calm, warm weather over a glossy sea brought us to the mouth of the Annisquam River, which provides a shortcut to Gloucester behind Cape Ann, cutting off fifteen miles of open ocean sailing. The Annisquam River and the Blynman Canal are like a foretaste of the Intracoastal Waterway, and in fact are sometimes considered to be part of it. Narrow channels wind through sandbars; people fish off the banks and dig clams on the bars.

The Gloucester harbourmaster greeted us in the river and told us the channel was shallow and crowded, and anchoring was forbidden – a pity, since it would have been a lovely place to stop. So we went on, nudging the sandy bottom twice and motoring within a stone's throw of expensive homes, funky cottages, and float-homes. Herons and gulls soared around us, and a variety of boats filled every available nook and cranny. The winding river soon gave way to the straight, grotty canal, which bent sharply through two bascule bridges and spat us out in Gloucester.

I was thrilled to be there. I had written about Gloucester and the Gloucester fishery, but I had never visited Lunenburg's archrival city before. It was bigger than Lunenburg, and much less charming – a fishy, salt-reeking industrial town with a waterfront that bristles with piers and warehouses. Brutal steel fishing boats lay cheek by jowl with elegant yachts. A beautiful clipper-bowed Friendship sloop tacked through the mooring field in the light breeze. Snowy-white swans visited from boat to boat, looking for snacks.

The harbourmaster assigned us to a mooring by radio, and when we went ashore to pay the rental, he gave me a package of information about the city and a souvenir floating keychain, which made Gloucester the only port thus far to have a welcome kit for visiting cruisers. In the tiny park by the wharf, metal dispensers provided free plastic "Mutt Mitts" for cleaning up after dogs. Leafing through the welcome kit, I discovered that the Cape Ann Historical Museum had a collection of Winslow Homer paintings – and was also the final home of Howard Blackburn's *Great Republic*. So I went to the museum and sure enough, there was Blackburn's twenty-five-foot sloop, looking remarkably fit and handsome; it would make a pretty respectable pocket cruiser even today.

Howard Blackburn was a legendary figure, a remarkable seaman in a town of great seamen. In the winter of 1883, Blackburn was a doryman hand-lining for halibut on the Grand Banks of Newfoundland off the schooner *Grace L. Fears*. In the fog and wind, his dory was separated from the mothership, just like Frank Knickle's. Blackburn lost his mittens and realized that his hands would soon freeze. So he deliberately gripped the handles of his oars, enabling himself to row even with frozen hands.

Like Frank's dory-mate, Blackburn's companion died of exposure. Blackburn rowed for five days to reach Newfoundland, where he was diligently cared for by a local family. All the same, he lost all his fingers, one toe, and both thumbs to the first joint. When he got home, Gloucester took up a collection and raised $500 to help him. Blackburn bought a cigar store and later branched out into saloons. During the town's periodic "dry" periods, he was a successful bootlegger. He ultimately became an important businessman in Gloucester.

In front of Blackburn's black-hulled sloop was another weathered boat – a much smaller one, only twenty feet long and perhaps three feet deep. To my delight, it proved to be *Centennial*, the first boat ever to be sailed single-handed across the Atlantic – by another tough Gloucesterman, Captain Alfred Johnson, who later became a very successful fishing skipper. As a result of a tavern discussion about how small a boat you could sail across the Atlantic, the twenty-eight-year-old Johnson crossed in 1876, in sixty-six days. When asked why he did the voyage, Johnson replied, "Because I was just as much of a damn fool as everyone said I was."

Johnson's example clearly inspired Blackburn, whose taste for adventure never died. In 1897, Blackburn led an expedition to the Klondike via Cape Horn. Back in Gloucester, he built the *Great Western* and crossed the Atlantic single-handed in 1899, sailing from Gloucester to England in sixty-two days. Two years later he sailed the boat I was looking at, the *Great Republic*, to Portugal in thirty-nine days.

All this with no fingers and only the stubs of his thumbs.

The museum had another surprise for me, a whole display dedicated to Phil Weld, once the publisher of the *Gloucester Daily Times* and the *Newburyport Daily News*. Twenty-five years ago, at an age when most men are contemplating retirement, Weld decided to compete in the Observer Singlehanded Trans-Atlantic Race, from England to New York. En route to England for the start of the race, his trimaran *Gulf Streamer* capsized in mid-Atlantic. Weld and his crew hung on to the outside of the hull for four days before they were rescued.

Nothing daunted, Weld had a new boat built and tried again. His fifty-foot trimaran, *Moxie*, was built by the Gougeon Brothers of Bay City, Michigan, the prophets of wood and epoxy boatbuilding, whose techniques I was using at the time in the construction of *Silversark*. Weld sailed *Moxie* to victory in 1980, setting a new record of seventeen days and twenty-three hours. By then he was sixty-five.

What a trio! And Joshua Slocum also visited Gloucester at the start of his solo voyage around the world, sailing out of the harbour with all the factory girls waving handkerchiefs from the factory windows. On the way into the harbour, we had noticed an antiquated brick factory sitting right down on the shore. MANUFACTORY, it said on the wall, GLOUCESTER SEA JACKET MARINE PAINTS. Could it have been the factory Slocum described?

Gloucester continues to generate stories of brutal suffering, heroism, and hardship, the most famous recent example being Sebastian Junger's riveting book *The Perfect Storm* and the subsequent movie, whose spectacular special effects brought me as close as I ever want to get to a full-scale storm at sea.

Lunenburg and Gloucester have long been competitors in Grand Banks fishing and in schooner racing. It is hard to imagine two more salty towns. I was exhilarated that we had visited both these legendary harbours – and had done it in our own little ship.

We motored out of Gloucester on another hot, calm morning, accompanied by an infestation of fast little biting flies. I had five welts on my legs before I even knew what they were up to, and later in the day they bit right through my socks despite a liberal spritz of fly repellent. We opened and screened all the hatches, and went around killing the flies that were already buzzing around the cabin.

For some eccentric reason, the flyswatter always drives Leo into a panic. Ashore, he hides in the most distant room in the house; on the boat he had nowhere to go. Marjorie had to take him on deck while I whapped the flies below.

Beating at the flies, we crossed Massachusetts Bay, the centre of New England's history, with the towers of Boston just visible in the thin haze to starboard. The bay was ringed with historic places. Boston, always the New England capital. Winthrop, named for the founding Puritan governor of Massachusetts. Cape Cod, where Thoreau walked the beaches. Provincetown, where the young Eugene O'Neill saw his early plays produced. Salem, forever infamous for the wave of hysteria that led its leaders to execute twenty of their own people as witches. But no place was more historic than our destination.

One might expect that a place famous for a rock would be on a rocky shore, but the approach to Plymouth is a long, narrow channel among sandbars and then behind a barrier beach. The outer harbour is shallow and the inner harbour was crowded. We would need a mooring. We filled the fuel tank at the town dock and called the yacht club. The club launch came out and led us to a mooring. What was it going to cost us?

"If you use the club's facilities," smiled the genial, middle-aged launch driver, "showers and launch service and all that, the mooring is forty dollars. If you don't use the facilities, it's free."

Not hard to figure out that one.

In the centre of the waterfront was a replica of the *Mayflower*, a stubby, ungainly-looking vessel with short masts, a spiderweb of rigging, and a towering stern castle. Like most famous emigrant ships, she looked slow and clumsy. I thought she would probably roll like a sow, and apparently she does. She is not really a replica, since nobody knows exactly the shape and dimensions of the original *Mayflower*; but she's a reasonable facsimile of a comparable ship of the period.

Seeking Plymouth Rock, we took the dinghy to a float beside *Mayflower II*, where a sign read, TIE-UPS 15 MINUTES MAXIMUM. Some of the dinghies at the float were almost filled with rainwater. Fifteen minutes is evidently a long time in Plymouth.

Plymouth's waterfront street has parks and promenades on the seaward side and the usual T-shirts and souvenir shops on the other, though the shops are housed in tasteful buildings that fit well with the dignity of the streetscape. A regular shuttle bus runs between Plymouth Rock and the recreated Plimoth Plantation, Massachusetts's living-history museum.

Plymouth Rock had to be right on the waterfront, since the Pilgrims stepped ashore on it. Sure enough, there was a kind of temple at the water's edge, a Greek colonnade consisting of a rectangular canopy supported by round columns. (The canopy was donated in 1921 by the National Society of the Colonial Dames of America.) Below the roof was a square well about six feet deep, and lying on the sand at the bottom of the well was what appeared to be a six-foot potato, with "1620" incised on its face.

Plymouth Rock. Ye gods.

We left early the next morning, motoring once again in quiet weather, bound at last for the Cape Cod Canal. The days were getting shorter; it was barely dawn at six. This morning, for the first time in some days, the cabin interior was heavy with dampness, condensation running down the windows even though both hatches had been cracked open all night. The days might still be warm, but the nights were getting cold.

South, south, south.

Morning condensation on *Magnus* affects both the inside and outside windshields. It was easier to steer out of Plymouth from below, where a little electric fan kept the windshield clear. I had scrunched *Magnus* against the wharf again in Plymouth, though not very seriously. *Cap'n Crunch Rides Again.* But it is not easy to make an accurate portside approach to a low-lying float with a steering wheel located on the starboard side – as both of *Magnus's* wheels are.

On the other hand, I had finally figured out why steering wheels on boats are so often located to starboard, unlike the wheels in our cars. A starboard wheel gives the helmsman an unobstructed view on that side – and that's the side where an approaching vessel normally has the right of way.

I had been reading James Michener's *Chesapeake*, with its vivid account of the tortures of Quakers under the theocracy of early Massachusetts, and I found myself thinking about the Puritans, who fled religious intolerance in Europe only to establish it in America. Their heritage persists; the United States, which scrupulously separated church and state in its constitution, still seems to be saturated with Puritanism, still sees every conflict as a celestial battle between good and evil. It is an odd view of life; it reminds me of the Gaelic saying that "many a delightful person has been spoiled by religion."

Magnus chugged into the broad entrance of the Cape Cod Canal, which saves mariners the long and dangerous passage seaward of the cape. We had timed our arrival to catch the south-bound tide, and *Magnus* went flying through at eight knots, swinging and twisting in the swift-running water. Marjorie had stationed herself on the foredeck, and she hung on hard while the boat bucked and reared. The canal felt more like a river, flowing fast between stone-armoured banks, passing houses and pathways and trailer parks.

Two towering highway bridges cross the canal, along with a double-towered vertical lift bridge for the railway. The canal shot us under the railway bridge and out into Buzzards Bay. I ducked below to check the chart for the entrance of Onset Harbor, our destination, "immediately south of the Canal," only to discover we had just passed it. We doubled back and motored carefully through the sandbars to tie up at the town wharf.

Onset is the home of Joe and Judy Tessier, friends of friends who had agreed to receive our forwarded mail. It hadn't arrived, and Joe was away, leaving Judy temporarily carless; she would call when she was mobile again. Onset lies on a winding sand-fringed waterway, and is organized around little waterfront parks and a village square. We browsed in bookstores and gift shops, and wandered into an Italian restaurant called Mark Anthony's, where we ordered ham-and-cheese sandwiches.

"Not very imaginative," said Marjorie as the waiter left, "but I've had such bad luck lately that I'm cautious."

True: she had been sabotaged by an Italian meal in Bar Harbor, and a pub supper in Portland, both of which had left her with symptoms of food poisoning. But the sandwiches at Mark

Anthony's were splendid constructs of smoked ham and tangy cheese in grilled panini rolls.

"I wonder what time Mrs. Magoo's going to phone," said Marjorie.

"Don't know," I replied. "Probably depends on Doo-Bop."

Waiting for Judy's call, we spent the afternoon back aboard *Magnus*, reading, writing, running the generator, changing the alternator belt and the engine oil. As I worked, I idly wondered about all the posters I'd seen for a Cape Verdean Cultural Festival held a few weeks earlier, with references to "our Cape Verdean heritage." I had seen some Portuguese-looking names around town as well. What would have induced people from an impoverished archipelago off the African coast to settle in the land of Thoreau and Emerson?

And then I remembered. Whaling.

Nantucket and New Bedford, both within forty miles of Onset, were the centres of American whaling. Yankee whaling vessels often visited the Cape Verdes to take on provisions and water – and crew. Cape Verdeans, said one skipper, were disciplined, frugal, and industrious – not unlike the Yankees – but they also worked cheaper than American sailors. By the end of the whaling era, a century ago, the whaling crews of New Bedford were disproportionately Cape Verdean. By then young Cape Verdeans were emigrating in great numbers to work in the mills and cranberry bogs of New England. Today, the Cape Verdes – having achieved independence from Portugal in 1975 – have a population of 418,000, and more Cape Verdeans live off the islands than on them, including 275,000 in the United States. Remittances sent home by expatriates constitute 20 per cent of the Cape Verdean economy.

Cape Verdeans represent the only major voluntary emigration of Africans to the United States – but the story has a darker side. During the slave era, England and France controlled the coast of Africa. The Cape Verdes thus became a crucial base for the

U.S. slave trade – in which New England merchants were heavily involved. Charles Darwin saw American slave ships in the Cape Verdes when he stopped there aboard the *Beagle* in 1832 and 1836.

After the Second World War, New England and the Cape Verdes were linked by a freight and passenger service, with as many as ten ships annually making the round trip. One of these was the *Effie M. Morrissey*, a Grand Banks schooner that participated in the international races and later made many Arctic voyages under Captain Bob Bartlett. At 110 years of age, she's still sailing, a National Historic Landmark based in New Bedford.

We ate Marjorie's Marvellous Chili and took Leo for his evening walk. On the wharf, a brown, wiry man named Nelson Russell quizzed us about *Magnus*; he had a ketch of similar size, moored just across the channel. Nelson and his wife had wandered the coast from Newfoundland to the Caribbean and South America. He had been doing the snowbird shuttle for twenty-seven years, leaving Onset in the fall and basing himself in Lantana, Florida, for the winter. He planned to leave in a couple of weeks, moving south in long offshore hops to Point Judith, Cape May, and beyond. At eighty-two, he would be sailing alone.

"My wife died four years ago, and I'm just lost," he said. "We were married for fifty-eight years – and that's not counting the five years in high school." I sympathized. Being widowed is one of the worst experiences life provides. But even at eighty-two, he could possibly remarry, as I had.

"Oh, I know that!" Nelson snorted. "It wouldn't be any problem to get married again. The women are coming out of the woodwork! They're absolutely shameless. I'm just not interested."

"Is it hard to manage the boat by yourself?" Marjorie asked.

"Oh, no. The boat keeps me sane," he said. "Some say it's a hobby, some say it's a sport. I say it's a disease. I said that to a fellow one time and he got quite upset. Who do you suppose he was?

Rush Limbaugh. And he dedicated a whole show to this fellow who had insulted his favourite sport."

Nelson is what I want to be when I grow up, I told Marjorie. The sailing part is negotiable. The outgoing, adventurous spirit is not.

Judy Tessier arrived, a cheerful woman with a lot of cruising experience. Our mail still hadn't arrived, but she took us home for showers, email, and coffee. What was our next port? Newport, Rhode Island, I thought. Judy nodded. Probably the capital of yachting in America, the place where the America's Cup races took place for decades, the summer retreat of the super-wealthy families of the Gilded Age, whose unbelievable "cottages" rimmed the bluffs of the town – Vanderbilts, Astors, and the like – Newport was an essential stop.

"Oh, yes," said Judy. "You don't want to miss Newport."

To hell with the mail. We were heading south. But Leo was having a bad day.

We had motored out into Buzzards Bay on a calm morning, with a sullen swell running. Now *Magnus* was rolling along – literally – in the sunlight, and the Wonder Whippet was in distress. His eyes were wild, and he was panting and whimpering. The only way to keep him calm was to stay physically connected to him. He lay on the settee bench with his head in Marjorie's lap, and whenever she got up, he tried to get up, despite the rolling of the boat.

Was he seasick? Marjorie lifted him into the cockpit and sat him on a bench. He seemed calm enough – but only if she sat there too. When Marjorie took a turn at the helm, I sat in the cockpit with Leo on my lap. If I moved, he was instantly alarmed.

Old dogs get anxious, querulous, and vocal. Until he was eleven, Leo hardly ever barked. Now he barked almost every time we left him alone. He used to burrow under the blankets and sleep his mornings away. Now he lay on top of the blankets and watched our every move. But today he was flat-out panicky. Did he desperately need to go ashore? Or was he just having an old-dog panic attack?

You can never know. So we rolled on down the coast past New Bedford and Padanaram, with the Elizabeth Islands stretching out to port – Woods Hole, Naushon Island, Robinson's Hole, Cuttyhunk.

We turned in to Westport – a one-time whaling centre, say the guidebooks, but it's hard to imagine whaling ships getting in and out of its harbour. The approach crosses a bar in just six feet of water, and the ebb currents can run at up to four knots. The channel is the mirror image of a question mark: sharply to port behind The Knubble, steadily around to starboard behind Horseneck Point, then up a narrow, twisting slot between sandbanks.

By now it was clear that Leo was desperate to get off the boat, and Marjorie couldn't help me find the way in; her efforts had to go toward calming the dog. As we headed in, I saw the swells rolling directly over the bar. The tide was not low, so we shouldn't bottom out in the troughs. I could see a mast moving behind The Knubble, and a sailboat soon emerged, lifting and sinking as it made its way toward us.

Up over the swells and down, with the depth meter showing 6.5 feet of water. Into the calm water behind the point, and then dead slow through the sandbars. The boat slowed down, dragging its keel through the sand. It came free, then dragged sand a second time, then came free again. Leo was virtually dancing in the cockpit. We pulled up to a fuel dock. While the attendant and I tied the lines, Leo tugged Marjorie up the flower-bedecked dock.

Halfway up the dock, Leo screeched to a halt, lifted his leg, and flooded the corner of a dock box. A woman standing nearby tore into Marjorie.

"He can't pee there!" she cried. "You shouldn't allow him to do that!"

"And just how would I stop him?" Marjorie demanded. "He's been on the boat for hours and he's desperate."

"Then you should teach him to pee on the boat!" declared Mrs. Snotbox.

"He's too old to learn to pee on the boat," said Marjorie distractedly.

"Then you shouldn't take him with you! Or you shouldn't stay out so long!"

Marjorie rounded on the woman and blew her stack.

"This dog is thirteen years old, and he's *dying*!" she snapped. "And you are an *ignorant* woman!"

She stormed off up the wharf. Returning a few minutes later, she picked up a water hose and rinsed the urine away. Glancing over, she was astounded to see that Mrs. Snotbox –

"You have a dog yourself!" she said, appalled. "You should know better. You don't *deserve* a dog."

She handed Leo back aboard. He was clearly more comfortable but still hyper.

"Dockage is too expensive," I said. "We'll have to take a mooring."

"Suits me fine," said Marjorie. "I don't even want to share a dock with that person."

Once on our mooring, we took Leo for a walk on the inside of Horseneck Beach. Westport Harbour is actually the estuary of two small rivers, whose low, flat valleys stretch inland in a carpet of bulrushes fringed with low trees. The town itself lies far upriver, and the harbour's only facilities are the marina and yacht club. For all that, it was a popular spot on a hot afternoon, with day-sailers and little catboats skimming between the moored yachts while a constant parade of sports fishermen ripped in and out of the entrance.

A woman was sunning herself on the beach with her dog. The dogs introduced themselves, and then introduced their people. Kate turned out to be a writer for a Providence newspaper, taking a day off to enjoy one of the last beach days of summer.

"It's our first beach day this year," said Marjorie. "We've been on the boat all summer."

We talked and talked – about the voyage, writing, dogs, and much else.

"We babbled like idiots," said Marjorie after Kate left. "We're still lonely, aren't we?"

"Yep."

"Do you think Leo's all right?"

"I don't know," I said. "He looks all right now." And indeed he looked fine, capering along the shore, nosing up to people, wading in the warm shallows.

I was actually quite worried. Marjorie is being a good sport, I thought, but this still is my trip more than hers. And what if Leo is really going downhill? What if he really is dying? Are we looking at vast vet bills, death, burial, cremation, what?

And, dammit, I'm not having much fun either. These long days of wallowing down the coast under power do nothing for my spirit, and living for prolonged periods in so small a space gets tedious. All we seem to do is work on the boat and run down the coast.

If Leo's going to be the way he was today, this will become a single-handed voyage with two passengers. What's the point of that? Why not haul the boat, rent a car, and call the boat transporter to truck *Magnus* back to Nova Scotia? When does it become idiotic to press on stout-heartedly?

Back aboard the boat, I turned on the weather radio. The news was not good. Hurricane Jeanne was on a rampage down south, and she was heading in our general direction, though the current predictions had her veering south and east of us, out toward Nantucket. But we needed a better place to hole up for a couple of days than a boondocks mooring in Westport.

I pored over the chart. When the marina launch came by, I flagged down the driver, a cheerful woman in her thirties, her blond hair and eyebrows bleached white by the sun – "a good-lookin' saltwater girl," as someone later described her. I wondered what she knew about ports in Rhode Island. We could go to the Great Salt Pond on Block Island, which sounded unique and beautiful, but lay even closer to the storm's predicted track. We could go to Wakefield, in behind Point Judith, but that meant working our way well inland through narrow channels and strong currents. Or we could go to Wickford, which sounded like a charming village well up Narragansett Bay, well off Jeanne's probable path.

"All nice, all well protected," nodded the Saltwater Girl. "But I'd go to Wickford. Easy to get in, easy to get out, and it's a really pretty little town. They've got good solid moorings, and you can tie up your dinghy right in front of the food store. Go to the Pleasant Street Wharf. Very casual, run by a bunch of old hippies, and they've always got a keg of beer on the go."

"My kind of place," I said.

"Thought so," she grinned.

I flagged down the Saltwater Girl again in the morning. I had awakened at dawn to hear the surf absolutely roaring on Horseneck Beach, which is completely exposed to Rhode Island Sound and the open Atlantic beyond. Was Jeanne already sending in a big sea that would make the entrance dangerous or even impassable?

"That's what I'm going out to see," she said. "Impressive sound, isn't it?"

She was back in minutes. The sound was puzzling; the surf wasn't big at all. If we wanted to go, we'd have no problem.

Nor did we. *Magnus* motored out through the cut over modest swells, and turned south down the coast. And Leo had a very good day.

Tied up at the dock of the Wickford Yacht Club on a warm September day. A couple of club members have taken our lines, and are making us welcome. The harbourmaster's name is Mark, and his powerful outboard skiff is tied up behind us. When he discovers Marjorie is from British Columbia, he beams. He's heading to British Columbia for a vacation next week, at the Wickaninnish Inn on Vancouver Island, a spot Marjorie knows well. We wanted to honeymoon there, but we couldn't manage it.

A power boat mutters slowly by, and the skipper comes on deck.

"I was in Nova Scotia this summer!" he calls. "Loved it! Beautiful place, friendly people. Welcome to Wickford."

Wickford stands on a point formed by the junction of two small rivers, their shared estuary well protected by two stone jetties – though a high tide and a high wind can reportedly raise the water enough to surmount the jetties. We're going to need a mooring, and we'll be staying till Hurricane Jeanne goes through. The consensus on the dock is that Jeanne is still tracking south and east, and should pass well away from us.

"We'll probably get a lot of rain, and that's about it," says Mark. "I've got moorings available, out there." He points to an area inside the south jetty. "And they're free."

"Ours are closer," says a club member whose accent bespeaks an upbringing in Hamburg or some other German city. "Very good, very strong. Und this late in the season, nobody vill trouble you to pay. From the mooring, you take your dinghy up ze other creek, and you tie up right in front of the food store."

We dinghied up Wickford Cove, past boatyards and moorings, and tied up at the town dock. Wickford's main street is lovely – eighteenth- and nineteenth-century buildings, not dickied up, just getting on with their lives. And Ryan's Market is just what you'd hope it to be, not a supermarket but a large, friendly, and well-stocked food store. Marjorie and I divided the shopping list, and I was wandering around the aisles when I heard Marjorie discussing meat with the butcher. *She talks funny*, I thought. *Why does she sound so odd?* Then I realized what I was hearing: we had been so long in New England that my ear was tuned to the local accent. This is a place where people buy "a bumpah stickah fer d' cah." Marjorie's Canadian voice sounded thoroughly foreign.

Like other regions, New England has its own internal stresses. Massachusetts is the queen bee in the New England hive, and the regional capital is Boston. According to Mainers and Rhode Islanders, people in Massachusetts are arrogant city slickers who like to throw their weight around. Torontonians are viewed the same way in Canada, Haligonians the same way in the Maritimes. Elsewhere in New England, people from Massachusetts are known as "Massholes." (Mainers are "Maine-iacs.")

In the fall of 2004, however, all New Englanders seemed absolutely united around one thing: the blazing performance of the Boston Red Sox. "I'm going home to watch The Game," people would say, and conversations would end, business would grind to a halt, pulses would race, people would nervously lick their lips. The Red Sox were on fire, and maybe this would be The Year – the year Boston would not fall apart, the year the Red Sox would not lose the crucial games at the last possible moment, the year Boston would win its first World Series championship since 1918.

It was The Year, as it turned out. In the American League Championship, Boston lost the first three games to the loathed New York Yankees, and then rallied to beat the Yankees four times in a row before clobbering the St. Louis Cardinals in the World

Series in four straight games. New England went bananas. But by then we were far away.

The next day Jeanne gave us torrential rains but little wind, just as the dockside sages had predicted. The overnight forecast called for winds of twenty to twenty-five knots.

But Jeanne fooled everyone. We woke up in the middle of the night to hear a malevolent wind screeching and roaring through the rigging, making sounds we had never heard before, while the boat bucked and wallowed so hard we had to cling to the mattress to keep from being rolled across the berth. Seizing the handholds, I crept from the V-berth and peered out a portlight into the night, seeing first the black sky and then the white water as the boat rolled far over with each gust. Even in the shelter of the harbour, the waves were three or four feet high, and all the moored boats were plunging and dancing wildly.

There was nothing to be done, so we lay down again, hanging on to the edges of the mattress and waiting for the dawn. I had two worries – first, that our mooring would fail, leaving us to drag helplessly across the harbour, and second, that someone else would drag and come crashing into *Magnus*. I had been reasonably careful with the mooring line, but not as careful as I might have been. I had not expected this black wild tumult, and in such conditions a mooring line can saw itself apart in the bow chocks with astonishing speed.

I fretted about this issue for an hour or so, then pulled on my rain gear and grabbed a flashlight. Emerging into the cockpit, I crept forward in a crouch. I was instantly soaked, and the raindrops stung my face. But the mooring line was fine – in fact, everything on deck was fine, though the dinghy was hopping and flopping crazily – and all the boats around us seemed to be staying in place.

By dawn the gustiness had subsided, but the wind had settled into a steady roaring gale. The boat was still rolling heavily, but more rhythmically and less violently. Looking out the harbour mouth, I realized that the stone jetties were completely submerged, the waves rolling completely over them. It was time to take Leo ashore, but trying to row in such conditions was lunacy.

"I wonder if he'll do his stuff in the cockpit?" said Marjorie. "Let's try."

We hoisted him into the cockpit. When he realized we were going no farther, he looked at us as though he wanted to take our temperatures.

We wedged ourselves into corners and immersed ourselves in reading. I peeked out the window to see a couple in oilskins let themselves off a classic wooden sloop and settle into a lean, graceful wooden skiff. The two of them shipped oars, shoved off, and rowed smoothly up the harbour, all four oars rising and falling in rhythm. They were long-term cruisers who lived aboard, I later learned, and they were rowing ashore to jobs at a local boatyard. So it was possible to row ashore – but there were two of them with no dog, and they weren't rowing a light plastic boat.

Leo lay on the settee, whining occasionally. Twice more we took him on deck; twice more he looked at us as though the wind had blown our brains out of our ears. At lunchtime, I looked out again – and saw a bright red kayak moving smoothly along beside the submerged breakwater. Hmm. A kayak, of course, is virtually unsinkable; it can roll completely over and come back upright, and the adventurous kayaker wasn't carrying a wriggling dog. Still, if he could do it . . .

In the early afternoon the rain eased, and I persuaded myself that the wind had dropped a little. Swaddling myself in oilskins and life jacket, I clambered over the stern, shipped the oars, and brought the dancing dinghy alongside the swim platform. Marjorie got Leo onto the heaving afterdeck, and I lifted him down into the dinghy.

Do or die time. I took a deep breath.

"Don't go!" cried Marjorie. "I can't stand it. Come back aboard!"

I hesitated. Leo would eventually relieve himself aboard – and his discomfort didn't really justify a risky trip ashore. I heaved him back aboard.

"I just saw the two of you there in the dinghy, and I thought, I could lose them both," Marjorie said, hugging us. "Or what if you couldn't get back aboard and I had problems out here? It's not worth it. Leo isn't going to die of a full bladder."

A husky outboard skiff was making its way across the harbour, heading toward us. It was Mark, the harbourmaster.

"How are you doing?" he called. "Need any help?"

"Well," I said, "I need to get the dog ashore. Maybe you could stand by while I row him in."

"Why bother?" said Mark. "Let me take you. Here, I'll come alongside."

His crewman grabbed *Magnus*'s gunwale, and I passed Leo over to him. He gunned the motor, and we splashed through the chop to the yacht club. Leo barely made it to the head of the ramp before the dam broke. He had been twenty hours without a pee.

"How hard is it blowing?" I asked Mark on the way back out.

"Forty knots, anyway. I heard it was sixty knots a few hours ago. You must have had an uncomfortable night."

"You could say that."

The wind died completely overnight. In the calm, sunny morning we dropped the mooring and motored to the yacht club dock. We needed to clean up the boat, drop off the garbage, bail out the dinghy, do some laundry, fill the water tank, walk the dog, unwind. A workman was up on the clubhouse roof, tacking shingles back in place. While I walked next door to see whether I could send email from the Pleasant Street Wharf, Marjorie started a load of laundry, pulled out her guitar, and perched on the after-deck. A large man walked down the dock.

"You'll have to move," he said. "That's the club's work dock. It's reserved for members, and I'm bringing my boat in right now."

"Where can we move to?" Marjorie asked, putting the guitar away.

"Maybe the dinghy dock," said the man. "Over there."

We moved. As I tied the lines, the Hamburger appeared.

"I vas wrong about ze mooring," he said. "Ze chairman of the mooring committee asked me to collect ze fee from you."

"How much?"

"Thirty dollars a night."

I gave him ninety dollars and he left. Now the workman from the roof appeared.

"You can't stay on the dinghy dock," he said. "That's reserved for dinghies."

"But there aren't any around, and there's plenty of room."

"I can't help that. I'm just telling you the rules."

"We're not going to stay long, but we do have a few errands to do."

"I don't feel too sad for you rich yachtsmen when I'm up there working on the roof in the hot sun," he said. "You can have an hour. After that, get back on your mooring."

I don't think so, I said to myself. Pleasant Street Wharf was genuinely pleasant, a small busy marina run by a couple of genial brothers who stored boats and tended moorings all over Narragansett Bay. I asked Chris Collins, one of the brothers, whether he had a mooring available, preferably something close to shore. He did. It cost twenty-five dollars a night. We filled up with diesel at his fuel dock, and I used his phone line to check our email and file my newspaper column.

Over lunch, Marjorie and I talked about yacht clubs and their members.

"You'd think one of them would have said, How did you manage during the hurricane?" said Marjorie.

"You would. But you know, cruising has completely changed during my lifetime."

"How?"

"When I was a kid, pleasure boats were made of wood, sails were made of cotton, and ropes were made of hemp," I said. "Maintaining a pleasure boat was a lot of work. Not many people did it. When a cruising yacht appeared at a yacht club, that was a rare event, and the crew was welcomed and given all the privileges of the club. It was a reciprocal deal. They knew you'd do the same if they came to your club. Even in the fishing villages, you were part of a freemasonry of the sea.

"But now the boats are all fibreglass and dacron, and their owners don't have to know very much or do very much. Every little cove is choked with local boats. Waterfront land is expensive. Taxes are high. There are liability issues. A lot more people are cruising, so cruising boats aren't an interesting event, they're a constant problem. I think yacht clubs want to behave like clubs, but they have to behave like marinas. So they're confused and resentful, and you never know how they're going to act."

"Maybe we should just use marinas," Marjorie said. "They don't have any of those complications. They're just selling a service and you're buying it. Very straightforward."

"You're right," I said. "And they want your business. Mind you, I feel pretty odd at marinas. I've never used them much before."

"But we have a dog," said Marjorie. "And we're in a new port almost every night, and in a strange country too. Anyway, we're out of here in the morning."

Stonington was our first port in Connecticut. It's considered among the most charming towns in New England. You can't prove it by me.

All the moorings in Stonington belong to the Dodson Boatyard, the only marina in town. We had motored all day in calm weather down the coast of Rhode Island, entering Long Island Sound between Watch Hill and Fisher's Island. I hadn't been able to raise Dodson's on the radio, so we made our way slowly to the Dodson yard, well up the harbour, and coasted to a stop just off the wharf.

"Berth for the night?" I called to a Dodson's employee.

"Nothing available!" she called back.

"Mooring?"

"No!"

"What?"

"We're hosting a race. Nothing available. Only thing would be Skipper's Dock, down the harbour."

It was the first of October, but Stonington's little harbour was crammed with boats.

Finding a place to anchor would be a good trick. We wove through the anchored boats to Skipper's Dock, an over-the-water restaurant with a long wharf. Free docking while you dine, overnight stays for "a nominal fee," says the Waterway Guide. The wind had come up, but a smiling couple from a trawler helped with our lines.

Leo strained at his leash as we headed up the dock. Oh-oh. No way off the dock except through the restaurant, dog and all. While Marjorie went ahead to reconnoitre, Leo and I waited under the deck, with the diners above us. Alas, he couldn't hold it any longer; he relieved himself right on the dock. I hurriedly pulled out a plastic bag. Marjorie returned.

"We can just keep him on a short leash and walk through the restaurant," she said.

"Too late," I said, showing her my plastic bundle.

"Oh. Well, let's go for a walk anyway."

I shoved the bundle in my pocket and we went up the stairs. People were laughing and sipping pale gold glasses of wine. Smiling, we picked our way through the tables to find ourselves on a narrow street lined with little old clapboard row houses – and with, hallelujah, a garbage can. Ten minutes later we were back at the restaurant. I collared the headwaiter.

"What's the fee for an overnight berth?" I asked.

"Forty bucks."

"Lord liftin' Jesus."

"Best deal you're gonna find in Connecticut," he shrugged.

We walked back down the wharf.

"Does that include power, water, showers, or anything?" Marjorie asked.

"Nothing," I said.

"Why don't we just go on?" said Marjorie.

"Good idea. There are places on Fisher's Island, just across on the New York side."

"Three states in one day," said Marjorie. "I like it."

It was slow going, motoring into the sunlight against a falling tide and a short, steep chop set up by the west wind. Spray splashed back over the windshield, and racing sailboats were flying across the Sound. Why are we always in a hurry, and why is the wind always adverse?

I went on deck to look around. Something was wrong. The dinghy – where was the dinghy? I scrambled up on the afterdeck. The dinghy was swamped, wallowing along under the water. While Marjorie kept *Magnus* idling into the wind, making no headway, I heaved the dinghy up to the boat and lifted the bow. Water poured out over the transom. I lifted it higher. More water poured out. I tied it high on the stern ladder, its transom still below the water. At least it was safe, and it wouldn't slow us down so much.

"I don't even approve of cruising this way," I said as Marjorie eased the throttle forward. "Motoring all the time, staying in marinas instead of anchoring, towing the dinghy – this isn't the way I cruise. Towing a dinghy is idiotic."

"We've been forced to tow it," said Marjorie reasonably. "We didn't start out that way. And if we're going to get south, we have to motor. What else can we do?"

"I know, but –"

"There, there," said Marjorie. "It'll be all right."

We came slowly into West Harbor, on Fisher's Island, and picked up a vacant mooring. I phoned the yacht club. An answering machine referred me to a number on the mainland. The manager's wife answered. Get a mooring from Pirate's Cove Marina, she suggested, or anchor out beyond the rock pile. Fine. From where we were, I could see two rock piles, and no way to determine which of the many vacant moorings belonged to Pirate's Cove. A youngish man was just furling his sails at a nearby mooring. I bailed out the dinghy and rowed over, looking for advice.

"We've got all kinds of vacant moorings around here," he said. "We had a racing meet in here last week, but those boats are all gone. Why don't you just stay where you are? It's better for you and for everyone else in the harbour to have you on a proper mooring rather than on your own anchor."

Fine by me. I rowed Leo ashore while Marjorie made dinner.

Over dinner we talked strategy. Our short daily passages meant that we were still making very slow progress south, and if we didn't get moving, we would freeze all the way down the coast. I wanted to reach Bridgeport the next day. Our friend John Pratt had offered us his berth there, since his boat was out of the water. John also had a package of mail for us, but he was going away on business in two days; if we got to Bridgeport tomorrow, we would have at least one day to see him. Alas, Bridgeport was fifty-odd miles away.

The problem was Leo, but I thought I had devised a solution. I need less sleep than Marjorie, and I was waking up in the night anyway – so why shouldn't I simply start the engine, drop the mooring, and start out single-handed? Marjorie could wake up later, and we would anchor somewhere in midmorning, take Leo ashore, and carry on.

"You're sure you can do this?" asked Marjorie.

"Absolutely. I've single-handed a wooden schooner all over Cape Breton with just a chart and compass. This boat's got all the gear, and a good engine too. John tells me there's a nice anchorage called Duck Island Roads, two breakwaters anchored by an island, about twenty miles away. That's four hours' running – good place to stop with Leo."

"Well, okay."

I dropped the mooring line at 4:00 a.m. and eased out of West Harbor in the dark. I love night sailing – lighthouses flashing on the horizon, the white of the wake on the blackness of the water, the lights of other boats slipping along in the darkness, the glowing red and green of your own running lights, the stars sprayed all over the dark sky. After a couple of hours the sky grew light, and the sun rose pink over the stern. When Marjorie awoke, Fisher's Island was far behind.

Two breakwaters stretch out at right angles from Duck Island, forming a triangle with the Connecticut shore. We were anchored behind the breakwaters before nine. Duck Island is a Natural Area Preserve, and the island proper is fenced to protect the nesting areas of herons, egrets, and ibis. I put Leo on his leash, and we took a leisurely walk down the beach – walks with a thirteen-year-old dog are generally leisurely – and we were on our way again in forty-five minutes.

Two and a half hours later, off Falkner Island, the engine faltered and died. *Magnus* rolled silently in the light chop.

I get needlessly flustered at such moments. We were in no danger – we were in the middle of Long Island Sound with a mild southwesterly breeze, gentle seas, lots of sea room, and plenty of help close at hand. We even had towing insurance with TowBoatUS. But my mind immediately started to buzz. Where were we? How far to Bridgeport? To the nearest alternative harbour? What was wrong with the engine? What about a tow?

"Hey," said Marjorie calmly. "We're a sailboat. We can sail."

Right. Of course we could. While Marjorie steered, I made sail. *Magnus* heeled slightly and forged ahead, holding her course and making four knots. The wind was light and flukey, and our speed rose and fell as the wind changed. Sooner or later we would make Bridgeport, but we would need some help working our way up the narrow creek to Captain's Cove Marina. I called TowBoatUS on the radio.

"Do you need a tow? We could tow you into Branford or New Haven."

No, I said, I wanted to give them a heads-up that we would probably need a tow once we were near Bridgeport. We agreed to talk again in an hour or so.

The afternoon drifted past, as *Magnus* eased her way along the sound. We passed Branford and slipped under the lee of a big freighter anchored off New Haven. John Pratt had phoned us to say he was in New Haven that afternoon, at a Yale University reunion, but he would meet us in Bridgeport.

TowBoatUS called on the radio. Look, said the dispatcher, I have a boat available now, and I may not have one later on. If you think you're going to want a tow later, take one now.

But we were still the best part of twenty miles out.

No matter, said the dispatcher. I can have a boat there in twenty minutes.

And he did – a big red-and-white inflatable with a little out-house for the helmsman, a massive set of towing bitts, and two powerful outboard motors. The skipper passed us a rope bridle with a long, husky towline and set off purposefully for Bridgeport. At the entrance to Black Rock Harbor he retrieved his line and lashed the big inflatable alongside *Magnus*. We came slowly up the slender creek and smoothly into a berth. John Pratt was waiting on the wharf.

"Pack your stuff for overnight," he said. "I'm taking you home for dinner. All three of you."

"But the engine – we –"

"We'll deal with the engine tomorrow," said John. "How long since you slept in a bed?"

"Two and a half months."

"Well, you're sleeping in a proper bed tonight."

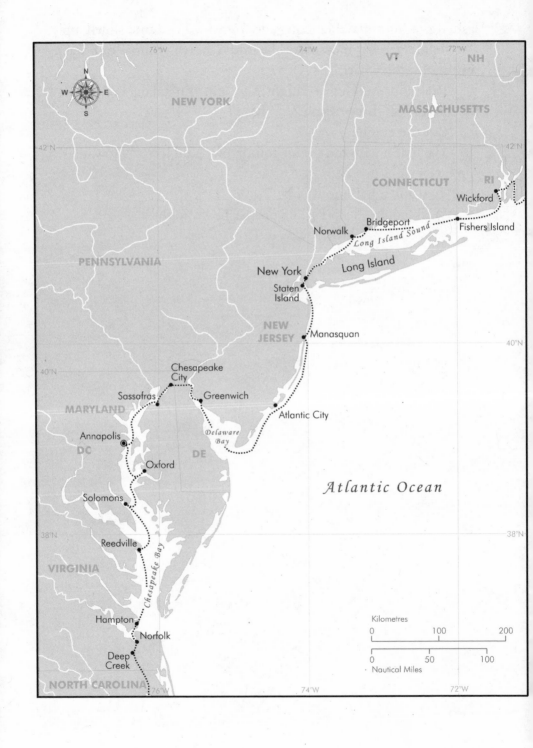

NEW YORK

MASSACHUSETTS

VT

NH

CONNECTICUT

RI

Wickford

Norwalk

Bridgeport

Fishers Island

Long Island Sound

New York

Long Island

Staten
Island

PENNSYLVANIA

NEW
JERSEY

Manasquan

Chesapeake
City

Sassafras

Greenwich

MARYLAND

Atlantic City

Annapolis

Delaware
Bay

DC

DE

Oxford

Atlantic Ocean

Solomons

Reedville

VIRGINIA

Chesapeake Bay

Hampton

Norfolk

Deep
Creek

Kilometres

0   100   200

0   50   100

Nautical Miles

NORTH CAROLINA

PART IV

THE CENTRE OF THE WORLD

"Turn the engine over," said John Pratt. I pushed the starter button, and the engine started right up.

"I'll be damned," I said, feeling remarkably silly. "You know, it never occurred to me to try that at sea."

"If a diesel doesn't run, generally it's not getting fuel," said John thoughtfully, gazing at the engine. "But there's fuel in the tank, and it's obvious that the fuel system is working. The engine runs. I wonder if there's air getting into the fuel supply." He squatted down beside the engine, pulling and twisting every connection in the fuel line – the joint between the tank and the shut-off, between the shut-off and the Racor filter, between the Racor and the lift pump –

"Aha. Look at this." He pulled the rubber fuel hose right off the brass fitting on the lift pump. "This should be clamped tight."

"That could be it, right there," said Tom McMullin, sitting up on the cockpit coaming.

"Or maybe not," said John. "But this hose clamp certainly needs to be tightened. Pass me a screwdriver."

With the clamp tightened, John methodically checked all the other joints. We tried the engine again. It started instantly.

"Well," said John, standing up, "that proves nothing. There's no good way to find out why an engine isn't running when it *is* running. Probably the best thing is just to continue with your trip and see whether it happens again. But let's install that notched V-belt while we're here."

"I don't want the engine dying in New York City," I said.

"I don't blame you," said Tom. "You don't fool around with Hell Gate. One time we were going through there and our engine died. That was pretty exciting. The currents are really strong. We've clocked over fourteen knots going down the East River."

"Install the belt and I'll finish this book," said Ruth McMullin, sitting at the dining table reading the galleys of Myron Arms's *Servants of the Fish*. Ruth is a former president of John Wiley and Sons, the venerable publishing house. Tom McMullin is a retired corporate lawyer. John and Ruth took their Yale MBAs together. They had just been to a class reunion, and – like us – the McMullins were staying with the Pratts.

John is a Connecticut businessman who had shown up at my door a dozen years earlier, looking for a Cape Breton location for a vineyard. A vineyard? In our climate? Not likely. But I didn't know John Pratt.

An engineer by profession, John owns the Petit Tool Company in Thomaston, Connecticut – a custom machine shop that also manufactures tools and parts for eavestrough installers and automakers. Shrewd and imaginative, with a boy's enthusiasm, John built a company that now supports him nicely without demanding his constant attention. He wanted a vineyard, and he believed that there had to be micro-climates in Cape Breton where grapes would grow. He found one in a dimple on Marble Mountain, beside the Bras d'Or Lakes. There he planted North America's most northerly and most easterly vineyard. Oddly enough, one local historian believes that Marble Mountain was Leif Eriksson's Vinland.

His grapes now produce a range of wines, marketed under the name Cote de Bras d'Or, which have lubricated many delightful evenings at our house, and also earned John a Cape Breton nickname. He is "Johnny Grape," just as I, because of my shock of white hair, have been known for thirty years as "Silver Donald." The name distinguishes me from the A&W franchise holder, the university registrar, the senator, and the former premier of Nova Scotia, all of whom are also named Donald Cameron.

Johnny Grape's Connecticut home is a soaring tile-floored atrium with an eighteenth-century cottage attached to one side. On the other side are a visitors' bedroom, a workshop, and a wine cellar. The atrium is dominated by a massive wood-fired Russian masonry heating stove. The house lies at a considerable remove from Martha Stewart, its atrium a constant swirl of dogs and cats and grandchildren and visitors. Music is always playing. Off the back porch, a room full of tortoises and tropical birds includes a parrot that shrieks and yells at John's wife, Charlotte, for hours on end.

Blond, funny, incisive, and calm, Charlotte explains that both she and John have attention-deficit disorder, which makes them impulsive, intense, distractible, and gregarious. Marjorie and Charlotte soon found they shared a passion for animals and a wacky sense of humour. When we talked about Marjorie's all-purpose nouns – ordering the whatcha-ma-doo from Doo-Bop – Charlotte laughed out loud.

"What's even crazier is, our husbands understand us," she said. "One time I was doing some caulking, and John was going to the store. I said, When you get somewhere, pick me up another thing of stuff. He said, Okay. And when he got to the hardware store, he bought another tube of caulking. Just what I'd asked for."

With the McMullins, we made a lively dinner party. Ruth and Tom had been competitive offshore racers who also cruised widely along the east coast. John had been crewing for them once when they put the boat on the port tack in Rhode Island and left it there through the Cape Cod Canal, and across the Gulf of Maine to Shelburne, Nova Scotia, without tacking or adjusting the sails for a couple of days and nights. It had taken *Magnus* more than a month to cover the same ground.

The McMullins had retired from Connecticut to Savannah, Georgia, and loved it.

"Are you coming to Savannah?" Ruth asked. "Oh, good. Then come and see us. We'll take you for a tour of Savannah. Where are you going next?"

"I'm not sure. We have to find some safe place for Marjorie and Leo for a few days while I go back to Canada to give a speech."

"Marjorie and Leo will stay with me," Charlotte announced. "She tells me she's never been to Macy's. Or Filene's. We'll have a blast!"

And so it was decided. Marjorie and I would leave the boat somewhere and get to LaGuardia Airport. When I flew out, John would take Marjorie home. He also arranged for his office to courier our mail, which was being collected every week by friends in Nova Scotia.

Later, I confessed to John that I was concerned not only about the passage through New York, but also about the treacherous coast of New Jersey, which is best covered in a single twenty-four-hour passage. I had been thinking I might want to leave Marjorie and Leo ashore for that one and find someone else to come along.

"I'd be very happy to join you," said John. "And Marjorie can just stay on here." And so that was decided as well.

Charlotte drove us down to the boat and saw us off. Our destination was Flushing, New York, right beside LaGuardia Airport.

"Toilet, New York," said Marjorie as we motored out of John's marina berth. "Didn't you tell me that Flushing is a sanitation depot too? Where they load up garbage barges?"

"Yep. But it's the closest spot to the East River that has any reasonable marinas."

"I'm scared of New York," Marjorie said. "Running down the East River dodging floating bodies. Where's Rikers Island?"

"Not far from Flushing," I admitted.

"A whole island of muggers and murderers," Marjorie said. "I'm not happy, Babycakes."

But we would not make Flushing that day. Once again, the southwest wind was up and we were butting into choppy seas. The day was bright and sunny, but it would take hours and hours to reach Flushing.

"Good," said Marjorie. "Let's go into Norwalk." We threaded our way through the crooked eastern entrance, which quickly got us out of the chop. Soon we were motoring up to the Norwalk Visitors' Dock in the middle of town. We hoped that Norwalk was not like Bridgeport, which is renowned for its nastiness and danger. Even the generally upbeat guidebooks caution visiting sailors against exploring that city. So we did no sightseeing in Norwalk, and we left first thing in the morning.

And that's when I confirmed that we truly were infested with trolls.

Magnus is a Norwegian boat, remember, a northern boat. Apparently she simply did not want to go south. Trolls were hiding in the bilge, grinning and cackling, holding us in the north as the grim winter approached. Look, *Magnus*, I would say, I am the master and commander here – the master, do you hear? You do what I command. Yah, sure, you betcha, *Magnus* would say in her distinctive Norwegian accent. The trolls would snicker – and then something else would happen to hold us in the north. A business issue, foul weather, dead batteries, fuel problems, an accident. I couldn't really blame *Magnus*. I could only blame myself. That's the genius of trolls. You don't notice their mischief. You think your problems are your own fault.

We left Norwalk on a cold, clear morning, with a falling tide and a following breeze, motoring down the well-marked ship channel. I wanted to reach New York by 3:30 p.m. to catch the ebb tide through the swirling turbulence of Hell Gate and down the East River. It would be the last daylight ebb for four days.

So *Magnus* ran aground.

I did not run aground, *Magnus* protests. De master and commander ran aground. Are you Bill Clinton? Don't lie. Admit your folly. Take de blame like a man.

Very well. As we ran down the channel, my attention was distracted. Suddenly I saw a high sandbar looming up ahead, marked by a tall green day-beacon close to starboard. The wide channel stretched out on the other side of the beacon. Ye gods! I was out of the channel, heading for the sandbar!

Marjorie watched astounded as I spun the wheel, zigged to starboard around the day-beacon, turned back to seaward – and felt the keel slide smoothly but firmly up onto a gravel bar. Marjorie stared at me. She thought I had lost my mind. She had been too stunned to speak. I had been in the narrow channel in the first place. I had deliberately turned out of it into a wide expanse of shoal water.

I called TowBoatUS on the radio. Their powerful launch arrived in thirty minutes, but *Magnus* had "sewed," as the nautical expression has it. The retreating tide had already left her firmly on the shoal. Nothing to do but wait for the rising tide, five hours away. The towboat departed.

The trolls were capering and clapping in the bilge. *Got 'im! Not going south dis week!*

The bottom wasn't rocky. The wind was off the shore. There was no sea running. *Magnus* would not bounce and grind. We were in no danger. Until the tide lifted her, she would simply lean over – and over – and over.

But we were about to be very uncomfortable. If your kitchen suddenly tilted thirty degrees, you could move only by scuttling along the downhill baseboard. The uphill cupboards would open and spill their contents on you. The dishwater would flow out of the sink.

We knew what it would be like because we had, um, been in this position before. Most sailors have, though few will easily admit it. The previous summer I had put *Magnus* hard aground in Tracadie, Nova Scotia, simply because I didn't understand how to manoeuvre her under power. I had tried to turn a tight circle inside a dredged basin with the current running strongly across our course. The boat slipped sideways toward a sandbar, and I had what Joseph Conrad calls a "short glimpse of the danger, full of agitation and excitement, like an awakening from a dream of incredible folly." Then the current pinned *Magnus* hard against the sand. The water swirled in little whirlpools around the water-line. In a wink, the boat was well and truly stranded.

"The only mission of a seaman's calling is to keep ships' keels off the ground," Conrad says remorselessly. "Thus the moment of her stranding takes away from him every excuse for his continuous existence." In Tracadie – and now in Norwalk – there was nothing to do but take out a small anchor to hold the boat from driving farther up the bar. There would be no chance of pulling her off until the tide rose again.

The tide dropped. *Magnus* slowly listed over to starboard, tilting more and more heavily as the water lowered her onto the gravel. The farther she tilted, the more difficult it became to do anything inside. The stove was tilted. The floor was tilted. The toilet was tilted. Simply walking from one end of the cabin to the other became an acrobatic performance.

Boats are designed to heel like this, though not for long – but people aren't. Marjorie chocked the dog into the downhill corner of a berth, and we settled ourselves in with our books. I felt sick at heart. Marjorie felt sick to her stomach.

"I'm seasick," said Marjorie. "I'm all right when the boat's moving, but my stomach can't stand this."

In Tracadie, we had rowed ashore and spent the afternoon with friends. In Norwalk, there was nothing to do but stare at the power plant on the shore. But then the action started.

Three hearty lads roared out in a sport-fishing boat, eager to rescue us. The Norwalk Shellfish Police – who enforce the oyster-harvesting laws – arrived in a powerful launch. They had come to rescue us too; someone had reported a sailboat capsized, with people in the water. Now the radio crackled: the U.S. Coast Guard wanted a situation report and administered a little quiz – how many aboard? Names, addresses, phone numbers? Taking on water? They said they would set up a "com schedule," calling every fifteen minutes hereafter.

Now a forty-foot coast guard vessel took up station nearby. They suggested we put on our life jackets. Why? I asked. Heeled far over, *Magnus* was in only two feet of water. We could have waded ashore.

"What's all this water on the floor?" Marjorie asked suddenly. Water? We ripped open the starboard storage compartments. Pots and cereal boxes were floating. I heard water trickling in, and trolls chortling. I burrowed aft, under the cockpit seat, chasing the noise.

Oboy. Water was seeping in around the bilge pump drain, and also through a screw-hole under the exterior trim. It hadn't done this last year, and it wasn't dangerous, but salt water can do a lot of damage to wires and motors and the like. And of course there is no pump in this part of the boat, which is supposed to be well above the waterline. I grabbed the hand pump from the dinghy. Hearing we were making water, the coast guard reached a frenzy of excitement. TowBoatUS called on the cellphone. Everyone wanted to talk to the master. I pumped and talked. The police launch came alongside with a pump, but their pump was too big. I continued with the hand pump. The cold wind rose, whistling in the rigging. The coast guard called. I pumped.

Shivering, I noticed that the police were wearing insulated orange exposure coveralls. I pumped. The coast guard called.

The Norwalk police were terrific – a handsome skipper, a burly mate, a ravishing deckhand who looked like the female lead in an Italian film. They were level-headed, funny, and companionable. The mate came aboard and carefully checked over the boat with me. The coast guard was still standing by, out in the deeper water. The police snorted. In Long Island Sound, they said, the coast guard was mainly a bureaucratic nuisance. The coast guard was now part of Homeland Security. They were watchdogs, and they would not undertake a rescue unless life was endangered, leaving all routine towing to the private sector. Instead, they would hang around demanding to be informed, asking questions and filling out forms, acting as though they had a role but really just getting in the way.

The water in the boat fell. The water outside rose. The boat popped upright. TowBoatUS returned and the police left. The towboat pulled *Magnus* free, towing her to the Norwalk Cove Marina. The coast guard vessel pulled in behind us to fuel up. I walked over and thanked them for their concern. They all nodded solemnly.

We set to work mopping up, wringing out, assessing the damage. The carpets were soaked, and salt water had intruded into the starboard lockers and under the drawers. The dockmaster at the marina thought *Magnus* looked down by the head, and must have water up forward. Impossible, I thought – but she was right. The water had run all along the side of the boat through the holes where the wiring runs. The lockers are watertight only if the boat is upright. Salt water had fried the battery charger, the pressure water pump switch – and Marjorie's laptop.

While Marjorie cleaned and scrubbed and aired things out, I called in the yard electrician and patched the little holes that had let the water in. The next morning, the yard crew slipped a pair of slings under the boat and lifted her out of the water. It was

October 6, and all around us boats were being lifted out and blocked in place for the winter. Owners were stripping off sails, rigging winter covers, putting antifreeze in their engines.

Magnus was undamaged, though the paint and gel-coat were completely worn off the bottom of the keel. Don't worry about that, said the yard crew, but when you haul her for the season, get the bottom of the keel barrier-coated with epoxy and painted. Do you want us to power-wash the scum off the bottom while she's in the slings? Yes, I said, and let's also get the yard's fibreglass specialist to smooth and paint the rough repairs from Jonesport.

I called a cab to take me to West Marine for a new charger. A dapper middle-aged man came out of the office and asked if he could share the cab; he had a pressing appointment in New York. He turned out to be a corporate lawyer with a lovely forty-five-footer. I assumed he was having her hauled out.

"No," he said, "I'm shipping her to the Caribbean with Dockwise."

Dockwise?

"It's a company with big self-propelled barges," he said. "They fill them with water till they sink a few feet below the surface. Then they open a door, and people sail their boats right into the barge. They strap the boats in place, pump the water out, and sail the barge down to the Caribbean. Or over to Europe, wherever you want. You don't have to unrig the boat or put anything away."

It sounded expensive.

"About $10,000," the lawyer said. "That's not a lot more than laying her up here, by the time you add everything up. It's easier on the boat – and now you've got your boat down south, and you can sail her any time you can get a few days off."

Sailing Away from Winter – On a Barge. I wonder how the trolls would deal with that? They had slowed us down and cost us a lot of money. But after one day's hard work, *Magnus* was ready to go again.

You betcha, said *Magnus*. I am wan tough boat.

You are, and I love you, I said. But let's get this straight. Despite the goddam trolls, tomorrow I am steering you *south*.

Ve gonna see about that, said *Magnus*. And I heard the trolls tittering in the bilge.

The second time we left Norwalk, we had just cleared the harbour when the engine began slowing down, almost dying, and then revving up again. I throttled back. We were not tackling Hell Gate and the East River with an uncertain engine. We turned around, and the engine ran perfectly as we returned to the marina. The trolls were still giggling in the bilge.

The same fuel connection had come loose again. No matter how hard I tightened the clamp, I couldn't squeeze the hose tight. It was simply too big. After a few failed experiments, I made a brass adapter from two hose fittings to reduce the hose size and make a nice tight fit. When I had the engine running smoothly – which proved nothing, since it had run equally well when we motored back in – we took our backpacks and headed across the bridge to "SoNo" – South Norwalk, a funky refurbished historical district where we loaded our backpacks with wine and enjoyed a Mexican meal.

The third time we left Norwalk, we butted into a grey sea under grey skies for eight miles before the engine died. I turned the key and it started. Under sails and slowly running engine, we made our way into Stamford, up the narrow East Branch to what the guidebook said was a reasonable marina. It was not; it was a fuel dock with some slips for residents of the adjoining condos. I found a busy mechanic named Vinny at the fuel dock and told him my problem.

"Dirty filters," he said flatly. "Change your filters."

I didn't believe it, but I had no better ideas. I changed the filters. Vinny nodded with assurance.

"You've solved your problem," he said. "Have a nice cruise."

Feeling more hope than confidence, we left Stamford. By now it was midafternoon.

"We can't make Flushing now, can we?" said Marjorie.

"Not in daylight. But Ruth and Tom really liked City Island. Let's go there."

New York City greets inbound sailors with a brick wall that reads, PRISON. The wall runs along the shore of Hart Island, the first of the many islands that make up the archipelago of New York. The next island is City Island, an old suburban outpost of the Bronx. Skyscrapers on the horizon, great bridges black against the amber sky.

New York City. Fancy that.

Because we had a dog, the Stuyvesant Yacht Club assigned us a mooring close to shore. Darkness had fallen when a teenager named Matt deftly manoeuvred the club launch up beside us. His companion was a pretty ten-year-old girl, a poised Noo Yawkah to the bone. Miss Bronx of 2011.

"You got a dawgy? He like it onna boat?" she said. "Wheah y' from? Caynada?" She paused, taking this in. "That's annudah *country!*"

"It is, dear, it is," said Marjorie, chuckling inwardly. "Maybe you'll come and visit Canada one day."

"Yeeah," nodded Miss Bronx. "But I wuddn wanna live theah. I wuddn wanna live anywheah but Noo Yawk."

Matt took us ashore with Leo, then returned us to the boat. We conferred quickly. It had been a long day, and we were both exhausted. This was New York City. Surely we could get a pizza? I called Matt on the radio. Sure, he said, I'll bring you ashore and they'll deliver the pizza right to the yacht club. In a moment, the launch was alongside again.

"Wheah's your dawgy?" asked Miss Bronx.

"He's down below," said Marjorie. "Does your mother know you're out here after dark?"

"Oh, yeeah," said the girl. "I'm allowed out with Matt until one." Her mother, it turned out, was a steward at the club.

Matt ran me ashore, and I ordered a pizza. It took a long time to arrive. It was about the worst pizza either of us had ever eaten.

The next morning I was beside myself with anticipation and anxiety. Our plan was to sail right through New York City and out to Great Kills, on Staten Island. We would go down the East River – a river with no source, but two mouths, one in Long Island Sound and one in New York Harbor. The tides rise through both mouths and meet in the swirling, narrow maelstrom of Hell Gate. The prudent skipper reaches Hell Gate at slack high water and rides the ebbing tide back down beside the East Side of Manhattan, passing under nine soaring bridges en route. To catch slack high water at Hell Gate, we had to wait at City Island till 8:30 a.m. I fussed with the charts, bit my nails, needlessly checked endless details.

"I've seen you wound up before," Marjorie said, "but never like this."

"This leg of the trip would be bad enough without trolls," I said. "I'm trying to think what I'd do if the engine died in the East River. But I can't know until I see the actual situation. All I can do is wait and worry."

We dropped the yacht club mooring at 8:40, motoring in the sunlight along the broad industrial river at 5.5 knots – under the Throgs Neck and Whitestone Bridges, past Flushing and LaGuardia Airport. Rikers Island appeared ahead, the Brothers, Ward's Island, Randall's Island, then Manhattan. New York is a city of islands, a vast urban hive sprawling across the delta of a great river.

In the calm clear morning, a big blue cutter from Newport, Rhode Island, came up behind us and passed us to port, another snowbird vessel heading for warmer weather. Two more sailboats followed in our wake. A tugboat came around a tight bend, pushing a snowy heap of water before her bow. The current began to swirl as we passed under a railway bridge and the Tri-Boro Bridge. As we rounded the next bend, the water ahead of us twisted in sinuous, sullen heaps.

"Hell Gate," I said, cranking the wheel back and forth to hold a course in the turbulence. Over to port was a boiling patch of standing waves, not moving, sharp-peaked and foaming. I steered away to starboard.

"Isn't that our course?" said Marjorie, pointing to the standing waves. Remembering her silence in Norwalk, I checked the chartplotter. She was right; I had been heading into the mouth of the Harlem River. I twirled the wheel, and *Magnus* crashed into the moving field of foam, thrown from side to side, speeding down the river. We bashed through the rough patch, and the current took us away flying – eight knots, nine, up to 10.5 knots. Five knots of our own, five knots of East River current.

Roosevelt Island spun by, and the Upper East Side. Marjorie took photos. I navigated and steered. We were whisking past joggers and cyclists, almost keeping up with the cars. Under the Queensboro Bridge, flying, flying. On the left, seedy Brooklyn wharves, grim old factories and warehouses, and a huge Pepsi-Cola sign. On the right, the elegant towers and riverside parks of Manhattan.

I glanced quickly to the right. Was that the UN Building? The Empire State Building? The Chrysler Building?

"Wow!" said Marjorie, out in the cockpit. "Look at that building! And that one!"

"Take a picture," I said, intent on the swirling river, whipping the wheel from side to side. "I'll look later."

Under the Williamsburg Bridge in a wink. Queer little water taxis painted to match New York cabs, brilliant yellow with a checkerboard belt. Small boats anchored and fishing – fishing! – in this most urban of rivers.

Fireboats and grubby creeks in Brooklyn. The towering spars of square-riggers at the South Street Seaport near Wall Street. Once upon a time, cruisers like ourselves could moor at South Street. I would have loved to do that.

A sharp right turn, and the most thrilling view of the day: the Manhattan Bridge and the Brooklyn Bridge, one behind the other – and, framed in their double arches, the Statue of Liberty.

The river expelled into New York's Upper Bay, full of tour boats and cruisers, ferries and freighters. We steered between Governors Island and the Battery on the Manhattan shore. A baroque red-brick building, with spires like minarets, stood all alone on an island. My God, that's Ellis Island, the gateway to America for untold millions of immigrants.

And now the Statue of Liberty, rising higher and higher into the sky as we approached. All around its base were boats – tour boats, sailboats, runabouts, trawlers, everything that would float – looking like insects beside the towering woman with the crown and the torch. A visitor from another planet would have assumed it was about religion, all the people out to worship at the representation of a goddess.

And in a way, that's just what it is. The model for the soaring copper statue was the French widow of Isaac Singer, the sewing-machine tycoon, but she represents the Goddess of Liberty. The structure that holds her upright was designed by Gustav Eiffel, the designer of the Eiffel Tower. The statue was a gift from the people of France to the people of the United States on the centennial of the Declaration of Independence – the world's second great revolutionary republic honouring the founders of the first. The giant statue celebrates the bond between the United States

188 • THE CENTRE OF THE WORLD

and its first foreign ally and supporter, a bi-national bond rooted in the American Revolution itself.

The French people undertook an immense public fundraising effort to design, create, and ship this colossal work of art to America. And the American public undertook a comparable effort to finance and build the pedestal on which it stands. As we approached, the statue simply grew bigger and bigger and bigger. Nothing really prepares you for its sheer scale. It is so perfectly proportioned that you forget it's as tall as a skyscraper. From the ground to the top of the torch, the statue rises 305 feet – more than thirty storeys.

How many hundreds of times had I seen photos of the Statue of Liberty? It's among the most famous and recognizable images in the world. I always find it deeply moving to remember that it was not a government project but a *gift* from one people to another. I can't think of another comparably magnificent gesture between peoples.

As we neared the statue, *Magnus*'s engine sputtered and slowed down. In the bilge, the trolls were laughing. Thought you could forget us and indulge yourself in lofty thoughts about the fellowship of humanity, did you? Ha! The skipper's mind raced. If the engine failed –? Marjorie was looking at me with alarm.

"It's okay," I said. "It was the East River that worried me. We can sail from here if we need to." The breeze was blowing from the northwest, down the bay toward The Narrows, where the Upper and Lower Bays meet. The engine sputtered and caught, sputtered and caught. If necessary, we could sail right to Great Kills, the little harbour where we intended to spend the night.

We throttled back, bore away to port, and rolled out the genoa. *Magnus* slipped down toward the Verrazano Bridge at the Narrows, past enormous anchored container ships and huge barges with tugboats locked into notches in their sterns. Under that last grand bridge, and out into the broad Lower Bay, with fabled Sandy Hook lying low on the eastern horizon. Around a lighthouse standing in

the water at Old Orchard Shoal. The engine sputtered and died. I
started it again, motored a few hundred yards, and it died again.
I started it again. We motored slowly into Great Kills, a little round
notch in the shore of Staten Island, and picked up a mooring. Déjà
vu: sixteen hundred miles from our home in Richmond County,
Nova Scotia, we were guests of the Richmond County Yacht Club
in New York.

Marjorie crawled into the V-berth with Leo.

"I feel sick," she said. "Too much adrenalin. I've never had a
high like that except getting married." In a wink, she was asleep.

In the bilge, the trolls were muttering and grumbling.

Magnus, I said, we're going *south*.

Ve gonna see about that, said *Magnus*.

Next door to the Richmond County Yacht Club is a Yanmar deal-
ership run by a former New York City detective – a tall, dark,
frowning man whose smiles, when they come, light up the sky.
Yanmars, says Mike, are "the best engines in the world." My
problem had to be pretty straightforward. He was busy, but he'd
make a little time.

Mike checked over the fuel system with great care. Yanmars,
he said, needed 5/16-inch hose all the way, so he removed the
little adapter I had made in Norwalk and replaced all the fuel hose.
We replaced both of the filters and several of the copper gaskets
on the fuel fittings.

"Start her up and run her wide open for an hour in reverse,"
he said. "Try to pull that mooring right out of the bottom." So we
sat on the mooring for more than an hour, churning up the bottom.
The little Yanmar never faltered. Mike declared the problem solved.
I wasn't so sure.

It would cost us $100 to leave the boat at the yacht club for a
week while I flew to Saskatchewan for my speech. The club
manager drove us into town. Great Kills is an old town, brick-built,

hot and dusty, settled largely by Italians. Marjorie got her hair done, always an anxious affair, but the Italian hairdressers were warm and funny, and they did a good job at a good price. I booked a taxi to LaGuardia for the morning. John Pratt would meet Marjorie there and take her back to Connecticut. The dispatcher said the trip should take us about forty-five minutes – a lot less time than I had expected.

Back at the club, we decided to order a pizza. Everyone we talked to recommended a little Italian restaurant only a few doors away. The young fellow who owned it was a brilliant chef and a business genius. I walked over and met him. One of his inventions was a pizza called "The Local Boy's Special." It featured "Sauteed Broccoli Rabe, Sweet Italian Sausage and Sundried Tomatoes on a Bed of Creamy Ricotta Cheese Topped with Home Made Fresh Mozzarella." Great, I thought, Marjorie is always up for new foods.

I bought one and took it back to the boat. We attacked it with enthusiasm, then suspicion, then concern, then distaste, then refusal. We finally threw it away half-eaten. It was the worst pizza we had ever tasted – worse than the one in City Island.

"New York," sighed Marjorie, "and we can't get a pizza nearly as good as what we buy from Ann Delorey in Arichat, Nova Scotia."

We went to bed hungry and woke up early, standing outside the clubhouse in the cool light of dawn, waiting for the taxi. The cabbie arrived twenty minutes late, driving a big old Buick. His name was Bill. He was an Italian American and an Automatic Talker. He wanted to know what route we thought he should take. His recommendation was to cross the Verrazano Bridge and circle around through Brooklyn. We solemnly concurred.

We crept through the traffic, across the bridge, through Coney Island and beside Sheepshead Bay while Bill delivered a fierce, mind-numbing monologue. I kept checking my watch. Bill was retired, a widower. His son had been a teacher, but his nerves drove him out of the classroom and into the fire service –

dangerous work, but worthwhile, did we know how many Staten Island firemen had died on 9/11?

He didn't need the money he earned as a driver. He drove taxi to keep his mind off his wife, who had died six or eight years earlier. He was a Bush supporter who reckoned that John Kerry had lied about his military record.

"I thought at first I'd vote for Kerry, but you can't have a man like that in the White House," he declared. "But I'm not a Democrat or a Republican, I'm an *American*!"

We crawled through the neighbourhood of John Gotti, the Mafia capo. I checked my watch.

"We got the best of everything in New York," Bill declared. "The best food, the best music, the best entertainment, the best crooks, the best con men . . ."

I checked my watch. An hour went by, an hour and a half. In the end, Bill took nearly two hours to reach LaGuardia, eating up most of the time I had allowed to get through security. I left Marjorie to pay the bill while I ran inside to the Air Canada check-in. Marjorie caught up with me. There was no sign of John Pratt.

"I have to go," I said. "I hate to leave you like this, but John has to be around."

"You go," said Marjorie nervously. "I'll be all right."

I flew down the ramp to the security gates, glancing back unhappily at the woman and the dog standing with their bags in the bustle of the airport. There was no line-up at the security gate, and I was through in an instant. You never know. As I cleared the gate, my cellphone rang.

"John was waiting outside," said Marjorie. "When I saw him, I grabbed him like an octopus. Have a good flight." And I did.

The New Jersey coast is a sandbar 110 miles long, with only a handful of inlets for harbours. In strong easterly winds, the seas break right across the inlets, making them treacherous to enter.

The best way to deal with this coastline is to avoid it, making one long passage offshore from Sandy Hook to Cape May.

John Pratt picked me up at the airport and took me back to Connecticut for a day. Then we drove down to Great Kills together, leaving Marjorie and Leo with Charlotte. In the morning we took *Magnus* out into Raritan Bay. The west wind was blowing hard, and a good-sized sea was running. In the open bay the wind piped up almost to gale force.

"I'm not sure this is a great idea," I said, hanging on as the boat rolled heavily.

"Your call, skipper," John shrugged.

"Let's go back."

That night the wind howled across Staten Island, shrieking in the rigging and making the moored boats dance at their anchors.

"Good decision," said John.

We tried again the next day. The wind was still brisk, but it was dropping. Raritan Bay was lumpy, but we would have some shelter once we rounded Sandy Hook. At John's suggestion, we had lashed the dinghy on the swim platform, hoping we had devised a better system than the one I had used in Nova Scotia, but the seas were tearing at it once again. When we tried to tow it astern, it ended up half-full of water, dragging hard against its lines and slowing us down. In the lee of Sandy Hook, I steered the boat into the wind while John climbed down into the dinghy and bailed it out. As we headed down the coast, the engine died.

I made sail while John bled the fuel line. The engine started, but half an hour later it died again. In the end, John bled it six times. The last time it ran only ten minutes. In the late afternoon, we were ambling along under sail just off Manasquan Inlet. A heavy swell and a fast-running tide were stirring up the water between the Manasquan breakwaters. We called TowBoatUS, who pulled us into the sandy estuary and up to a marina.

The next morning we took the entire fuel system apart. We lifted the supply line out of the fuel tank and checked it for cracks and pinholes. We dismantled and cleaned every joint and component. We added a rubber bulb to make it easier to prime the system. John had brought a new lift pump. We installed that. We devised a method to by-pass the whole fuel system, running the engine by drawing fuel directly from a jerry-can rather than from the built-in tank. We collapsed the dinghy and lashed it on deck, snugged up the rig, and ran the engine for an hour at the dock. At three in the afternoon, we headed back out to sea.

Along the shore, speedboats were racing along while sails moved slowly against the horizon. Sports fishermen were anchored here and there, fishing in the shallow water. John was at the wheel and I was down below when I glanced up and saw an anchored sport fisherman dead ahead, its skipper waving frantically.

"John!" I shouted. "Hard a-starboard!" John spun the wheel and we missed the boat. His vision had been blanketed by the low-cut genoa jib, and he hadn't seen the boat at all.

The forecast called for a light westerly becoming a light easterly in the evening, and then a light southerly. The southerly should find us at Cape May, in time for a favourable tide to carry us up Delaware Bay. We motored till midnight, down to Barnegat. The seas kept building. *Magnus* thumped into them, throwing spray all across the boat. When we changed course toward Atlantic City, she began rolling heavily, really heavily, more heavily than I had seen her do before. Eventually, she was rolling twenty degrees to each side.

And then the engine died.

We charged on deck into a roaring east wind – a steady twenty-five knots, we judged, with gusts to thirty. Whitecaps loomed out of the darkness, borne by steep six- to eight-foot seas. Insulated in the pilothouse, we hadn't noticed the slow growth of the tumult outside.

"It's best not to look behind," grinned John. Naturally, I looked back. A whitecap came surging out of the night, rising well above the rail before lifting the boat and passing harmlessly underneath us. We unfurled the jib and trimmed it for a southerly course to carry us as far from the coast as we could manage. Then John climbed down into the engine room.

"Look!" he said, lifting up the priming bulb. It had been sucked flat. We had a brand-new problem. Crud in the fuel tank, loosened by the mad antics of the boat, had plugged the fuel line. John reversed the priming bulb and pumped air back into the tank, clearing the line. The engine started.

We carried on, motor-sailing with the jib. The brilliant neon lights of the casinos in Atlantic City were visible on the horizon twenty miles away. Thunder crashed and lightning flashed. Rain poured down. *Magnus* shouldered her way through seas bigger than she had ever seen since we bought her, smashing and spraying and shaking in the blackness. Concerned about losing the engine again and being trapped against that forbidding shore, we edged out into the easterly wind, making short tacks out to sea and long tacks down the coast, pursuing a shallow zigzag course toward Cape May. The boat surged off the seas and crashed down into the troughs. Everything trembled – the rig, the furniture, and my confidence. Holy Lord liftin'. Am I doing this for pleasure?

Yeah, I thought, we're doing this for pleasure. And then the wind hauled to the south – right on the nose. That removed the danger of running ashore, but it slowed us even further. We raised the mizzen. As the dawn approached, we were both tired, taking turns grabbing snatches of sleep.

"Don!" John's urgent cry brought me instantly awake. A huge tug, two miles off, was hailing us. We were on an uncomfortably close course.

"Small Canadian sailboat," said the skipper of the tug, "what are your intentions?"

"Are you the tow off my starboard bow?" I asked.

"Yeah. I'm a really, really big tow too."

"Our intentions," I announced, "are to tack out of your way. Right now."

We tacked back toward the coast, and John confessed he was glad to do it, since we had also been sailing toward a collection of thunderheads and lightning strikes. The dawn came up grey and chilly, the land hidden in the mist, the restless dark seas rolling and tumbling. And then the wind died.

"We've been towing a line," said John, pulling a loop of heavy braided rope out of the water. "Is this yours?" Uh-oh. Sometime in the night, the seas coming over the bow had tugged a loop of the anchor rode free, and the rest of the line had slipped out after it. I didn't know that was possible. We hauled it in and heaped it in the cockpit. It made my blood run cold; if it had looped around the propeller, it would have disabled the engine.

We furled the jib and motored toward Cape May. I had always intended to go through the Cape May Canal rather than rounding the cape itself, but now I thought the east wind would probably have raised dangerous seas, which would be breaking into the entrance of the narrow inlet. In addition, we had been listening to radio traffic from a fellow who had gone aground right in the canal in front of the ferry terminal and was desperately trying to get off before the ferry arrived. He was not having a wonderful morning.

So we went around. The chart showed shoals all around the cape, with narrow channels between them. The water turned slick and then popply, showing the strength of the tide carrying us into the bay. While John slept, I picked my way between the foaming shoals off Cape May and out toward the ship channel up the wide, featureless expanse of Delaware Bay, its low distant shorelines invisible in the mist.

The wind and rain returned, but now the sea was only a modest chop. At noon we changed course for the sinuous Cohansey River, halfway up the bay. "It looks like an intestine on the chart," said John. Winding among salt-marsh grasses, we eased into the last wild marshland in New Jersey. Visible over the marshes were the masts of boats at Hancock Harbor Marina, near Greenwich. Three twisting miles later, we were tied up, after twenty-four memorable hours at sea.

We snugged up the boat, signed in at the marina, and called Connecticut. Our wives had had "an illegal amount of fun," said Marjorie, and would have a superior roast beef dinner waiting for us the next day.

"We've learned a lot," said John as our rental car cruised north on the Jersey Turnpike. "We've given *Magnus* a real test, and she's come through with flying colours. Not a bad thing to have done. We were never in danger, and we came up against nothing we couldn't handle. And the engine has run beautifully for twenty-four hours without any sign of an air leak."

Luck had been with us as well. A week or two later, I talked with some local sailors who thought I'd been either brave or foolish to steer through the shoals off Cape May. The shoals keep moving, they said, which means the charts are always out of date. I had watched the chart, the GPS, the sounder, and the water around me very carefully, but apparently cul-de-sacs sometimes develop in which the water shoals from fifteen feet to three feet in a boat-length. Experienced sailors here go through the canal – and if they can't do that, they sail right over to Cape Henlopen on the Delaware side before turning up the bay.

"We need to pump out the fuel tank and secure the anchor rode and do a few other little things," John continued. "But it's been a good experience, and you're past all the worst parts of the trip. If you want extra crew for crossing the Gulf Stream, I'd love to come along."

"I'd love to have you," I said. Calm, knowledgable, and interesting, John had been a perfect companion. I'd sail with him anywhere.

"When I hugged you after the Jersey coast, you were like a bag of bones," said Marjorie, squeezing my hand. "Charlotte and I were wide-eyed all night when you told us about it."

"We were glad to see Greenwich," I said. "Isn't it nice?"

Waiting out a grim forecast, Marjorie and I were wandering around Greenwich (pronounced "Green-Witch"), a town of about a thousand whose central area is a National Historic District. Greenwich was once an important port, one of only three ports of entry in New Jersey, and in December 1774 it hosted the last "tea party" of the American Revolution. Boston's was the first and the most famous – but similar forays were later made against tea cargoes at New York, Annapolis, and Greenwich as well.

We walked along Greenwich's one quiet main street, lined with well-kept historic houses, kicking our way through vivid fallen leaves, still enjoying what Marjorie called "the longest autumn in history." There wasn't a soul on the street. In front of one house stood a table with jars of pickles and loaves of home-baked bread and a coin-box with a sign telling us to take a loaf of bread if we wanted one and to drop two dollars in the box.

"This is New Jersey?" said Marjorie in disbelief. "Where crooks and mobsters hang out?"

I shook my head, equally astonished. All around Greenwich were broad marshes of tall brown reeds, narrow tidal creeks, and wide flat fields with combines raising clouds of dust as they harvested the soybean crop. The whole district exuded an aura of rustic harmony that reminded Marjorie of her beloved Fraser Delta. And yet we were – as the eagle flies – about twenty-five miles from Wilmington, thirty-five miles from Philadelphia, fifty-five miles from Baltimore, eighty miles from Washington, and a hundred miles from New York.

Greenwich is pretty much at the centre of the centre of the world, roughly midway between the political powerhouse of Washington and the financial powerhouse of New York – at this point in history, the two pre-eminent cities on Earth. New Jersey is the most densely populated state in the Union. And yet here was some lady selling bread on the honour system, on a village high street so quiet as to make the sleepy main drag of D'Escousse seem a roaring broth of commerce.

I mentioned our amazement to Bob, the eighty-two-year-old veteran of the Battle of the Bulge who worked part-time at the marina. ("It gets me out of the house and gives me something to do," he had explained.) Now he shrugged and laughed.

"This is *south* Jersey," he said. "It's a different world."

We fought our way out of the Cohansey River against a stiff tidal current, the tan-coloured marshes illuminated by a pink and plum sunrise. The sun rose into the clouds, and the day turned grey and calm. *Magnus* motored up the bay past tidal creeks and nuclear power plants, keeping clear of dredges and freighters.

The engine never faltered. A Jersey mechanic had "polished" *Magnus*'s fuel, pumping all the diesel out of the tank and passing it through a set of filters, rinsing the tank out with the now-clean fuel, and filtering it again. A lot of little flakes like fish-scales had come out of the tank, possibly the gel-coat inside the fibreglass tank slowly breaking down. Meanwhile, I had pulled the copper supply line out of the tank and bored a dozen holes near its lower tip, ensuring that even if one inlet hole was blocked, fuel would flow through the others.

Delaware slid by to port, New Jersey to starboard. Confronted with what they saw as a vast wild continent, our ancestors had an endearing habit of naming their new settlements for the ones they had left behind: New London, New Hampshire, New Glasgow, Nieuw Amsterdam, Nouvelle France, New York. New Jersey was about as little like old Jersey as one can imagine, but it impressed me again with the long reach of that tiny island in the English Channel. In Isle Madame, our Cape Breton home, the merchant class was largely made up of French-speaking Jerseymen, "les Jersais" – Levescontes, Jeans, Maugers, Bourinots – drawn to Cape Breton soon after its capture from France. The "Jersey" in New Jersey comes from Sir George Carteret, governor of the island of Jersey, whose nephew Philip Carteret became the American colony's first governor. Elizabeth, New Jersey, is named for Sir George's wife. Like Carteret Street in Halifax, New Jersey's Carteret County is named for the family. Old Jersey's influence soon faded in New Jersey, but the names remain.

Near Reed's Island, *Magnus* crossed the bay to the Delaware shore and soon turned into the broad, straight Chesapeake and Delaware Canal. Halfway through the canal, Chesapeake City provides free overnight berthage at its town dock in a shallow basin off the canal. We tied up there in the early afternoon.

Chesapeake City is as surprising, in its own way, as Greenwich – a compact little town of 735 souls housed in compact little homes almost directly underneath a high-level bridge. It owes its existence to the fourteen-mile canal, which was first proposed by the Dutch in the seventeenth century, and actually completed in 1829. The canal shortened the distance between Baltimore and Philadelphia by three hundred miles. One of its early proponents was the percipient Philadelphian Benjamin Franklin.

In its first version, the canal was a narrow waterway with four locks, tended by lock-keepers and kept filled by steam-powered pumps. It was widened and deepened down to sea level in 1927, and it now carries 40 per cent of the ship traffic in and out of Baltimore. Chesapeake City was and is the transfer point for Chesapeake and Delaware harbour pilots – and the town grew up to house the people who worked there.

But as employment at the canal dropped, the town gradually transformed itself into a tourist destination, considered by *Travel & Leisure* magazine to be "a Top 10 crowd-free weekend getaway near America's largest cities." Like Greenwich, it is right in the centre of the centre of the world, about midway between Baltimore and Philadelphia, and its intimate little streets are crowded with former workers' houses that now serve as small inns, shops, taverns, and restaurants, while the former pump-house for the canal's locks has become a museum.

In the morning we motored on down the canal and into the Elk River, which opens into Chesapeake Bay. The engine faltered just once –

"– troll burp," said Marjorie –

– and that raised the hair on the back of my neck, but the little Yanmar quickly settled back into its steady rhythm.

Chesapeake Bay is a magnificent inland sea that forms the estuary of countless stately rivers – the Susquehanna, the Potomac, the York, the Rappahannock, the Patuxent, the Choptank, the Chester, the James, and many more. All these rivers and their tributaries produce a shoreline intricate beyond belief, a maze of creeks and bays, islands and promontories.

The Chesapeake is full of contradictions. Great cities stand here – Baltimore, Washington, Norfolk – but many parts of the bay, particularly on the eastern shore, remain remote and rural. Outside the main channels, Chesapeake Bay is rarely more than twenty feet deep, but enormous foreign-going ships routinely traverse its waters. It is a cruiser's paradise, and it is also home to the biggest naval base in the world. The rival capitals of the civil war, Washington, D.C., and Richmond, Virginia, are both located on Chesapeake rivers, and lie just a hundred miles apart. Eight presidents have come from rebel Virginia, including four of the first five: Washington, Jefferson, Madison, and Monroe. Chesapeake Bay is a whole world in itself, and a person could easily spend a lifetime exploring it. Many have. I had intended to spend a month here, but we were lucky to get two weeks.

South, south, south! But I still want a month in the Chesapeake some day, and maybe more.

Our first stop in the Chesapeake was the Sassafras River, on the eastern shore not far from the canal. I wanted to visit Mike Arms, formally known as "Myron" Arms, the author of a couple of books that I greatly admire. His new book was *Servants of the Fish*, which Ruth McMullin had read in Connecticut. Mike and I had corresponded at some length, and I had provided a pre-publication testimonial for *Servants of the Fish*, but we had never met.

So we moseyed on down the bay in the pearly-grey morning, and after a dozen miles we turned in at the mouth of the Sassafras. A couple of boats were tacking down the wide river as we entered. The Sassafras is shaped like a scale model of the greater bay, a tapering sheet of water fed by small tapering creeks along both banks, with alluring autumnal woodlands and rich green fields running up the rounded hills and back into the twisting glens.

The Sassafras switchbacks abruptly at Ordinary Point, first to starboard and then to port, narrowing steadily as it slips into the countryside. *Magnus* slid gently along past the scattered homes and farms, the odd anchored boat, the occasional cottage. Three miles farther inland, an elegant green cutter lay at anchor: *Brendan's Isle*, the vessel Mike has sailed repeatedly to Arctic landfalls – and icefalls. We set our anchor. A long ranch-style house stood on the crest of a hill, with a pasture stretching down to the water. A lean, sandy-haired man buzzed over in an outboard skiff. Mike Arms.

"Come on up to the house," he said. "What we thought we'd do tonight is anchor out down the river with a couple of friends and have dinner aboard. The last overnight of the season. Does that appeal to you?"

It did. Two hours later, having met Kay Arms, the dogs, and the Norwegian Fjord ponies, we were anchored just inside Ordinary Point in company with *Brendan's Isle* and the two Southern Cross 31s that had been tacking down the river as we came up. Dave and Karen and Ben and Carol are all experienced cruisers, with lots of experience in the Chesapeake, the ICW, and the Bahamas. But only Mike and Kay have cruised the Arctic, and Mike tells some stories over a potluck supper featuring home-made biscuits, salads, and a delicious chicken-based "white chili."

He tells, for example, about the way he felt his throat tighten when *Brendan's Isle*'s keel ran smoothly up on the rocks as she entered an uncharted bay in Labrador, hundreds of miles from any possible help. Then, astonishingly, the keel slid farther forward – and the vessel floated off. But now it was trapped inside the bay, behind a rocky bar.

"I sent a couple of the young folks out in the dinghy to take some soundings," Mike recalls. "They came back and said we'd crossed over a solid line of boulders, no break in it anywhere. But there was, obviously. We sounded till we found it, and here we are."

Mike built this beautifully finished vessel from a bare hull, and she has carried him – sometimes with Kay, sometimes with sail-training students – to Labrador, Greenland, northern Norway, the Faeroe Islands. One such voyage led to the book that first brought him to my attention. Sailing to Labrador in 1991, he was frustrated and puzzled to find miles of sea-ice where no ice should be. The anomaly led him into an extensive research project – and another voyage – which eventually yielded a fine book of scientific adventure, *Riddle of the Ice*.

I loved *Riddle of the Ice*, which introduced me to the idea that the world's climate is substantially shaped by a Great Ocean Conveyor Belt that moves distinct bodies of ocean water around the world. This vast circulation, scientists believe, warms the north and cools the south by carrying cold North Atlantic water deep under the surface to rise in the South Pacific before turning north again as warm shallow currents. The conveyor belt appears to be a major factor in the whole global climate.

Climate change is one explanation for the collapse of the cod population, which in turn threatens to collapse the population of Newfoundland. That's the subject of Mike's new book, *Servants of the Fish* – a portrait of Newfoundland after the cod, set in the context of another voyage. I had wanted to do such a book myself, but my time for that had passed. *Servants of the Fish* proved to be another multifaceted exploration – a voyage in realms of the intellect and the spirit as well as the ocean.

Cruising around the great island, meeting old friends and making new ones, Mike repeatedly links human experience to the scientific and economic questions. What happened to the cod? And what will become of the communities that relied on it? He concludes – like most other thoughtful observers – that seals, migration, and climate change had very little to do with the cod collapse. The cod disappeared because human beings caught almost all of them – along with more than 90 per cent of the world's halibut, marlin, tuna, swordfish, and other large predatory fish.

What will sustain the communities that once relied on the cod? Mike visits new ventures in tourism, aquaculture, the burgeoning shrimp and crab fishery. All of these can help. But nothing will really replace the vast bonanza of the codfish.

"Ours is the generation," he concludes, "that has finally been forced up against the limits." In essence, he notes, we are all Newfoundlanders, facing the same dilemmas, trying to learn "to live sustainably on a planet that is fragile and finite and surprisingly small." We are a predatory species, and what predator ever truly understands that its prey is not infinite?

The four couples went to bed early, as sailors tend to do, rowing to our anchored boats in our dinghies while the moon shone bright over this bewitching landscape. We rose early too, and in the silent peach sunrise, I walked Leo on the deserted beach, looking back at the four sailboats lying motionless on the glassy water. The morning was so still that the world seemed to be holding its breath.

Leo and I turned a corner on the beige sand, and suddenly a whole congregation of Canada geese noisily took flight, squawking and yammering at our intrusion. Chesapeake Bay is where large numbers of Canada geese spend the winter, and their presence confirmed that we had really, truly sailed a long way south.

"Oh yes," said Mike as we idled past *Brendan's Isle* saying our farewells and heading for Annapolis. "I was talking to Henry Fuller in Baddeck, and he told me there was a gale blowing and it was bitterly cold. Down here it's, what, sixty degrees? And the leaves have just started to turn. So glad you stopped here. Wonderful to meet you. We'll see you in Cape Breton next summer. Have a terrific cruise."

We were having one already. What unites cruising people, perhaps, is a thirst to know this world deeply, in all its splendour and diversity and terror. All our cruises are voyages of exploration. But Mike Arms ranges farther than most of us, and his lucid, stimulating books help us all to see further.

There was less to Annapolis than I expected.

The city looms large in history and nautical culture. It is the capital of Maryland, and for a few months it was the capital of the United States; the Treaty of Paris, which ended the American Revolution, was ratified here in 1784. Annapolis claims to have the largest collection of eighteenth-century buildings in the United States. George Washington resigned his army commission here, and the city is famous as the site of the U.S. Naval Academy, where that marauding rascal John Paul Jones is interred. As for boating culture, a famous chandlery named Fawcett Boat Supplies is right on the harbour, and the annual Annapolis Boat Show, held each October, is the most important nautical marketplace on the east coast. A major social occasion for cruisers, the boat show had taken place just a couple of weeks before our arrival, and I was sorry to have missed it.

On the other hand, Annapolis is small – only 35,000 people – and it's crowded and expensive. Anchorages are inconvenient, and only rental moorings are available in the harbour proper. One row of marina berths is known as Ego Alley, for the showoff boats that moor there during the season. The fuel-dock attendants were impatient and dismissive, especially when confronted with a little boat that took only forty-three gallons of diesel. The thick-witted harbourmaster's idea of "Internet access" is a phone jack in the wall, without even a table nearby.

On the third hand, however, the narrow cobbled streets of the little downtown are crammed with shops and coffee houses – one of which, the City Dock, boasted free wireless Internet service. Bobbing about in Ego Alley was an emblem of modern cruising: a sailor sitting in his dinghy with a laptop and talking on his cell-phone. Across the narrow waterway a traditional skipjack sloop bore the sign SAVE THE BAY. Shabby and neglected, the skipjack looked as though it needed saving itself.

A shallow pool by the wharf is decorated with bronze statues of Alex Haley, author of *Roots*, and of his ancestor Kunta Kinte and his family, who arrived in Annapolis as slaves in 1767. Annapolis is a semi-Southern town, its prosperity originally based on tobacco. We were getting south, all right.

Annapolis is also a dog-friendly town, Marjorie reported. She had noticed dogs and dog owners everywhere, and when she lingered outside shops selling clothing, crystal, and incense, the managers waved her in, whippet and all. That evening, a woman stopped on the street and bent down to scratch Leo's ears.

"Hi, Leo! You're with your daddy now!" she said. She stood up and smiled at me. "He was in my shop today. He's a fine dog."

We noticed another oddity in the harbour: Canadian flags, two of them, on boats moored off the town dock – the first we had seen since August. As we scanned the fleet, we realized that we had caught up with at least the tail end of the great southbound migration, a fleet of boats from the whole of the northeastern United States and eastern Canada. Many come down the coast; many others come from the Great Lakes via the Hudson River. In the fall, Chesapeake Bay is a funnel for southbound boats.

"See you down south!" called the skipper of a pilothouse cutter from Illinois, as he dropped his mooring the next morning.

I rowed Leo ashore, and tied up the Porta-Bote at a float beside the replica schooner *Pride of Baltimore II*. To my surprise, two other Porta-Botes were also tied to the float.

"Is that something new?" asked a well-dressed, middle-aged woman standing on the dock, looking at the dinghy.

"It's a folding boat," I said. "And it's terrific. Sturdy, rows well, motors well . . ."

"Which boat are you from?"

"The little blue ketch," I said, pointing.

"Are you Canadian? Yes?" Her eyes locked on mine like lasers. "*I am so embarrassed about what our country is doing in the world*," she said. "Our behaviour is immoral and disgraceful. I want to apologize. Please understand that this government does *not* represent the people we really are."

I was completely taken aback. My mind raced. What does one say –?

"Don't be embarrassed," I said after a moment. "It's not your fault."

She relaxed perceptibly.

"No," she said, "that's true. It absolutely is *not* my fault."

"We've been in the States for a couple of months now," I said, "and you'll be pleased to know that we've been treated with kindness and generosity everywhere we've been."

"I *am* pleased," she said. "I'm *very* pleased. Thank you for telling me that."

DEFEND AMERICA: DEFEAT BUSH. The election was only a couple of weeks away.

We motor-sailed on to the Choptank River, the setting of James Michener's *Chesapeake*, via Knapps Narrows, an appealing little land-cut reminiscent of the Annisquam River, with houses and marinas lining the banks. Many of the houses had their own small wharves, and lifted their small motorboats clean out of the water on electric lifts.

A skipjack was moored in the canal, and when we emerged into the Choptank we saw another, ghosting with all sail set. The sloop-rigged skipjacks were built for shell-fishing, long the mainstay of the Bay; indeed, the name "Chesapeake" is an Algonquin word for "great shellfish bay." Shallow, fast, and manoeuvrable, the skipjacks were perfectly designed for the work, and they are still a lovely sight, with their slender bowsprits thrusting ahead of them and their sweeping booms trailing over their sterns. They were the last American vessels to fish under sail, though few if any still go "drudgin'" for oysters, crabs, and clams; most are now excursion boats and museum vessels. But to see a white-sailed, white-hulled skipjack drifting along the Choptank in the calm white morning was like seeing an exhalation of Chesapeake history.

Like the Sassafras, the Choptank is only the central stem in a branching system of creeks and rivers that meander far back into the land. Seven miles up the river we turned up the Tred Avon River, and then into Town Creek, which creates the peninsula on which the town of Oxford is set. In the sunlight, with houses set back from the water, Town Creek itself was a postcard of serenity. It has at least four branches, with several marinas and clusters of boats moored all along its banks. The trees along the creeks were glowing with yellow and gold. With no clear plan, we idled up to the fuel dock at Bates Marine, tied up, set Leo on the dock, and were greeted by a smiling blond woman of forty or so.

"And how are you this morning?"

"Well, delighted to be in Oxford. I've been looking forward to seeing this town for years."

"Well, we're just as delighted to have you here," she said. "Welcome to Oxford."

"Could we land the dog for a moment, and could you give us some advice about anchoring and stuff?"

"Sure! Take the dog over there – there's another dog there, but he's friendly. Let me get you some brochures and a map. Anchor anywhere, but maybe the best place is by that point – close to town, and there's a dinghy dock right there. If you're looking for a good meal, the best place is Latitude 38, just down the road, and they'll send a car to pick you up . . ."

Does it get better than this? I didn't even have to call customs. I had called in from Chesapeake City, and when I checked in again from the Sassafras River, the pleasant woman in Baltimore almost scolded me.

"What you callin' me again for? You called me yesterday."

Well, I explained, we'd been told it would be wise to call in from each and every port we visited.

"Well, that's silly," she said. "Ah understand, Ah understand, you're tryin' to do everything right – but, Cap'n, you don't have to call in again anywhere in Maryland. Just enjoy yourself."

Oxford's streets were almost deserted, the comfortable houses slumbering under a high canopy of leaves. It had no tacky souvenir shops or fast-food joints, despite its popularity as a cruising destination. It seemed frank and genuine, a town of people who love the water and shape the town to suit themselves.

One house had a plaque commemorating the breeder of a holly hybrid, which made me note the changing vegetation as we crept south. Mike Arms had a thousand holly trees at his farm when he bought it, and he had been hauling them out for years. Farther down the bay we heard that the hollies are protected – but our informant also said that if you want to grow holly, you don't have to do anything. Just leave the land alone, he said, and hollies will grow – along with pines, which also thrive in the bay's sandy soil.

The next day took us back across the bay to Solomons, where friends of Ruth and Tom McMullin had offered us a berth at their private dock. Solomons is another bewitching tracery of meandering creeks and wooded inlets. We took the first and second right turns, then a left, and found ourselves gliding up to the dock where David Arbuthnot was waiting to take our lines.

"Welcome to Solomons!" he said. "You're in good time for dinner."

Two other couples came to dinner, Gresh and Renie by car and Joel and Mary with their friend Sue on a Sabre 38, which we tied across the end of the wharf. Hors d'oeuvres aboard the Sabre, and then up a flight of steps and through the fallen leaves to the airy, generous house that David and Sally had built for their retirement.

It was the kind of dinner party that lingers long in the memory – bright, worldly people with shared interests and wildly divergent experiences, sharing a delicious meal and discussing subjects that really mattered to them. Before retirement, David had been in international business management, based in Paris, and Sally in publishing. Gresh had been in overseas sales, based in Singapore and Hong Kong. Renie was English, and had just obtained her U.S. citizenship. She and Gresh had raised a blended family of seven, and when the time came to leave Hong Kong they had taken two years off and sailed their boat to the United States via East Africa and England. Joel was an economist, and Sue the widow of a military officer.

By now the presidential election was only four days away, and everyone at the table – except Sue, a pretty and graceful woman – passionately hoped that Bush would lose. Sue wasn't sure.

"Normally I'd have discussed it with my husband," she said, "but I can't do that now, and I really don't know what I'm going to do. Maybe I won't know till I get in the polling booth."

But although Bush was anathema to the others, Kerry hadn't generated any special devotion.

"Fellow offered me a Kerry/Edwards bumper sticker the other day," said Joel. "I said, Don't give it to me, I won't put it on my car. Okay, said the fellow, what about an 'Anyone but Bush' sticker? Give me that one, I said, I'd put *that* on my car."

Joel was a short, bushy-browed, self-confident man with a huge resonant voice and a penchant for theatrical gestures; it was hard to believe that such a vivid personality could be an economist. (An economist is someone who is good with numbers, but doesn't have the personality to be an accountant.) He had an admirable command of language, and had thought of being a writer. He would have been a good one, and probably a very successful one.

"Bush presents himself as a conservative," said Joel, "but he's not a conservative, he's a radical. He's running up unbelievable deficits, and that's going to murder the U.S. dollar. Investors are already putting their money elsewhere."

So where should one invest to avoid the crash of the greenback? Switzerland? Germany? I had my own answer to that one. The Canadian dollar was rising steadily, and so was the Canadian market – so a Canadian could simply stay home. Investing in Canada hadn't occurred to anyone at the table. Canada is still not a sexy country, even for investors. Sigh.

Everyone at the table had relocated to Maryland from the northern states, but Solomons was about as far south as they cared to go. David Arbuthnot had already explained to me that real-estate prices were much lower in the Northern Neck of Virginia, just across the Potomac River, but Virginia was a "red" state, Southern, rural, and agricultural, heavily influenced by evangelical Christianity, comfortable with Bush. Maryland was a "blue" state – urban, affluent, liberal, and multicultural.

In Solomons, David explained, people were oriented toward Baltimore and Washington, just an hour away, cities with international links and a broad outlook on the world. The Northern Neck looked toward Richmond, a much more insular city and the former capital of the Confederacy.

As the election campaign had progressed, it had occurred to me that the bitter divisions in the United States reflected the fault-lines that led to the Civil War. T.S. Eliot – an American – once opined that no civil war ever truly ends, and I remarked at the table that the American Civil War really didn't seem to have ended; it had just entered a new phase. And the South – having recruited a patrician New England family, the Bushes, to lead it – was winning.

That idea went over like a toast to Osama bin Laden. No, no! You've got it all wrong. It has nothing to do with the Civil War.

But I thought you didn't want to live in Virginia because –

No, no, that's cultural and social. Nothing to do with the Civil War.

Oh.

The conversation broke into fragments and turned elsewhere. Gresh was interested in our voyage and wanted to know where we had been. Had we visited Mystic Seaport, Port Jefferson, Great Salt Pond on Block Island?

None of them, I said.

"You missed everything!" Gresh cried.

How could you not? I asked. We were travelling through the most historic parts of the United States, and there is so much to see in these fascinating states that nobody will ever see it all. Besides, we were as much interested in the people as in history. Should we have skipped this dinner party and visited a museum instead? Traversing the entire east coast in about ninety days, we would inevitably miss a lot – but even here the ground was covered with leaves, and we could feel the chilly breath of winter not far behind us.

I notice, I wrote in my journal, *that place names are becoming places. I've long been aware of Annapolis, Southwest Harbor, Oxford,*

Gloucester – but now I know how they look and feel and smell, how people speak, the trees, the quality of the light, and so forth. As these places become real, I forget what I thought they were like; I only know what they actually are like.

We stayed a day in Solomons touring with the Arbuthnots while a weather system blew through. When we tried to leave, we had problems with the battery combiner, which distributes the electrical charge to the two separate battery banks. A quick phone call to West Marine turned up a replacement in Alexandria, an hour away, and the Arbuthnots loaned us a car to pick it up. As we headed down the bay the following morning, we reflected on the generosity and hospitality we'd found everywhere. The Arbuthnots had treated us like family. Yet we were almost complete strangers – friends of friends of friends.

The dinner crowd had suggested we go back across the bay to Crisfield to sample the bay's best crabcakes at the Captain's Galley. Marjorie wanted to spend election night in a cozy little bar where we could do anthropological research while eating well and drinking carefully, and our new friends had unanimously recommended Stella's Second Floor in Onancock. But it was November 1, the recommended date for *leaving* the Chesapeake. We were still at least two days from Norfolk, and the wind was blowing straight down the bay. It was time to make time. So *Magnus* charged down the bay under genoa with her engine running hard, making something over eight knots. Speed was becoming important as the days grew ever shorter.

"Are those *pelicans*?" said Marjorie, pointing at a flock of big brown birds sitting on the water.

"Brown pelicans," I nodded. "We'll see them all the way south from here."

"I've never seen a pelican before in my life," Marjorie said. "What neat birds. Look at the way they coast through the air. When they fly they fold back their necks like a heron. Where are we going, by the way? Remember, I want to sit in a local bar, eat soft-shell crab, and watch the presidential election results."

"I was thinking about Reedville," I said.

Marjorie opened the cruising guide. Reedville, Virginia, on the bay's west shore, was formerly a menhaden processing centre. Today it "is enjoying a renaissance, and recent additions to town include a waterfront restaurant with dockage, an ice-cream parlor, an art gallery, and several Victorian B&B's." It also boasted a fisheries museum and several marinas.

"Sounds fine," said Marjorie.

We made our way into the Great Wicomico River – there is also a Little Wicomico – and nosed into Reedville. Both shores were lined with the ruins of fish-processing plants. Tied to the crumbling wharves to port were five or six grim, rusty grey ships – small mothballed naval vessels, I guessed. A sharp turn around a tall, crumbling smokestack brought us into a web of cozy-looking creeks with pretty houses and private wharves lining their banks. Ahead of us was the Crazy Crab Restaurant and its marina. We pulled up to the fuel dock, tied up, and looked around. The restaurant was locked tight. There wasn't a soul to be seen. We were looking right up Main Street, and not a person nor a vehicle was moving.

A fibreglass skiff roared around the bend, propelled by a big outboard. The lanky character at the helm wore a variegated tattoo, shaggy hair, a sleeveless T-shirt, and a reversed baseball cap. He had bulging biceps and a nine-day beard. He nodded, skipped ashore, and vanished. When he materialized again, he stopped beside *Magnus*.

"Nice boat," he said. "Real nice boat."

"Thanks," I said. "She's pretty unusual. Not everyone admires her."

"The people that admire her are the ones that know the sea," he said. "Scandinavian?"

"Norwegian," I nodded.

"Thought so," he said. "Short ends, canoe stern, she's got that sturdy Scandinavian look." He stuck out a hand. "Scott Rogers. Here, lemme give you a business card. Take a couple of 'em."

M/V WORK HORSE, read the card. Maritime Logistics. Blacksmithing. Marine Towing/Salvage/Diving. All Types of Welding. Metal Sculpture. Trucking. Mooring Service. Hydraulic Jacking and Rigging.

"Tell me, Scott," I said, "if I were looking for the throbbing commercial heart of Reedville, where should I look?"

Scott put a hand on a wooden hand-rail. "Might as well look for a pulse in this," he laughed. "Everything in Reedville is closed on Mondays. Not much happening on the other days either, but on Mondays Reedville is *dead*." He laughed again. "I love it here."

He was from Massachusetts, he said, and when he stumbled into Reedville he knew where he belonged. He went back and packed up his whole business – tugboat, barges, crane, and a sixty-five-foot Sparkman and Stephens sailboat – and moved it all south in one big raft-up.

"Did two-and-a-half knots," he said. "If there was *any* wind, I didn't go out. Good decision, though. I just bought one of those old menhaden schooners, the grey ones you saw when you came in?"

"I thought those were mothballed navy ships."

"Naw, naw, they're menhaden schooners. I sold one of the transmissions for more than I paid for the ship. I got thousands of gallons of diesel, hydraulic fluid, lubricating oil. And I got a contract to tow the ship out and sink her off Ocean City next summer for an artificial reef."

He jumped into his skiff and roared away. We took the dog for a walk in the cool gold autumn sunlight. Reedville's houses were huge and ornate, gracious mementoes of a prosperous past. But the only commercial premises open on Main Street were the

Northern Neck Bank and a Chinese herbalist and acupuncturist.

We found the Reedville Fisheries Museum, which is said to tell the story of Reedville and the menhaden or "pogy," a stubby, oily little fish related to the herring. In 1976, William Warner noted that Reedville's seagoing purse seiners brought in about 500 million pounds of menhaden annually, "making Reedville the leading fishing port of the United States in tonnage landed." Menhaden gave Virginia the second-highest fish landings in the nation, behind the Louisiana shrimp fleet but ahead of all New England. The fish was used for fish meal and oil, crab bait and cat food. The ruined buildings at the harbour mouth were old menhaden plants, but Scott Rogers had also pointed out the new Omega Proteins reduction plant that converts menhaden into omega-3 oils and still processes 234 million pounds annually.

"You should be here in a sou'east wind, when they're cookin' fish," Scott Rogers had said. "Phew!"

We walked around the museum to look at a beautiful skipjack, *Claud W. Somers*. Two genial fellows were painting *Elva C.*, a fifty-five-foot fishing vessel built in 1921. No, they said, the Fisheries Museum was not open on Monday – or Tuesday, or Wednesday, or Thursday. It only opened on weekends.

Did we want to eat out? "Pretty much everything's closed Mondays," they said – even during the high season, never mind November. But the Legion was putting on a chicken and pea supper that night, in behind the fire hall.

Well, no, we didn't particularly want to eat out. We went back to the boat. There was still no sign of the marina management. Two more boats came into the deserted marina that Monday, but the proprietors never appeared. So we cast off and moved to another marina that was willing to sell us fuel – and had a restaurant that opened at lunchtime.

On election night, however, we found no little tavern, no place to hang out and take the political pulse of the district, if it has one. Instead, as this savagely contested election played out, we lay in our berth on the boat and listened to the local radio station, which played golden oldies and gave us about thirty seconds of CBS network news every hour. I have no idea whether people in the Northern Neck knew there was an election.

We learned about the Bush victory at noon the next day from an Ohio couple named Paul and Diana who keep their big catamaran in Reedville during the summer, and in the Bahamas during the winter. A Bush Republican, Paul had fully expected John Kerry to win. Reviewing the results, we realized that *Magnus* was tied up right at the political fault-line, the Maryland-Virginia border. Maryland, along with every other state we had visited, had voted for Kerry. Virginia – and every other state on the rest of our route – had voted for Bush.

Yo' in Bush country now, bubba. Say, ain't that the flaig o' Soviet Canuckistan?

The Bush victory appalled Frank, a single-hander in a tiny twenty-three-foot junk-rigged steel boat. ("And we thought *Magnus* was odd!" said Marjorie.) Frank was from California and had bought the boat in Sarasota. He had taken eighteen months to reach Reedville, where the local yard would do some work on his boat before he went back down south again – brrr! – in February. Frank was almost an Automatic Talker, aghast at the current direction of the United States, apprehensive about the infringements on civil liberties in the Patriot Act, sick about the invasion of Iraq. He wanted no part of a country that would re-elect Bush.

We waited another couple of days while a storm system blasted through. We were still in the centre of the world – just seventy miles south of Washington, forty miles north of Norfolk, the biggest naval base in the world – but in Reedville we felt as though we had been rolled backward in a time machine. Cellphone service had not fully arrived in Reedville. The community had heard of the Internet and looked forward to hearing more about it. To buy a quart of milk, we had to borrow a car and drive to Kilmarnock, seventeen miles away. Rural Virginia makes the rural Maritimes seem frenetic.

But we had a good ol' time in Reedville. We hung around readin' books and doin' chores, lunchin' at the marina restaurant on soft-shelled blue crab and sugar toads – which are actually a little fish, deep-fried whole. Lying in bed, we listened to the snickerin' of the owner's goats and the bayin' of his nine rabbit hounds, two Labs, one Jack Russell, and one Dalmatian. Lotta dawgs.

Reedville felt strangely familiar – a hauntingly beautiful scrap of tidewater, inhabited by folks whose lives were centred right here and who liked their lives very much. No wonder Scott Rogers loved it.

"How y'all doin'?" inquired a fisherman. Good, I said. You?

"Gettin' by just fine," he grinned. "Gettin' by just fine."

We left Reedville not because the weather sounded good, but because the previous three days had been horrible and the following three days sounded worse. Though the forecast called for fifteen- to twenty-knot southwest winds, right on the nose, we decided to grit our teeth and smash through to Hampton Roads, at the mouth of the bay – the end of the Chesapeake, the beginning of the Intracoastal Waterway.

We motored past the derelict menhaden schooners – how can you call a motor ship a "schooner?" – and out into the open bay. As always on these Chesapeake days, we found ourselves part of a steady trickle of southbound yachts: two far ahead, three far behind, a couple farther out in the bay, all plugging south.

The wind, dead ahead, set up a nasty chop, and *Magnus* took so much water over the bow that it made no sense even to use the wipers. The bay is so shallow that its channel markers are not buoys but steel structures driven straight into the bottom. Lighthouses stand like minarets in the water – Smith Point off the Potomac, Windmill Point off the Rappahannock, Wolf Trap near

Mobjack Bay, Thimble Shoal off Hampton Roads. Around Windmill Point and Wolf Trap there were whole fleets of small boats sport-fishing, trolling along with rods bristling from their gunwales. Coastal Line-Dippers, waterborne variant.

This was our last day on the bay, I reflected. I had quickly learned to love it, and I continued to be amazed that such huge areas of natural splendour could exist right in the middle of the megalopolis that stretches from Boston to Richmond and Norfolk. The bay has 11,600 contorted miles of shoreline, and on many of its stretches you would hardly guess there was a town anywhere near, let alone whole clusters of cities and suburbs.

"But we don't know what's already been lost," says Mike Arms. "We're seeing it *now*, and you're seeing it for the first time. Our baseline is now. Human beings have such short memories. We don't see what used to be there."

Very true. I have no idea what the Chesapeake looked like in the 1950s, never mind the 1600s, but it was very different from today. Parts of six states drain into Chesapeake Bay, and the population in the watershed has doubled from 8 million to 16 million in my lifetime. Every day, a hundred acres of forests and wetlands fall to urban development. The bay receives runoff from sewage plants, septic systems, roads, parking lots, and innumerable upstream farms that now rely heavily on chemical fertilizers. Nitrogen and phosphorus enrich the water, causing "blooms" of algae, which in turn are consumed by bacteria. The bacteria suck the oxygen out of the water, making it impossible for other life forms to survive. As a result, about 20 per cent of the bay is now a "deepwater dead zone."

Thousands of acres of underwater grasses – which are nurseries for the famous crabs – have been killed off by the cloudy water, which prevents sunlight from reaching them. Crab populations have dropped precipitously; many of the crab dishes on Chesapeake restaurant menus are prepared with imported Asian crab. And the oyster population has crashed. Once the lifeblood of the bay communities, oysters have declined to just 1 per cent of their 1950s numbers. Oysters are particularly important because of their ability to filter impurities from the water; at their peak, the bay's oysters were capable of filtering the entire volume of the bay's waters in less than a week.

It's the same story as the Atlantic cod, the old-growth forests, the Pacific salmon, the prairie soils. Too many people, too much technological firepower, too little respect, too little humility. Fools that we are, we have gone to war with nature. If we win, we die.

The water calmed as we approached Thimble Shoal, off Hampton Roads. Big ships were coming and going, and we hugged the buoys at the edge of the channel. Hampton Roads is an estuary within an estuary, a large open basin where many rivers meet the bay – small ones like the Nansemond, the Pagan, the Lafayette, and the Hampton, and two great ones, the Elizabeth and the James. The Elizabeth River is the first leg of the ICW.

Numerous cities ring Hampton Roads – Norfolk, Newport News, Portsmouth, Hampton, Virginia Beach. Taken together, they make up a metropolitan area of 1.6 million people. The local Chamber of Commerce says that Hampton Roads is "the world's largest natural harbor." Maybe. Halifax, Rio, and Vancouver might argue.

I had a friend in Virginia Beach – Walter Rawle, an electronics engineer from New Brunswick who had been a colleague when I was a university dean. And Walter, now working in the defence industry, had a colleague, Wayne Baker, who was the dockmaster of a waterfront condo in Hampton. Baker was out of town when we motored up the Hampton River, but he had a neighbour named Wayne Rodehurst, also a cruising sailor. We would be Baker's guests in Hampton, and as we swung our bow toward downtown Hampton, Rodehurst was standing on the dock in front of a row of brick townhouses, waiting to take our lines.

"Hampton," said Wayne Rodehurst as we drove along looking for a hardware store, "is the oldest continuously occupied English-speaking settlement in the New World, founded in 1610. It doesn't look old because it's been burned four times, and there's hardly anything historic left to see. But it's all historic ground. There are signs all over the place saying things like, 'Pocahontas peed here.'"

Wayne is a dignified and reserved man, a former college president – but he's full of surprises. He and his wife, Mary Lou, cruised continuously for seven years after his retirement, covering more than sixty thousand miles. They migrated south a dozen times, sailed north to Ontario in the summer, cruised down the St. Lawrence, and moseyed around the Maritimes on their way back. Their immaculate Tartan 27 was still tied to the wharf in front of their townhouse, and they still enjoyed shorter cruises on the Chesapeake in the season. The boat was businesslike and simple – kerosene lights, heat from a flower pot inverted over the galley stove. He and Mary Lou were a wealth of information and good advice.

Hampton, for us, was both a staging point and a mad social whirl. It was the last city we would see before Charleston – a place to load up with food, have some minor sail repairs made, change the oil, put new watertight gaskets on the hatches, get the water tank flushed out, and buy elements for the drinking water filter. I spotted a North Sails Loft nearby. I wanted to get the genoa repaired and get a new brown cover for the mizzen. I was eager to see Walter Rawle again, and to meet his new family. We were looking forward with some mild apprehension to visiting Jack and Catherine Colgan, friends of my brother who were glad we had been slow to arrive in Hampton Roads, because they had been vigorously campaigning . . . for George Bush. Oboy.

And, of course, we wanted to see the places that Pocahontas peed – and not only Pocahontas, but also Captain John Smith, George Washington, Patrick Henry, Thomas Jefferson, and other famous Virginians. Hampton may be all new, but the restored colonial Williamsburg was not far away.

When he showed up, Wayne Baker proved to be a genial giant, a massive red-bearded man of Scots ancestry who would have looked terrifying with a claymore in his hand. Susan, a pert, bright woman of much more credible dimensions, teaches art history at a local college. They hosted a party for us the following night, inviting the Rodehursts, the Colgans, the Rawle family, and a couple of sailing friends who also lived in the condo complex.

I hadn't seen Walter Rawle for ten years or more. In Cape Breton, he had been working on microwave landing systems for aircraft, and had taken an interest in my youngest son, who was then studying electronics. A blocky man with a bushy moustache, he had recently remarried. Robyn, his new wife, had an engaging eight-year-old daughter named Olivia. Robyn was noticeably younger than Walter.

"Shocking," said Marjorie with a mock frown and a sidelong glance at her own noticeably older husband. "How did you meet?"

Robyn laughed. Walter was a serious runner, a frequent entrant in fifty-mile races, and the two had met, she said, when she was driving along and saw Walter pelting along on the shoulder of the road.

"He had such nice legs, I couldn't stop looking," she explained. "I nearly ran my car off the road. I thought, I've got to meet that man – and here we are."

Robyn, Marjorie, and Olivia discovered a shared interest in horses and riding. Robyn was training to become a specialized dressage instructor, and owned her own horse now, a thoroughbred named Palomar. Marjorie had gone a long time without riding.

"So come riding with me!" said Robyn.

Jack Colgan was a midsized dynamo – compact, energetic, definite. Catherine was willowy and stylish, a native of nawthun Loozy-anna. Like many people in the Chesapeake, they head north when the temperature rises, and their summer home in

Quebec was near my brother's. Jack had been naval attaché at the U.S. embassy in Ottawa, where Catherine was a cultural attaché.

Jack and Catherine had plans for us. We were coming for supper on Tuesday. Jack would pick us up and take us for a tour of the Norfolk naval base on the way to Virginia Beach, where they lived. Any food allergies? No. Could Leo come? Yes. All right? All right.

When the party ended, we stayed up late talking about literature, politics, and culture with our hosts. As Marjorie said later, Wayne and Susan were "instant old friends." Like many liberal Americans that week, they were almost in despair about their country as a result of Bush's re-election and intensely interested in Canada as an imaginable alternative to Bush's America. They were not alone; the Canadian immigration website had just seen a sharp spike in hits from Americans. Susan had just finished Yann Martel's *Life of Pi*, a book Marjorie and I both loved. Wayne reminisced about the pleasures of Scotland, which he had recently visited.

"They had an open-bagpipe night at a pub over there," he said in his soft Virginian voice, "and I guess one of the pipers got a little tipsy and fell over on his pipes, which gave this kind of dying squawk. So then the cry went up all over the pub, 'We have a piper doun! Piper doun!'" He laughed delightedly. "You know, only in Scotland."

Wayne worked with Walter Rawle at a security company founded by ex-Navy Seals, creating animated digital models of real prisons.

"You can go into the prison on your computer screen and see exactly everything that's in there. If you go through a door, you see which way the door swings and what picture's hangin' on the wall on the other side. So if there's ever a riot or anything like that, you know exactly what you're dealin' with, where the access points are, all that kind of thing. The officials can view every inch of the place and figure out exactly what's goin' on where."

Did he have techies available who might look at Marjorie's laptop, which hadn't worked since it was contaminated with salt water in Norwalk?

"Sure, lemme take it in." Alas, the techies simply pronounced it dead on arrival. We dropped it in a dumpster a few days later.

Our mail arrived. While Marjorie went riding with Robyn, I tried to set up the Pocketmail kit I had ordered. An email system much favoured by cruisers, Pocketmail consists of a pocket computer that is held against a telephone, much like an old-time acoustic coupler. Whistle. Chirp. Email.

Alas, I couldn't get it to work with my cellphone. Then I remembered that the cellphone was supposedly also a modem, capable of downloading email directly. Did I have the "dongle," the specialized adapter cord? Did I have the software? By God, I had both. I installed them. The system worked like a charm, and at tolerably high speed too.

This stuff takes a lot of time, I wrote in my journal, *but this is the end of rowing ashore with the computer and looking for an Internet café. From now on I can do it right from the boat. But why didn't I remember this weeks ago?*

Walter picked me up and we all went out to a Mongolian grill for supper. He was thinking of moving back to Canada. He had a good job possibility in Halifax, not far from his elderly parents, and he thought he could start his own business on the side. He and Robyn could have a farm and horses within easy reach of the city.

Robyn was willing, but apprehensive. All that snow, all that cold, a foreign country, so far away. We did our best to reassure her. Nova Scotia is beautiful, property is reasonably priced, horses are available. And she came from Cincinnati, only 250 miles from Canada.

"The poor woman," said Marjorie later. "The idea of living in a foreign country has really thrown her off balance. At one point she asked me, 'What do Canadian women wear?'"

"What did you tell her?" I asked "Mukluks? Bearskin coats? Scratchy woolen lingerie?"

Marjorie smiled.

"I just said, 'I'm a Canadian woman. Look what I'm wearing.' And it was exactly the same as what she was wearing."

The next day Jack Colgan appeared on the dock to take us on a tour of Naval Station Norfolk, the largest naval base in the world. We had seen the enormous grey ships looming across Hampton Roads when we entered, but up close, the sheer scale of the base was astonishing. It's a whole city. The navy owns 36,000 acres and nearly 7,000 buildings in the Hampton Roads area, employing 108,000 military personnel and more than 41,000 civilians.

Seventy-eight naval vessels call Norfolk their home port – aircraft carriers, battle cruisers, missile destroyers, frigates, assault craft, submarines, and God knows what else. The base boasts seven miles of wharves and piers. The base airfield oversees more than 100,000 flights a year, which works out to one flight every six minutes. In fact, the first flight from a ship took place here in 1910, when a Curtiss biplane slowly flew off a fifty-seven-foot wooden ramp built on the deck of a heavy cruiser. The navy is worth $11 billion a year to the local economy.

Jack Colgan was utterly at home on the base, joking with the guards and tooling around the grounds with all the familiarity of a tour guide. In a real sense, the navy genuinely was his home. He had spent his life flying for the navy, instructing in flight schools, and serving as a navigation officer on aircraft carriers before ending his career as a naval diplomat. He met his first wife while she was still a student, married her shortly after she graduated, and immediately left on a cruise that lasted many months.

From the base, Jack drove us to downtown Virginia Beach, an old resort district whose art deco hotels and waterfront were reminiscent of Miami.

"The first time I ever heard the name Virginia Beach was when I was studying Edgar Cayce," I said. "He lived here, didn't he?"

"I'll drive you by his house," said Jack cheerfully and did. It is a modest beach cottage, white and black and grey, with a wide porch running across its front and a shed dormer on its roof. But it was the home of one of the most fascinating people of the twentieth century, "the sleeping prophet" whose medical and metaphysical insights still echo around the world. The psychic "readings" Cayce gave in a state of trance have been described as "the finest devotional material of the 20th century."

Jack and Catherine live in a rambling one-storey house surrounded by tall pines. We steered clear of politics, but one could hardly miss the photos in the hallway of the Colgans with the Bush family, the portrait of Dubya at Yale, the photo of Catherine with Pierre Trudeau, the letter from the White House in which President Reagan congratulates them on their marriage. Jack was widowed in Ottawa, but he and Catherine have now been married eighteen years.

Catherine had prepared a genuine Southern meal for us – sweet squash, salad, savoury rice, perfectly done catfish, and a pie so rich I had to bring mine back to the boat in a doggie box. I wondered why they had chosen to retire in Virginia Beach, noting that the Chesapeake generally seems to be a very popular retirement area.

"Cum-heres and cum-backs," nodded Jack. "That's what they call people like us. We had a house in San Diego too, and we thought about retiring there, but we just didn't feel as comfortable as we do here."

I had not expected to like the Colgans so much. Perhaps most of us tend to demonize people we disagree with, making them into monsters and caricatures. Jack was as gleeful about Bush's victory as a Red Sox fan after the World Series, and one might have predicted that he would be a chest-thumping macho sort of guy with no sensitivity toward gays, or a man who would bury his deepest feeling. But he was nothing of the kind.

He volunteered the story of his second son, a fine artist who lived in San Francisco and whose work was exhibited as far away as Russia. Several of his paintings were hanging on the wall, and they struck me as quite extraordinary, almost Egyptian in their stylized, impersonal beauty and power. In his thirties, the young Colgan came home for a visit and spent a wonderful holiday with his father. Then he went back to San Francisco and jumped off a building. He had AIDS, and at that time AIDS was a death sentence.

"He thought his sexual orientation was 'a curse,' which didn't give him any choice or control," Jack said softly. "I'm sure he didn't have any choice in it. I think myself it's genetic."

Just once we came close to a little flare-up, when Marjorie commented on how little most Americans seemed to know about Canada. Oh, no, Catherine protested, I think Americans know a lot about Canada, and we're very fond of Canada –

"Catherine," said Marjorie, "I've just had a woman ask me what Canadian women wear. And she's *married* to a Canadian."

There was a brief moment of shock and then a gust of laughter.

"Did you tell her that Canadian women put their underwear on one leg at a time?" asked Catherine.

Back on the boat, we compared notes on the evening, one of the great pleasures of married life.

"They're very good company," said Marjorie.

"They are," I said. "I didn't expect to feel so warmly toward Jack in particular. But he has a lovely open, sunny nature, and a great appetite for life."

"The original happy warrior," said Marjorie.

Leo had been a bit troublesome at the Colgans, querulous, anxious, and slow to settle down – though he had eventually fallen into a deep and untroubled sleep. Old dog stuff, said Marjorie, but in general he's doing wonderfully.

I had to agree. In the morning I heaved him up on the dock and realized I had forgotten his leash. He took off at a brisk trot, intent on finding a patch of green. Then he went exploring. Before I could catch him, he had gone up to a man stretching himself on his patio. Tail wagging, he sniffed at the man, and then trotted smartly through the patio doors and into the townhouse.

"Leo!" I snapped. "Leo! Come here! Come! Now!"

Leo paid no attention at all.

"Sorry," I said to the man. "I'll have to go get him."

"Raht," the man nodded dryly. "Dawg minds reel goo-ud."

We intended to leave on Wednesday, but the sail repairs weren't completed – and the next day was a holiday. We called the Bakers and the Rawles and invited them out for dinner at a fine little Italian restaurant nearby. Robyn couldn't make it, but Walter arrived with a CARE package for Canadian travellers: a short-wave radio so that we could listen to the CBC, a CBC short-wave broadcast schedule, a handheld VHF radio, and a can of Tim Horton's coffee.

"What are your plans for Veterans Day?" Wayne asked.

"If we can rent a car, I'd like to see colonial Williamsburg," Marjorie said.

"Good idea," said Wayne. "Susan, whyn't we take them?"

"Sure," said Susan. "It's a long time since we went there ourselves."

Years ago, I trained as a guide at the Fortress of Louisbourg National Historic Park, Canada's nearest counterpart to colonial Williamsburg. Fortress historians were frequently in touch with Williamsburg historians, and Louisbourg administrators often compared notes with Williamsburg administrators. Two very similar projects, set in the same period – but they started from very different assumptions, and they provide two very different experiences.

The French fortress is in an isolated location, and its site was abandoned after it fell to the British for the second and last time in 1758. It has been reconstructed by the federal government with meticulous fidelity to a specific moment in time – the summer of 1744, just before it was captured for the first time by Pepperrell's ragtag citizen army from the American colonies. It stands alone at the tip of a peninsula, well away from any reminders of the twenty-first century. A bus drops you at the gate, where you're greeted by armed French guards who examine "passports" and warn against spying. The fortress is a time warp; its whole idea is to immerse the visitor in the ambiance of 1744.

Williamsburg, by contrast, has been continuously occupied since the early seventeenth century, serving as Virginia's capital from 1699 to 1780. The reconstruction of its colonial district was largely financed by John D. Rockefeller, Jr., and it is now the world's oldest and largest living history museum – but many of its homes continue to be residences, and the district is an integral part of a modern city of 12,000. The College of William & Mary – the second college in the American colonies, after Harvard – was founded by King William III and Queen Mary II in 1693. Its laptop-toting students still occupy its original campus and some of its original buildings at the end of Duke of Gloucester Street.

If Louisbourg immerses you in the past, Williamsburg infuses the present with the artifacts and experiences of the past. Its shops and restaurants are real shops and restaurants, and in the politest possible way, they want your money – just as they would have in the eighteenth century. The bookstore is a real bookstore that serves the students of William & Mary. The historic district has no wall, no gate, no admission. You just saunter in and stroll around the generous, car-free streets.

Look, there's the Wren Building, allegedly designed by Sir

Christopher Wren, and still part of the college. Here's the Capitol, where the legislature used to meet. Here's the colonial governor's palace. Here's the shoemaker's shop, the tavern, the milliner, the apothecary, the silversmith's shop. Here's a replica of a 1750 fire engine. You, there, give us a hand with the bucket brigade.

And just when you think you're in a theme park, you get a sharp reminder that all this is real. The present chancellor of the college is Margaret, the Lady Thatcher – but the first American chancellor was George Washington, an alumnus who was certi-fied as a surveyor here in 1749. Its other alumni include Thomas Jefferson, James Monroe, and Chief Justice John Marshall. It gave its very first honorary degree to Benjamin Franklin.

All this historical grandeur aside, William & Mary – like colleges everywhere – is a genteel money-laundering operation. No matter what kind of a brigand or robber baron you may be, a donation to a university will buy you a veneer of respectability; uni-versities need money and aren't unduly fussy about the source. This college, for instance, was founded in part by a contribution of three hundred pounds sterling derived from the proceeds of piracy.

Wayne and Susan led us around a corner and down a side street to Berret's Seafood Restaurant and Taphouse Grill for a memorable Chesapeake dinner of crab cakes and an ambrosial bowl of a classic local dish, "she-crab soup." The soup is made by blending the crab meat with the internal egg sacs of a ripe female crab and then adding sherry, butter, cream, and spices. Some authorities consider this the absolute pinnacle of crab cookery, the highest and best use that can be made of a crab. They have a strong argument. The soup was enough to induce ecstasy.

"Don," said Marjorie that night, "the trolls are at it again."

"How so?"

"They know we're starved for social contact. They know we love to eat well and drink wine and laugh with friends. If we don't get out of Hampton soon, we'll never leave. This is just too pleasant."

"Maybe these folks are really lotus-eaters, snagging wayfaring mariners with ambrosial food the way they almost snagged Ulysses."

"I never knew lotus-eaters had beards," said Marjorie, thinking of Wayne.

"We'll go tomorrow," I said.

But we didn't. When I checked with North Sails in the morning, the genoa was ready but the new mizzen cover wasn't. I picked up the genoa and hoisted it back on the roller-furler. It looked great, its new brown fringe nicely matching the brown stack-pack on the mainsail. Richie, the sailmaker, said the new matching mizzen cover would be ready by two. It was, but by then the wind was coming up, the rain was pouring down, and darkness was approaching. The days were getting short.

Wayne Rodehurst came down to the wharf and invited us for cocktails. Lotus-eaters and trolls, a fatal combination. We accepted.

Before cocktails, we walked to the nearby Virginia Air and Space Center, which serves as the visitor centre for NASA's Langley base. We saw *The Polar Express*, an animated 3-D extravaganza, in the centre's Imax theatre and bought some space-age toys as Christmas gifts for my grandchildren. We wandered through the museum afterward, looking at historic aircraft and space memorabilia, including the landing capsule from the Apollo 12 moon mission. I found it unexpectedly moving to look at the frail-looking, battered little ship that had gone so far.

That evening we talked with Wayne and Mary Lou about their own little ship, which had also gone far – about engine failures in the Gulf Stream, glorious days in the open sea, hard thrashes to windward to get south. We talked of obstacles overcome and rewards accepted, about the political and management issues involved in a crew consisting of a married couple.

"Our rule," said Wayne, looking over at Mary Lou, "was that if either of us had real misgivings about a passage, we didn't go. And of course a lot depends on the boat itself and the crew. What's comfortable for one boat and crew isn't necessarily comfortable for another. There's no shame in staying somewhere until you're happy to go on."

That's the exact same rule I've seen in a dozen other settings – non-profit publishing, university administration, community organizations, marriages. In the groups that function best, major decisions are made not by vote but by consensus. Everyone has a veto, but nobody uses their veto casually. But if, in the end, the participant is genuinely and immovably uncomfortable with a decision, the group accommodates that discomfort.

We woke up on Saturday morning after a night of drenching rain to hear the wind still moaning in the rigging. An exceptionally high tide had immersed most of the dock and reached eight feet up the lawn. A car on a dock opposite was standing in water up to the rocker panels. I had to put on my rubber boots to take Leo ashore.

The forecast was foul for the next three days. But it was time to defy the trolls and bid a regretful farewell to the lotus-eaters. I wanted to get across to the Elizabeth River, through Norfolk, and into the ICW proper, where we could make some time no matter how the wind blew, but even the crossing of Hampton Roads could be miserable in this kind of weather.

In a fever of indecision, I went up to see Wayne Rodehurst, who knew these waters very well. He and Mary Lou agreed that we might have an hour of discomfort, but after that we should be in sheltered waterways. As we spoke, the wind dropped dramatically. Wayne went upstairs to take a look from the bedroom window. He came down to report that Hampton Roads looked like a millpond, though it was difficult to be sure, since he was looking at the backs of the waves.

I went back to the boat and reported to Marjorie.

"Let's go," said Marjorie.

And we went.

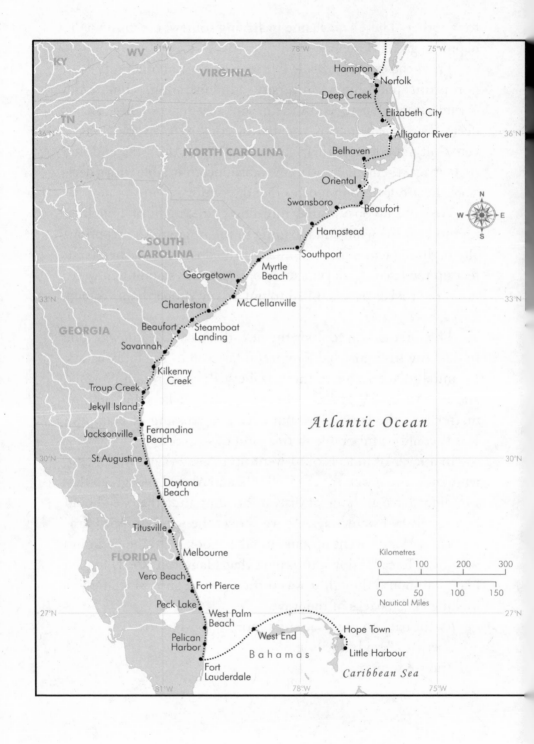

KY
WV
VIRGINIA
81°W
78°W
75°W
Hampton
Norfolk
Deep Creek
Elizabeth City
TN
36°N
Alligator River
36°N
NORTH CAROLINA
Belhaven
Oriental
Swansboro
Beaufort
Hampstead
SOUTH
CAROLINA
Southport
Myrtle
Beach
Georgetown
McClellanville
33°N
Charleston
33°N
GEORGIA
Beaufort
Steamboat
Landing
Savannah
Kilkenny
Creek
Troup Creek
Atlantic Ocean
Jekyll Island
Jacksonville
Fernandina
Beach
St. Augustine
30°N
30°N
Daytona
Beach
Titusville
FLORIDA
Melbourne
Kilometres
Vero Beach
0   100   200   300
Fort Pierce
Peck Lake
0   50   100   150
27°N
West Palm
Beach
Nautical Miles
27°N
Pelican
Harbor
West End
Hope Town
B a h a m a s
Little Harbour
Fort
Lauderdale
Caribbean Sea
81°W
78°W
75°W

N
W   E
S

PART V

DIXIE

Not too bad at first – in fact, not bad at all – but out in Hampton Roads the olive-coloured water quickly heaped itself into steep seas, while the coast guard gave an emergency warning of imminent forty-knot winds.

Oboy. Autumn, says naturalist William Warner in *Beautiful Swimmers*, ends with a "dry gale" that comes up suddenly out of a blue sky.

> The wind rises in a few minutes from a placid five or ten knots to a sustained thirty or forty. . . . Short and steep seas, so characteristic of the Chesapeake, rise up from nowhere to trip small boats. Inattentive yachtsmen will lose sails and have the fright of their lives. Workboat captains not already home will make for any port . . . the big northwest blow will last for at least twenty-four hours, churning the bay milky white with steady forty-knot winds, fifty or higher in the gusts. When at last it stops, the water is gin clear and a new cold creeps over its

surface. . . . Autumn, a charmingly indecisive time on the Chesapeake, has given way to winter.

Brrrr. South, south, south!

The rising northwest wind chased us into the Elizabeth River between the twin cities of Norfolk and Portsmouth, *Magnus* corkscrewing and rolling before the short brown seas. The wind was distinctly chilly. The river was rimmed with container terminals, grain elevators, and piers, both commercial and military. The channel is not wide, and we wallowed along the edge of it as a Japanese container ship backed out toward us, tugboats huffing and puffing to heave her bow out to seaward. The river gradually bends away from the open water, but the waves and the lusty wind chased us into the heart of the port.

And here, where the eastern and southern branches of the Elizabeth River join, is red buoy R36 – Mile Zero of the Atlantic Intracoastal Waterway. We were in The Ditch at last.

A few marinas announced themselves from the shore, and we noted a couple of anchorages filled with yachts – but the dominant feature of the river is naval installations and hulking grey ships. As we approached three tall lifting bridges – two railroad bridges, one highway bridge – a naval picket boat took up station beside us, pacing us. We took no photographs.

In its thousand-mile length, the ICW is crossed by about 130 bridges, of which 85 or so open to allow the passage of boats with tall masts. Some are bascule bridges, which lift up from a hinge on one side, like a trapdoor. A few are swing bridges. These three in Norfolk were vertical lift bridges – paired towers with a horizontal deck between them. The two railway bridges keep their decks up unless a train is expected; but the highway bridge has to open to let a boat pass through. I radioed the bridge-master.

"Come raht on up, Cap," he said. "Be open when y' git here."

It was hard to believe that this monstrous piece of engineering would whisk a section of highway high into the air before *Magnus*'s mast slammed into it. But it did. For the first time – but by no means the last – I was filled with admiration for the timing and judgment of the bridge-tenders, who raise and lower their spans just long enough to let the boats through with the minimum disruption of road traffic.

Beyond the three bridges, the river traffic eased. The river wound through a low, reedy industrial landscape, twisted a couple of times, and brought us to the ICW's first bascule bridge, at Gilmerton. The bridge-tender was waiting for a train, which meant we had to kill time by circling in front of the bridge. Unaccustomed to bridges, and forgetting that they will open at any time for commercial traffic, I timidly hung much too far back, thus missing a chance to get through quickly during an unscheduled opening for a tugboat. Ah, well. One learns.

Past Gilmerton, southbound boats choose one of two routes, which merge again at the Alligator River in North Carolina. Some vessels continue on the Elizabeth River to Great Bridge, through a lock into the Albemarle and Chesapeake Canal, and thus into Currituck Sound, North Carolina. But the older alternative route is by far the more romantic – the oldest manmade waterway in the United States, the Great Dismal Swamp Canal.

Who could pass up an opportunity to travel something called The Great Dismal Swamp Canal? We swung up Deep Creek and motored into the canal's first lock in the cold light of an autumn afternoon. The water swirled around us, covered with foam. Shivering in the biting wind, we emerged from the lock into the canal, and promptly tied up behind a Mexican restaurant in the quiet village of Deep Creek itself, once a roistering haunt of shingle-makers and lumbermen who worked deep in the swamp itself.

"Don," said Marjorie, "there's something wrong with the toilet."

There was. It was full.

Oboy. The Air Head is a wonderful device – it is astonishing how composting shrinks the solids – but it does need emptying from time to time. Seasonal cruisers can let the contents season (so to speak) over the winter, and spread the resulting crumbly black compost on their flower beds in the spring. Travelling sailors, says the cheerful manufacturer, can simply bag the partially digested contents and heave them into the nearest dumpster.

But how do you get the contents into the bag? Is that really the kind of task you want to perform in the public eye? And do you want to answer a lot of questions from the owner of the dumpster?

"Say, fella, what's that you're heavin' in mah dumpster?"

"Oh, nothing. Nothing."

"Sure seems like sumthin'. Here, lemme have a look . . ."

Well, later. We went off for a good Mexican meal, postponing the moment of reckoning until after dark. Then I took a flashlight, muscled the Air Head into the cockpit, demounted the liquids tank, and removed the seat from the solids tank. I slipped an inverted garbage bag over the latter and upended the whole thing.

Whoops! Voices on the canal bank! I turned off the flashlight and crouched low in the cockpit. A couple of kids with bikes wandered past.

"Look, that boat's from Caynada."

"Long way."

Yikes. Was I on the verge of creating an international incident? CANUCK CRUISING CAPTAIN CAPTURED, TURDS IN TOW. *Just compost, says red-faced skipper caught red-handed with sack of sewage . . .*

The kids moved off. I scuttled around the cockpit, rinsing the Air Head with buckets of canal water, double-bagging the nasties, lugging the Air Head below. Back on deck, I scanned the canal bank. I could see the dumpster behind the Mexican restaurant, only a few yards away. Clutching my black bundle, I

scuttled up the canal bank, opened the side door of the dumpster, pushed a cardboard box aside, shoved the plastic bag inside,
and slid the door closed.

I looked around, stood up straight, thrust my hands in my
pockets, and ambled slowly back to the boat, whistling. Who,
me, officer? Never saw that stuff before. Just taking a walk on
the canal bank for a bit of fresh air before turning in. Yes, a bad
business. Hope you catch the culprit. Good night, officer.

"Well?" whispered Marjorie.

"Done," I replied.

We left early in the chilly morning with Marjorie at the wheel,
motoring down the arrow-straight aisle of water through the vivid
autumn forest, leaving a soiled brown and beige wake behind us.
The water was the colour of Cape Breton tea.

The first attraction of The Great Dismal Swamp Canal is its
name. You think, That can't be real – but it is. The swamp was
named in 1728 by Colonel William Byrd II, a founder of a distin-
guished family. A ribald, acquisitive, and opinionated character,
the early Byrd wrote lively diaries. He "rogered" his wife regularly, he reports, and once gave her "a flourish" upon his billiard
table. He also left a lively account of his experience leading the
survey commission that established the first Virginia–North
Carolina boundary line. It ran right through the swamp, which
Byrd described as "a vast body of dirt and nastiness."

Because the swamp almost prevented travel between
Chesapeake Bay in Virginia and Albemarle Sound in North
Carolina, Byrd suggested a canal. In 1764, six investors formed a
company to buy forty thousand acres of the swamp, log its hulking
cypress and juniper trees, build a canal, drain the swamp, and
sell the land for farming. One of the six was a surveyor, who laid
down the canal's route. His name was George Washington.

Washington sold his shares in 1796 to "Lighthorse Harry" Lee, the father of General Robert E. Lee, who never paid him. The canal slowly advanced, dug initially by slaves. It opened in 1805. Though it has been enlarged several times since, the U.S. Army Corps of Engineers still only guarantees six feet of water.

The greatest attraction of the canal is the Great Dismal Swamp itself. Such marshes once occupied 30 million acres of the southeastern United States, and even in its modern, shrunken state, this vast ecological nursery still covers 300,000 acres, including a 110,000-acre National Wildlife Refuge. It is home to black bears, white-tailed deer, bobcat, otter, and more than two hundred species of birds. It is one of the few places on this continent where peat is being formed.

Interestingly enough, the swamp is about twenty feet above sea level. Hence the lock at Deep Creek, which lifted *Magnus* nine feet when she entered the canal. And although the amber water looks dirty, it is actually super-pure. It's freshwater, coloured and chemically purified by tannic acids from the juniper, gum, and cypress trees. Bacteria can't grow in it, so it stays palatable long after most freshwater has gone skunky – a quality that made "juniper water" from the Dismal Swamp invaluable to the skippers of early sailing vessels.

U.S. Highway 17 runs exactly parallel to the canal, though the dense ferns, trees, and underbrush usually hide the motorists from the cruisers. Halfway along the route is the North Carolina border. A couple of hotels at this shadowy, ambiguous border crossing – deep in the swamp, far from towns and officials – once did a thriving business by catering to duellists, fugitives, and couples in need of quick, unscrutinized marriages. Their location at the state line made for an easy getaway from irate parents, bailiffs, or creditors. One hotelier even advertised the speed of his marriages. "In half an hour after their arrival," he wrote, "'the blushing bride salutes her wedded lord.'" A local newspaper, reporting on one swamp wedding, blandly noted that,

"The fortunate groom was just nineteen, and the fair bride was just forty-five."

Today, the North Carolina Welcome Center serves both motorists and boaters as they cross the border, providing parking space off the highway and free dockage on the canal. Three or four boats were already tied up there, and Marjorie steered *Magnus* onward without stopping. It was a day fit for a magic realist – the black-green trees, the gold and russet leaves, the hard sky capping the long slot of waterway like a cold blue roof.

The ghosts around us, rising like vapours from the still water, included innumerable runaway slaves, for whom the swamp was a natural sanctuary. In the nineteenth century, the swamp sustained an entire fugitive economy based on hunting, lumbering, and shingle-making. Both Thomas Moore and Longfellow wrote poems set in the swamp, and the legendary Nat Turner, leader of the most important slave revolt in U.S. history, is thought to have hidden out here.

Magnus churned down this vibrant aqueous highway for twenty-three miles, past ancient rotting pilings with small trees and vivid bushes growing from their tops, past the conical roots of dead cypress trees, past towers of vine climbing the trunks of gum trees and junipers. The leaves were past their peak, but still flared scarlet and gold in the bright, chilly sunlight. Five herons flew ahead of us, rising and taking wing whenever we caught up with them. A small flock of Canada geese crossed the slit of open sky above. The geometric V of our wake lapped the banks of the canal behind us, while the narrow strip of unruffled water stretched out ahead, straight as a highway. It felt like a time out of time.

The little ketch reached the end of the canal at the South Mills lock. In 1862, the Confederacy's Third Georgia Regiment repelled a Union force charged with cutting rebel supply lines by blowing up this lock. After the North captured Norfolk, Confederate soldiers hid in the swamp, making guerrilla raids on Union vessels and forces.

Today, the lock was under the control of two beagles and an engaging woman who operates both the lock and the adjoining road bridge. ("I s'pose they're rabbit haounds," she said, "but th' only thing they hunt's biscuits.") While we slowly dropped down to the level of the Pasquotank River, she regaled us with stories about her pet raccoon, rescued as an infant from a burning stump.

The Pasquotank begins as a narrow, twisting stream, slowly widening as it approaches Albemarle Sound – a backwoods river with only a few fishing camps on its banks. After a quick twist through a railway swing bridge, it delivered us into the declining metropolis of Elizabeth City, population seventeen thousand – the capital city, in effect, of the Dismal Swamp and its canal. Lumbering in the swamp is all but over, alas, and the canal itself has been largely supplanted by the newer route through Coinjock and Currituck Sound. It is an open secret that the U.S. Army Corps of Engineers would love to close it, a notion that makes Elizabeth City apoplectic.

So Elizabeth City eagerly attracts traffic into the canal, rejuvenating its downtown and providing free overnight dockage for transient boaters. Every afternoon, a golf cart appears at the little park by the transient docks, driven by Fred Fearing, now over ninety years of age, who greets the crews and presents roses to the ladies. If more than a couple of boats are tied up, he invites all the crews to his nearby home for tea and hors d'oeuvres. In the past, Fearing was part of a whole group of retirees known as "The Rose Buddies," but the others have all died, and he now carries on the tradition alone.

I wanted to meet Fearing, but the town berths lie between pilings – a style of berth new to me but much favoured in the South – and a stiff breeze was blowing across them. A block away was a large city park with a seawall. We knew how to dock *Magnus* along a seawall, and we did. Alas, we never met Fred Fearing.

But we were certainly in the snowbird migration. At six-thirty the next morning – the first good day after several days of strong northerly wind – a stream of seven boats pulled out, heading south. We stayed behind for a day, poking around the sleepy, pleasant little city, picking up a few groceries, finding an optometrist to repair my favourite glasses. Moored in the centre of town, we felt a bit exposed, and once, when I came back from walking the BFD, Marjorie reported that "some weirdo" had been peering into the boat, waving at her.

"He was really creepy," she said. "I already figured out that if he came aboard, I was going to use the kitchen knife on him. But it's a friendly place otherwise. When I was out this morning, everyone I saw smiled and caught my eye, and said, 'Mawnin!'"

"Really?"

"Black and white alike. But you remember those glitzy golden shoes I liked? I went in the store and asked if they had any in size six, and the salesman said, 'Oh, no, we don't have much in that size. Almost all the shoes we carry are size eleven and twelve.' Eleven and twelve? 'Yes,' he said, 'and thirteen and fourteen too. That's not only here, but through the whole state.' Do you think that can possibly be true? Is there something in the gene pool that gives all North Carolina women feet like snowshoes?"

"I don't know," I said, "but they don't get their hair cut on Mondays. I went looking for a barber and I found seven hairdressers – and every one was closed."

I really did need a haircut. My hair had been cut in Portland, Maine, on September 18. By the time we left New Jersey on October 25, it had fluffed out into a halo of white curls.

"Sugar Toes," Marjorie had said sweetly, "you need a haircut. You look like a dandelion gone to seed."

"I'll get one in Chesapeake City," I had said. "Cast off."

But nowhere among Chesapeake City's little quaint shops could I find a little quaint barbershop. Nor had I found one in Annapolis or Oxford. In Solomons, we had patronized a ship chandlery, the post office, and an upscale food store, but not a barbershop. In Reedville, we had driven a borrowed car to nearby Kilmarnock, where we found motor oil, groceries, Chinese food, and a vivid pink laundromat. I saw a barbershop in the distance as we drove out of town. In Hampton, I discovered one hair-styling shop – which boasted chiefly of its prowess in putting in dreadlocks. My hair was now long enough for dreadlocks, admittedly – but the vision of a chalk-faced man in white dreadlocks would have been an apparition to frighten small children.

Cruising books lead you to imagine idyllic sailing, exotic foods, snorkelling, snoozing, and sun-downers in the cockpit. Well, yes – but few writers admit that such days are sandwiched between intense attention to the forecasts, the navigation and the diesel engine, and long trudges through small-town streets, carrying heavy burdens of food, dirty clothes, and motor oil. What is easily accomplished in your home – laundry, for instance – can fill an entire day. You overlook theatres, galleries, and museums. You're focused on the hunt for an oil filter or a quart of milk.

Or a barbershop.

With the skipper still looking like a dandelion, *Magnus* slipped down the broad expanse of the lower Pasquotank and out into the open water of Albemarle Sound. The sounds of North Carolina are broad but shallow – no more than twenty feet deep in most places. In a breeze, they can kick up a nasty short sea, but they also provide almost the only sailing opportunities along the entire ICW.

But there was no breeze at all. Albemarle Sound was as flat as a tabletop. We motored into the Alligator River Marina, a novel establishment – a highway truck stop with a marina behind it, the same facilities serving both travellers, with hurtin' music blaring from its outdoor speakers. The next day we hooked up the aerial to the short-wave radio that Walter Rawle had given us, and as we motored through the Alligator-Pungo Canal – which runs through the East Dismal Swamp – we listened to the sound of home, Shelagh Rogers's morning show on CBC Radio. Among her guests that morning was our friend and neighbour, Farley

Mowat, talking about his new book, *No Man's River*, a story of
the Canadian Arctic after the war, when northern natives travelled
by canoe and dogsled, and lived or died as the deer herds waxed
and waned. Farley sounded much younger than his eighty-four
years, warm and engaging, still passionate about the Earth and the
human assault on it. Hearing him speak was like having him
aboard, travelling with us as we made our way down the Pungo
River into the Dowry Creek Marina.

We had the radio on again the next morning, motoring down
the Pamlico River toward the junction with the Neuse. The
Pamlico and its sister river can be Bad Neuse, quickly raising nasty
short seas when the wind comes up, but that day was breathless,
overcast, and hazy – the morning sky peach and silver, the glassy
water coral and grey. Random black dots in the misty vague distance marked a widely spaced string of other boats migrating
south. *Magnus*'s wake spread out behind us in a huge wide V, occasionally peaking up in a molten geometry of smooth pyramids
when our wake crossed another. For the moment we had nothing
to do but let the autopilot steer us to Maw Point Shoal, which
marks the turn into the Neuse. Homesick and relaxed, we were
happily listening to Shelagh Rogers on *Sounds Like Canada* on
the short-wave radio.

Low distant points of land seemed to float above the water,
almost invisible but for the tufts of umbrella-shaped trees growing
on them. There would be houses on those shores, and many
would be adorned with tall flagpoles and big American flags un-
dulating lazily in the breeze. This is an American habit one soon
gets used to, the Stars and Stripes flying everywhere – on car
aerials, in flower beds, on shops and offices, on house porches.
The flag is on bumper stickers, on restaurant menus, spattered
across the rear windows of pickup trucks, anywhere and everywhere. Canadians, vigorously understated in their patriotism,
don't normally feel moved to assert that their menus and trucks
are located in Canada. Americans feel otherwise.

Mind you, *Magnus* had just sailed through a particularly rich swatch of American history. In many respects, the United States was invented in Virginia, and its destiny was decided on Civil War battlefields all over the mid-Atlantic states. This history is the foundation of the American national story, the story that unites this sprawling, diverse, deeply regional country. Its events are heavily documented, celebrated, and memorialized. The story is about freedom and democracy, about immigrant people in a new world boldly taking command of their own affairs, constantly striving for a fresh, new way of organizing a society based on liberty and justice for all.

Of course the story stubs its toe on the harsh realities of slavery, expansionism, the extirpation of the natives, the excesses of capitalism, and the like. There is always a gap between story and history. It is nevertheless a great and noble story, this conscious and continuous creation of a nation based on a grand philosophy, and since the withering away of Marxism it is almost unique in the world.

And so the United States loves to recognize achievement and to honour the achievers. When presidents leave office, they retain their Secret Service protection, establish libraries to hold their papers, and continue to be addressed as "Mr. President." Presidential homes become national historic sites – shrines, almost – and are federally funded and cherished and promoted. Every structure, it seems, is named for some achiever. The Washington Monument. The Kennedy Space Center. Tycoons arrange for their own memorials: Carnegie Mellon University, The J. Paul Getty Museum, The Ford Foundation.

The memorials can be exceedingly modest. Along the New Jersey Turnpike, for example, every roadside rest area is named for a Jersey worthy. Tacos and toilets at service nodes named for J. Fenimore Cooper, Woodrow Wilson, Walt Whitman. At the local level, the impulse can be downright absurd. The Colonel Lucius J. Berdphart Memorial Highway, the Commissioner O. G. Hosafat Municipal Reservoir, the Frank Lee Trivyal Colosseum.

I do not exaggerate. The next day we would see a historical marker commemorating the first motorized school-bus service in North Carolina.

But that's better than what we do in Canada. As *Magnus* crossed the Pamlico and turned up the Neuse to the little town of Oriental, CBC News reported that the family home of the late prime minister John Diefenbaker – which Diefenbaker physically helped to build a century ago – would finally be moved into a collection of historical buildings in Moose Jaw. For years it has been lying neglected on the grounds of the legislature in Regina, where it has fallen into disrepair, been boarded up, and been used as a pen for Canada geese.

O Canada.

Oriental – named for a ship of that name – styles itself "the sailing capital of the South" – or at least of North Carolina. I had expected a fair-sized place, but in fact it's a very small town: 2,700 boats but only 875 people. Its free dock was full, so we snugged into a very tight corner at a nearby marina, with a big blue Hunter from Michigan on one side and the main street of Oriental on the other. I picked up the BFD. I had learned to cradle him in my left elbow, leaving my right arm free to grab the rigging, climb ladders, and so on.

"Careful," said Marjorie as she almost always did.

"No, no," I said. "This time I'm going to be cavalier about it. If Leo falls in the water, what the hell, he's only a dog."

"Don!" said Marjorie, genuinely shocked. I snickered. As I set the BFD down on the shore, a bushy black dog bustled up to us, looking very assertive. I hauled Leo's leash tight.

"That's Kona," said the skipper of *Boxer*, the neighbouring Hunter, a lean man with greying blond hair flowing down to his shoulders. "Don't worry about him. He belongs to *Toucantoo*, over there. He's completely friendly."

Kona proved to be perhaps the most competent boat dog we ever saw, lounging on the deck, jumping on and off the boat on his own – and he was perfectly trained. At the door of a restaurant, his master would say, "Stay, Kona" and go in for his meal. Kona would lie by the restaurant door for hours, wagging his tail at passersby.

"Take lessons," I said to Leo.

Despite its yachty reputation, Oriental was a relaxed, low-key little town of modest houses and old stores, friendly to dogs and families. A young couple named Sam and Jane were travelling with their two children and their black Labrador retriever on a beautiful varnished ketch called *Linnet II*. We met them as they zoomed through the level streets, parents and children all doing their errands on in-line skates. The post office was chatty and friendly. The barber seemed genuinely sorry to tell me he was too booked up to cut my hair. An old black man on an equally ancient bicycle pedalled slowly past the post office. He wore a red shirt and an orange vest, and he gravely lifted one hand in salute to the several cars and trucks that tooted at him as they went by. Oriental felt cozy, unpretentious, and intimate, like a village in the Maritimes.

But the food was not like the Maritimes at all. At The B&B Cafe, Marjorie had a platter of tuna, shrimp, spicy sausage, rice, cayenne mayonnaise, and black beans, while I chose St. Louis–style ribs, cooked for five hours, smothered in barbecue sauce, with big fat onion rings and coleslaw done with a tart vinaigrette. The men at the next table said things like "Great Heavenly Days!" and compared notes on the rotten state of the tobacco market. Meanwhile, back at the marina, it was party time under the grass roof of the open-air tiki bar. The drinks were flowing, and the laughter came in waves. It was the middle of November, and the revellers were wearing shorts and golf shirts. This was the South, all right.

All the way from Staten Island, I wrote in my journal, *I've had the sense of being part of a ghost migration. Everywhere we went, we were told that five – or eight, or twelve – Canadian boats had passed through last week. By now Carol and Jim Organ are way ahead; I got an email from them in Lake Worth, Florida. So I thought we were real stragglers. But it's at Hampton Roads that the south-pointing funnel really narrows – that's where we first saw Sam and Jane on Linnet II, and several boats left there one morning, calling to us that it was time to go. Half-a-dozen snow-gulls left ahead of us in Elizabeth City, and the next day we met four boats converging on the Alligator River. Five came into the marina with us that night, and four of those left at dawn with us. At Dowry Creek, eight or ten boats came in after we did, and although we were the first out in the morning, several followed. We could hear more on the radio as we came around to Oriental, and when we got here there were half a dozen, including Linnet II. And tonight another batch came in, including two sailboats from Quebec.*

So we're now clearly part of the pack, and I'm not sure just how I feel about this. All my cruising has taken me far away from any pack; that was the whole point of cruising. On the one hand it's reassuring to know we're not that late, and some of these folks will be very enjoyable. Others, I'm not so sure. We won't be lonely again, anyway. However, I suspect it would be quite possible to drink your way all down the coast to Miami, and a lot of people probably do. There's a certain useless feel about some of these very capable people.

There's also a big difference between people who are partying and filling in time, and people like Sam and Jane who are clearly exploring the world by boat, together. They're like late-blooming hippies, and they feel like part of my tribe. I don't feel very much at home with the crowd at the tiki bar. On the other hand, I have a certain reserve, and so does Marjorie, and my discomfort may be nothing more than shyness. I suspect we'll enjoy an evening or two at marina bars, but we won't make a habit of it.

Be this as it may, we're certainly now part of this odd community, all drifting south.

Another day of nosing through creeks and canals brought us to Beaufort. We tied up at the town docks and went rambling through the town. I was browsing in the Golden Dolphin, a waterfront gallery, when a salesman named Harry Bryant approached me.

"Can Ah he'p you find anythin'?"

"My wife," I said. "She's shopping somewhere along Front Street. She –"

"She was heah," he said instantly. "She met a tall, handsome fellah with a big sailboat, and they went off togethah. I don't rightly know which way they were headed."

"Oh, that fellah? That was me," I said. We laughed. "I see you're having a sale."

"We are," Harry nodded. "The building's been sold. The new owner owns the Carolina Panthers. Ah don't know what he intends doin' with it. He cain't tear it down, because there's a moratorium – and the Historical Society wouldn't allow it anyway. But he's got a big boat, and there's a dock out back."

Beaufort, I had quickly learned, takes great pride in its built history. Almost every house downtown has a plaque giving its name and date. Most were constructed in the eighteenth and nineteenth centuries. The stately houses across Front Street were magnificent, and many of them had been converted into inns. But the Golden Dolphin's building seemed a rather commonplace concrete block structure.

"Ah, but that facade could have been added later," said Harry. "They used to manufacture engines in this buildin', and put 'em in the boats built down at the boatshop, the shop that belongs to the Maritime Mew-zeum now. Look!"

He seized me by the arm and steered me inside. Up among the blackened rafters was a cluster of drive shafts and flat-belt pulleys, leftover artifacts from an old industrial workshop. Interesting and unexpected. But my attention had been distracted by a fine photo beside the cash register – a wild horse running free among sand dunes.

"Shackleford Banks?" I asked. Shackleford Banks, part of the Cape Lookout National Seashore, is one of the most magnificent barrier island beaches in the world. Its wild ponies are famous, and the island lies only a couple of miles from Beaufort. You can take a tour boat out there, or rent a kayak and paddle out yourself.

"No!" cried Harry. "Those horses are *right heah*, on Carrot Island, right across the harbour."

Wait a minute. *Magnus* was tied up right in the middle of downtown Beaufort. When I looked toward the boats moored across the harbour that morning, I had been delighted to see half-a-dozen dolphins off the end of the dock, their dorsal fins gracefully rising and slipping away as they browsed for food. Behind the anchored boats was Carrot Island, which encloses Beaufort Harbour. The island is near enough that a middling swimmer could reach it – and there were wild horses on that island? Wild ponies as well as dolphins, right in downtown Beaufort?

"Yes!" cried Harry. "There's about *sixty* ponies on that island."

Marjorie was still invisible, concealed in the retail fog. As I walked down the dock to the boat, I looked over at Carrot Island again – and there they were, five tawny horses meandering along the beach.

Beaufort (pronounced "Boh-fort"), North Carolina – not to be confused with Beaufort (pronounced "Bew-ford"), South Carolina – is a favourite stop on the ICW. Its ocean inlet also provides safe access to the open sea for skippers heading offshore on direct passages to the Bahamas and the Caribbean. In the spring and fall, cruising boats stream through Beaufort and its sister community, Morehead City. The downtown waterfront welcomes them with marinas, bookshops, galleries, and Internet cafés. On weekends, the Friends of the Library run a book sale from a gypsy caravan in the parking lot of a downtown bank. The North Carolina Maritime Museum is open seven days a week – and provides a courtesy car for the use of visiting sailors. And we enjoyed the Southern fare at both the restaurants we tried.

"With food, you can't miss," Harry had declared. "In this town, even the hamburgers are good."

Because the whole region is composed of sand, this part of North Carolina is also a beach-lover's delight. Beaufort lies near the southern end of the long arc of sandy barrier islands known as the Outer Banks – sweeping miles of beaches, stretching in both directions and fronting directly on the ocean. The Outer Banks are separated from the mainland of North Carolina by the wide, shallow sounds we had just traversed. The sounds were the favourite haunt of Edward Teach, otherwise known as Blackbeard, a sometime resident of Beaufort whose home – Hammock House, built in 1709 – is the oldest house in town. A popular "Ghost Walk" held each evening in Beaufort includes a visit to the house.

Blackbeard was the freebooter who created the popular archetype of pirates and piracy, an early practitioner of the arts of image and spin. He was no slouch in battle – his ships once blockaded the port of Charleston, and he was capable of defeating a Royal Navy ship one on one – but he deliberately set out to create a terrifying image for himself, twisting his huge black beard into braids and setting a length of slow fuse afire at each side of his face when he leapt aboard the ships he pillaged. Superstitious folk from South America to New York literally believed him to be the incarnation of the devil. This fearsome reputation saved him a lot of trouble; it induced most skippers simply to surrender without a fight.

When he tried to retire from piracy, Teach obtained a royal pardon from the governor of North Carolina (who was rumoured to be in cahoots with him) and married a girl from nearby Bath. She was allegedly his fourteenth wife, though his first thirteen "marriages" seem to have been brief liaisons with strumpets. But the retirement didn't last, and the master pirate's gory end took place about fifty miles from Beaufort, at Okracoke Inlet, in a furious battle against two British naval vessels. Teach took five pistol bullets and twenty severe sword cuts before he died. His severed head was hung from the bowsprit of the naval sloop *Pearl* and later exhibited at the entrance to the Hampton River. Carolina folk tales report that his headless ghost can be seen wandering the coast on stormy nights, sometimes exhibiting a mysterious light, howling and searching for his head.

The reputed wreck of Blackbeard's ship was discovered lying in twenty feet of water in 1996. Its ship's bell and other artifacts are on display at the Maritime Museum on Front Street in Beaufort, and souvenir shops still thrive on his reputation. "Work," says a T-shirt in Scuttlebutt, a shop selling nautical books and bounty, "is for people who don't know how to PLUNDER!" Beaufort merchants, I surmised, had not forgotten how to PLUNDER; Marjorie was still wandering among those enticing shops. Ah, well. Eventually she would wash up at Golden Dolphin, and Harry would greet her. I knew what he would say.

"Your husband was heah!" he would declare. "And a pretty young thang was heah too. She had a cute li'l sailboat, and the two of them went off togethah. I don't rightly know which way they were headed."

"Yes," Marjorie would reply, "that was me."

We left Beaufort following the suggestions of John Wilson, the local skipper of TowBoatUS. Sailing directions and guidebooks always recommend the use of "local knowledge," which is a bit like recommending good health. How do you get it? The skippers of TowboatUS and its competitor, SeaTow, spend their days towing boats off local shoals. They know exactly where the problems are.

The previous day, I had radioed TowBoatUS for advice about Bogue Sound, where the channel appeared to be a narrow canal just under the surface of a deceptively wide sheet of water. A few moments later, John appeared beside *Magnus* in a big red TowBoatUS inflatable. We looked over the chart together. The seaward side of the channel through Bogue Sound was steep, he said, and the other side was gentle. Favour the gentle side; if you do go aground, you'll probably be able to back right off.

A long-time cruiser himself, John had just bought into the local TowBoatUS franchise, thus neatly solving the problem of what a full-time sailor does when he gets beyond earning his living by such arduous and nomadic activities as repairing, rigging, and delivering boats. He loved this part of North Carolina, and he was fascinated by the fast-vanishing local cultures of the coast, the Elizabethan speech of the Outer Banks, and the African-derived Gullah language spoken on the coasts of the Carolinas and Georgia.

Up at the showers I had met another John Wilson, the long-haired skipper of *Boxer*, the big Hunter from the neighbouring berth in Oriental. He was not a happy cruiser. He and his wife had recently had an accident, and his wife had cracked a couple of ribs. That shook his self-confidence. I sympathized; the trolls had combined with the Jonesport wharf to shake mine too. He was an appealing man, tall, loose-jointed, palpably intelligent, an unreconstructed survivor from the dissident 1960s. He had recently retired as a philosophy professor in Flint, Michigan. The American-born son of two Canadians, John normally kept his boat in Ontario.

"I thought it would be easy once we got to the ICW, like a highway for boats," he said, "but it isn't that way at all." I had just been thinking the same thing. Every day required planning, and the narrow channels demanded careful steering and constant alertness.

"Have you noticed all the Maine Bigwhiskers around here?" asked Marjorie as we picked our way out of Beaufort and down the long invisible channel through Bogue Sound.

"Yes!" I said. "They're a long way from home. Lot of Christians around too, did you notice? The folks at the Golden Dolphin Gallery are evangelicals."

"The laundromat in the General Store was closed 'in observance of the Lord's Day.'"

"I wanted to go to that special service for boaters at the little park there," I said. "The theme was supposed to be 'Sailing Directions for Heaven.' I actually intended to go – just out of a spirit of anthropological inquiry – but I got tied up and missed it."

"And wasn't it good to see Jim and Sandy Shulz again, even just for a few minutes?"

"Yes. But what a time they've had."

Jim and Sandy were the couple we had met on the catamaran in Portland. They left Maine well behind us, and then came to grief on the Jersey coast. The Jersey passage was Sandy's first overnight sail, and – like John Pratt and me – the Shulzes un-expectedly found themselves in big seas and heavy winds. They decided to seek shelter in Atlantic City. Huge waves were pouring through the narrow entrance between the stone breakwaters. Just a hundred yards from safety, *Adagio* was picked up by a big comber and dropped on the stones. The next wave lifted her up again and threw her into the harbour – but one hull was badly damaged. They limped to a wharf. Water was pouring in.

They held the water back with hastily rigged pumps and luckily found a boat-lift wide enough to accommodate *Adagio*. The local fibreglass repairman did an excellent job. But the event delayed them for two weeks, cost their insurance company $12,000, and badly shook their self-confidence too.

"We never thought we'd see you again," said Sandy. "We thought you'd be in Florida by now."

"I thought so too," I said. "But there's always something to keep the rabbit's tail short."

And, I might have said, to keep your own hair long. I had found no barber in Alligator River or Dowry Creek or Beaufort. I actu-ally entered a barbershop in Morehead City – the real thing, circa 1935, multiple mirrors, straight razors, vile green potions in jars on the counter. The barber's next victim was patiently waiting in a cracked and lumpy leather chair. He said the barber was in the back room. The back room looked like an even older shop. The ancient barber was sitting in an ancient chair, facing the counter and talking on the phone. He ignored me. I coughed and shuffled, snapped my fingers, yodelled and tapdanced. I studied the back of his Brylcreemed head. He never even looked around.

But now we motored out of Bogue Sound, through a twisting passage among spoil-bank islands created by dredging wastes, and arrived in the little fishing port of Swansboro. The proprietor of Casper's Marina is "Miz Susan," Susan Casper, a slight, bright, ethereal woman. Did we need diesel, water, showers? Yes, all of the above. And did we need anything else?

"Yes," I said. "A haircut."

"Charley's Barbershop," she said. "A couple blocks over that way." My heart lifted. Then Miz Susan paused.

"No, Charley's closed on Mondays."

My heart fell. Is there any place in America where a man can get a haircut on a Monday? By now my hair was so long that a Beaufort waitress, approaching from behind, had taken Marjorie and me to be mother and daughter.

"There might be a hairdressing salon open," Susan said. "Would that do?"

"Yes, yes," I said desperately.

After four phone calls, Susan Casper found a salon that could shear me that afternoon. It was three. Could I come over right now? Yes, three-thirty would be fine. I seized my wallet and hot-footed it through the red-and-golden leaves in the micro-suburbs of Swansboro to Corbett Street. Corbett Street has no sidewalks, only burgers and malls. It is that part of every American town where, as John McPhee puts it, "the city has burst its seams and extruded Colonel Sanders." In the lee of Hardee's Restaurant I found Sensations Hair Styling.

The impeccably coiffed and manicured receptionist took my name and address and typed them into her computer, so she could remind me when I needed another haircut. She gestured toward a slim young woman, dark-haired and dressed entirely in black. The

Dark Lady of the Scissors approached me and put out her hand.

"I'm Yvette," she said, "and I'll be doing your hair today."

"Yvette," I said, "you really have no idea just how glad I am to meet you."

"That nice guy from *Boxer* stopped by," said Marjorie, after admiring The New Me. "John Wilson? They're at a marina across the harbour. I like him."

"Me too. Okay with you to be gone by seven in the morning?"

The days were short now – daybreak was about seven, dusk about six – and the ICW is no place to navigate in the dark. By now we had a routine. I got up first and put on the coffee. While I heaved the BFD ashore for his morning constitutional – Marjorie's habitual "Careful!" drifting out of the hatch behind me – Marjorie made his morning snack of kibbles and a scoop of meat, with a Lasix pill buried in the meat to prevent fluid forming in his lungs, a few drops of digoxin for his heart condition, and a sprinkle of glucosamine for his arthritis.

Then Leo would snuggle into our berth while Marjorie opened the curtains, mopped condensation off the windows, made sandwiches, and filled a Thermos with coffee. Meanwhile, I checked the engine oil, started up the instruments, and got the day's electronic charts up on the laptop, pulled out the guidebooks and the paper charts, and switched the electrical system from shore power to ship's power. Then we went on deck, started the engine, checked the dinghy's towline, and brought the anchor up short – or, if we were at a marina, retrieved the electrical power cord and got the docklines aboard. Finally we slipped the engine into gear and departed, steering from the cockpit until *Magnus* had cleared the harbour and started down the long magenta line on the chart that marks the course of the ICW.

Breakfast was a bowl of cereal or some fruit, occasionally bacon and eggs, prepared and eaten underway. And then we settled down to a long day of navigating and steering. Our objective was to make thirty to forty miles a day, running for six or eight hours and tying up by midafternoon. Once moored, we would call the U.S. Customs, take Leo ashore, and do the necessary errands – signing in at the marina, picking up a quart of milk, buying fuel or filling the water tanks, perhaps taking a shower. *Magnus* has her own shower, but showering ashore avoided a clean-up in the boat.

All of this usually allowed us time to walk around the town a little before the sun went down. Then we went back to the boat, where Marjorie made supper while I wrote notes and planned the next day's run. After taking Leo ashore once more, we turned in early, reading till nine-thirty or ten. If the forecast was decent, we would be up at six, preparing to leave again by seven.

So we were on the dock at Swansboro in the early-morning light along with the crews of *Skippy V*, a houseboat-style motorboat moored right behind us, and *Maximum Comfort*, a centre-cockpit sloop. In Swansboro, for the first time since Norfolk, we had serious tidal effects to consider. The ocean lies just beyond the sandy barrier islands, and it rushes in and out through a narrow tidal inlet. That morning, the bubbling current was threatening to sweep *Magnus* into the bow of *Skippy V*.

"Just back her away hard," said the skipper of *Maximum Comfort*. "We'll hold her at the dock while you get your lines aboard. Then you just give it to 'er in reverse. Once you're clear of the dock, make your turn and off you go."

The strategy worked – but the current was so strong it nearly carried us right back down into *Skippy V*. I goosed the engine, and we cleared by a whisker. Let that be a lesson to you, I told myself. From here on you'll be crossing tidal inlets every few miles, and the tides are going to get higher and the currents stronger all the way to Georgia.

Our course that lovely morning lay through the Marine Corps firing range at Camp Lejeune – no landing/no stopping, no passage at all when the Marines were doing target practice.

Happily, they were not firing, and we motored for eleven miles through a curiously unspoiled landscape with no sign of habitation, except for military equipment apparently abandoned along the banks. We quickly discovered that speed differences among tall vessels matter less on the ICW than one might think. We were the first to arrive at the first bridge, but we had to wait for the bridge to open. So *Skippy V* and *Maximum Comfort* caught up with us. *Skippy V*, travelling at eight knots, reached the next bridge far ahead of *Magnus*, and *Magnus* was far ahead of *Maximum Comfort* – but *Skippy V* had to wait for an opening, and all three went through together again.

By now the sky was clouding over, and isolated raindrops spattered the windshield. The forecast called for strong winds and rain the following day. *Skippy V* and *Maximum Comfort* announced that they were pulling into the Harbour Village Marina, just ahead. We joined them – and so, a bit later, did *Boxer*.

That night John Wilson came aboard with his wife, Sandy. While we had made elaborate preparations for this trip, John and Sandy had made a nearly spontaneous decision to take the boat south. One of their anchors was still stowed on the forecabin sole. They were doing the trip on the cheap, without such aids as electronic charts or a radar. In Delaware Bay, they had been smothered in fog so thick that they had resorted to following another sailboat that did have radar, and when they got to the Chesapeake and Delaware Canal, they found it closed because of the fog, which left them playing blind-man's buff with a fleet of freighters until the two sailboats crept into Delaware City.

Over a glass of wine, they told us about their accident. They were motoring in the Alligator-Pungo River Canal when, without warning, the boat stopped as abruptly as if it had hit a wall. Sandy happened to be standing in front of the main hatch, and the impact threw her right down the companionway into the cabin. When she landed, she broke one rib and damaged others.

"I do yoga," she said, "and I made myself relax even when I was falling. But when I hit, I knew it was really bad. So I concentrated on my breathing and tried not to move. But that was only a week ago, and it sure hurts."

"I felt terrible about it," said John. "Some barge must have dumped a load in the channel or something, because I know we were right in the channel. There should have been plenty of water. It just destroyed my confidence. I'm really hating this trip. I'll be glad to have done it, and I'll remember it into my senility and dotage, and I'll force my grandchildren to listen to my stories about it over and over again – but I will *never, ever* do it again."

Chuck and Lynne on *Skippy V* were tied up next to us, and they had also experienced a nasty grounding in the Alligator-Pungo. They had been forced out of the channel by a tug and tow that had gone aground and had been towed off. The second towboat had also gone aground, and its skipper was not yielding any part of the channel to anyone. Four or five oncoming boats were forced aside, and *Skippy V* had hit an underwater stump, damaging one of her propellers. The boat had to be hauled out in Belhaven for repairs.

As we talked on the dock, Lynne looked around at the spitting rain and the trees bending before the wind.

"Well, I guess this settles the question of where we're spending Thanksgiving," she said.

Marjorie and I looked at each other. Thanksgiving? That was six weeks ago. No, wait – in the United States, Thanksgiving is in late November.

"Would you like to have Thanksgiving dinner with us?" asked Lynne. Of course we would.

Lynne served up a grand meal of chicken, yams with mandarin oranges, Brussels sprouts, and – something totally novel – a wonderful pumpkin mousse. Big, spare, and easygoing, Chuck had spent most of his life in Alaska, first with the air force and then with two major corporations. He had owned a house there, but he had chosen to rent the house out and live in a cabin with wood heat and no running water. He only left the cabin when he got together with Lynne. Then, when the two decided to sell out and go cruising, she also insisted on a really comfortable boat.

Skippy V was certainly comfortable. She was fifty feet long and sixteen feet wide, more like a motorhome with a pointed bow than a conventional boat. Lynne was growing a small garden in containers on the upper deck. Inside, *Skippy V* resembled a small apartment, with regular kitchen appliances, a washer and dryer, and a queen-sized bed. In protected waters, she was so stable that nothing was chocked in place or fastened down: the flowers stood in vases on end tables, and we pulled our chairs up to the table as though we were ashore. "Happy Thanksgiving," said Chuck. We all raised our glasses. We had plenty to be thankful for.

The four boats went on together the next day in a little flotilla, aiming for Carolina Beach, just north of the Cape Fear River. But the current there was running hard, the water was shallow, and the dock was exposed to wakes and chops. *Boxer* and *Maximum Comfort* looked it over and quickly decided to go out into the Cape Fear River and down to Southport. After tying up briefly, *Skippy V* and *Magnus* followed. Before long, John Wilson was calling us on the radio. The current in the river was ebbing fast, he said, and *Boxer* was scooting along at better than ten knots. *Magnus* poked through a short canal and out into the broad sunny river. Catching the same tide, she went flying down the river at similar speeds. We were in Southport, fifteen miles farther on, in ninety minutes.

Southport is a pretty little place, a couple of thousand people, tranquil clapboard houses under towering live oak trees draped in grey beards of Spanish moss. I noticed the unusual name "Ruark," which I'd encountered only once before in Robert Ruark, a kind of dwarf Hemingway – a syndicated columnist, hunter, adventurer, and novelist (*Something of Value, Uhuru*), who was famous in my youth. Sure enough, here was a plaque recording Ruark's origins in Southport. He spent his summers with his grandfather here, an experience he recorded in *The Old Man and the Boy*, published just a year after *The Old Man and the Sea*.

Our next day's destination was Barefoot Landing, a factory-outlet mall in Myrtle Beach, South Carolina, which provides a free dock for transients. The day would include two of the ICW's most famous hazards – Lockwood's Folly Inlet, where the currents run fast and the water is shallow, and the Rock Pile, a cut through the bedrock so narrow that a barge and a pleasure boat couldn't pass side by side within it.

But the morning brought a near-disaster.

Over the passing weeks, Leo had become more and more youthful. He was full of life and energy, charging down the floating docks and jumping over the rail to get in or out of the boat. In fact, I had learned to take a leash with me when we went for his morning walk, just to ensure that he didn't run away and make a foolish leap back aboard in his eagerness for his morning snack. This particular morning, the boat was wet with dew and the dock looked slippery, so I snapped his leash on before we even left the boat.

Leo instantly jumped up on the cockpit seat and flew over the rail – but his leash wrapped around a cleat, stopping him in mid-air. He dropped like a stone into the narrow gap between the boat and the floating dock. I was on him instantly – I don't know how one moves so fast at such moments – and as he bobbed to the surface I took an iron grip on the scruff of his neck and heaved him bodily up on the dock. He gave a mighty shake. My mind was racing. Marjorie would have a fit. Leo still needed to relieve himself. Better take him ashore anyway.

Leo was willing; he trotted straight up the dock for twenty feet – and then his hind legs wobbled and fell out from underneath him, and he collapsed on the dock. He was panting, and his eyes were glassy. I thought he was having a heart attack and dying before my eyes. I scooped him up and hurried back to the boat, calling for Marjorie. Leo was absolutely limp in my arms.

We laid him down on the floor of the cabin. He was breathing, but although his eyes were open he seemed unconscious. Then he started trembling uncontrollably, his teeth chattering like castanets.

"I think he's in shock," I said.

"Definitely," said Marjorie. We had both taken first aid in Nova Scotia. "First thing –?"

"Keep him warm," I said.

"Especially since he's soaked," said Marjorie. "And keep him calm."

We wrapped him in a towel and in his baby duvet – his favourite blanket, a gift from Wayne and Susan Baker in Hampton. We lay down beside him, warming his body with ours. We talked quietly to him, and to each other. I called *Boxer* and *Skippy V*, and told them to go on without us.

After a time, Leo's breathing steadied. He raised his head and lapped a little water. We lifted him up and installed him in the big forward berth, under our own duvet. For three hours, he scarcely moved. And then he started struggling to his feet.

"I bet he has to pee," said Marjorie. "Did he pee this morning?"

"No." We carried him outside and up the dock to the shore. We set him down, and he peed as though he would never stop. Then he turned and started for the boat again.

"He wants his morning snack," I said, marvelling at his perkiness. Twenty feet from the boat was a wet smudge on the dock and two little stools.

"This is where he collapsed," I said, picking up the stools in a plastic bag. "I think he must have blacked right out."

"How does he look to you now?"

"Just fine. Amazing."

He *was* fine. We never saw another sign of distress. But we never let him jump ashore again either.

That evening John Wilson phoned to see how Leo was doing. *Boxer* and *Skippy V* had crossed into South Carolina and were watching the Myrtle Beach Christmas parade of boats. *Boxer* was planning to stop the next day at Barefoot Landing.

"Meet you there," I said. "How was the run?"

"Fine," said John. "Lockwood's Folly was just dredged, and the Rock Pile was okay. There's a barge tied to the shore in the middle of it, and you have to pass the barge really close. Otherwise, just stay in mid-channel. So Leo's okay?"

"Leo is wonderful," I said quietly. "Leo is just wonderful."

Barefoot Landing was bizarre – more than a hundred shops clustered around an artificial lake and not a one of them selling a single damn thing that a sensible person would ever think of buying. Overpriced T-shirts, candy and fudge, stuffed animals, polyester beachwear, tasteless baseball caps, hideous pictures, sunglasses, circus souvenirs. Stores with names like Instant Karma, Magnet World, Peanut Shop, Black Market Minerals, Dress My Cell, and – my favourite – Bible Factory Outlet. Buy Direct from God, I suppose. John and Sandy walked right on through Barefoot Landing to Wal-Mart and Piggly Wiggly, which sell things that people might actually need.

But the dock was free, and three of the five boats tied up there that night were Canadian. One – *Janbaree III* – was a brand-new Maritime-built Cape Islander, registered in Ottawa but just launched in Maryland. Jan and Barry, the owners, were old Waterway hands, former sailboat owners glorying in their new-found ability to tick off eighty miles a day. As they came in, Jan stood on the foredeck with a beautifully coiled line and threw it unerringly. She was, said Marjorie, "one of those fearfully capable cruising women that I really want to throttle – but unhappily, I liked her."

Happy to have found congenial company, the crews of *Boxer* and *Magnus* took to travelling in company. The days began blurring together. Up in the morning, motor through the marshes, end the day in some funky little place. A bit of touring, shopping, boat chores, perhaps a shared meal, and an evening conference over a glass of wine – though John drank only coffee. How far would we go tomorrow? How many bridges? When did they open? Was there an inexpensive, dog-friendly place to tie up or anchor? What sights did we want to see?

Because we had electronic charting and radar, *Magnus* led the way. By now I had figured out the way the currents worked when the ICW crossed the ocean inlets more or less at right angles. If the tide was running out of, say, the New River, as we approached it the current would suck the boat along the Ditch toward the outflowing river – and then, beyond the river, the outgoing current would hold us back. We might do eight knots down-current as we approached the river, and four knots against the current once we passed the river.

To port, the barrier islands were erupting in lavish monster houses, some of them with screened patios so large they looked like the vast birdcages at the London Zoo. To starboard, swamps and mudbanks, cypress woods and virtual jungle. And then the waterway would loop deep inland, running through a serpentine river, choked by bushes on both sides, broken only by an occasional fishing camp or sawmill.

The engine was still doing "troll burps," slowing down and then coming quickly back to speed. I concluded that the burps might not get any worse, in which case they were nothing more than a nuisance – or they might get bad enough to stop the engine altogether, in which case the problem could be analyzed and solved. I could only hope the trolls would not kill the engine at a dicey moment – crossing an inlet, for instance.

Boxer was having engine trouble too. Her Westerbeke diesel ran beautifully until the boat reached about 5.5 knots. Then it would shake and vibrate alarmingly. The Wilsons had poured a lot of money over the problem in New York, and again in North Carolina. But nothing had worked. As Marjorie noted, John was "a Fret Monster," constantly worried about the boat, the route, the engine. He even fretted about his own skills, though he was a superb sailor and boat-handler. I once watched him berth *Boxer* in a strong beam current so smoothly that the dockhand whistled.

A good landing, I said.

"Masterful," said the dockhand.

Georgetown, South Carolina. Another sleepy little place with perhaps the nicest waterfront we'd ever seen – a long boardwalk on pilings with slips running out from it and numerous micro-parks connecting the boardwalk to the pleasant main street just one short block away. The downtown businesses had entrances both on the street and the boardwalk, and the cafés had decks overlooking the river. DO NOT FEED THE ALLIGATORS, said the signs, but we had yet to see a gator. Perhaps it was too cold for them; we had been enjoying the longest autumn on record, but it was December by now, the nights were dipping down toward the freezing mark, and the mornings were downright chilly.

McClellanville. A fishing hamlet on a shallow side creek, full of shrimp boats, with a funky, casual, down-at-heel marina, pelicans resting on the pilings, ruinous trawlers mouldering away in the mud, clumps of oysters growing all over the pilings, ole yaller dawgs patrolling the wharves, just my kind of place. The manager was away when *Boxer* and *Magnus* arrived, but an amiable young guy waved us in. "Duane hadda go to Charleston, ast me to give y'all a hand," he said.

Duane proved to be sandy-haired, moustachioed, and funny. The smallest of the dogs was an illegally cute yellow Lab puppy –

Welcoming guests aboard for drinks, Hampton, Virginia
(WAYNE BAKER)

Author Myron Arms with Norwegian ponies: *Brendan's Isle* and *Magnus* moored in background, Sassafras River, Maryland

Moored at Deep Creek on the Great Dismal Swamp Canal

Feeding the alligators in Georgetown, South Carolina

Rafted up with John and Sandy Wilson on *Boxer* in McClellanville, SC

The skipper at the
inside helm, steering
south

Gullah woman
weaving baskets
at the Charleston
Market, SC

Statuary in the famous
Bonaventure Cemetery,
Savannah, Georgia

Niece Jocelyne
Coburn with her
friend Kobe, Fort
Pierce, Florida

Toy boat *Magnus* with serious motor-yacht, West Palm Beach,
Florida

Mimi Rehor and a wild horse, Great Abaco Island, Bahamas

The crew at Club Soleil, Hope Town, Bahamas, with the famous Hope Town lighthouse in the background (LINDSAY DELAPLAINE)

View of Hope Town from the lighthouse

Music at Pete's Pub, Little Harbour, Bahamas. From left:
Carol Moseley, Pete Johnston, Greg Silver, Bob Ahlers,
Marjorie (with guitar)

Marjorie and Leo enjoy the beach at Hope Town

"jest a dumb-ass Lab," said Duane. John wondered whether we might get some fresh shrimp and eat it together. Sure, said Duane, you can buy it straight off the boat – "or if you look real pitiful, they'll probably give it to you. Here, I'll come with you." He and John shortly returned with ten pounds of shrimp.

"Twenty bucks," said John. "For ten pounds. Well, I'm sure it's more than ten pounds. The fellow just grabbed a bunch of shrimp and said, *Thet looks lahk ten paounds.* Duane and I are going to shell 'em and cook 'em. We'll do two lots. I'll do half of them sautéed in butter and scallions, and Duane'll do the others in garlic oil sauce, which is the way he likes 'em."

"I'll do hors d'oeuvres and a salad," said Marjorie.

"I'll do rice," said Sandy.

We all ate in *Boxer*'s spacious cabin. Duane brought his wife, Ruth, and their twelve-year-old son, Myles, a captivating kid who knew an enormous amount about fish and fishing, and quizzed Marjorie closely about the West Coast fishery; at one point he ran ashore and got a magazine with a photo of a spring salmon to confirm that this was what she used to catch. It was. With me, he talked knowledgably about the ice-resistant concrete pilings designed for the Confederation Bridge to Prince Edward Island. ("We've been studying Nova Scotia this past week," he explained, "and next week we're doing Egypt.") Myles was attending a "magnet" school of the arts, Duane explained, and he had been admitted on the basis of his drawing – but he was clearly getting a first-rate academic education as well. Duane and Ruth were delighted; South Carolina's underfunded public school system, they said, was the worst in the nation.

Duane and his family left after supper, but Marjorie brought the guitar, and we stayed on *Boxer* till nearly midnight, playing folksongs and talking while the Wilsons ran up and down to the marina office tending their laundry. The washer and dryer stood in splendid isolation in the middle of a wide-open workshop, and they were free, but they ran on quarters. To use them, you put in a quarter, then lifted the front panel and took the quarter out. When the machine stopped, you put the same quarter in again. It was a good system, but it took all evening to do the clothes.

From my notes: *John really detests the South, though Sandy's mother's family are all good ol' boys from Arkansas, fellas who "like to drink whisky in a Dixie cup with their meals." He tells about attending a Texas chili cook-off, and hearing the Texans discuss what they planned to do with some Northerners in attendance. The mildest idea was to "serve 'em chili so hot even God couldn't eat it." As the afternoon progressed, the boys kept drinking beer and getting more aggressive. "Things were getting a bit chewy," said John, "so Sandy and I made it a point to be gone by sundown." He believes that a subterranean dimension of Bush's appeal in the South is the belief that he'll keep the blacks in their place, despite dressing his windows with Condoleezza Rice and Colin Powell.*

I've relaxed another notch. Chores that won't prevent us from getting to Florida won't get done until we do get to Florida – like the element on the kerosene stove that is acting up. And we're far enough south now that we know we'll be in mid-Florida, at the least, before Christmas. Our beloved niece Jocelyne has a booking into Orlando on the 18th, and a return flight from Miami to Vancouver on the 30th. So we'll rent a car and pick her up, continue down the ICW, and put her back on the plane after Xmas.

Charleston. A glorious Suth'n lady, with a lurid past.

"The city was *de*secrated by Yankee *aggress*ors durin' the Wah for Suth'n IndeePENdence," cried Charles. "Oh, no! Oh, my! Ah mean it was *cap*tured by Union troops durin' the CIVil Wah. Ah forgot – Ah'm the only Suth'ner on the bus!"

Looking for a quick overview of this legendary city, we had gone with the Wilsons to the Charleston Visitor Center, formerly part of the railway station. We had been lured onto Charles's tour bus by a sleazy looking shill with a cast in one eye, a fedora, and a black leather sports jacket. Charles himself was slight, with small eyes and an icy smile; shorn of his moustache, he would closely resemble Dubya himself.

Charles loudly pronounced himself "Canadian-friendly," but he proved to be a serving of instant, condensed bile. His passengers consisted of two couples from Michigan, a couple from California, and a brace of Canadians, and he disliked us in that order. He suspected the Canadians of holding un-American opinions, he knew the Californians were from outer space, and he viewed all Northerners as hereditary enemies. He also despised feminists. I was pleased to be spared his opinions on blacks or Asians or gays or Jews – although he did point out the first synagogue in America, which still serves a large Jewish community in Charleston.

Nasty though he was, Charles gave us a terrific tour, a rapid-fire patter with a wonderful inflected style of speaking, almost like an evangelist's rap. Some sentences ended up, some down, some flat, and he had a great feel for the rhythms of language. Showing us the military academy known as The Citadel, Charles drove us around the school's central square, decorated with Vietnam-era helicopter gunships, jet fighters, and other weapons. He pointed at a Sherman tank. Once, he said, some students put some gas in the tank and took it for a drive.

"But they ONly knew how to *sta't it* – they had NO ahdea how to *stop* it, and the only way they could DEW that was to drahve it into a *tree* . . . Aftah that, the FACulty brought the tank *back*, and made thuh engines . . . inOPerable."

The Citadel became nationally famous in 1994, when it admitted a student named Shannon Faulkner – and then changed its mind upon learning that Shannon was a woman. Under pressure, the school ultimately let her in – but she was hazed so relentlessly that she dropped out in a week. The ensuing lawsuit, Charles told us, broke the gender barrier.

"Abaout two HUNDRED women . . . attend The CITadel today," he said. "Naow we got four MEN on this bus today, and haow many of *you* GENNELMEN think it's a good AHdea to have *women* servin' in the MILitary?" John and I put our hands up. Charles glared at us.

Why would anyone – man or woman – want to attend The Citadel? The discipline is rigid, the culture is macho, the hazing is vicious, and the history is embarrassing. The school was founded in 1822, says Catherine S. Manegold, author of *In Glory's Shadow* about the Shannon Faulkner case, "as a private militia to protect Charleston's ruling white elite" after an aborted slave uprising.

"From that time until the Civil War poor white boys were called to town to act as racial guards," Manegold says. "Cadets used the school as a springboard to the business class. The wealthy in return enjoyed those graduates' loyalty and often a life-time's faithful and disciplined service, too." Today, about a third of the cadets join the military, Charles said, "usually as commissioned OFFicers." It was an eerie, threatening place, all the severe-looking young men marching around with their wedge caps tilted forward, black leather cases under their arms, their heads all but shaven. It felt like cold, organized meanness.

Charles toured us past the old rice mills, the covered market, and dozens of mansions and historic town houses. Many were "Charleston single houses," just one room wide, with a porch running around two sides. At street level, the porches have formal entry doors that open not into the houses but into the hidden gardens, full of leaves and blossoms, with Spanish moss pendant on the massive live oaks. The remarkable taste, cohesion, and inventiveness of Charleston's historic architecture stems from a civic ordinance dictating that no building should ever be taller than the spire of an early church, which stands, Charles reported, "two hundred sixty-*five* . . . FEET, seven and three-quarter *inches*." Another ordinance requires that all modifications and repairs be done with historically accurate materials. The result is a beautifully coherent city, full of colourful painted stucco, elaborate wrought iron, wooden fretwork, gracious porticoes and balustrades.

Charles drove us through an intersection celebrated in *Ripley's Believe It or Not* as "The Four Corners of Law," defined by buildings devoted severally to federal, state, municipal, and canon law. Graduates of the College of Charleston, he said, don't wear gowns; instead the men wear white dinner jackets with red-rose boutonnieres, while women carry one red rose for each year it took them to complete their degrees. It must be lovely.

For all his prickliness, Charles had some surprising attitudes. When he was drafted, he said, he considered expatriating himself to Canada, and if he had known that President Ford would eventually declare a general amnesty, he might have done it – but it was just too much to give up his country, his friends, and his family forever. So he went to Vietnam. John Wilson's fur bristled; he had been so deeply opposed to the Vietnam War that he had an arrest sheet two pages long for his protest activities. When Charles noted that President Bush had recently visited Canada to improve relations and deal with border security, I stayed silent, but John vigorously shook his head. Charles asked why.

"I think he went to try to prove to the Canadians that he's not quite as evil as they think he is," said John. Charles glared again.

Charles stopped the bus for his passengers to stretch their legs, while he went into a store and came out with a tray of pralines and glazed pecans. As he passed them around, he pointed out some former rice mills and remarked that in the early days a plantation owner worked in the fields alongside his slaves – because the slaves generally knew how to grow rice and the owner didn't. But the usual discipline for slaves was flogging, said Charles, "and Ah could *nevah* underSTAND how a man could work . . . *side by side* with anothah MAN . . . and then turn *around* and have him . . . *flogged*!" The answer? An owner could bring a slave to the town workhouse and pay twenty-five cents to have him flogged by someone else.

For Charles, the Civil War was only yesterday. Over yonder was a football field being excavated because the Yankees had dumped Confederate soldiers and sailors there in an unmarked mass grave. Out on the horizon was a fortified island called Fort Sumter; the Confederate bombardment of the island was the starting gun for the Civil War. And here was a replica of the Confederate submarine *Hunley*, the first sub ever to sink an enemy ship. In February 1864, she attacked the *Housatonic*, a Union ship blockading the port. She rammed the *Housatonic*, embedding a torpedo in the wooden planking, and then backed away for some distance before pulling the fuse line. The torpedo went off, and the ship sank in five minutes. The sub commander signalled with a blue light that the mission was completed and then dived – and stayed on the bottom for the next 112 years. When the sub was located, all the men were still on duty, sitting at the cranks they had used to turn the propeller. They had apparently submerged to wait out the commotion on the surface, underestimated their need for air, and died quietly of anoxia, starvation of oxygen to the brain.

John clearly thought that Charles was dying of anoxia right before our eyes.

Steamboat Creek, South Carolina. A concrete wharf and launch ramp on a backwater off the North Edisto River. No town, no farms, nothing around but marshes and muddy fields. *Magnus* lay tied to the wharf, *Boxer* anchored in the creek. We had consulted Skipper Bob's indispensable *Anchorages Along the Intracoastal Waterway*, looking for dog-friendly places to anchor. We had dubbed this spot "Leo's Landing," and Skipper Bob had guided us well. There aren't many places in these swamplands where you could take a dog ashore without sinking to your thighs in the muck. But this was one of them.

The land was so flat that we could see the masts of other boats apparently moving through the grass and reeds. They were in the ICW, a couple of miles away. Good old boys came and went from the concrete wharf, launching outboard runabouts and using their husky pickups to pull them out again. A couple of genial fellows well into their seventies puttered up to the wharf, white-haired, pink-cheeked, almost angelic. Their boat bristled with fishing rods. How had they fared?

"Oh, got a couple of trout, but it don't matter," smiled one. "Was a good day. Any day we c'n get out on the creek is a good day."

Any problem if we tie up here overnight? We're not really supposed to, but?

"Nah, not much action this time o' year. Nobody's gonna bother yuh."

The next outboard to arrive was steered by a misplaced Maine Bigwhisker in camouflage clothing and a square-topped baseball cap, almost Civil War style. His companion was a high-testosterone dog that looked like a great big Jack Russell. What kind of dog was he?

"He's jest an ol' mongrel dawg," said the Bigwhisker. "But he's m'buddy. Only reason either one of us is still livin' is, we ain't worth a bullet to put either of us down."

The night was exquisitely dark, with a huge spray of stars across the black canvas of the night. In the morning it was heavily misty, and we waited half an hour till the visibility improved. As we turned back into the North Edisto, a Canadian ketch emerged from the Wadmalaw River and fell in behind us. *Zingarou II* was from Thunder Bay, and the Wilsons had met her in Tonawanda, New York. She was a Bruce Roberts design, which her owner had taken eighteen years to build. Now he called on the radio. Could *Zingarou II* tag along behind us? Sure, but –

"I thought we'd be following boats that knew the way," I said to Marjorie. "But here we're leading this little flotilla."

A demanding run through a maze of narrow passages and shallow water brought us to Beaufort – that's BEWfurt, not BOWfurt, fella – in time for the Christmas parade and an unexpected reunion with Jim and Sandy Schulz.

We had missed the Christmas boat parades in Myrtle Beach and Charleston – but the Christmas street parade in Beaufort made up for it. This was a *real* parade, an *American* parade, a parade that went on and on and on. All of Beaufort was on display – the Beaufort High Eagle Pride Marching Band, black kids jiving in green track suits and Santa hats. The Beaufort High cheerleaders. The Classic Car and Truck Club, and the Beaufort Square Dance Club, square-dancing on a flatbed. There were floats from the Ducky Car Wash and the Port Royal Bulldogs State Cheerleading Champs. The Christian Motorcyclists Association displayed their motto, "Riding for the Son." The state representative rode in a Jeep, the mayor in a golf cart. The local Marine Corps base sent a brass band.

And there was more – much, much more.

The Drumming Seagulls. The Beaufort Police. The Beaufort County Black Chamber of Commerce. Highway 21 Drive-in and Open Air Market. The Miss Beaufort Pageant. Low Country Window Tinting. First Presbyterian Church. The Beaufort County Sheriff's Office. Beaufort Pediatrics. The Society for Creative Anachronism, a crowd of medieval knights doing battle with swords and shields. The Boys and Girls Club of the Low Country. TJ's Auto Repair. L&L Garage Door Service. Five or six fire departments, sirens wailing, red lights flashing . . .

And that's *still* not all. For a town of ten thousand, Beaufort was clearly a buzzing hive of activity.

A pleasant-looking woman hurried up to us.

"You're on *Magnus*? From Halifax?"

"Well, we're from Cape Breton, actually –"

"So am I! I'm Gail. You've got to come over for a drink. My husband will be here in a minute –"

Gail had been married for forty-six years to a Dutch-born Ontario farmer named Meindert Wolff. They spent their summers in Ontario, their winters in Beaufort, which they loved – the friendliest people, the best climate (not too hot, not too cold), the right-sized town (not too big, not too small). They took us for a tour of the antebellum houses on Old Point, Beaufort's oldest and most exclusive neighbourhood. Because the Union took Beaufort early in the Civil War and used it as a headquarters, the town – unlike many Southern towns – was never burned. If the houses seemed familiar, it might have been because such films as *Forrest Gump* and *The Big Chill* were shot there.

They had a home across the river, with a private dock. Over a good snort of rum, Meindert invited us to call on the way back.

"Use the dock," he said. "Stay as long as you want. Doesn't matter if we're here or not – just tie up and make yourself at home."

Thank you. But we had Georgia on our minds.

Savannah. Ah, Savannah!

When we checked in at the Thunderbolt Marina near Savannah, I remarked that I wanted to see Bonaventure Cemetery, a spooky ambience featured in John Berendt's novel *Midnight in the Garden of Good and Evil*. The attendant nodded.

"That book really put Savannah on the map," he said. "That and the Savannah College of Art and Design."

The day was hot, and I was back in shorts; it was December 7, but we had caught up with summer again.

"What's a cold winter day in Savannah?" I asked.

"In the fifties, generally. High thirties at night. If we get four or five days in a row where the temperature goes below freezing, everyone calls that a hard winter. Okay, you're all checked in. Showers and laundry over there, and you'll get a newspaper and a box of Krispy Kreme donuts delivered to your boat in the morning. Enjoy Savannah."

Oh, yes. In another lifetime, I will live in Savannah. As Bill Bryson says – and Bryson is not easy to please – "I did not know that such perfection existed in America."

And such dark subtlety. In Berendt's book, there is a moment when half-a-dozen people are chatting at the most exclusive and elegant party at the year, held at the Mercer House, a sumptuous mansion built by the great-grandfather of Johnny Mercer, the legendary songwriter. Now it belongs to Jim Williams, the connoisseur, art and antiques dealer, and real-estate entrepreneur played in the film by Kevin Spacey. Williams has just been charged with the murder – in the house – of his bad-ass young homosexual lover.

The company is glittering: diplomats, financiers, heiresses, corporate lawyers, and the like. The manners are courtly. The catering is impeccable, the drinks are superb. In one little grouping, the talk turns to the guns people carry. Colonel Atwood produces his .22 Magnum. Two of the women ooh and ahh; both their husbands committed suicide with guns exactly like this one. Dr. Fulton shows off a .22 Derringer concealed inside a wallet. When the bandit demands your money, you pull out the wallet and shoot him dead. His wife, says the doctor, packs a .38. Another woman nods; she carries a .38 as well. A third woman shows off a pearl-handled revolver, which she holsters in her bosom.

Darkness and elegance. Violence and repose. Formality and bawdry. Savannah is a stylish, black-hearted temptress who seduces everyone she meets. She is anything but bland. We adored her on sight.

Our guide that day was Ruth McMullin, whom we'd met at the Pratts' in Connecticut. She picked us up at Thunderbolt and drove us down to Bay Street, which runs along a bluff parallel to the Savannah River. The old cotton warehouses along the river drop right over the edge of the bluff. They are two storeys high on Bay Street, but five storeys high on River Street. The lowest floors have been converted to shops, restaurants, and pubs, all facing the river across a narrow grassy promenade.

In a tacky souvenir shop, I posed beside a lifesized mannequin of a Confederate general in full uniform, while Marjorie stood beside a full-sized pirate. (In *Treasure Island*, notes Berendt, the treasure map bears an inscription that it was given to Billy Bones by Captain Flint at "Savannah this twenty July 1754.") A few doors away is River Street Sweets, where Southern candies are made before your eyes – pralines, glazed pecans, chocolates, sugar and spice pecans, log rolls, caramel, taffy. Behind a counter just inside the door, a man is making pralines, a naughty confection of sugar, butter, and pecans. A tray of samples lies on a counter in front of him. People walking down River Street duck inside, pluck a praline, and walk on.

At the end of River Street, a statue of a girl stands on a scrap of parkland where a narrow road made of ballast stones from ancient ships winds its way up the bluff. "The Waving Girl" is said to represent a lighthouse-keeper's daughter whose lover sailed away and never returned. All her life she waved a sheet of cloth at every passing ship, hoping her lover would be aboard. The story is not true. The truth is much more prosaic. The hell with the truth.

The Waving Girl wears clumsy shoes. Originally she was barefoot, but "this is the South," said a woman we met, "where you don't wear white before Easter or after Labor Day." The sculptor was ordered to add shoes.

Darkness and elegance. Savannah is a shady city lit by wandering shafts of brilliant sunlight, a city of billowing live oaks draped in Spanish moss. The streets are laid out in a grid interrupted by twenty-one squares. Each square is a little gem, full of magnolias, azaleas, oleanders, and myrtle, usually with a monument or two, often faced by grand churches and ornate townhouses. Street after street, square after square. Brick houses, stucco houses, houses with spectacular columns and grand porticoes, houses adorned with fantasies in wrought iron. Savannah has more than a thousand historic houses, many of them still serving as residences. And all the historic architecture is cushioned by shrubs and trees, the sunlight filtering through the leaves.

Savannah was barely touched by the Civil War. As General Sherman and his armies were marching through Georgia, from Atlanta to the sea, Savannahians conferred. They sent out their mayor to meet Sherman, promising to hand over the city intact provided that Sherman preserved it. Sherman agreed and sent a telegram to President Lincoln. I BEG TO PRESENT TO YOU, AS A CHRISTMAS GIFT, THE CITY OF SAVANNAH. The city was then the leading cotton port in the world.

Savannah's streets and squares were designed by the remarkable James Oglethorpe, Georgia's founder – social reformer, parliamentarian, and soldier. Oglethorpe intended Georgia to be a classless society where slavery was forbidden (along with liquor) and where each householder owned and worked his own land. Georgia welcomed such persecuted minorities as Jews and Lutherans and also the three founders of Methodism – John Wesley and his brother Charles, and George Whitefield, all of whom lived and preached in Savannah for brief periods. Whitefield in particular was the leading figure in the Great Awakening, a wave of religious ecstasy that swept the American colonies in the eighteenth century. He is considered the founder of American evangelicalism. He has a lot to answer for.

Ruth led us to the Gryphon Tea Room for lunch. A refurbished pharmacy, the restaurant still boasts some of its original stained-glass windows along with banks of oak-faced apothecary drawers. It stands opposite a former armoury that was the first building occupied by the Savannah College of Art and Design (SCAD). Established in 1978 with just seventy-one students, SCAD now enrols more than seven thousand students on campuses in Savannah, Atlanta, and Lacoste, in Provence. It has been a galvanizing force in Savannah, buying and renovating more than fifty buildings in the heart of the city – old schools, warehouses, residences, movie theatres, churches and synagogues, department stores, railroad buildings, and residences. And pharmacies: the Gryphon itself is owned and operated by SCAD.

Darkness and elegance. Bonaventure Cemetery lies right on the Intracoastal Waterway, on the Wilmington River near Thunderbolt; we had cruised right by it. The cemetery is so large and leafy that no city sounds penetrate its shady recesses. The ever-present live oaks and Spanish moss are accented by the enormous array of lifesized, ghostly white Victorian statues. Here lie Jim Williams and Danny Hansford, poet Conrad Aiken and songwriter Johnny Mercer. I find myself humming. "That Old Black Magic." It's a Mercer tune, of course.

Black magic, all right. This is the cemetery used by Minerva, the voodoo priestess. On the opposite bank of the river lie the Georgia Sea Islands, home of the Gullah people . . . *Kumbaya, my Lord, kumbaya* . . . the setting of Pat Conroy's novel *The Water Is Wide* and the film version, *Conrack*, which gave me my first look at those beautiful islands.

Ruth drove us out to the McMullins' big, gracious home on Skidaway Island for dinner. Limes and fat yellow lemons were growing on their deck, which looks out over miles of tan-coloured marsh and wandering silver water. They no longer owned a sailboat, but they spent a lot of time kayaking and birding in the marshes. They were passionate about their new home, and had already lent their formidable talents to such organizations as the University of Georgia's Marine Extension Service, where Ruth teaches as a volunteer, and the Coastal Georgia Nature Conservancy, where Tom serves on the board.

"The coast of Georgia is amazing," Ruth said. "It has seven hundred thousand acres of marsh, which is one-third of all the marsh that remains on the east coast of the United States. It has thirteen barrier islands, and only four are accessible by car. That's why Tom and I love to explore in our kayaks. Right outside the back door are deserted beaches and islands with birds, dolphins and maritime forests, and they're accessible only by boat."

All this at their back door, and lovely Savannah at the front door. No wonder they're happy.

We sailed out of Savannah into three days of misery. The Georgia ICW is one hundred and forty miles long, with only two towns – Savannah at the beginning and Brunswick at the end. This is a continuation of the Low Country, the endless flats and marshes we had covered in South Carolina. Large "sounds" penetrate the barrier islands and give access to the sea. In the sounds, the tides rise and fall as much as nine feet, which makes the currents shoot through the narrow back channels of the ICW like fast rivers. Strong easterly winds push ocean water inland, concealing the reeds, while strong westerlies blow the water out to sea. The water is shallow at the best of times, and the Georgia command of the U.S. Army Corps of Engineers had responded to budget cuts by simply ceasing to dredge the ICW channels. Skipper Bob confirmed our fears: it is hard to find a spot where there's enough water to anchor, where the current isn't too swift, and where there's a place to land Leo. We would need to dock at marinas.

We conferred with the Wilsons. Thirty-one miles from Thunderbolt, Kilkenny Creek offered a marina with "a laid-back atmosphere." Fine. But the second day we could see nothing but "a small marina restricted mainly to local craft" at Troup Creek, nearly sixty miles farther on – much farther than our usual day's run. From Troup Creek it was a modest day's run to Fernandina Beach – Florida at last.

All right.

Leaving Savannah we passed a creek that used to be called Back River. It had been renamed the Moon River, to honour the Johnny Mercer song. Mercer seemed to me now like the voice of

Savannah, plangent and melodic, easy and bittersweet, an amalgam of beauty and regret. He had written an astonishing collection of standards. "Lazybones." "Blues in the Night." "Laura." "One for My Baby, and One More for the Road." "And the Angels Sing." "Autumn Leaves." I hummed as I twirled the wheel.

It was a tiring day, cranking through the narrow creeks and crossing the wide water of Ossabaw Sound. Georgia's own Hell Gate lies between the Ogeechee and the Little Ogeechee Rivers. The Hell Gate channel is allegedly marked by a back range, two beacons that the helmsman is supposed to keep in line as he looks over the stern, but one of the beacons was lying on its face in the mud. It marked nothing but the general neglect of the ICW in Georgia. We got through only by dragging *Magnus*'s keel through the mud. And the trolls were still making the engine burp.

The next day was our worst run on the whole ICW.

On the chart, the shoreline of central Georgia looks like a wicker basket full of snakes, a haphazard maze of creeks, sounds, rivers, and cuts. The ICW hip-hops from one waterway to the next, gradually wriggling its way south. To be precise – if I must – our route lay down the Bear River to St. Catherine's Sound and up the sound to the North Newport River. Through a dredged cut to the South Newport River and thence to Sapelo Sound. Up the sound to the Front River, through Creighton Narrows, and across the Crescent River to Old Teakettle Creek. Down Doboy Sound to the North River and thence into the Little Mud River. Down Altamaha Sound, up the Altamaha River, through Buttermilk Sound, and down the MacKay River to Troup Creek.

Good grief.

Five boats left Kilkenny Creek that morning. *Blue Moon* and *Toucantoo* – whom we'd met in Oriental – elected to sidestep all the intricacies of the ICW by sailing out into the ocean and going offshore to Brunswick, probably arriving after dark. We were tempted to join them, and so were *Boxer* and *Tayo*, skippered by a cheerful Québécois named Didier Durand. But the forecast was for a solid twenty knots of westerly wind, and the breeze was already brisk. After a quick conference in the pre-dawn, the three of us decided to stay inside and worm our way southward via the ICW.

I had changed the oil and again bled the air from the fuel system. I thought I had figured out what the trolls were up to; the fuel system seemed to be sucking air somewhere between the fuel tank and the fuel filter. I fixed it. *Tayo* got away first, and we could see Didier's jib over the endless marshes as he rolled and unrolled it whenever the wind came fair. Suddenly *Magnus*'s engine slowed down, then slowly speeded up, then slowed again. The trolls were roaring with laughter. Somehow I had made the problem worse. I swore. This was going to be a long run, barely manageable in daylight with the engine running well. If the engine died in all that wind and current, miles from nowhere, what would we do?

The wind kept rising. As *Magnus* bucked up St. Catherine's Sound, the seas rose to three feet or more. Solid spray came flying over the bow. The rig shuddered, shaking the whole boat. I called *Boxer* on the radio. Just how strong was the wind? A steady twenty to twenty-five, said John, and gusts to thirty.

Now we seemed to be shaving the bottom of the winding creeks. As we realized later, the strong westerly was blowing all the water out of the creeks, and the tide was falling too. We followed range after range, lining up the markers ahead or astern, concentrating furiously on staying the middle of channels that were both shoal and constricted. The wind was shrieking in the rigging. The engine continued to falter.

We came off the Rockdedundy range into the Little Mud River at dead low tide. All day I had been nosing slowly back and forth across the creeks, seeking the deepest water. This time I couldn't find it. The display on the depth sounder got lower and lower – 4 feet, 3.6, 3.2. We must have been pulling through soupy mud already. The sounder reading dropped to 2.8 feet, and then the display went to solid bars. There was not enough depth to register.

"Don!" came John's voice on the radio. "We're right in the channel and we're hard aground."

With her four-foot draft, *Magnus* was still chewing through the muck, churning her way forward. The water behind her looked like brown paint.

"We can't stop, can we?" said Marjorie.

"If we do, we'll be stuck too," I said. "And we can't tow them or anything. We better go on. We'll wait for them when we get out into the Altamaha River, up ahead."

Behind us, John and Sandy were looking at each other in horror.

"No!" said John. "They're *leaving*!"

We called them on the radio. They were in no danger, and the tide would soon be rising. We would wait for them outside. But when we reached Altamaha Sound, we still only had seven feet of water. The wind was screaming, and the channel was too narrow for us to anchor. Out in the ocean, we learned later, *Toucantoo* and *Blue Moon* were being beaten about so badly that they turned back.

"We'll catch up with you later," said Sandy's voice. "We've got company anyway. Three or four other boats are stuck here now too."

Up the Altamaha – and we bumped twice more in the channel. Up ahead, another sailboat slowly took shape. It was lying down on its port side right in the channel, hard aground beside a channel marker. Marjorie called the skipper on the radio. He was fine, if a bit chagrined; he had been forced to the edge of the channel by a passing boat, and he was waiting for the tide to lift him off. On the radio, we heard three or four other grounded boats calling for help and advice.

Six more ranges, six more narrow channels, and we finally emerged into the MacKay River. We could hear *Boxer* calling to a marina back on Buttermilk Sound, a marina we knew nothing about. We tried to call, but our radio seemed to be acting up. The sun was setting blood-red over the brown marshes. Marjorie felt sick. I felt a little guilty, quite triumphant, and nearly exhausted. Leo was bursting. We turned into Troup Creek. We had put fifty-eight miles behind us.

Two charming kids, Kyle and Travis, took our lines, supervised by their father – whose accent was so strong I could barely make him out. *Tahrgude, naow!* Troup's Marina was a grey-weathered set of pilings and floating docks. It had no showers or electricity, but it did have a tavern at the head of the wharf, with a pool table. The price was reasonable, and we felt as though we'd landed in the middle of a family.

"Y'all goin' to the cookout?" asked one of the boys.

Cookout?

"It's a pig-pickin'. Roastin' a whole hog," said the boy. "Starts at six, in back of the marina." He looked up. "Here comes anothah boat."

The new arrival was *Tayo*; we had passed her in one of the sounds. Marjorie was not up to a pig-pickin', but when I arrived, Didier and his wife, Henriette, and their daughter, Catherine, were already there, paper plates loaded with food, talking intently with members of the Troup Creek Boating and Fishing Club. The ticket was six dollars, and you could eat as much as you wanted. The club holds a social every month, usually a fish fry or what-ever, but this time it was a whole roast hog, accompanied by salads and hot baked beans. Absolutely delicious.

I felt very foreign among the thick Georgia accents. Every now and then Rick, the emcee, would emit a piercing whistle, followed by "Lis'n up!" Then he would make an announcement or confer an award. One white-haired grandmother won a trophy for trap shooting – or so I thought, but I was never sure what Rick was saying.

A short woman with a near-impenetrable Southern accent herded *Tayo*'s crew into posing for a snapshot.

"Get this fella in too," a tall man said. "He come from Canada too."

"Yeah," said Didier, with just the hint of an accent. "We're d' Canadian navy."

The three Québécois and I laughed and threw our arms around one another. Flash. Four Canadians, captured on film.

At home we might have been shy with one another, I reflected, conscious mainly of our differences. For all I know, Didier and his family may be *indépendantistes*, supporters of a sovereign Quebec. But abroad, we shared more than we had realized. After six months in the United States, Marjorie and I had concluded that Canada truly exists not on the map, not in our institutions or ethnicity, but between the ears of Canadians.

For example, Canadians evidently have a distinctive style. Who knew? When we told an expatriate friend that we had found generosity and warmth all down the U.S. coast, she said, "Well, you have that Canadian charm. You approach people with that, and they respond. But don't misunderstand. If you approach Americans aggressively, they can do that too." Laughter is the Canadian social lubricant – and the Canadian private code includes a wry sense of humour. Whenever the crew of *Magnus* met another Canadian crew, we almost immediately found things to laugh about – "we're d' Canadian navy" – and the laughter sounded like home.

The humour threw John Wilson off balance. Again and again, we would say something goofy, and John would take it seriously. Marjorie would shake her head and waggle her finger at him.

"Ees leetle joke, John!" she would say. "Ees *fonny*, no? Leff, John! *Leff*!" And John's luminous, brilliant smile would burst in the cabin like sunlight.

We loved the boisterous energy of the United States, its sense of national responsibility, its kindness to strangers, its pride, its expansiveness, its ebullient music and art and literature. But we were also learning how deeply Canadian we were, how shaped and formed by our own odd country, how attuned to its habits and values. Canada lies deep in our assumptions, our attitudes, our understanding of social structures.

The strangest thing a traveller ever encounters is himself.

Next day, the winter caught up with us. We had entered Troup Creek in shorts and sleeveless shirts; we left it in mittens, jeans, flannels, and padded vests.

"It's the trolls," said Marjorie.

"Trolls?"

"We're only one day from Florida," she explained. "The trolls are still working on the engine, but they can't stop us now. So they're importing Norwegian weather."

I heard giggling in the bilges.

"Thor's whiskers!" I cried. "I believe you're right!"

Our destination was Jekyll Island, just thirteen miles away, where we planned to rendezvous with *Boxer*. Jekyll Island is Newport South: a rustic retreat for the robber barons and plutocrats of the Gilded Age. As I tossed the lines to the dockhand at the Jekyll Island marina, I remarked that even I, a Canadian, found the weather chilly.

"Ah find it plumb cold," he grinned. "Damn near down to freezin' last night."

Boxer arrived, and the four of us borrowed the marina's courtesy car to tour Millionaire's Row. Here were "cottages" built by such families as the Morgans, Astors, Rockefellers, Vanderbilts, and Pulitzers. The Crane cottage – which belonged to the plumbing fixtures family – had twenty-two rooms, twenty baths, and no kitchen. All meals were taken at the huge Queen Anne clubhouse of the Jekyll Island Club – "the richest, the most exclusive and most inaccessible club in the world," as one magazine described it in 1904.

I also went to the local drugstore to buy an elastic cuff and some heat pads for my right arm. The ICW had given me tendonitis from steering all these weeks through its kinks and bends and meanders.

That night we finally had a traditional Low Country Boil at a local restaurant – boiled corn and potatoes, spicy sausage and shrimp. John had spent part of the afternoon tightening *Boxer's* stuffing box, and we laid out a plan: Fernandina Beach the next day, then Jacksonville, then a lay-day to tour St. Augustine. On to Daytona for three days, while we picked up our niece Jocelyne, and onward to Melbourne or Vero Beach for Christmas.

"I want Christmas at a marina with a swimming pool, a hot tub, a tiki bar, an inflatable snowman, and good access to the beach," said Marjorie. "Jocelyne's coming all the way from British Columbia, and I want her to go home with a suntan."

"I will make it so," I promised.

The weather was bitter as we motored behind Cumberland Island and crossed St. Mary's Sound into Florida, tying up at the pretty little town of Fernandina Beach. Marjorie had been agitating about Christmas preparations for months.

"Babycakes," she had said in August, when we were sailing down the coast of Nova Scotia, "we need to start thinking about Christmas."

"Not yet," I had replied. Marjorie loves Christmas, loves preparing for it, loves finding and sending perfect gifts to beloved people. Very endearing, and reminiscent of my mother, who started her Christmas shopping at the Boxing Day sales. I, however, am an ex-Grinch, not yet entirely reformed. I have had plenty of miserable Christmases and watched other people have worse ones. I once owned a four-by-eight sign that read, BAH, HUMBUG!

"Snuggle-bucket," said Marjorie in September, when we were sailing down the interminable coast of Maine, "we need to start thinking about Christmas."

"Not yet," I replied. "We don't even know where we might find ourselves at Christmas."

"Pork chop," said Marjorie in October, when we were sailing down Chesapeake Bay, "we need to start thinking about Christmas. It's already past Thanksgiving."

"Not yet," I said. "We're in the States. They haven't even held Thanksgiving yet."

"Dearest and best," said Marjorie in November, when we were snaking through the sluggish brown rivers of South Carolina, "we need to start thinking about Christmas."

"Not yet," I said. How can a man think about snowmen and Santa Claus when he's trying to get from the Wadmalaw River to the Dawho?

"Joyful one," said Marjorie now in Florida, "it's December. Hanukkah has started, Christmas is upon us, New Year's is breathing down our necks. Hello? Hello? We need to start thinking about Christmas."

"I suppose," I conceded glumly. We were drinking coffee at a sidewalk café in Fernandina Beach. It is hard to think about Christmas when the palm fronds above you are swaying in the breeze, and pelicans are soaring over your head.

"To start with," said Marjorie, "we need some Christmas decorations for the boat." True, I thought. We'd seen boats festooned with lights, ingenious Christmas trees mounted on their bows, stars and wreaths and garlands hanging from their rails and their rigging.

"Where?" I asked. Center Street in Fernandina Beach is upscale gift shops, fine dining, jewellery, book stores. Not a tacky Christmas decoration on sale anywhere.

"Fred's," said Marjorie. "That's where the woman in the post office said we should go." Bloody hell. The woman had been doing covert research.

Fred's proved to be a squat down-at-heel building, probably a small former supermarket. John and I sat outside with Leo while Marjorie and Sandy plunged in. Marjorie emerged with a smug grin.

"Jackpot," she said. "Come."

I handed the leash to John. Fred's – which styles itself "America's Hometown Store" – was a truly amazing emporium, somewhere along the spectrum between the Dollar Store and the Noo Too Yoo Consignment Centre, but a trifle less classy. Tacky ceramic statues, ghastly table lamps, assorted plastic containers, tinny electronics, minor pieces of flimsy furniture, an odd selection of foodstuffs. And Christmas decorations, at bargain prices.

We bought a tinsel garland to rim the front of the cabin. We bought three golden bells on a ribbon, and a single bell for Leo's collar. We bought a candle surrounded by pine cones encrusted with fake snow to illuminate the Christmas table. We bought a short string of lights that I could wire to the overhead, and a long one that would almost reach the masthead. We bought a wreath to hang on the bow.

"Sugar plum," said Marjorie, surveying this heap of treasures on the galley table, "when shall we put them up? Now?"

"In due course," I said.

That night, northern Florida suffered "a hard freeze" – temperatures below freezing for several hours, with enough windchill to feel like the low twenties. The forecast called for cold weather, followed by cold weather. Temperatures were fully fifteen degrees Fahrenheit lower than normal. Cold air masses were moving down from Canada. (Judging by U.S. broadcasts, Canada's main export appears to be cold air masses.) The robotic announcers of the National Oceanographic and Atmospheric Administration were instructing astonished

Floridians on the dangers of cold weather. Cover sensitive vegetation with cloth, not plastic. Wear several layers of clothing.
Bring pets indoors overnight.

No, I thought guiltily, these cold air masses come from
Norway, not from Canada. The trolls might not have prevented
Magnus from reaching Florida, but Norwegian weather would
certainly prevent us from enjoying it. When we left at daybreak
for Jacksonville Beach, Marjorie wore a down jacket and woollen
gloves, while I wore a fleecy, a foul-weather jacket, and mittens.
John and Sandy were wearing sweaters, ski suits, insulated
mittens, toques, and full facemasks.

"God bless a motor-sailer," I said, shedding my outer clothes
and settling into the inside helm seat as we started down the long,
straight channels that carry the ICW southward behind the
barrier islands of Florida. The furnace kept *Magnus*'s cabin toasty,
and I was steering in my shirt sleeves. *Boxer* didn't even have a
canvas dodger to break the wind.

We tied up beside a highway bridge at Jacksonville Beach. It
was December 15. Clearly we weren't going to be in South Florida
by Christmas. We could certainly get south of the frost line,
spending Christmas in Vero Beach or Fort Pierce, or possibly as
far south as Stuart. I scanned the *Waterway Guide*, looking for a
marina with a swimming pool, a hot tub, a tiki bar, a restaurant,
and good access to the beach. One marina looked perfect: the
Harbourtown in Fort Pierce.

"It's in a jettied basin," I told Marjorie. "No currents. It has
a restaurant and a pool and wireless Internet, and there's shopping
within a block. There's a bridge right next to it leading across
the ICW to the beach. Fort Pierce is a town of some size too.
You know, movies and stuff."

"Maybe a vet?" said Marjorie. "I'd like to get someone to
look at that lump on Leo's leg."

"Just a fatty tumour, isn't it?"

"That's what the vet said. But it's growing fast. It was only the size of a marble when we left, and now it's the size of a golf ball. And it's right at the joint of his foreleg. I don't want a veterinary crisis when we're in the Bahamas. Who knows if there's even a vet over there? Anyway, it sounds as though you've found the right place. Go ahead and make a reservation. Christmas in Fort Pierce."

As she spoke, Marjorie was performing her usual miracle, producing a really delicious meal of smoked-salmon fishcakes, tomato salad, tinned peas, and fresh carrots. *I don't know how she does these things with only one burner, which is all we've had for weeks,* I wrote in my journal. *I just don't have time to play with the stove and still keep driving south.* But when we looked for a bottle of wine, we found all but one had vanished.

"The trolls," said Marjorie in disgust. "They're turning down the temperature *and* drinking the wine as well." I peeked into the wine rack we had carefully built in under the fridge. Totally empty.

In the morning the temperature was just above freezing, and we had a cold run through the dredged canals down to the Tolomato River. Bold signs warned us about manatees and alligators, but we saw no such beasts. I suspect they were numbed and had sunk. In Usina Beach, we passed a backyard with oranges and lemons on the trees. We reckoned they had been tied there as Christmas decorations.

I had my mittens on again as I went on deck in St. Augustine Inlet. We circled for twenty minutes in a rattling north wind near the Castillo de San Marcos, our teeth chattering, while we waited for the next opening of the famous Bridge of Lions. At the St. Augustine Municipal Marina, we tied up, fled below, cranked up the furnace, and prepared to have a glass of wine.

Oh, yeah. The trolls had drunk all the wine. Add it to the shopping list.

Meanwhile, St. Augustine!

Even in the cold, St. Augustine is cool, with tile-roofed stucco churches, grand hotels, and farmers' markets clustered around serene squares and tree-covered plazas. The Spanish explorer Ponce de Leon is said to have landed here in 1513, searching for the legendary Fountain of Youth. (Tourist operators contend that he found it. For a modest fee, they will show it to you.) The town was established in 1565, which makes it the oldest continuously occupied European settlement in North America. Its historic buildings include the Castillo de San Marcos, dating from 1672, when the town was still Spanish.

We were looking for wine. We passed Flagler College, once the Ponce de Leon Hotel, built by Henry Flagler, the Standard Oil magnate whose railroads and hotels practically created modern Florida, starting in the 1880s. Flagler ran a railway down the length of the coast, dotted the right-of-way with grand hotels, and established tourism and agriculture as Florida's main industries. We looked for a vintner on Aviles Street, the oldest street of all. We wandered into the courtyards of Spanish colonial houses. And then, at the end of King Street, we found the San Sebastian Winery, located on the city's second river, the San Sebastian.

A winery tour and a wine-tasting was just beginning. What better way to spend a cold, wet afternoon? We watched a video, walked through the winery, and quizzed Ted, our guide, which gave a pleasant air of virtuous educational initiative to the afternoon. Then we gathered around a U-shaped bar while Ted explained what we could learn from a wine's colour, how to "open it up" by swishing it in the glass, how to assess its aroma and its taste.

Ah, delightful. We both liked the Castillo Red, and Marjorie thought well of the Rosa. I liked the sherry and wanted to try the sparkling Blanc de Fleur. We tasted eight wines, ending with a hot mulled elixir. We found ourselves very cheerful, quite oblivious to the cold.

Ted delivered the coup de grâce. Significant discounts on various vintages, and 25 per cent off on a case of any twelve bottles.

Four Castillo, two Rosa, a port, and a sherry, and let's see, a couple of Blanc de Fleur to go with Christmas dinner . . .

"You gotta great businesh model," I said, drawing my whimpering VISA. "Get 'em half-looped an' then offer 'em a great deal. Irreshistible."

"Certainly hope so," he purred with a conquistadorial smile.

Ah, Shaint Augustine. Wunnerful town. We sailed south the next day and had never a speck of trouble. No doubt the trolls were, as we say in the Maritimes, tee-totally ossified.

Jocelyne came swinging out of the arrivals gate, tall and slim and pretty, nineteen years old and on top of the world, her smile lighting up the Orlando airport terminal. I thought again: This girl makes my spirit sing. And Marjorie's. For both of us, spending time with Jocelyne is like relaxing in clear sunlight.

The weather was still cold, and Daytona Beach is not the most fetching town in Florida – parts of it are squalid and dangerous – but Jocelyne was happy to be in a place of sand and palm trees, far from university examinations. We drove to the famous twenty-three-mile driving beach, where the world land speed record was set and broken fifteen times, starting in 1903, when Ransom Olds – as in "Oldsmobile" – flew down the beach at the breakneck speed of forty-eight miles per hour. The National Association of Stock Car Racing was formed at a meeting in a Daytona Beach motel in 1947, and the first Daytona 500 race took place here in 1959. If America is in love with the automobile, this is one of the places where the two first stole a kiss.

Since this beach was all about automobiles, and the tide was low, we drove our rented car out on it. When Jocelyne saw the drive-in church – or RIVE IN CHRISTIAN CHURCH, as the fractured sign described it – she cried, "Stop the car! I have to take a picture! It's just too weird!"

Magnus was moored at the Seven Seas Marina, a rundown, do-it-yourself boatyard of real people and real boats. Linda, the woman whose voice had guided me in, told me her grandfather had moved here from West Virginia and in his retirement had built a rudimentary house on an island in nearby Mosquito Lagoon. He had built a little skiff for his granddaughter, and he towed it behind his boat when he went fishing.

"Lots of times I can't remember coming home," she said. "I'd fall asleep in my little boat in my sleeping bag. But my grandfather insisted I had to push for shrimp along with him. He said if I was going fishing, I had to catch my own bait. The shrimp were in the seagrass, and you'd walk through the grass pushing a box-shaped net ahead of you, towing the boat behind you. Then you'd dump your net right in the boat, sort through it, and put the shrimp in a live-bait well. It was a wonderful way to grow up."

So that's how Florida used to be.

Jocelyne slept in the aft cabin the next morning while *Boxer* and *Magnus* started down the Indian River, the 170-mile section of the ICW that runs behind the barrier islands all the way to the St. Lucie River. Sandy and John saw their first manatee; cocooned in our wheelhouse, we had missed them, just as we had missed the wild boars they saw in Georgia. As the day went on, an enormous blocky building slowly arose from the sandy barrier islands: the Vehicle Assembly Building at the Kennedy Space Center.

As I tied our lines in Titusville, the florid skipper of a blue trawler cried, "Five minutes! But they've stopped the count."

"It'll be half an hour," nodded the lean, silver-haired skipper of a white ketch. "Maybe more."

"Excuse me?" I said, straightening up. "Are you fellows saying there's a rocket launch going on?"

"Sure is," said Blue Trawler.

"Monitor Channel 13 on your VHF," said White Ketch.

I scampered off to alert Marjorie and Jocelyne, who had already taken Leo ashore. I was as excited as a kid at the circus. When I *was* a kid, rockets and astronauts were a distant fantasy. (When Jocelyne was a kid, she wanted to be an astronaut.) But even now it is a rare thing to see a silver rocket rise on an orange pillar of fire and scorch away into the sky. It only happens in a few places on Earth – most notably on Florida's "Space Coast," the region around Cape Canaveral. Titusville is at the heart of that region – and we had arrived at precisely the right moment.

Then the let-down. The count down started, then stopped again. NASA wouldn't say when it might resume. The rocket might not be launched until much later.

I went off to browse in the marina store, thinking about the human advance into space in my lifetime – the electrifying *beep-beeping* of Russia's Sputnik satellite, launched when I was twenty; the flight of Yuri Gagarin; the arcing sub-orbital sleigh-ride of Alan Shepard down the South Atlantic, starting right here in Florida. I was a new father when the ecstatic voice of John Glenn spoke to us from orbit, trying to tell us all – live – about the awesome beauty of this green, spinning planet.

I recalled that shadowed, glittering prince, John Kennedy, declaring that the United States would – before the end of the decade – send a man to the moon and bring him safely back. Impossible, of course, but a grand project, an ambition worthy of a great nation. When it actually happened, Kennedy was dead and I was in Dublin, now a father of four, watching Neil Armstrong become the first human to leave the Earth and land somewhere else. The world was shrinking like an ice cube in the sun. Via Welsh TV, a Canadian family in Ireland was watching a live broadcast from an American on the moon.

And now I was a grandfather, cruising the Florida coast in a motor-sailer, and the world was wrapped with satellites. God knows how many satellites spin around us, carrying our broadcasts, our telephone conversations, our entertainment, our daily news. Satellites serve farmers and fishermen, spies and surveyors, realtors and merchants. I even steered *Magnus* by satellite signals. As a result, space had reportedly lost its magic. Over the years, shuttle launches and space walks had become routine events, barely worthy of media attention except at moments of disaster. Nobody cares about space any more.

So say the pundits. But when we visited the Kennedy Space Center a few days later, we were thrilled – and so were the hordes of other visitors. The vast Vehicle Assembly Building is a structure big enough to assemble a thirty-six-storey rocket and turn it upright. On a movie screen we saw Alan Shepard, remembering that he had looked back from the moon to the Earth, and found himself crying softly to think that those who shared that tiny, fragile planet were in conflict with one another. Another screen showed Kennedy, declaring that we choose to go to the moon because it is in our nature not to do the things that are easy, but the things that are hard.

You could spend days at the Space Center, walking through the space shuttle *Explorer* and watching IMAX films, touring the Rocket Garden and the launch complexes and the art gallery, touching pieces of the moon and of Mars. We stood inside the actual control room as the Apollo 8 mission was "launched." The offstage engine roared, and the light from its burning fuel brightened the room. Then we entered the huge hangar that houses the overwhelming Saturn V rocket, which propelled human beings to the moon.

A dockhand ran into the Titusville marina store and snapped me out of my reveries.

"She's off!" he shouted. "Goin' up now!"

I ran outside, and there it was, a brilliant tangerine flame below a silver line, tracing a white plume across the brilliant blue sky, curling toward orbit under a pale half-moon and fading into the stratosphere. And it still gave me a lump in my throat.

Melbourne the next day, and then onward on December 23, heading for Fort Pierce. Just south of Sebastian Inlet, *Boxer* called on the radio.

"We've got a diesel leak. Have to anchor while we figure it out."

We anchored beside *Boxer* in the calm grey morning, while John located the leak in a metal fuel line and patched it with epoxy. The weather was still cold. The patch held for an hour or so, and then started leaking again. By the time we pulled into Vero Beach, *Boxer* was losing fuel steadily – and she immediately went aground at the entrance to her marina slip.

Vero Beach Harbour was choked with boats, some of them rafted together on the town moorings. Dinghies came and went, often loaded with kids and dogs. In an adjoining slip was *Zingaro II*, the unique ketch from Thunder Bay that had travelled with us in South Carolina, and when we went ashore we met Chantal and Yves on *Chewan*, from Quebec. Chantal was a dog groomer who volunteered to trim Leo's long nails and encouraged us to have his tumour examined after Christmas.

Many cruisers spend the whole winter in Vero Beach. It's a charming, safe town, and the marina is located in a small park on a perfectly protected creek. John went off to order a new fuel line from Westerbeke and returned to report that Westerbeke would air-courier the fuel line to Vero Beach overnight. By eleven the next morning, however, the part had not arrived. It was Christmas Eve. We had reservations in Fort Pierce, and John Pratt had couriered our Christmas packages to the marina there. We decided to leave the Wilsons in Vero Beach, make the two-hour run to Fort Pierce, rent a car, and pick the Wilsons up on Christmas Day.

"You're going to spend Christmas in *Fort Pierce*?" said another cruiser, overhearing the conversation. "Have you been there? No? Ah, well."

Oh-oh.

By suppertime, we understood. Fort Pierce was the most down-scale city on the coast, joined neither to the prosperous Space Coast to the north nor the opulent Gold Coast to the south. It allegedly has the highest murder rate in the country, though other cities dispute that. Don't walk more than a couple of blocks from the marina, people warned us, except to score drugs. The marina itself was exactly as advertised – well protected, with a restaurant and a pool. But it was old and rundown, and our finger pier was narrow and rickety. Hurricanes Jeanne and Francis had pum-melled the facility. The pool was unusable – and even if it had been available, the weather was awful.

A snowstorm in Kentucky the previous night had grounded all UPS and FedEx flights, delaying *Boxer*'s fuel line – and also our Christmas packages. The marina and the restaurant were closing early for the holiday. A few coloured bulbs flickered here and there among the moored boats. We wanted to rent a car – an escape vehicle – but on Christmas Eve the car-rental agen-cies were closed too.

"Don't worry about it," grinned a fellow on the wharf. "Around here we don't rent cars, we just steal 'em. Saves the trouble of bringing 'em back. We'll get you a car. Any particular make? Any special colour?"

Marjorie was devastated. Jocelyne's carefully planned, magical Christmas was evaporating. We would spend the holiday trapped and isolated in a seedy marina, surrounded by yeggs, without the gifts our friends and family had carefully forwarded. We would be lashed by the wind, soaked by the rain, and cold enough that we would need to run the furnace. She could have wept.

"Marjorie," said Jocelyne, "It's okay, it's fine. I'm just happy to be here."

"Jocelyne's right," I said. "We've got food, we've got wine, we've got gifts for one another. We've got decorations for the boat – how bad can it be?"

"Let's decorate the boat," said Jocelyne.

We ran a tinsel garland and lights around the cabin, and tied the wreath to the bow pulpit. We strung lights to the mast-head, with a controller that flashed them in different sequences. We tied a bell to Leo's collar and found Christmas music on the radio. The radio was playing "It's Beginning to Look a Lot Like Christmas."

"Let's compose our own Christmas carol," I said to Jocelyne. "Something suitable for the occasion. An anti-carol. Like, *It's beginning to be a dog-shit Chris-muss . . .*"

"Right!" said Jocelyne. "*Ev'ry where we go – o – o . . .*"

"*We're surrounded by gangs of thugs –*"

"*Who are dealing illicit drugs –*"

"*Ecstasy and LSD and snow!*"

The anti-carol came together quickly.[8] With two goofy characters singing raucous songs to her, Marjorie could hardly remain disconsolate. We had enough gifts for one another to make three very plump stockings. Next morning we opened them, and that afternoon Marjorie whipped up a splendid Christmas dinner of pâté de foie gras, followed by sauteed chicken breasts with cranberry sauce, vegetables, and dressing.

We walked on the dock and found we were not entirely alone. In the slip right next to ours was *Seeker*, a big Hunter sloop with no mast. It had been blown over in the hurricane that wrecked the marina, and was awaiting delivery of its new rig. It belonged to Dave, an English ex-stockbroker who was married to Toni, an

---

[8] The full text – pulled by the pitifully pusillanimous publisher – can be found at www.silverdonaldcameron.ca.

Irish ex-belly-dancer. When not cruising the Bahamas, they lived (naturally) in Montana. At the end of the dock was *Somerset*, a forty-foot catamaran owned by a huge Great Dane named Kobe, whose attendants were from Ottawa – Tim, an architect, and Carol, a consulting veterinarian who commuted to work at a pharmaceutical company in California. They had lost their nearby house to the same hurricane and were living full-time on the boat. Carol agreed that the tumour on Leo's foreleg should be removed, and she knew a good local vet clinic. When business reopened, we booked the BFD for surgery on January 3.

Fort Pierce, though scruffy, was not quite as bad as advertised. After Christmas, the Wilsons came on down from Vero Beach, their fuel system working perfectly. The weather remained cold and raw, but we rented a car and toured, socialized with our neighbours, and stocked up on supplies for the Bahamas.

There was one incident, on Boxing Day, that shocked us, and the rest of the world. Marjorie and Jocelyne were in the marina's lounge, where crowds of people were visiting and playing cards. Marjorie glanced over at the TV and gasped.

"Did you hear that?" she said to Jocelyne. "Did they just say that *twenty-three thousand* people had died in a tsunami in Southeast Asia? Did I hear that right?"

Jocelyne nodded. "That's what I heard." Marjorie looked around. The chatter continued. Nobody else seemed to be paying any attention. Twenty-three thousand? Could that possibly be right?

On December 29, we drove down to Miami with Jocelyne, toured the art deco district, walked on the beach, and ate good Mexican food. Then we put our precious girl on a plane for Vancouver and drove sadly back to Fort Pierce in time for New Year's Eve. With Dave on flute, Toni on mandolin, Tim and Marjorie on guitar, we held a memorable party, starting in the marina restaurant and ending up aboard *Somerset*. It was going to be a happy new year. We were going to the Bahamas.

The moment Jocelyne left, the weather – naturally – turned warm. Around the marina, Bahamas fever was growing.

Crossing from Florida to the Bahamas means crossing the Gulf Stream, the great river in the ocean that sweeps from the Caribbean up along the coast to Newfoundland, where it turns east, delivering its remaining warmth to northern Europe. The Gulf Stream is responsible for palm trees growing in Cornwall, County Cork, and northern Scotland. In the Straits of Florida, compressed between Florida and the Bahamas, the stream runs at up to three knots. Because the Gulf Stream is going to carry your vessel steadily north as you cross it, you would ideally start from a point well south of your destination in the Bahamas. Palm Beach, almost due west of Grand Bahama Island, is the northern-most practical departure point.

The next issue is the weather. Northerly winds blowing against the northgoing stream will kick up steep breaking seas that can overwhelm a small boat. An east or southeast wind slows the boat's eastward progress while the stream carries it north. Motoring straight into an easterly, a yacht might take twelve miserable hours to travel forty-eight miles. In that time, the stream will have carried the boat thirty-six miles north.

A comfortable crossing requires a wind from the south or west. Alas, such winds are rare in winter. Florida's typical winter weather cycle begins with a "norther" – a strong north wind driven by a cold front. After the front passes, the wind swings to the east and stays there for days. And days. And days. Then it veers briefly to the south and perhaps to the southwest. That brief interlude of southerly breeze is the "weather window." That's when you sail to the Bahamas. Very soon – perhaps even the next day – the wind will go around to the north, and the cycle will begin again. It may be weeks before you get another window.

Seeker got her new mast, and Dave and Toni threw a mast-warming party, with much more music. There I overheard the skipper of a sixty-foot motor-sailer saying that he had recently conferred by radio with skippers who had been waiting for three weeks in Palm Beach, fifty miles south. They thought a window was opening up for the end of the week.

I told Marjorie what I'd heard.

"Let's go," she said instantly.

Leo had his surgery. John and Sandy cruised on down the ICW. Marjorie and I scurried around Fort Pierce in a borrowed car, loading up on food, fuel, cash, and other necessities. The vet filled out a health certificate, and we faxed it to the Bahamian government. Toni drove me to the post office to mail home some boxes of un-needed winter clothing. When I went to check out, the marina applied a generous discount to our bill. But I had to confess that we had lost one of our two washroom keys. We had ransacked the boat looking for it, and Marjorie finally concluded that she had left it in one of the shower rooms. Nobody had turned it in, however. The manager shrugged: Don't worry about it. Have a good trip.

On January 5, with a very subdued post-operative Leo nestled in blankets and pillows, we finally left Fort Pierce – which, in the end, had served us very well. Motoring south in the Indian River, we overtook two other Canadian boats, one from Hamilton and the other from – believe it or not – Winnipeg. They were intending to anchor in Peck Lake, a wide spot on the ICW, and go on to Palm Beach the next day.

We picked our way through the confusion of "The Crossroads," where the ICW crosses the St. Lucie River, and ran through a long canal to Peck Lake. There we found *Adagio*, with Jim and Sandy Shulz. The two Canadian boats soon joined us. Just before the crews gathered for happy hour, we rowed our bandaged dog ashore. By now the temperature was nearly 80°F, and we were wearing shorts. In January. Hallelujah! We took Leo for a short walk through the palm trees and underbrush, and emerged on a sweeping beige beach where rolling waves crashed ashore from the turquoise sea. Sharing a beer, we gazed at the eastern horizon. Just over there lay the Bahamas.

We caught up with *Boxer* in West Palm Beach. This town had also been pounded by hurricanes; both here and in Peck Lake we saw the masts and rigging of sunken sailboats poking out of the water, a spooky sight. Palm Beach proper, on the barrier island, is well and truly the Gold Coast, winter home of the wealthy and powerful – Lord Black, Teddy Kennedy, and other unfortunates. We joined *Boxer* at the Rybovich Spencer marina on the mainland shore – a huge facility, specializing in the care and feeding of mega-yachts belonging to the likes of Jimmy Buffett, who lives nearby. Among these mini-ocean-liners, our "yacht" looked like a dinghy.

Both in the marina and at several local anchorages, boats were waiting for the promised weather window. John and Sandy, however, had decided to take a berth at Rybovich-Spencer for a month, rent a car, relax, see the sights, and try to deal once and for all with the engine vibration. Would they come on to the Bahamas later, as they had planned? Maybe – but for now they had had enough. They were warm and comfortable, and the Palm Beach area offered theatre, music, art, and movies. They were bone-weary, and they wanted to stop and relax.

So did we – but in the Bahamas, not in Florida. Alas, no weather window materialized. The wind remained stubbornly in the southeast. From Fort Lauderdale, fifty miles farther south, however, a southeasterly would have sufficed. From "Fort La-La," the Gulf Stream actually shoves a boat toward Grand Bahama. The course from Lauderdale covers sixty-nine miles as opposed to fifty-four from Palm Beach, but – said the old hands – a boat can actually cross more quickly from Lauderdale. We would have better odds of catching a suitable window there.

Onward, then, though leaving the Wilsons behind was like saying goodbye to family. As we motored away, the ICW quickly became an exclusive highway – a slot of well-churned water between concrete walls in front of mansions, haughty clubs, glitzy condos, flossy marinas, and pretentious hotels. Mega-yachts, tour boats, sea buses, speedboats, huge sports-fishermen, police patrol boats, and migrant sailboats followed one another in bow-to-stern progression through an endless succession of opening bridges. The wakes echoed back and forth between the concrete walls, creating chaotic wave sequences. Humble little *Magnus*, salt-stained and chalky after nearly six months of cruising, plugged along among the gold-platers. We passed high-rise towers and magnificent tile-roofed homes in sea-foam green, pale blue, coral, deep yellow. Idling through this boggling opulence, we gawked like hillbillies.

We anchored overnight in an artificial lagoon called Pelican Harbor. Canals radiate off the lagoon like spokes from a wheel, each canal lined with pastel palaces and apartment blocks. There was no public landing place to take the dog ashore. But Marjorie spotted a couple of dogs playing in a yard, so I dinghied in and got permission for Leo to come and visit – and to come ashore in the morning too.

Next day we motored through Fort Lauderdale, the "Venice of America" and "Yachting Capital of the World." The city was built by dredging canals through the shallow lagoons, then building streets and houses on the flat peninsulas created by the dredging. The ICW winds through Port Everglades, Fort Lauderdale's cramped harbour, which is filled with enormous cruise ships, gigantic container vessels, coast guard cutters, tugs, ferries, water taxis, and an infinite variety of pleasure boats. The traffic was more dense than New York. The waterfront houses were more grandiose than ever.

"I didn't know there was this much money in the world," said Marjorie. She did not sound envious.

Beyond the harbour, we passed through two bascule bridges into the modest city of Hollywood. Somewhere up north, the Wilsons had met a local sailor named Eric Dybing, who had recommended waiting for a window either at a free anchorage nearby or at the Hollywood Municipal Marina. Unsure whether we had identified the anchorage correctly, we went to the marina. When the weather window came, we would call our trusty Johnny Grape, John Pratt, who had offered to fly down from Connecticut and sail across the Gulf Stream with us. We would fuel up and scoot back to Port Everglades, and – for the first time since she left New York – *Magnus* would turn her bow to the open sea.

But not just yet. Day after day, the winds remained in the east, leaving us stuck in Hollywood.

As readers of Carl Hiaasen and John D. MacDonald know, South Florida is a strange place – swamps and citrus, plutocrats and paupers, thugs and theme parks, vast housing developments that serve as holding tanks for the not-quite-deceased. The dead-flat landscape is rigorously stratified. The wealthy live on the narrow barrier islands, facing the Atlantic beaches, and along the Intracoastal Waterway. The paupers live on the mainland, ten blocks west of the ICW. The middle class lives farther inland, in sprawling subdivisions with names like Pembroke Pines and Walnut Creek. Everything is temporary. Everything is for sale. Along the ICW in South Florida, a cruising sailor of modest means often feels like trailer trash.

The happy exception is Hollywood.

Admittedly, Hollywood can be nasty. I had been there ten years earlier with my film-maker friend Charlie Doucet, researching *The Living Beach*. When our motorhome broke down, we were towed to a frightening compound in Hollywood, where snarling guard dogs patrolled the grounds and the steel fences were topped with razor wire. We stayed in a seedy Hollywood hotel that was comprehensively, and ineffectively, sprayed for cockroaches during our visit.

But this time Hollywood was thoroughly enjoyable. The marina is right on the ICW, beside a small recreational lake, and the beach, just across the bridge, features a "Broadwalk" – that's how they spell it – modelled on the Boardwalk of Atlantic City. A wide paved promenade, the Broadwalk provides unimpeded public access to the beach. It stretches a mile and a half along the sand, with cafés, low hotels, and souvenir shops on one side and the wide beach beside the aquamarine water on the other.

Hollywood's barrier island is only a block wide, full of small motels, efficiency apartments, and modest restaurants. The traditional winter home of thousands of Québécois, Hollywood is said to include the largest French-speaking population in the United States, and its businesses *parle francais*, provide *piscines chauffées*, and carry Radio-Canada on their TV menus. Ah, said a marina worker, himself Québécois, "in de winter, h'it's a little Quebec 'ere."

The Hollywood mainland is low-rise, low-key, and colourful, structured around the broad expanse of Hollywood Boulevard, which runs straight inland from the bridge. The spine of the city includes an Art Park, a new public library, and a funky little brick-paved, tree-lined downtown full of pastel-painted early Jazz Age buildings. A little Toonerville trolley shuttles between the downtown and the beach.

We had just tied up when we met Chantal, who had trimmed Leo's nails in Vero Beach. She and Yves had run aground and wrapped the dinghy painter on the propeller shaft. *Chewan* had been hauled out to have the shaft replaced – but the new shaft was too long, and when they turned sharply to enter the marina, the prop embedded itself in the rudder. Yves was frustrated but philosophical.

"Imagine if this 'ad happen in the Gulf Stream!" he said. "No steering, no power, four foot seas behind, a cruise ship coming up and a freighter ahead . . . ! No, this is the place to 'ave the problem. We'll get it fix', and we'll go to the Bahamas."

Right, I said. But there are worse places than Hollywood to spend the winter.

"No!" Yves roared. "We're goin' to the Bahamas, and that's *that*! We didn' come all this way to not get *there*!" That afternoon, TowboatUS towed them back to the repair yard.

The days slipped by. The crews of a couple of boats from Quebec didn't speak much English, and we don't speak good French – but with a kind of instinctive courtesy and amusement, each used the other's language when we met. A Sabre 38 registered in Fargo, North Dakota, of all places, was skippered by Allan, a poet, a translator of *Beowulf*, and an amateur meteorologist with broadband Internet service. He gave us regular bulletins on the weather windows that always, it seemed, were about to open – but never did.

I wrote a column, caught up with my journal, answered the mail. Marjorie scoped out the town and stocked up again; we were steadily consuming our drinking water, canned goods, wine, and beer – all of which were meant for the Bahamas. We had a quick lunch with my old friend Roy MacKeen, a Cape Bretoner who had spent nearly thirty years acting as a ship's agent in Florida and the Caribbean, especially the Bahamas. He gave us a list of useful Bahamian contacts and information, and made some suggestions about boat-handling and small improvements to the boat and its gear. I scrubbed *Magnus*'s filthy waterline, changed the air filter, replaced the missing bolt on the swim ladder. Cleaning the engine's raw-water filter, I lost its O-ring overboard. Oh-oh. We couldn't run the engine till I got either a new O-ring or a new strainer.

"Talk to Doug," said the marina attendant.

I wanted to talk to Doug about the stuffing box on our propeller shaft anyway. A sturdy, bearded man of forty-five or so, Doug was a waterfront figure right out of Travis McGee – a professional captain in charge both of *Snafu*, a sport fisherman, and a 70 mph, 2,000-hp speedboat. In addition, Doug salvaged sunken boats, did mechanical repairs, and seemed to know everyone in town. His intense blue eyes missed nothing, and he listened with equal intensity. He thought the stuffing box was fine, and as for the O-ring – well, let's see what we could find. We climbed into his brawny diesel pickup and drove to the Tru-Valu Hardware, talking about boats and tools and adventures and epoxy.

Hanging out with Doug was like being home in Cape Breton. A truck pulled up beside us at a Stop sign, the black driver waving and grinning. He swapped a bit of gossip with Doug before the light changed. Doug teased Adrienne, the manager of the hardware store – where we did find a rubber washer to replace the O-ring – and in the parking lot he was hailed by Fred, the seventy-four-year-old "reserve captain" on a boat that Doug operated. Fred had just sold his boat to "some idiot who's been twenty-three years in the Navy and he can't read a chart. I taught him everything I could in three and a half hours. He's heading for Jacksonville. Hope he gets there. I can't go offshore with this medication I'm on – if I hurt myself, I can bleed to death internally and not even know it."

"Listen," said Doug, "there's a skipper's job coming up on a tavern taxi-boat, seventy bucks for a four hour shift, plus the tips. You should look into it. I'll get you the guy's name." Fred thought he might.

A couple of days later I dismantled the manual bilge pump in the engine room. Why was it not working? Aha! The flapper valve in the bottom of it had been installed upside down. But I couldn't unscrew the body of the pump without a vise. I took it over to Doug.

"Why not two pipe wrenches?" said Doug. Why not, indeed? When we reassembled the pump, it worked perfectly.

"Do you always solve everyone's problems as smoothly as you solve mine?" I asked.

"Nope," said Doug. "Most people don't bring me such good problems to solve. Nah, nah, you don't owe me anything. That's okay, Bubba."

Eric Dybing, the Wilsons' friend, came by for a beer. An ardent voyager, and the owner-manager of a security agency that specializes in protecting celebrities and executives, Eric was energetic, charming, ebullient, and full of information. He was married – no surprise – to an adventurous Québécoise. The anchorage we had missed was right in front of his home, just before the last bridge we passed.

"This is the best departure point for the Bahamas," he declared. "Steer east and the current will carry you to West End. Go on to Lucaya, and don't miss the restaurant where they feed the bull sharks daily. You can send any extra crew home on the *Cat*, the big ferry from Nova Scotia – you know it? It runs between Lauderdale and Lucaya in the winter. In Lucaya, you can anchor in the canals of a big subdivision that was never built. Then go to the Berry Islands. It's only about fifty miles." He walked us through a complete cruise, right down the Exuma chain to Georgetown – where to anchor, where to find a cheap marina, where to snorkel, where to beachcomb, what precautions to take. ("In Nassau, for security, take two bottles of wine and give one to each of your neighbours.")

His ideal day in the Bahamas? "Wake up and get a little breakfast. *Read your book.* Go for a swim and spear a nice fish for dinner. Take the fish to another boat. They'll invite you for dinner. Go back aboard your own boat. *Read your book.* In the afternoon, take your sweetie for a walk on the beach. Do whatever occurs to you. Go for a swim. Lie in the sun. Go back aboard. *Read your book.* Go over to the other boat for supper. Have a drink. Tell some stories. Go back aboard. *Read your book.* Then the next day, do it all over again. Do it all the way down to Georgetown. Then do it all the way back."

Count me in. But first there was the little matter of getting across the Gulf Stream. The weather systems came whistling through, one after another – first the ripping north wind, then the days of easterly wind, then the quick swing through south to west. But the westerlies lasted only a few hours, not long enough for the Gulf Stream seas to "lie down" – window open, window shut, bam-bam! – and then we were back to the ripping northerlies again.

"Yeah, I'm going to the Bahamas too, but if this keeps up, maybe I'll just go south and leave from Miami," said a cruiser I dubbed the Lone Ranger. I never knew his name, but *Lone Ranger* was the name of his boat, and it suited him too – a man in his sixties who had been single-handing his trawler for two years. Lean, brown, scruffy, and unshaven, he had just made the Great Circle tour up the Mississippi, through the Great Lakes and down the ICW – his third transit of the ICW in the two-and-a-half years he'd been a full-time liveaboard.

"I've been divorced for twenty years," he said, "and I thought that living on a boat wouldn't be any great change, but it is." I wanted to know how he managed the ICW, which requires such continuous attention that a single-hander wouldn't even have an chance to relieve himself. The Lone Ranger smiled.

"I get up in the morning and drink a strong coffee and smoke a pipe to get things moving," he said, "and I keep a bucket beside me at the helm. You're right, it's not easy – I've been through more than a hundred locks and God knows how many bridges, and I'm always worried about docking. I don't think people understand what the boating life is all about. They think you spend your time anchored in a beautiful tropical cove, enjoying a drink – but that's not what it's like at all. Did you hear the forecast today? Nothing but garbage, even the extended forecast. North winds, fifteen-foot seas. Good Lord."

I had an ulterior motive in approaching the Lone Ranger; I was looking for a buddy-boat, another cruiser that would be heading for the Bahamas when the weather broke, a boat to cross in company with us. For first-timers especially, crossing with a buddy-boat is strongly recommended. Your buddy may be able to help if you get into trouble – and at least someone else will know you're out there. The Lone Ranger didn't seem a likely prospect – but then we got an email from David and Sally Arbuthnot, back in the Chesapeake. *Easy Time* and *Calypso*, two sailboats belonging to friends of theirs, were somewhere in Fort Lauderdale, waiting to cross – maybe we'd like to look them up? I emailed them immediately.

We rented a car and drove back to Fort Pierce in torrential rain to have the staples removed from Leo's wound. As we drove back to Hollywood, Marjorie was listening to a Spanish radio station – featuring oddities like Neil Diamond singing "Sweet Caroline" in Spanish – and she suddenly burst into a flood of Spanish nonsense. *Huevos y tocino! El burro es muy peresoso! El burro es rojo! Dos frios cervesos, por favor! Ceilito lindo!* She has a sharp ear for the nuances of voices and accent, and she sounded genuinely Spanish. We laughed all the way home.

But the long wait for the weather to break was making us both snappish. The next morning was cool and rainy, and we slept late. Marjorie had had bad dreams about the death of a favourite horse, and she got up cranky, banging her elbows on things and sighing heavily; she has a remarkable gift for heavy sighs that direct the blame for all her sorrows toward her innocent husband. Then she launched into a litany of complaint. The boat was too small, everything was damp, the rain was pouring down, she was a long way from home, she had been swept up in my ambitions and had no life of her own. Eventually I blew up.

"Enough, Marjorie, enough!" I snapped. "You've done nothing since you got up but sigh and mutter and bitch and complain. Enough!" She looked at me wide-eyed and innocent.

"But I'm not finished," she said plaintively. The two of us burst into laughter.

"And anyway, it's disgusting that you're so cheerful," she said.

"Frightfully sorry," I said cheerfully.

"No, that won't do," said Marjorie. "False contrition is revolting in a man your age."

And then she put her hand in her pocket of her raincoat and said, "What's this?" She made a very funny face, burst into stage tears, and sobbed, "I'm s-s-so *ashamed*" – and pulled out the missing washroom key from Fort Pierce.

Ron and Suzie Williams on *Easy Time* were indeed waiting to cross, and they had a car. Along with *Calypso*'s owners, Frank and Rita Gerrett, they came to meet us, a quartet of good friends who had made the crossing before. They were moored in two different locations on the other side of Port Everglades. The three boats could assemble just inside the inlet and then cross together.

We discussed the weather outlook. For the first time in a couple of weeks, it looked promising.

From my notes: *Allan says that Friday looks like the window: E winds today, SE 10-15 knots Wed and Thurs, S and SW Friday, then NE on Saturday. Will check the Internet to see what Barometer Bob is calling for over in the Bahamas, and then call John Pratt.*

The forecast held.

On Thursday afternoon, another cruiser helped us to fold up the Porta-Bote and lash it on the foredeck, right in front of the inside helm. To my surprise, it didn't interfere with visibility at all. Then we filled up with diesel and motored slowly north along the ICW through two bridges to the Dania Cut-off Canal, which gives direct access to Port Everglades. As *Magnus* puttered slowly up the canal, a stubby man on a wharf started capering about and shouting to us.

"Hey!" he shouted, pointing at the word *Halifax* on our stern. "Ever get to Cape Breton?"

"We live there!" called Marjorie.

"Yesss!!!" he shouted, raising both fists. I replied with the code phrase of the Cape Breton patriot.

"Down wit' d' Causeway!" I cried.

"Yesss!" he shouted again, shadow-boxing and jigging on the dock.

"The Cape Breton mafia is everywhere!" I shouted.

"It is, it is!"

We tied up at the Royale Palm Yacht Basin at 5:10 p.m. At 6:00, fresh from Connecticut, John Pratt came striding down the dock with his sea-bag. We did the pre-departure checklist, had a drink, ate roast chicken with baguettes and fruit, and tried to sleep.

At 2:30 a.m., we took the Wonder Whippet down the silent wharf for his last contribution to American soil, brought in the electrical cord, turned on the navigation lights and the electronics, and cast off. *Magnus* idled down the dreamlike dark canal in the quiet night, slipping into Port Everglades beside the towering walls of cruise ships. We scanned the black water for the lights of *Easy Time* and *Calypso*. I called on the radio.

"*Easy Time, Easy Time*, this is *Magnus*."

"Hi, *Magnus. Easy Time*. We can see your nav lights." The Gemini catamaran was dead ahead, but *Calypso* had been caught behind a Fort Lauderdale bridge. She would follow an hour later. A sloop named *ZigZag* was slicing through the darkness beside us. John shouted to them. Were they heading for West End? They were. Four boats would be crossing today.

Magnus raised her head to the ocean swell. The bright towers of Fort Lauderdale slid behind us. The fairway buoy winked ahead. The forecast called for moderate westerlies, ten to fifteen knots, but the west wind coming off the land was all of that and perhaps more. The sea was beginning to build. Ahead of us, *Easy Time*'s masthead light was weaving and swaying. At the fairway buoy, I set a course for West End.

"How should I steer?" John asked.

"Oh-seven-four," I said. "Really, just follow that catamaran." *Magnus* was rolling heavily in the following seas.

"She'd ride better with some sail up," said John. "Should I roll out the genny?"

"Yeah." We unrolled the big genoa jib, and the steady pressure of the wind immediately dampened the rolling. The boat was still heaving, though, and everyone was holding tight to the handrails. The wind seemed strong. The lights of *Easy Time* and *ZigZag* were swinging across the black horizon. Ron Williams's voice came crackling over the radio. *Calypso* had left Port Everglades, but she was out of sight astern.

"*Magnus*, how are you doing? Your lights are rolling a lot."

"Yeah, we're rolling," I said. "You?"

"We are too. There's a lot of wind."

"How much, do you know?"

"Twenty knots on the anemometer, gusting higher."

"We had a lot worse than this on the Jersey coast," John said quietly. "Too late to turn back anyway." True: slogging back against wind and sea would have been a miserable ordeal. Leo whimpered quietly. Marjorie reassured him.

The lights of Florida shrank and then vanished, leaving only a loom of amber light painted on the sky. The seas rose. The dawn drained the darkness away and revealed a busy ocean – seas five to six feet, whitecaps all the way to the horizon. The water was an amazing colour, rich and hard, a deep indigo blue we had never seen before. Something skittered low above the water and then plunged into a wave – a flying fish, the first one I had ever seen. *Magnus* rolled far to port, and something crashed. Two plastic drawers had flown out of the galley cabinet. One was cracked, the other broken. I shoved them back and tied them in place with Leo's leash.

The brightening sky was spangled with broken clouds and spots of sunlight. The horizon turned misty, then cleared, then turned misty again. The masts and sails of *Easy Time* and *ZigZag* faded into the mist, then showed themselves again, then faded once more.

Following them, said John, was "like chasing a mirage." *Magnus* was utterly happy, coursing along under genoa and engine, tossing and rolling, making as much as eight knots through the water.

"I would like a breakfast beer," said John. "Just one. Beer quenches your thirst and keeps your stomach happy, did you know that?" I fetched him a beer and tried one myself. The hours ticked by, John steering, me watching and navigating, Marjorie organizing food and passing it around, Leo snoozing in the forward berth. Dark blue seas curled up astern, lifting the boat and breaking along her sides in a smother of white. Every hour, *Easy Time* called *Magnus* and *Calypso*, checking progress, comparing notes. Every hour I noted our position, watched the boat's slow crawl across the electronic chart.

By noon, *Easy Time* had land in sight. We soon saw it too – casuarina trees fringing the sea, a faint shape that slowly became the bulb of a water tower. A band of pale water appeared, a buff-coloured line of stones: the breakwater of West End.

I called ahead to Old Bahama Bay Marina. A warm Bahamian voice came back.

"Gled to have you. No problem wid a berth. We be lookin' for you."

In between the tall stone breakwaters now. Clear pastel green water. Low buildings around a dredged basin, a handful of other boats, and lots of empty berths. A smiling black youth with corn-rowed hair standing on the dock, waving us in. He caught our lines and wrapped them around the pilings. His name was Kyle. You gave us a fine welcome, I said.

"You come so far to be here," said Kyle with a huge smile. "We got to make you welcome."

The Bahamas at last, after three thousand miles. Six months to the day since we left home. A great sail, said John. We're here, I said to Marjorie. I don't believe it, she replied.

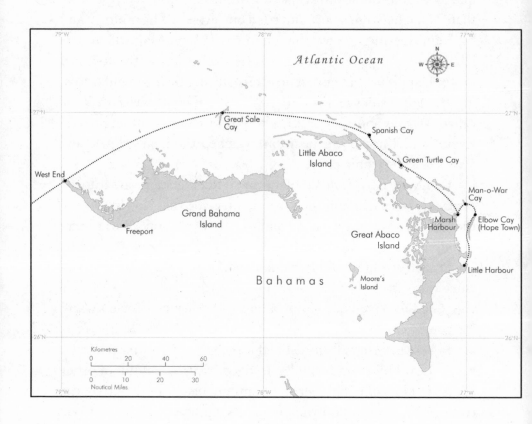

PART VI

ABACO

Champagne cruising. The kind of sailing you get in your dreams.

A warm southerly breeze presses the stout little ketch with its burgundy canvas across the dancing turquoise water. She is bound for a deserted tropical island. The boat heels slightly under a tall azure sky. The sun is brilliant but not burning. The horizon is a complete circle, without a speck of land in sight. The water is twelve feet deep, and so clean that you can see the sand and the weeds on the bottom.

You don't have to follow a channel. There are no rocks or reefs anywhere nearby. No bridges, no drying sandbars, no narrow landcuts. Nothing to worry about. You can sail any course you like. Up ahead of you, you can see just one other boat – and the skipper is fishing as he sails. It's late January.

This is one of the most memorable days of your life. Soak up every moment. When you are old, you will remember this day and smile. A voice inside scoffs: Bubba, you're old now. Another voice answers: Not today.

We almost didn't go. This morning in West End, *Magnus* seemed to have quite a lot of water in the bilge, and I thought the freshwater tank was emptier than it should have been. The stuffing box was seeping too much. The computer was cranky, and though the forecast was uncertain, it appeared that another front would blast through shortly. Our route would lead us north of Grand Bahama Island (of which the west end is West End) and into the Sea of Abaco. Our destination was the eastern end of that sea, an area known as The Hub of Abaco, an inland sea ringed by a necklace of islands, the Abaco Cays – pronounced *"keys,"* as in Florida. It would be a hundred-mile, two-day run, broken by an overnight stop at remote and isolated Great Sale Cay. We could be weatherbound at Great Sale. Should we wait out the front with *Easy Time* and *Calypso*? Or should we emulate Bill and Tina on *ZigZag* and go on?

"Look, the weather is gorgeous," said Bill, "and if we wind up with a rolly anchorage in Great Sale, so what? This is a go-day. If it blows hard tomorrow, it won't kick up much of a sea, because you're in shallow water on the banks, and the wind is sup-posed to be northwest, which is just going to push you where you're going."

John assessed the issues with implacable logic. Even if the fresh-water tank emptied itself, we had enough water that we wouldn't die of thirst, check. The stuffing box was leaking a bit, but it was nothing that the pumps couldn't handle easily, check. The com-puter was nice to have, but we could easily navigate without it, check. Nothing we'd heard about the weather sounded threaten-ing, and right now the weather was gorgeous, check. Good old John. We cast off, threaded our way through Indian Cay Passage behind Bill and Tina, and entered a fragment of paradise.

Although the Abacos were new to John, the Bahamas were not; he owns a home in Harbour Island, Eleuthera. The country consists of 300,000 people living on 700 islands strewn over more than 1,000 miles of ocean. The islands are actually hill-tops standing on two enormous plateaux, the Great Bahama Bank to the south and the Little Bahama Bank to the north. The barely submerged banks are separated by a trench of water a thousand feet deep, but the water over the banks is shallow. *Plenty of watah in de Bahamas, mon*, runs a local saying, *but some of it spread mighty thin.*

Ambitious to a fault, I had originally planned for us to visit Nassau, the capital, and also the Exuma chain and Eleuthera – all on the Great Bahama Bank – as well as the Abaco chain, on the Little Bahama Bank. The best authorities advised against it. Too much charging around, not enough enjoyment. The first-timer should just go to the Abacos, said Skipper Bob's *Bahamas Bound*, and save the rest for later. The advice fit our mood. After six months of plugging south, we were ready to stop and smell the frangipani.

The south-facing anchorage at Great Sale Cay looks like the gap between a forefinger and a thumb. Four boats were already there, and *ZigZag* went in ahead of us. We tucked in behind the thumb, ran over close to the finger, and anchored. Marjorie and I took the BFD ashore. We had never seen such a shoreline – rough, jagged limestone rock that would easily have ripped a hole in an inflatable dinghy. Leo picked his way along and did his business. We heard a splash and looked around. John had plunged off the swim platform and was vigorously swimming around the boat.

I set the GPS to warn us if the anchor dragged and left the mizzen up to hold the boat into whatever wind might blow. At bedtime, Leo wanted to go ashore again – not a great idea in the pitch dark on a vicious rocky shore. I took him for a walk on deck, up to the bow and back – and when he hopped back into the cockpit, he stopped abruptly.

"He's peeing!" cried Marjorie. "Good dog! Oh, good dog." He had never done it before, and – despite our constant encouragement – he never did it again.

In the middle of the night, the wind came up ahead of the front, whining in the rigging – thirty-five knots, we heard later – and I checked our position several times during the night. *Magnus* never budged. The sea was choppy in the morning, the wind blowing hard from the northwest, just as predicted. John and I carefully took Leo ashore and assessed the situation. *ZigZag* was going on? We would go on.

We rolled and crashed to windward under power till we cleared the cay, then made sail and began a roaring downwind passage into a narrowing funnel between the islands. High gun-metal and charcoal clouds chased across the sky, and the sea was a turquoise tumult, whitecaps foaming over pastel waves. The chart was peppered with exotic names: Strangers Cay, Double-Breasted Cay, Paw Paw Cay. As we squared away for Hawksbill Cay, John pointed astern. A bulging wall of cloud was bearing down on us. Ahead of it, the wind picked up.

"There's the front," he said.

The front rolled over us and onward to the south, bringing a bit more gusty wind and intermittent rain. But the boat was belting along at more than eight knots. Umbrella Cay slipped by. Allans-Pensacola Cay. We passed Centre of the World Rock, altered course to pass between Hog Cay and Crab Cay, and steered into the marina at Spanish Cay.

While we took the BFD ashore, John vanished. He came back a few minutes later, grinning, with a bottle of amber liquid in his hand.

"Try this," he said. "I think you'll like it."

Like it? It was a rum liqueur called Nassau Royale, and it was ambrosial. Like it? It was smooth, flavourful, appallingly easy to drink. "The Spirit of the Islands," said the bottle. "A delicate blend of exotic ingredients with a hint of vanilla . . . it's light as the Bahama breeze, as enticing as the Nassau sunshine." Like it?

"John," I said, just before I slid off my seat and into my berth, "it'sh a good – good thing I didn' know about thish before now. Where has thish been all my life?"

Spanish Cay – which was named for a pair of Spanish galleons that sank offshore in the seventeenth century – had been hard-hit by Hurricanes Frances and Jeanne, which followed almost identical tracks down the Abaco chain. Jeanne in particular had moved very slowly, stalling for fifty-two hours near Spanish Cay and subjecting the area to fifteen straight hours of winds above a hundred miles per hour. We had seen heavy damage at West End, where the sea had punched through a big piece of the breakwater and closed the hotel. The hurricane damage to the Spanish Cay marina had been pretty well repaired, but on the offshore side of the island we saw eroded shorelines and badly damaged build-ings – including the carcass of Wreckers Bar, right on the white sand beach, which the hurricanes had wrecked.

The marina provided wireless Internet service, so we stayed a second day while I caught up with business. Marjorie cleaned and organized, and John moseyed around the boat repairing things. He examined all the running rigging, tightened the stuffing box, filled the gas tank on the dinghy, fixed the broken drawers, and designed restrainers to keep them permanently in place. We went walking and were stunned by the beauty of the beaches and the water, and by the lush vegetation – coconut palms, royal poincianas, frangi-pani, bougainvillea, hibiscus.

The Bahamas – we soon began to see – are often an emul-sion of poverty and plutocracy, without a whole lot of folks in between. Spanish Cay once belonged to Queen Elizabeth II, and later to the Texas investor Clint Murchison, sometime owner of the Dallas Cowboys. Since Murchison's death the island has changed hands several times, and the current owner is develop-ing it both as a private resort and also as a site for exclusive homes. His name was Don, and we found him making a pot of excellent she-crab soup in the kitchen of the restaurant when we went up for dinner. As well as Spanish Cay, he owned restaurant chains in Florida, Texas, and Louisiana. The island has its own five-thousand-foot airport, and Don commuted by private jet. He also owned a boatbuilding business in British Columbia, where he was having his own mega-yacht built. Such boats, he confided, cost "about $14 million, but you can make a couple of million on 'em if you manage things well."

Oh.

Green Turtle Cay, just twelve miles on, was another world. Green Turtle has two anchorages, White Sound to the north and Black Sound to the south. White Sound is the tourist district, with hotels, lodges, and modern marinas. We took the very shallow passage into Black Sound. We filled up with diesel at The Other Shore Club, a small, rickety marina that also showed some storm damage. The dockmaster, Kevin, is – according to the sign on his truck – the Bahamas' greatest rock star, leader of a band called The Gully Roosters. We were in shorts, but Kevin was wearing a toque; he thought it was cold.

"You look like a Canadian," said Marjorie.

"What, a black Canadian?" said Kevin. "Oh, I don't think so!"

"There are plenty of black Canadians," said Marjorie. But Kevin clearly didn't believe it. For him, presumably, Canadians are white and live on boats.

It was an easy walk to New Plymouth, a picture-perfect village of five hundred souls with narrow concrete streets, a shallow green harbour, and a range of shops and services. Tiny houses on tiny lots, painted aqua, peach, lime green, deep coral, vivid pink, dandelion yellow. Tidy little stores, decently stocked. A century-old gaol. Dogs and chickens and kids. Golf carts and miniature Suzuki pickup trucks and vans. An historic Loyalist cemetery.

Loyalist? Yes, indeed. The Bahamas are predominantly a black nation, but in the Abacos the proportion is roughly 50/50 – and the whites, known as "Conchy Joes," are the descendants of

Loyalists who left the United States after the Revolution, settling in British colonies like Nova Scotia, New Brunswick, Ontario – and the Abacos. These Loyalists, unlike the Canadian ones, came from the South – from Florida, Georgia, and the Carolinas. Many black Bahamians are descended from Loyalist slaves.

"Let me buy you your first conch fritters," said John, leading us to a tiny restaurant with an outdoor gallery.

Conch – a huge underwater snail – is a staple food in the Bahamas. The meat is tough but tasty; it's beaten flat and fried to make "cracked conch," or diced and served raw with citrus juices, pepper, and onions as a conch salad. Conch fritters are made of ground conch deepfried in batter. They look a little like deepfried scallops, and they are simply delicious, especially with a Kalik (pronounced "click"), "the beer of the Bahamas."

Green Turtle is not quite in the Hub of Abaco. The major settlements – Hope Town, Man-O-War, Marsh Harbour – lay a bit farther southeast. To reach them, we had to transit the only really treacherous spot in the Abacos, the Whale Cay passage.

The cays stand on the very edge of the Little Bahama Bank, and the tides force huge volumes of water between the cays when the tide changes. In addition, waves from distant storms rear up into great combers when they suddenly encounter the steep wall of the banks and crash into the narrow cuts between the cays, a condition known in the Bahamas as a "rage." Most of the time, small craft can avoid the cuts – but the water between Whale Cay and Great Abaco Island is too shallow for most boats to negotiate. Deeper boats have to go out into the open ocean to get around Whale Cay – and in a rage, the passage can be rough enough to roll a freighter over and sink it.

We motor-sailed through the passage on a glorious sunny day. It was challenging enough, with swells of ten to twelve feet. Approaching boats – and there were several – simply vanished when they dropped down into the troughs. The swells were breaking all around, presumably on nearby reefs – but no; a closer look at the chart showed they were simply big breakers. The route led out to seaward and then parallel to the rounded bump of Whale Cay. It re-entered the Sea of Abaco through a narrow but well-marked passage behind Great Guana Cay, and led back into protected open water – the Hub of Abaco.

The seas flattened out. Tropical islands lay all around the horizon, boats sailing serenely between them, tiny ferries hustling back and forth. We raised all the sails, cut the engine, and sailed quietly through the turquoise water. Marjorie sat on a cockpit seat with Leo on her lap, both of them gazing off across the water. Ahead was Marsh Harbour, the largest town in the Abacos, the third-largest in the country, where John would catch a plane and we would catch our breaths.

Picking up a piece of paper, John smiled at me and drew a circle with the letters "TB" inside it and drew a slash across it. No Troll Burps. He put his finger to his lips. Don't say it out loud. Don't alert the trolls. He was right. Since Georgia, the trolls had been drinking our wine and spoiling our weather – but they had left the engine alone.

We called the Marsh Harbour Marina, made a reservation, furled the sails as we motored slowly through the busy harbour. Cruising boats were anchored everywhere. As we entered our berth, a slim, mahogany-tanned man with a short, greying beard took our lines.

"Donnie Schmeisser," he said, holding out his hand. "From Lunenburg. You're from Halifax?"

"From Cape Breton, actually," I said, shaking his hand. "Don Cameron."

"Not *Silver* Donald Cameron?"

"Well, yes."

"Silver Donald, Silver Donald, I'm some glad to see you," said my new friend feelingly. "I'm glad you made it. I been following your trip in your column every week on the Internet. Donald, Donald, I was sayin' to myself, get a move on. Get south, get south. You're gonna be *cold*, buddy." He paused for a moment. "Oh, by the way, they're reading from your work over at Hope Town tonight."

Say *what*?

"There's a cruiser's net every morning on the VHF," said Donnie. "Tells you what's going on around the Abacos. And what's going on tonight is a reading of cruising literature at the Hope Town Marina. Fellow from Ontario is reading something you wrote. You should get in touch with him. He'll be right happy to know you're here."

Excellent, but I'll do that later. Right now we're interested in a drink or two, and a good meal.

"You got here on the right day," said Donnie. "Tonight is rib night at the marina. The barbecued ribs are really, really good. And there's dancing afterward. Music by Browntip's Rake 'n' Scrape. Browntip plays a musical saw."

All *right*!

Seven in the morning. Sunrise, low tide, and I'm heaving Leo up onto the finger pier at Marsh Harbour – thirty-eight pounds of whippet, relaxed but ready. He lands four-square on the wooden deck. I scramble up behind him, and we walk to the shore for his morning constitutional.

The wharf is damp with overnight rain. The boat is wet, and there's water in the dinghy. The air feels fresh and cool, the early sun hidden behind a fence of backlit clouds. But the upper sky is clear, and a light northerly wind holds the anchored boats in formation. It's like a summer morning in Nova Scotia – but on a comparably warm and bright northern morning, the sun would have risen at 4:30, not at 7:00.

The BFD and I walk past Donnie and Marilyn Schmeisser's spacious trawler, *Xanadu*. This is the Schmeissers' third winter in the Bahamas, and they're a fund of information. How to get hooked up to the Internet. Where to shop for groceries. How to get the forecast. Where to find marine supplies. Where to find seclusion. Leo tugs me around the corner of the Jib Room, the marina's bar and restaurant, heading for a patch of coarse green grass dotted with palmettos, just in behind the industrial-sized barbecue. He sniffs the terrain, does his stuff, and we turn back to the boat. He's tugging hard on the leash, anticipating food.

Over the last six months, I reflect, he and I have done this routine in city streets, seaside parks, village squares, marshes, parking lots, beaches, bridge abutments. We've done it in sun, rain, wind, and fog, trudging up wharves, rowing over choppy water, and putt-putting through the darkness with the outboard. Marsh Harbour is our fifth port in the Bahamas, our eighty-third port since leaving home.

But these mornings in Marsh Harbour are fundamentally different, because we aren't intent on going anywhere any more. We'll visit other places, certainly. But we were going to the Bahamas, and we're there. We're settling into Marsh Harbour for a while, and it's a startling shift of gears. "Cruising the East Coast" involves a lot of travelling. "Cruising the Abacos" means living aboard your boat in the Abacos for some weeks, exploring the islands as much or as little as you choose. The Hub of Abaco is a protected inland sea that reminds me a bit of Chesapeake Bay – but it has no cities, no great amount of commerce, no naval bases. It's actually more reminiscent of the Bras d'Or Lakes, back home in Cape Breton. Its size is similar, and it offers similarly wonderful cruising – plenty of islands and tidy little settlements within a couple of hours' sail. Like Cape Bretoners, we soon learned, Abaconians have a distinct accent, a laidback style, and a fondness for rum.

The difference is palm trees, turquoise water, conchs, tropical fish – and grand sailing in January.

I take a deep breath on the wharf now, before lifting the BFD back aboard. The sun is up, gilding the anchored boats, the marina, the palm trees, and the low, chalky cliffs. A soft breath of wind brushes my bare legs and ruffles the vivid water. The dog tugs at the leash. Eighty-three ports behind us, and breakfast ahead of us. Good morning, Marsh Harbour, good morning.

"Good mornin', Abaco!" cries a cheerful Texan voice on Channel 68. "It's 8:15, and the Abaco Cruisers' Net is on the air – keepin' you amused, bemused, and confused, and hosted this morning by Jeff and Mary on *Agur's Wish*, with Stanley the Killer Bichon, in beautiful downtown Marsh Harbour!"

The Bahamas telephone company, Batelco, is expensive, inconvenient, and hopelessly unreliable. So Abaco communicates by VHF radio – cottagers, boaters, grocery stores, everyone. You call a Marsh Harbour taxi on VHF Channel 6.

Enter the Abaco Cruisers' Net, which has been providing information to cruisers and cottagers on the VHF for thirteen years. Cruisers take turns hosting it. With his warm voice and relaxed manner, Jeff Reid does it superbly. He's a big gregarious guy, with a greying blond ponytail, on a graceful Tashiba cutter. I know Stanley the Killer Bichon too. I see the little white dog strutting down the wharf like a rooster, taking Jeff for regular walks.

"And we all want to know what the weather is gonna be," Jeff says, "so here it is, courtesy of BarometerBob.com."

Barometer Bob is an amateur forecaster who maintains a fine Bahamas weather site on the Internet. He used to do the weather every morning, but he's had health problems this winter. Today he's providing the forecast, but Jeff is reading it. It's not good – strong westerly and northerly winds all week. It's blowing like stink already.

"And now we want to know the sea conditions in the Sea of Abaco," says Jeff, "and for that we go to Troy on Great Guana Cay." Troy is inaudible this morning, but Jeff remarks that from what he can make out, the dogs have described it well: "Ruff! Now we'll check the passages." He does a little poll: someone says that

Tilloo Cut sounds passable, but nobody reports on Whale Cay or any of the other four or five passages.

"Well," says Jeff, "as they say in *Blazing Saddles*, 'son, you're on your own.' And now we go to Miss Pattie for any emergency messages." Today Miss Pattie does have an urgent message for a Canadian boat, which she describes in detail. Someone says that the boat is at Snake Cay, in the remote southern district of Abaco. Miss Pattie – Pattie Toler – is married to Barometer Bob. A full-time Abaconian, she is the Net's solid foundation. She organizes the hosts and relays messages from cruisers too far off to be heard by the host, and also provides an emergency email service.

Community news. The Hope Town Sailing Club is holding a race. The library in Treasure Cay is having a yard sale. Mimi Rehor reminds cruisers that A Buck a Book, a book exchange that raises money for the wild horses of Abaco, is open this afternoon. The Net continues with trivia questions, headline news, financial news, and "invitations" from local businesses. Jeff asks for people flying back to the United States or Canada who are willing to carry stamped, flat, unsealed mail for other cruisers, bypassing the Bahamas' torpid mail system.

Open Mike. *Interlude* is looking for a refrigerator repairman. *Muskokie* thanks those who helped when the skipper accidentally deep-sixed his spectacles. *Principessa* wants information about clearing customs in Fort Pierce, Florida.

Jeff invites new arrivals to introduce themselves, which we did the other day. Today nobody answers. Okay, any departing boats who want to say farewell? Jeff hears one, but I can't hear it.

"Okay, it's time to do the weather recap, and then the Abaco Cruisers' Net will be clear."

And that's how you find out what's going on in the Abacos.

The Marsh Harbour Marina is across the harbour from the town proper. If we were going to stay for a while, we needed ground transportation. Fortunately, *Magnus*'s previous owner had left two 1946 Japanese Katakura Porta-Silk bicycles on the boat. The bikes were hinged near the pedal cranks and folded up to the size of a suitcase. Many cruisers carry folding bikes, though very few are as bullet-proof and heavy as the Porta-Silks. Certainly nobody else had a bike that said, "Made in Occupied Japan." These bikes may originally have been designed for Japanese paratroopers. Imagine that: Japanese warriors in full battledress drifting down from the sky, each one clutching a twenty-seven-pound folding Porta-Silk bicycle.

I had stowed the bikes away in the engine room when we left Cape Breton and brought one of them out just once, in the nice flat city of Hollywood, and unfolded it for Marjorie. Marjorie had not been on a bicycle for, well, some time. She went wobbling off in the general direction of the nearest Publix supermarket and quickly came wobbling back.

"It's not straight," she said. "I'm afraid it's going to fold up while I'm riding it." I had not assembled it correctly, and I folded it up again and stowed it away. Now it was time to try the bikes again. I heaved them up on the wharf and unfolded them. They have small wheels, no gears, tall "praying mantis" handlebars, and coaster brakes; to stop the bike, you pedal backward, hard.

We went for a ride.

Small wheels and tall handlebars make the bikes very quick to turn. Overall, they seemed nervous, fidgety, and hard to stop. Marsh Harbour's roads are narrow, and sidewalks occur erratically. True to their British heritage, Bahamians drive on the left – but they drive American-style left-hand drive vehicles, which leave the driver whizzing along the shoulder of the road. Keeping out of their way on a wobbling, twitchy bike was a challenge. Biking uphill, without the help of gears, was another challenge. Stopping the bikes was a third challenge.

We rode around the head of the harbour, picked up some groceries, and headed back. By now our legs were weak, sweat was running down our faces, and our chests were heaving. We felt rotten, which pleased us; that's how you identify good exercise.

Riding by the head of the harbour, we had noticed a big square yellow-and-white castle – a real castle, crenellated battlements and towers, the whole package – overlooking the harbour from a hillside. Oh, yes, people said. Cottman's Castle. He was the Out Islands doctor. Wonderful man. He wrote a book called *Out-Island Doctor*. You should read it.

Evans Cottman spent twenty years as a mild bachelor biology teacher in Indiana, living with his parents and his maiden aunt. But under this bland exterior beat the heart of a thwarted adventurer. In 1939, having researched the warm places that he might explore during his summer vacations, and move to permanently when he retired, he visited the Bahamas. He met Percy Cavill, one-time swimming champion and inventor of the Australian crawl, who was then happily living in absolute poverty as a beachcomber in Andros. He travelled in mail-boats and local sailing skiffs to Long Cay, Crooked Island, and Acklin's Island – still among the more remote parts of the Bahamas – and fell utterly in love with the islands.

"The moon had risen," Cottman writes. "It was just past the full, huge and yellow and slightly bent. Against the moon-touched sky the palm trees seemed etched in ebony. Not a frond stirred. . . . I had been fascinated with the island in the daytime. Now I was spellbound. I walked slowly. It seemed to me I could feel the moonlight like warm water pouring over me, soaking into me, moving with the blood through my veins."

Such things, he thought, "could only happen in a strange and wonderful country. And I had the feeling that if I could manage to see more of the country, even more strange and wonderful things would happen."

They did. On his third summer visit Cottman bought ten acres on Crooked Island, started a homestead, and went to Abaco to have a boat built for himself. There, the forty-something teacher fell in love. The bride was in her late thirties, a Marsh Harbour native, and deaf. Cottman, meanwhile, had learned that the need for doctors in the Out Islands was so severe that the Bahamian government would give an Unlicensed Medical Practitioner's certification to people with a reasonable background in science. Cottman had a masters degree in biochemistry. He applied and was accepted.

With a new family – the Cottmans soon had a daughter – and a new profession, Cottman blossomed in the Bahamian sun. He loved medicine and never stopped learning about it. He dealt with everything from toothache to tuberculosis, from industrial accidents and heart attacks to wife-beating and knife-fights. Travelling on native sloops, he sometimes slept on deck with the pigs and sheep, poking the pig with a safety pin to discourage undue intimacy. He marvelled at the differences between the islands – one cay full of poor people, but clean and smiling; another population surly, dishonest, and living in squalor.

His wife eventually persuaded him to move to Marsh Harbour, where local craftsmen built him a ketch-rigged motor-sailer called *Green Cross*. He learned to sail and single-handed the boat not only around the Abacos, but as far south as Andros, the Exumas, and Long Island, including a memorable passage *inside* Whale Cay in stormy weather.

"Done reach" is the Bahamian expression for "has arrived." Wherever Cottman went, children ran ahead of him, shouting, "De doctah done reach!" He discovered that "communication with my patients was generally easier if I spoke their dialect." So he would "sound" a patient with his stethoscope and ask, "You does plague wid gyahss?" And the patient would reply that, yes indeed, he was bloated with gas. "You does plague wid de runnin'?" The patient might shake his head: no, he didn't have diarrhea. Cottman's last "office" was the second floor of the Methodist church, accessible only by an outside staircase that had been carried away by a hurricane. Cottman built a ladder, rigged a block and tackle above the doorway, and assisted little old ladies up the ladder by tying a rope around them and hauling on the tackle.

What shines out of Cottman's autobiography is his sheer appetite for his new life – his love for his family and for the islands, his endless curiosity, his good humour, his complete acceptance of the Bahamians and the realities of their lives in what was still very much an isolated and impoverished colonial backwater. A second chance at life is not given to many people. But the career of "de doctuh" is a reminder that human beings are full of surprises – and that the person who will most profoundly surprise you may be yourself.

When it comes to phone service, the Abacos are behind. When it comes to the Internet, they're ahead – and the Internet also provides an alternative to the phone.

All the way down the coast, I had been becoming more familiar with wireless Internet services, which are increasingly common in U.S. marinas. Come up to the dock – or even anchor off – and turn on your wireless-enabled laptop. Bingo! You're online. Sometimes there's a sign-up process, and sometimes there's a fee that you can charge to your credit card. You don't have to lug your laptop ashore, or dial up through your cellphone, or hunt around for an Internet café. Often you can simply turn on the computer and log on through someone else's wireless router. For someone like me – who does business on the Internet all the time – wireless is a huge advance.

And once you're on the Internet, you can make phone calls through the laptop, using a service like Dialpad.com or Skype.com. Just put on a headset with a microphone – or use a phone plugged into your computer.

The Abacos have gone a step further. Two companies – Out Islands Internet and Coconut Telegraphs – provide wireless Internet throughout the Hub of Abaco. It's a brilliant solution to the problem of providing broadband Internet service in a sparsely settled archipelago. With the right equipment you can pay $60 or $70 a month and get on the Internet from almost any little cay. You can sail the Hub and surf the Web at the same time. At least in theory.

In practice, there are at least three levels of equipment. We had the basic device, a little card that plugs into the laptop. The next level is a separate device with a small antenna that plugs into a USB port with a cable, which means you can place the antenna anywhere you want. The third level is a wireless "bridge," a much more powerful (and expensive) setup that can be permanently mounted on the boat. I rode over to the town and asked about buying a wireless bridge and omni-directional antenna. Well, no. The equipment was on order and might be in "next week." Would they call me when the equipment arrived? Oh, certainly.

Welcome to Bahamas mañana, the cavalier approach to time, money, and business for which the islands are famous. Needless to say, nobody ever called.

I decided to play the celebrity card. I emailed both services and said I'm a writer, doing columns and a book. I want to do a piece on wireless Internet in Abaco, and would appreciate any help. This brought back a very knowledgable and intelligent response from a young woman named Tara Hingle at O.I.I., who proved to be one of the owners of the business. Tara suggested a USB device, which she had in stock. When I arrived at the O.I.I. office, of course, Tara was away, and the staff knew nothing about the device. I went to a nearby store that did have it – but for $120, about double what it should have cost. I biked on down Don Mackey Boulevard, the dusty main street, to a tiny little store which also had it – for $90.

The Abaco wireless system wasn't perfect; wireless operates on line-of-sight principles, and the quality of the connection would vary from moment to moment depending on what got in the way. I never did manage to link both our two laptops, nor did I ever really master Internet telephony. But we used O.I.I.'s service for the rest of our time in the Abacos, and despite many frustrations, we always contrived to make it work. At its best, it was excellent. At home, I reflected, my only access to the Internet was a slow connection over the telephone. Whatever its shortcomings, wireless in Abaco was better than what I had in rural Nova Scotia.

It was an odd sensation, of course, sitting in the cockpit in shorts, reading emails from Nova Scotia about blizzards and ice pans and frozen pipes. I tried to feel guilty. I failed.

"Good morning, everyone," said a woman's voice on the Cruiser's Net. "This is Mimi at A Buck a Book, reminding you that our book and video exchange is open today from four to six, and that all the proceeds go to support the wild horses of Abaco. We're easy to find . . ."

The wild horses of Abaco?

I found A Buck a Book in a steel shipping container at the end of a scruffy little mall. Behind a chainlink fence, a dozen semi-feral "potcake" dogs barked and scurried and whined. A Bahamian "potcake" is a stew; by analogy, a potcake dog is a genetic stew. A small, slim woman in her sixties, with long blond hair, emerged from the shipping container, wearing a denim shirt and jeans. She hushed the dogs.

"I'm Mimi," she said, shaking my hand firmly. The shipping container was lined with shelves of books and videos. Cruising sailors bring used books to her, and pay a dollar for each book they take away. On a table in the middle of the container was a DVD called *The Wild Horses of Abaco* and a model of a sturdy-looking brown-and-white paint horse. Yes, she said, wild horses lived in the pine forests of Great Abaco Island – unique horses that had survived here for five centuries. She could take us for a tour.

She picked us up at 8:45 at the marina in an old Dodge minivan, filled with tools and gear. As we drove out to the horse

preserve, she talked passionately about the horses and her relation-
ship with them. Marjorie, who is also devoted to horses, quizzed
Mimi intently.

Her name is really Milanne Rehor, but she is known everywhere
as Mimi. She had lived aboard her sailboat in Marsh Harbour for
thirteen years. She had heard faint rumours about wild horses in
Abaco before she first sailed to the Bahamas, and sought them out.
They were trembling on the verge of extinction. She began a one-
woman campaign to save them, riding through the woods on a
motorcycle with a blow-gun, tranquilizing them and injecting them
with vaccines and medications, bringing veterinarians to care for
them, publicizing their uniqueness and their plight.

She was driving us through a flat, featureless woodland of
tall, slender Australian pines with an understory of brush. When
she turned off to a secondary road we saw a few hovels surrounded
by trash, owned, said Mimi, by Haitians. She turned again, into
a faint track through the woods, and stopped at a pool of water.

"I thought you'd like to see a blue hole," she said. "Be careful
of the poisonwood. Do you know how to identify poisonwood?
No? Here's some." The plants looked a bit like laurel, and they
can grow up to twelve or fifteen feet high. Simply brushing against
them can produce a painful rash. Mimi suggested that we remove
our clothes carefully when we got home, and wash them before
wearing them again.

Blue holes are unique to the Bahamas – tidal shafts of freshwater floating over salt water. The tides percolate through the
island's porous bed rock, seeping in and out through the limestone. This blue hole was 270 feet deep, eerie in its stillness, so
clear we could see ledges and protrusions far under the surface.

"I don't like looking into it," Mimi said. "It gives me reverse
vertigo."

We drove on. A few moments later, Mimi waved at a guard
and drove through a small gate. A buzzard flew up ahead of us.
Suddenly Mimi stopped.

"There they are," she said, pointing into the forest.

And there they were indeed – seven small horses, brown and black and dappled, foraging together in a clearing where limes and cherry tomatoes grow wild. They were ripping and chewing the rough, sharp leaves of the palmettos.

"They like palmetto leaves," said Mimi, plunging through the bushes toward the horses. "And bananas. And avocados. I love to see them when they've been eating avocados – they all have these foolish green smiles."

She walked right up to the horses, greeting each by name. Marjorie and I followed cautiously behind. These were wild horses, after all, but they certainly knew Mimi, who took out a rubber curry and began to stroke the nearest horse. The little mare calmly looked around at her, then turned back to the palmetto leaves. Mimi invited us to stroke her too. The horses were utterly unconcerned. Marjorie tried to feed an apple to the little mare, but the horse rejected it. If it had been a banana or an avocado, Mimi said, it would have been gone.

They are small horses, Marjorie noted, about thirteen or fourteen hands, pony-size. And they are genetically unique. Arab horses have half a backbone fewer than other horses; the Abaco horses, Mimi said, have one fewer than an Arab. They had convex Roman noses and wavy manes and tails. Their ears were big enough to make me wonder whether they hadn't had intimate relationships with donkeys, which are not a whole lot smaller.

Mimi calls herself the "curator" of this herd, and the word is well chosen, for these are historic horses. Out on the vicious coral reefs that fringe the Abaco cays lie the bones of at least a dozen Spanish galleons, and the ancestors of these horses swam ashore from those wrecks. They have survived countless forest fires and hurricanes, but twentieth-century logging and farming ravaged their habitat, and new plantings provided them with feed that made them fat and sickly. Nevertheless, the herd numbered about two hundred until the 1960s. Then a young girl tried to ride one, and was killed in the process.

Suddenly the horses were considered dangerous. All but three were hunted down and slaughtered. Fortunately, one of the three survivors was a stallion, and two were mares. The present herd – just twelve individuals – is made up of their descendants.

Mimi has become their self-selected curator simply because she loves them and she cannot bear to see them vanish. There is a certain spiritual purity to her feeling for them. She does not love them for their potential as servants to humans. She does not want to ride or harness them. She just wants them to thrive as one more bright thread in the intricate fabric of life. She has no idea why this mission became the focus of her life. She has no background with horses at all.

"All I really know about horses is what I learned as a little kid, reading *Misty of Chincoteague* and *King of the Wind* and books like that.

"But these horses are so brave, and so tenacious. We had a mare with an injured back leg that eventually buckled sideways. When she was autopsied, it turned out that she had no tendon in that leg, none. Maybe she injured the leg on a thorn, and maybe the thorn had pesticide on it, or something like that – we have no way of knowing. Another simply went off in the woods and died, and the vet refused to do an autopsy, so we don't know what happened there either."

In 2002, after a decade of research, DNA analysis identified the horses as a new strain of the endangered Spanish Barb, directly descended from the horses brought to America by Columbus and the conquistadors, and more remotely descended from the horses of Africa's Barbary Coast. Mimi's horses are designated by the Horse of the Americas Registry as the Abaco Barb – a unique sub-species and possibly the purest herd of Spanish Barbs still in existence. Mimi has persuaded the Bahamian government of their tourism value, and the government has now set aside 3,800 acres of Crown land as a guarded preserve for them.

We stopped to pick wild cherry tomatoes growing on vines in a lemon tree, and while we were picking the horses moved off. We found them again maybe half a mile down the fence and followed them back to their original spot. Marjorie walked near them, and the stallion didn't like it. Bringing up the rear and herding the mares, he watched Marjorie warily and lashed out a hoof at her when she got too close, back at the original pasture.

"That was just a warning," said Marjorie. "And I don't mind. If he'd wanted to kick me, he could have."

Mimi has established a non-profit organization, Arkwild Inc. (www.arkwild.org) to raise funds and generate publicity. A 4-H Club in Salmon, Idaho, pressured Breyer Animal Creations, manufacturers of an extensive line of horse models, into producing an Abaco Barb model. Breyer (www.breyerhorses.com) now sells a model called Capella and donates a portion of the profits.

Can the Abaco Barb survive? With so small a herd, the odds can't be good. On the other hand, not many endangered species have curators like Mimi – and that single fact might just be the salvation of these sturdy, persistent little horses.

The horses' pasture had previously been a 3,700-acre citrus grove, but at the end of 2004, citrus canker was discovered there – a disease that kills citrus trees within two years. The entire farm was quarantined, and the trees were being destroyed. Not far from the horses' preserve, we came upon a man driving a D8 bulldozer, pushing down rows of trees and piling them into heaps for burning. Ripe grapefruit and oranges lay scattered all over the ground.

The closure of the citrus farm had thrown 150 people out of work, mostly Haitians. The Haitian presence is a major issue in the Abacos; hardly a week went by without a story about Haitian refugees and illegal immigrants in *The Abaconian*. The immigration is driven by a kind of osmotic pressure. Haiti is not far away; the Bahamian border is infinitely porous; the Haitians are starving and desperate. And, like immigrants everywhere, the Haitians will do work that the Bahamians reject. If the Americans can't prevent illegal immigration from Mexico, how can the Bahamas possibly control the steady seepage from Haiti?

Bahamians say that the Haitians will soon outnumber the native Bahamians, if they don't already – and the country now includes many native-born Bahamians who are the children of Haitians. The ambiguous status of the Haitians has led them to live as squatters in shanty-towns, and the Bahamian government seems to be making a serious effort to deal with the issue, awarding citizenship to those who qualify and integrating them into the Bahamian community, and deporting those who don't qualify. The underlying concern, of course, is that Haiti's political culture is one of repression and violence – and so the integration of the Haitians (who are clearly not going away) is a matter of real urgency.

Mimi drove into the citrus farm with a bag of rice for a Bahamian friend left without work and without income by the closure of the farm. Only three Bahamian families remained at the farm settlement; most workers had been Haitian, and most had left. The Bahamians and Haitians had lived in separate compounds, and the difference was striking. The Bahamian houses were poor but orderly; the Haitian housing was jumbled and squalid. The dusty laneways were deserted except for a solitary woman who walked by with a stainless-steel bowl balanced perfectly on her head.

This is a remarkable environment for an American woman living alone on a boat, supported only by a tiny inheritance. But nothing fazes Mimi. She told us she had recently been driving with a friend and smelled something funny in the smoke from a yard fire. When she investigated, she found a Haitian burning a live dog. It wasn't his first offence; he'd been caught hanging a dog before.

"I've told you," she told him firmly, "if you've got a problem with a dog, call me. If it needs a new home, I'll find one. Whatever the problem, I'll fix it. But you can't do this."

And with that she went to the police. Wasn't she frightened in such situations?

"Oh, no. I might be more fearful if I were twenty-five or thirty, with a long life ahead of me, but at my age I'm fatalistic. If something happens, it happens, and I've got things set up so that the work with the horses will go on." She laughed. "A Haitian threatened me once, and I went toward him with my fists clenched. I was going to plough him one. Well, this upset everything he understood about women and men. He backed away and backed away, saying, 'Can't do that. Woman can't hit man –' I said, 'Wanna bet?' And eventually he ran off.

"Of course I'm quite vulnerable – I've been thirteen years in the Bahamas on a tourist visa, and I could be told to get out any time. But I know myself very well. Where else could I live on a boat and do this? And if I weren't doing this work here, I'd be doing something like it somewhere else."

Johnny Grape flew in with Charlotte, and the four of us had a riotous reunion – rum, wine, Nassau Royale, and steaks at the Jib Room. In the morning, John took us all to meet his old friend Skeet LaChance in a low brown house across the road, its backside at grade, its front held up on poles, with a sweeping view across the Sea of Abaco to Great Guana Cay. The house stood on the bare black-and-white limestone bedrock. As we were to learn, it had once been surrounded by soil and gardens, but the two hurricanes of 2004 had stripped all that away, along with the sundeck and part of the roof.

A burly, bearded man in his seventies, Skeet had been one of the Bahamas' leading divemasters and still headed a motorcycle gang called The Scurvy Few. Debbie Currie, his winsome blond companion, was much younger. Older man, younger woman – "always a shocking situation," as Marjorie noted. Skeet wore a grey beard and a white umbrella parakeet on his shoulder. Disney was casting *Pirates of the Caribbean II* in the Bahamas just then. It occurred to me that Skeet should have auditioned, but he was recovering from treatment for cancer, and Debbie had just had a hip replacement.

Like Mimi, like others we would meet, Skeet was a deeply individual individual – a refugee from the tamed, regulated, urbanized modern world, a man who needed an environment where the social mesh is loose and wide. In this, too, the Abacos resemble Atlantic Canada, also a favoured destination for the scurvy few.

If Skeet had lived three hundred years earlier, he might well have been a pirate, like most residents of the Bahamas at the time. This is not an insult; the pirates were no more bloodthirsty and violent than the navies of the day, and they were considerably more democratic and egalitarian. Sparsely settled, neglected by European governments, close to the routes of the treasure ships, the Bahamas effectively belonged to the pirates – a thousand or more – who made their headquarters here. They were driven out in 1718 by Governor Woodes Rogers, himself a reformed pirate, and the motto of the Bahamas became *Expulsis Piratis, Restituta Commercia* – roughly, "pirates expelled, commerce restored." But, says one old Abaco hand, piracy and commerce are not entirely different, and the pirates haven't altogether gone away. Abaconians evidently retain a certain sneaking affection for them; Matt Lowe's Cays, just outside Marsh Harbour, and the M/V *Stede Bonnet*, once the local mail-boat, were both named for pirates.

"Wracking," however, really has gone away. Stripping wrecked vessels was once a major Abaconian industry, licensed and regulated by the government. The Abaco barrier reef is more than a hundred miles long, and it lies close to some of the principal shipping lanes of the world. Nobody knows how many ships may have been wrecked on the reefs, but the number must be in the hundreds, perhaps the thousands. In 1856, half the able-bodied men of Abaco held wrecking licences, including a Methodist minister who once spied a wrecked ship from his pulpit. Realizing that his parishioners couldn't see it, he asked them to bow their heads in silent prayer – and then slipped out the door to reach the wreck ahead of everyone else.

The wrecking industry was ended by the British government's decision to erect lighthouses at strategic points in the Bahamas. Still, the bones of those lost ships still lie on the reef – including all twelve galleons of the Spanish treasure fleet wrecked "at Abaco" in 1595. A man like Skeet LaChance probably has a notion of what "at Abaco" might mean. But – writes Dave Gale, a friend of Skeet's and an experienced treasure diver himself – those who think they know probably don't, and those who probably do always lie. Including Dave Gale.

We sailed for Man-O-War Cay in bright sunlight, before a brisk northwesterly breeze, Johnny Grape at the wheel again. Cruising in the Abacos is very different from any other cruising you've done, he remarked. It's only an hour to Man-O-War. You know what I notice about cruisers? They're mostly senior citizens. That's who can afford to go. How do you feel about finding yourself in a community of retired people?

"Cruising Greybeards," I agreed. "Another species, like Automatic Talkers and Maine Bigwhiskers. You ever notice how many cruising skippers down here are grey-haired and bearded? I think they intend to look like pirates, but they generally look like retired professors, which is probably what they are."

"You've thought about this," said John.

I had, and it made me uneasy. When we left, I expected to meet a wide variety of people – nature freaks camp-cruising in dinghies, young families poking south in dowdy old ketches, sleek stockbrokers in fast motor-yachts, drifting hobos in grotty ex-fishboats, students in cramped sloops, evangelists navigating by faith and laden with Bibles. But the ICW was populated by middle America and middle Canada in retirement, chugging south in packs like migrant suburbs. The truly disquieting thought was that I was just another aging bourgeois, diligently pursuing a fake adventure with the odds stacked heavily in my favour. When Marjorie and I married, the idea had been that Marjorie would keep me young – but I worried that instead I was making her old. In her mid-forties, she was about the youngest person on the ICW.

Yet although I was sixty-seven, I wasn't retired. How would a writer retire? And why? I still felt like a young comer with a reputation to make. I had never been in better physical shape. I wanted to see more and learn more. And I enjoy diversity. That's why I didn't like school, boxed into classes where everyone was the same age. In the oddly sedate milieu of cruising, I felt as though the lifestyle around me was older than I was. When Marjorie and I were in marinas and chose to play music in the cockpit, for instance, the music never precipitated a party. With younger people, it might have. Instead, I worried that we might be disturbing the people around us. John nodded.

"I also don't like pointless people," he said. "By that I mean people who have no real ambition, no raison d'être, no life agenda. People who have truly retired and aren't doing anything with their lives. But that isn't just a question of age."

"It's not," I said. "We've met plenty of older people who are absolutely an inspiration."

I told him about the morning that a woman in her seventies knocked on the hull and asked to examine our mainsail stowage system, which she thought could be adapted for her boat. Her name was Annie. When she was divorced in her sixties, she kept the family sailboat, a twenty-eight-footer, and sailed it single-handed to England. There she met Neville, who was rather older than she. Together they built a wooden catamaran called *Peace IV*, which they subsequently sailed twenty thousand miles. It was anchored in the harbour. When she saw me tying a rolling hitch, she showed me how to tie a camel hitch, an improved rolling hitch created by circus people to tether camels. Now that she was back on the western side of the Atlantic, she looked forward to visits from her children, of whom she had "far too many." But she had acquired many of them by "the easy method – just open the door, and they'll come in. You tell the state and their parents that they're with you, and that's it." Old age? Pagh! Old age is what you make it.

"Here's an interesting thing," I told John. "Cruisers here in the Bahamas are not the same as cruisers on the ICW. Everyone here is reasonably competent and self-confident, because the Gulf Stream passage filters out anyone who isn't. And there are practically no big yachts here in the Abacos. The boats are generally forty feet or less."

Later on, a very experienced sailor asked me what I thought that cruisers had in common. I could think of lots of things – a sense of adventure and some capacity to manage money, for instance. Yes, he said, but there's something more important: they're all achievers. They may be labourers or lawyers, but they're *good* labourers or lawyers. And they generally have "a very low greed quotient." That's true – and, generally speaking, cruising people refuse to be dominated by their own fears. They aren't immune to fear, but they don't let it rule their lives.

Man-O-War hove up ahead. Its harbour is like a very short T, with coves running both ways from its exceedingly narrow entrance. We turned to port and crept up the narrow waterway, swerving to stay clear of a ramp-bowed workboat that looked like a landing craft. Little docks ran back into the mangroves, and the harbour was crammed with boats.

Physically, Man-O-War village is much like New Plymouth, though smaller – narrow concrete streets, small and tidy pastel houses, well-tended mini-gardens. Cars are forbidden on Man-O-War; people get around on golf carts. Two streets run parallel to the harbour shore, crossed by eight streets that run right across the cay to the Atlantic beaches. An elderly woman motored up to us on a golf cart and offered us fresh-baked bread. The waterfront confirms what the guidebooks say: this is probably the most marine-oriented community in the Abacos, with two excellent boatyards, a fine hardware store, a marine railway, canvas shops, a sail loft, a ferry dock. The small passenger ferries that criss-cross the Hub of Abaco belong to Albury Ferries, based in Man-O-War. All of them are white fishing-style boats named "Donnie" – *Donnie V*, *Donnie III*, *Donnie VII* – so they're universally known as "the Donnie-boats."

Man-O-War, says historian Steve Dodge, is "a more disciplined community than most." It was founded, Dodge notes, by Benjamin Albury, a boy from Harbour Island, near Eleuthera, and Eleanor Archer, a girl from Marsh Harbour. In 1977, 230 of the 235 residents were descended from "Pappy Ben" and "Mammy Nellie." It is a seriously Christian community. No alcohol has ever been sold on the cay, and when community leaders decided that too many young people were smoking, local stores were persuaded to stop selling tobacco altogether. Man-O-War has traditionally been an all-white community, with a black labour force that still migrates from Marsh Harbour by Donnie-boat in the morning and back in the evening. When non-residents began buying properties here, the town barred them from the town proper, but allowed them elsewhere on the cay – "to insulate the settlement from foreign influence," says Dodge.

In the twentieth century, Man-O-War became famous as the boatbuilding centre not only of the Abacos, but of the Bahamas. This little island launched a stream of vessels – fishing smacks, sponge schooners, Abaco dinghies – built from such local woods as horseflesh, corkwood, madeira, and pine. The first book I bought on the Bahamas, back in 1973, has beautiful black-and-white photos of wooden vessels being built on the beaches of Man-O-War Cay. The days of wooden boatbuilding are gone, but the Alburys of Man-O-War still produce husky, seaworthy outboard-powered fibreglass skiffs. The technological innovation that transformed the Abacos, Steve Dodge remarks, was not television or the Internet, but the outboard motor.

The proudest memorial of the old ways is the graceful seventy-foot schooner *William H. Albury*, built in 1963 under the supervision of William H. Albury himself – "Uncle Will," a master boatbuilder who constructed more than three hundred vessels of all sizes. The ship named for him, now based in Marsh Harbour, represented the Bahamas in the U.S. Bicentennial Parade of Sail in New York in 1976 – an occasion freighted with irony, since it was the triumphant revolutionaries of 1776 who drove people like the Alburys out to the Bahamas in the first place.

A beautiful, stubborn place. After John and Charlotte had left, I talked with Donnie Schmeisser about Man-O-War. With its tidy, tightly linked community, its superb boatbuilding, and its suspicion of outsiders, could Man-O-War be called the Lunenburg of the Abacos? Yes! said Donnie. Yes, that's exactly what it is.

Returning to Marsh Harbour one day, I noticed that the steering seemed queer. Turning the wheel hard over didn't make *Magnus* turn very much. When she did turn, I had to put the wheel hard over the other way to make her straighten out again.

Browntip was cleaning bottoms that day – that's Browntip the musician, virtuoso of the musical saw, master of the revels at the marina's weekly steak and ribs nights. I don't know his real name. A patrician-looking, cheerful man, he's as comfortable in the water as a blacktip shark – but he's a brown man, so he's universally known as Browntip. His day job is cleaning boat bottoms. He arrives in his battered blue runabout, suits up, starts up an air compressor, and jumps in the water, tethered to the compressor with a long yellow hose.

I hired him. And while you're down there, I said, check out the rudder. He did. Nothing wrong. I checked the steering system inside the boat, testing every component from the wheel to the rudder head. All fine.

A temporary glitch of some kind? Alas, no. When we left the marina again, the boat would hardly steer at all. Back in the berth, I put on my own mask and snorkel, and dove down to take a look. All okay. Now Marjorie held the wheel while I tried to move the rudder. Aha! The rudder moved about twenty degrees without moving the wheel. The only steering component I couldn't see was the section of the rudder stock, which passed through the hull inside a tube. The stock had to be broken inside the tube.

I cursed feelingly. The boat would probably have to be hauled, and the nearest boatyard was the Marsh Harbour Boatyard, a dozen sea miles away. We would need a tow, and we could expect to spend several days living aboard the boat high and dry in a hot, dusty yard. When could the work be done? How long would it take?

"Look, this is the Bahamas," said George, whose boat was moored near ours. "Things run on island time. Don't expect anyone to deal with your troubles any time soon." He turned to Jason, the Bahamian dockmaster.

"Am I right?"

Jason laughed and nodded. Another neighbour shook his head. "I bet you're looking at four thousand dollars."

Not this kid, I thought grimly. Think like a rustic engineer from Cape Breton. Can't we stand the boat ashore and do the work between the tides? No? Okay, I bet we can do it in the water. We'll get a diver to remove the rudder, take the broken part to the boatyard for repair, and reinstall it the same way.

On Tuesday, I talked the problem over with CJ's Welding and called the redoubtable Browntip. *Magnus*'s rudder post is made in two pieces, bolted together just above the rudder. On Wednesday, Browntip went down with wrenches and Vise-grips. First he removed the rudder, then I dropped the stock down to him. And there was the problem: a corroded weld, hidden inside the rudder tube.

Hopping in a taxi, I took the stock to CJ's Welding and the rudder to the boatyard. The machine shop made a new and improved stock, and the boatyard put a hole in the trailing edge of the rudder. If this problem ever arose again, I could tie a rope through the hole in the rudder and steer with the rope. A power outage delayed the work until Friday afternoon. That evening I called Browntip. Saturday morning at eight, he was making bubbles under the stern. By nine he had the rudder back on. Four days, start to finish.

"You'll remember the Browntip!" laughed Browntip as he waved and put his runabout in gear.

"Wow," said George. "What did it cost you?"

"Four hundred and change," I said. "If this is island time, it's okay with me."

Much of what we had heard about the difficulties of cruising the Bahamas simply isn't true – at least in the Abacos. Water was said to be scarce and expensive. It's true that the islands rely on rainwater and on desalinized seawater, and yes, it can cost twenty-five cents a gallon. If our fifty-gallon tank is empty, it might cost $12.50 to fill it. If we use it carefully, it lasts a week. How bad is that?

Prices in the Bahamas were said to be very high, because everything is imported and taxed. And yes, manufactured goods and processed foods are pricey. But staples like rice, potatoes, and meat don't cost much more than they do in Florida – and anything imported from the British Isles, like British biscuits or Irish butter, is cheap. Marinas in Abaco charge half what they charge in Florida. People complain about the cost of a one-year cruising permit – $150 for boats under thirty-five feet, $300 for larger ones. Your boat may be worth anything from $50,000 to a couple of million – and you're paying less than a dollar a day to cruise in Paradise. I think it's a bargain.

I was a little envious of Browntip. I wanted to go diving.

"I don't like putting my face in the water," said Marjorie, wrinkling her nose. "I can't go scuba diving, my ears won't take it. And I don't like the idea of a fish brushing up against me. Eeew!"

"Twinkletoes," I said, "if you only see what's on top of the water here, you won't have seen the Bahamas. Trust me. It's fantastic."

I once had a scuba certificate, but it had long since elapsed. I wanted to get it back, but in the meantime I had been snorkelling – lying face-down in the warm salt water, breathing through a snorkel, drifting with the wind and the current. Diving is the closest any of us will ever get to flying, and the view is amazing.

I had no idea what I was seeing. Marjorie and I had attended a seminar on sport fishing, not because we had any real intention of fishing – though many cruisers do catch fish for the table, and seem to do it easily – but because we were curious to know about the local fish and about spear-fishing. The instructor talked about equipment I'd never seen and fish I didn't know: marlin, grouper, snapper, kingfish, bonefish, dolphin, grunt, jack. "When an eighty-pound wahoo takes your line, you'll know it," he said. Wahoo?

The fish mainly live on the reefs and around "structure" – coral heads, rocks, wrecks, anything that provides food and shelter. But I had found that all kinds of sealife showed up when I simply went drifting off the beach. And the Abaco reefs are everywhere – between the cays and the open sea, and scattered within the protected Sea of Abaco itself.

We bought Marjorie a mask and some fins. She took them into a swimming pool, tried swimming with the fins, and practised putting her face in the water and breathing through the snorkel. Her breathing sounded "funny, as though I'm listening to someone else."

When we went to the beach, she lay down in knee-deep water and was delighted with the view of the bottom.

"Come on," I said. "Let's go out to the reef."

"I'm not a very strong swimmer."

"It's only thirty yards," I said, "and it's almost impossible to sink in this water anyway."

We snorkelled out to the reef, Marjorie still quite surprised to realize that she didn't have to thrash around to stay afloat, that she could just hang on the surface, breathing easily through her snorkel. We saw a few scattered fish as we came over the sandy bottom – but the reef itself was another world. A dozen varieties of fish nosed around great burgundy balls of weed-covered rock and big brown nodules of sponge. A starfish larger than any we'd ever seen before lay on the bottom.

And the fish came in every size, from pinsized transparent minnows to fat, deep fellows a foot or more in length. Some were alone, and some in schools that wheeled and dove and scattered. Their colours were astonishing – deep reds, electric blues, lemon yellow, drab grey and brown, glossy silver and leaf green. Back on the shore we took our little plasticized field guide and tried to decide what we'd seen. We were pretty sure of stoplight parrotfish, yellowhead wrasse, bluehead wrasse, grey snapper, and yellow jack. We thought we might have seen tiger grouper, yellowtail snapper, blue tang, and yellow goatfish. Yellow goatfish?

"So, you liked it?" I said.

"Unbelievable. One of the most beautiful things I've ever seen," said Marjorie. "You know, I realized when I was watching them that the fish don't want to brush against me any more than I want to brush against them.

"That wasn't easy for me. I found it really scary being over my head and so far from the shore for so long. But I went ahead and did it anyway. And I am so proud of myself."

"I'm proud of you too," I said.

"Life is too short to be cowardly," said Marjorie.

Our Cape Breton friends Jim and Carol Organ had been one day ahead of us in Jonesport, but they had leaped down the coast in long offshore hops, reaching Nassau in time to fly home for Christmas. While we had been tiptoeing our way down the coast and over to the Abacos, they had plunged hundreds of miles farther south, down to the Turks and Caicos Islands, close to Haiti and Cuba. We had sought their advice before we left. Now they were homeward bound through the Abacos, and at last we could tie up together and compare notes over dinner. Jim is a Newfoundlander, and aboard their boat one evening, Carol served a grand Newfoundland-style dinner of salt cod, potatoes, pickled beets, green peas, and "scruncheons" – scraps of fatback pork rendered into something resembling crispy chunks of bacon.

"Donnie," said Jim, "I figured out the Bahamians this trip. Didn't know what to make of 'em at first, but I finally figured it out – they're black Newfoundlanders. They're just exactly like us, Donnie! Shy when you first meet 'em, but once they get to know you, you're their friends for life. Wonderful people. Do anything for you. They're just Newfoundlanders, only they're black.

"So, did you enjoy the trip down?"

We did, I said, but we found ourselves terribly lonely for a while.

"That's why we came south in long jumps," said Carol. "We wanted to stay in a few places long enough to know people. But you know what else we did? Whenever we came into a new anchorage, we'd pick out a boat that looked interesting. Then we'd row over and introduce ourselves and invite them over to our boat."

"If you do that, you make a lot of friends pretty fast," Jim nodded. "Almost every time we anchor now, there's someone we know."

Marjorie and I looked at each other and nodded. That would have been a smart idea.

"The ICW is really exhausting though, isn't it?" said Carol. "And another thing we found, it's hard living so close together for months and months, with no chance to get away from each other. You have a little spat, and you can't go somewhere else in the house to get away and cool down."

"At home I'd go to my workshop," Jim nodded. "But you don't have a workshop on a thirty-two-foot boat. This has been a really cold winter too. We shouldn't have cold fronts coming through one after another the way they are, not this late in the season, but they're still coming. The winds should be mostly easterly, and not much over fifteen knots, but we're still getting real northers every few days."

"Listen!" said Carol. We fell silent. All over the harbour we could hear the sound of people blowing blasts on conch shells to honour the sunset, as they did every night at dusk.

"Nice to be here," grinned Jim.

"Magnus, Magnus, Magnus," crackled the VHF. "This is *Isle of Somewhere,* over."

Lane and Betty Befus had heard that *Magnus* done reach. They were the couple who had arranged the Hope Town reading of cruising literature the night of our arrival in Marsh Harbour. Lane had read my story, "Going to Hell for a Pastime," which they had clipped from *Canadian Yachting* in 1982. Apparently they often read it aloud for pleasure – both to each other and to groups in cruising circles. They wanted to arrange another reading – but this time they wanted me to read the story, and anything else like it. And they wanted to hold the reading in Hope Town, on Elbow Cay.

And so, on a glorious sunny afternoon, *Magnus* slipped out of Marsh Harbour and sailed for Hope Town. The Sea of Abaco was stunning that day – the water a brilliant bright blue-green over the white sandy bottom, low islands all around, the massive lighthouse of Hope Town poking above the horizon like a tall red-and-white layer cake. This is the Bahamas' most famous lighthouse, one of only three in the world still illuminated by kerosene. The boat moved along as though suspended in liquid glass, the bottom clearly visible below. We sailed up to the Parrot Cays, the home of Dave Gale, a New York–born refugee from civilization whose *Ready About* is a delightful account of his life in the Abacos. *Magnus* turned for the narrow entrance into Hope Town Harbour, twisting to port under the looming bulk of the lighthouse, and steering as if to head up a narrow concrete street. We passed a tiny island with a single house on it, turned to starboard, and entered Hope Town.

I instantly fell in love.

Funky, salty, picturesque, and lively, Hope Town crowds the eastern shore of a totally protected harbour, a circle of water with three creeks running off it like spokes vanishing into the mangroves. Pastel houses, micro-streets, a dozen spindly wharves and one big one. Boats coming and going all around the harbour, and a crowd of anchored cruising vessels in the middle. On the western shore, three or four marinas clustered under the lighthouse, facing the town.

Lane Befus had booked us a slip in the Hope Town Marina at Club Soleil. Club Soleil is a small old resort, a few shocking pink buildings with half-a-dozen rooms and eighteen marina slips. The proprietor, Rudy Malone, took our lines, tying the fastest bowline I ever saw. He was a thin, easygoing angular man with a ready smile and a wry sense of humour. The marina hadn't fully recovered from the summer's hurricanes. It still didn't have functioning showers, for instance. The whole place was just ticking over – the spacious restaurant closed, the rooms mostly vacant – because Rudy had sold it to a Florida developer who intended to build condos on the site.

But it was lovely. Rudy was serious about his fishing – he caught a huge fifty-five-pound grouper while we were there – and totally relaxed about his business. Could we use the idle restaurant for a reading? Sure. For a music session? Sure. Were we going to town to pick up a bunch of people? "Use one of my skiffs."

The second time I approached Rudy, he said, "Oh, you'll have to talk to Uncle Rudy about that." He had morphed into Buddy Malone, a nephew who lives on a project sailboat in the marina and sometimes manages the place in Rudy's absence. I was embarrassed at my error, but Buddy just laughed. The whole Malone family looks the same, he said.

I noticed another project boat on the dock, a hurricane-wrecked Columbia 30 with no sails, its portholes covered with clear plastic and duct tape. It had been patched together as living quarters for an Italian artist named Rita and a potcake dog named Sophie. Between Rita's boat and ours was a tiny sloop crammed with two young couples intent on perfecting their guitar licks. Down the wharf was a short boat owned by a short woman with a short dog: a twenty-foot Flicka, crewed by Nancy Bell and her corgi.

Across the wharf an immense Nova Scotia flag billowed from the rigging of a gorgeous green ketch. *Te Amor* belonged to Cam and Jan Albright, who operate a Nova Scotia campground in the summer and sail the Abacos in the winter. Cam looked like an old hippie in a bright figured shirt and a Russian hat, and Jan was a robust blonde with corn-rowed hair who boasted of being the only woman she knows who both dives for conch and also makes a "famous" conch stew. On the other side of us was a tiny, tidy twenty-four-foot outboard-powered trawler crewed by two enormous dogs, a Bernese mountain dog and a Newfoundlander. The dogs' staff consisted of Frank and Cathy Hearn, an early retired couple from Toronto who heaved and hauled the dogs ashore (or into their inflatable dinghy) by means of a custom-built gangplank.

The fleet also included two cruising tugboats: *Bluejacket*, from Rhode Island, owned by Bill and Suzie Merrill, whom we knew from Marsh Harbour, and *Isle of Somewhere*. Lane Befus had been a photographer, and Betty an English teacher. Before they went cruising, they had driven the Pan-American Highway and made a travel film about it. They were cruising with Buddy, a ten-year-old husky-terrier cross – a *what*? – whom they had inherited from a recently deceased friend. Buddy was not a sea dog. He had fallen in the water fourteen times. But he had quickly learned that urination in the cockpit would be rewarded by a dog biscuit. Now he went out constantly to do "pee squirts," said Lane, garnering a bikkie every time.

My kind of people. My kind of place.

The reading attracted a larger crowd than an average reading in a Canadian library – thirty or forty people in the darkened interior of Rudy's cavernous dockside restaurant. Rita brought up some catalogues and samples of her work – powerful portraits of some of the strong women in her life. "Going to Hell for a Pastime"[9] is a fictional account of a disastrous week of cruising in Cape Breton. It takes its title from Samuel Johnson's remark that "the man who would go to sea for pleasure would go to hell for a pastime." Sailors – who have a wide experience of maritime mishaps – always roar with laughter at the narrator's account of the embarrassments and discomforts he and his wife experience as guests on his brother's sailboat. The Hope Town crowd loved it.

Rudy's prices were reasonable, so we settled into the marina for some days, trucking back and forth across the harbour in the dinghy. Hope Town itself is as charming a village as I have ever seen. It lies on a thin isthmus, and consists of two narrow streets with interconnecting lanes. Along the lanes stand a pastiche of little pastel-painted houses, tightly crowded together, none more than thirty feet high. Motor vehicles are barred from the town proper. Along the shore are gift shops, a dive shop, an administrative centre with a mini-jail, small grocery stores, a fish market, a bicycle shop, a lodge. The fine little museum is named for Wyannie Malone, Rudy's ancestor, a widow from South Carolina who was prominent among the town's Loyalist founders. Behind

9 "Going to Hell for a Pastime" is posted at www.silverdonaldcameron.ca.

the two streets rises a line of sand dunes. Beyond the dunes is a magnificent ocean beach, two miles of pink coral sand with a snorkelling reef just offshore.

We walked the narrow streets, ate conch fritters and cracked conch in the shoreside restaurants, bought what are alleged to be the best key lime pies in the world at the famous Vernon's Grocery and Bakery. Vernon's last name is Malone; he is Rudy's brother. *Hours of Operation*, says a hand-lettered sign on the door, *Open when we're here . . . Closed when we're not!* We trudged over the dunes and down to the long pink beach. The azure surf was warm and flecked with fine sand. We capered in the surf and swam in the warm salt water while the Wonder Whippet scooted in and out of the swash like a youngster. The azure sea shaded into deeper blue as it stretched out toward the horizon. Over there somewhere lay Africa.

We lay on the beach and read. Only one other couple was enjoying the two miles of beach. They had spent many hours there, and they were brown as teak. They came from Toronto. Canadians are a living joke in Florida and the Bahamas. In January and February, residents shiver in sweatshirts and toques. Others think the water is warm and the weather delightful. They are the first in shorts, the first into the pool. They are the Canadians.

We met Lane and Betty Befus at the town dock.

"What do you think of Hope Town?" Lane asked.

"Fabulous," I said. "Absolutely fabulous."

Lane lowered his voice to a near-whisper.

"I could live here," he said.

"So could I," I replied.

We also spent happy days just hanging around the marina, reading and writing and visiting. Club Soleil had a pool that was usually deserted, a fine place to read and cool off. Marjorie came back from the pool one day suffused with wonder.

"I went up there to read, but I didn't read at all," she said. "I just lay back in a lounge chair and listened. The air was just alive with birdsongs – all kinds of them, different coos and trills and warbles. I couldn't see many of the birds, but what I did see were those tiny Cuban emerald hummingbirds, you know? They hang in the air, and then you blink and they're gone. And then there were three or four Man-O-War birds – did you see them?"

"I did." Four or five of them had been circling high above the marina, gliding almost motionless through the upper air. The Man-O-War birds are officially called Magnificent Frigate Birds, and they truly are magnificent, with their raked and angled eight-foot wings and their long forked tails.

We caught close views of the emerald hummingbirds on the paths and roadways that led up into the bush behind the marina, where we often walked over the hill to look out on the Sea of Abaco. We led the BFD around through a boat-storage yard to another marina at the base of the great lighthouse. The lighthouse is not locked – nothing in the Abacos seems to be locked; as in Cape Breton, the crime rate is zero – so we went in and climbed the five hundred steps that spiral up inside the lighthouse. The view was worth the climb – the whole Hub of Abaco on one side, with Hope Town and the Atlantic spread out on the other side. Looking down, we saw the buildings and wharves of the marina, and a little blue boat that had come all the way from Nova Scotia.

We were reminded that no place is immune to misery and sorrow one night when an inflatable launch with a flashing red light tied up beside Rudy's restaurant, with a group of sombre-looking men gathered around it. Among the men were Rudy and Buddy, who are both active in the volunteer Bahamas Air Sea Rescue Association. They had been out to look for a man who had been heard shrieking for help. Alas, they found him too late; the man had drowned. He had been drinking all day, and was thought to have fallen overboard.

Our neighbours, Greg Silver and Denise Saulnier, flew down from Cape Breton. They had rented a house at the south end of Elbow Cay, a few miles from Hope Town.

"Look at you two!" said Denise. "You look wonderful – fit and tanned, and you've lost weight – and Leo, you look wonderful too."

"You both look ten years younger," said Greg.

The voyage had changed us. Only now did I realize that I had, in a sense, sailed away from old age and gained a new sense of freedom. At home I had been haunted by the perception that my life was winding down – but I now felt that I'd simply entered another phase of it. Marjorie and I had been discussing all kinds of new ventures – selling our home and building a new one, starting another business, even building a new boat. *I may not do any of these things,* I had written in my journal, *but for whatever reason, I'm feeling far more free. I feel as though I should begin these things if I'm inclined – and if they aren't finished on my death, so what? But the odds are I'll live another 20 years, and that's plenty of time to do these things and enjoy them. Another parallel with Cape Breton: both places seem to free people from the arbitrary constraints of age.*

Greg and Denise rented a golf cart, and the four of us – with Leo – prowled the length of the island. One memorable evening we went for dinner at the Hope Town Harbour Lodge. We started with a shot of Nassau Royale. Denise's eyes grew wide.

"This stuff is lethal," she said. "This is much, much too good. It should be called 'Grandma's Ruin.'"

We were served by a breathtakingly beautiful young Bahamian waitress – almond eyes, chocolate skin, ice-white teeth. She looked like an African princess. Conch fritters, snapper, a small filet mignon. Afterward we wandered into the lounge. Should we have another Nassau Royale? Wellll – perhaps just one. A man from Virginia was playing an electric piano – lovely old standards, Johnny Mercer and Hoagy Carmichael, slow-dancin' music from my youth. I thought it was the best-sounding electric piano I had ever heard, and told him so. Yes, he said, it was a great piano, with properly weighted keys and a foot pedal. It was just like playing an acoustic piano, but it was always in tune. Would I like to test-drive it?

I was just sozzled enough to do it. I sat down and belted out some of my old fraternity-house boogie-woogie. The piano was just as nice as he said it was – a Yamaha P80, with a full eighty-eight keys. It occurred to me that I could possibly store a keyboard like that aboard *Magnus* and not be restricted to the guitar, an instrument I do not play even tolerably well. Denise took a turn at the keyboard, and then I played a few more of the old slow numbers – "Don't Blame Me," "I'm in the Mood for Love," "I Only Have Eyes for You." Denise and Greg are superior ballroom dancers, and they were soon circling around the floor. Others followed their example, and soon the little dance floor was filled.

I am playing the piano in a bar in the Bahamas, I thought. How did this happen?

The Sea of Abaco ends at Little Harbour, where the cays converge with the mainland of Great Abaco Island. Turn east here and you can sail out between the reefs and cays into the open Atlantic. Great Abaco runs south for another thirty-five miles toward Harbour Island and Eleuthera, but without any harbours or outlying cays, and with only one tiny settlement, the fishing hamlet of Cherokee Sound.

Little Harbour itself is no metropolis even now, and it was essentially uninhabited when the schooner *Langosta* sailed into its compact, circular anchorage and moored here in 1951. The schooner belonged to Randolph Johnston, a sculptor and art professor, and his wife, Margot, a gifted ceramicist. With them were their three young sons. The Johnstons were prototypical dropouts, sickened by the slaughter of the Second World War and appalled by the nuclear recklessness of the Cold War. Growing up in Toronto, Randolph Johnston had been inspired by *Robinson Crusoe* and *Swiss Family Robinson*. Having learned that the Bahamas still offered free land to homesteaders, the Johnstons cruised the islands for a year, looking for their own desert island. They found it in Little Harbour.

They lived four years on the schooner, and one year in a bat-infested, mosquito-whining cave. Over a decade, they built a home and a foundry, and resumed their art. Eventually, Randolph Johnston produced lost-wax bronze sculptures that won him a world reputation. When the schooner eventually rotted away, his youngest son, Pete, converted the wheelhouse into a little pub on the beach. The wheelhouse is long gone, but Pete's Pub still prospers.

On our eighth wedding anniversary, Marjorie and I set out from Hope Town toward Little Harbour with Greg and Denise. Our course snaked through reefs and sandbanks. A long line of largely deserted cays lay to the east, and the wild low mangrove shoreline of Great Abaco lay to the west. The route took us through the Pelican Cays Land and Sea Park, one of the finest snorkelling areas in the Abacos, down past the ruins of Wilson City, once the site of a major sawmill operation, and past the Bight of Old Robinson, a wide, shallow bay pocked with blue holes.

At low tide the entrance to Little Harbour between North Beach and the blackened limestone bluffs of Tom Curry's Point provides only three and a half feet of water. We eased across the bar and found ourselves in a circular cove of blue-green water containing fifteen or twenty moored boats. Some were familiar from other ports and anchorages: *Merganser, Xanadu, Easy Time*. To the west, high black bluffs were pierced by deep, mysterious sea-caves. Three hurricane-wrecked sailboats lay strewn along the high tide mark. To the south were sandy beaches and a few summer homes. And to the east, standing on the sandy neck that separates the harbour from the open sea, was Pete's Pub, with its adjoining art gallery, foundry, and other buildings. A deck with a wide flight of wooden steps led down to the water. A dozen dinghies were tied to the steps.

We picked up a mooring and dinghied ashore. The early afternoon sun was hot, and we went for a swim at North Beach, walking past the gallery and the foundry. The gallery includes works by other artists, but it is dominated by the Johnston bronzes. Here is the infinitely wise and experienced face of St. Peter, from *St. Peter: Fisher of Men*, a work in the collection of the Vatican. An undersea scene cast in bronze supports the glass top of a coffee table – waving seaweeds, sponges, elkhorn coral, a big winged ray suspended in the air, supported just at the tip of the tail: bronze scuba under glass.

Randolph Johnston's work embodies a vision by turns stark and sensual and tortured. In *The Kiss*, two lovers twine about one another like vines, young and sleek and full of potency. *The Old Woman Who Never Dies* is like a ballerina, one graceful hand flung skyward to touch a bird. But *Quiet Desperation* shows both the bland mask of a man in midlife – and also the anguished and distorted visage concealed behind the mask. And I will never forget the frightening sculpture of *Death and Everyman*, a terrified, well-muscled man being pursued by a fleet-footed spectral figure with its advancing foot touching a human skull.

Three intricate bronzes portray scenes from Hemingway's *The Old Man and the Sea*. These are the work not of Randolph, but of Pete, who is also a jeweller and a goldsmith, and whose own sons are also sculptors. In his journal, Randolph described Pete as "the rebel's rebel, the individualist's individual, the implacable foe of regimentation in any form." His work contains a lovely quality of freedom and gaiety that seems entirely his own.

The bronzes were – and are – cast in the foundry next door. Among the cactus and palms in the scruffy subtropical garden outside are a handful of enormous bronzes – a vast turtle, a dolphin, an immense ray. The foundry itself is a rambling, shady building open to the air. A high roof, steel beams, heavy posts, open doors, workbenches, many works in various stages of development – "it's a shop, a wonderful shop," I told Greg, and he grinned. He shares my love for workshops.

Lost-wax bronze is an intricate and risky technique that has been used by artists for at least five thousand years, and Richard Appaldo, Randolph Johnston's last student, gave us a tour of the process. The artist carves an original in any convenient material – wood, clay, plasticine, whatever – and then coats the original in ceramic, creating a hollow mould to be filled with molten bronze. The result is an exact replica of the original carving – but cast in bronze, which essentially lasts forever.

Richard arrived in Little Harbour on his own sailboat, more than twenty years ago. He has that remarkable French knack of seeming young and lean and ardent even though the arithmetic says he must be well and truly into middle life. But he may just be getting started. Age "is surely relative," Randolph Johnston wrote as he entered his seventies. A powerful, fit man, he then looked a bit like Sean Connery, with his bushy head of receding white hair, white beard, and dark eyebrows and moustache. "I know how old I am. But I do not feel old. I still work long hours and enjoy every minute of it."

I hated to leave the Johnstons' foundry. It made me home-sick for my boat shop, far away in Nova Scotia. If I had visited this workshop in my youth, if I had been infected with the passion and discipline of the Johnstons, I might well have been moved to spend my life in such a shop, pursuing an art that blended the physical and the aesthetic. But that will be another lifetime.

It was time for a sundowner. Formally dressed in swimsuits, we repaired to the pub, greeted once more by Donnie and Marilyn Schmeisser. Our quartet found places around the triangular bar – the bow of a boat, if one looked more closely. The bar was shel-tered by a shingled roof mounted on posts – a folk-art installation in itself, festooned with decorations and mementoes. No walls. Coconut palms growing up through the tops of picnic tables standing in the sand. Graffiti everywhere, chiefly the names and dates of visiting boats. Flags, T-shirts, and bras stapled to the rafters, contributed by long-departed sailors. A traffic light: red, green, yellow. Street signs, kegs, driftwood, nets, licence plates, fishing floats, an ancient bronze cannon, anything to add character.

We ordered drinks – Kalik beer, Bahama Mama, Goombay Smash. Leo rooted for grubs in the sand. People sat around the carved bartop, drinking and chatting. Two couples reclined in lawn chairs facing the bar. I thought, I have wandered into a story by Somerset Maugham.

Our little party fell to reminiscing. Eight years earlier, Greg had flown from Nova Scotia to Vancouver and played the fiddle at our wedding party. Since then we had been neighbours in Cape Breton, and now Greg and Denise were with us again in the hot southern sun.

"Cape Breton!" cried a grey-haired man in a lawn chair. "Did you say Cape Breton?"

"I know you!" cried Greg. "You were in Cape Breton –"

"– last July," said the man. "You and I played together at the marina in St. Peter's."

He was Bob Ahlers, a fiddler from Albany, New York. His wife, Carol Moseley, plays guitar and flute. They sail a MacGregor 26 trailer-sailer called *Time Enough*. The previous summer they had towed their boat to Nova Scotia, sailed the Bras d'Or Lakes, and played in a Cape Breton jam session with Greg. Now they were cruising the Bahamas with Sam and Arlene Wykoff, a New Jersey couple on another MacGregor called *Puff Stuff*. After launching in Key Largo, Florida, the two boats had sailed the Exumas and Eleuthera, and were returning to Florida via the Abacos.

"We were going to sail on today," said Bob cheerfully, "but we got rummed-in."

"Got your fiddle aboard?" Greg asked.

"Sure!" said Bob. "You?"

"You bet. And Marjorie's got her banjo and guitar. Want to play a few tunes?"

"Absolutely!"

The musicians went for their instruments – three fiddles, two guitars, a flute, and a banjo. We ordered conch fritters, followed by lemon-pepper hog snapper and grilled mango grouper, with buttered garlic bread on beds of salad greens with a tangy vinaigrette. Every Saturday during the summer months, the pub roasts a whole wild boar, but the season was too early for that.

The food cooked. So did the musicians, switching from Appalachian tunes and Cajun melodies to folksongs, Irish airs, Cape Breton jigs. The fiddles spoke together like old friends. Guitar chords coloured the air. Carol switched from guitar to flute, Denise from fiddle to guitar, Marjorie from guitar to banjo.

"They're awfully good," a woman from England whispered to me. "Have all of you been travelling and playing together for long?"

"No," I said. "The fiddlers have only played together once before in their lives."

The food arrived: sharp, sweet, delicious. A stocky man appeared, with a greying moustache and a gold pendant. As the tunes resumed, he beamed. The music, he said, was "wonderful. Wonderful! This is what the place is for! Drinks all round!" He was Pete Johnston, and at his command young servers circulated with trays of champagne.

Eight years before, Greg had played Celtic tunes for our wedding, and now the ensemble was playing them again. There is a unique poignancy in Celtic music – sweetness and an almost manic joy coupled with an underlying sadness. The joy of life and the sorrow of mortality, as inextricably combined as vines woven through a fig tree. Music is of the moment and in the moment, and it flies as fast as the moments themselves, standing out against eternal time as brilliantly as the tracery of lightning against a storm-blackened sky. A marriage is also composed of flying moments, and anniversaries are poignant as well as joyful. Happiness celebrated, memories cherished, accomplishments recognized. But the moments behind us are gone, and the moments ahead remain mysterious.

In truth there is really only one moment: this one. Marjorie and I had shared eight years of loving, laughing moments. As the music floated out into the warm soft night, we were using this splendid moment richly and fiercely and joyfully. A better anniversary would be hard to imagine.

The music was still ringing in our ears as we crashed into our berths and fell asleep instantly. As the boat slowly swung on its mooring in the middle of the night, however, a brilliant shaft of moonlight moved over my face and woke me. I slipped out of our berth and climbed on deck. The boats lay on the water like sculptures of boats set into black glass. The moon coasted high in the dark sky, and its light washed the low hills in blue light.

I heard an odd noise from the stern. Something was swimming back there. I flattened myself on the afterdeck and slithered aft. Poking my head over the edge of the deck, I looked down. A cluster of little figures in Speedo trunks were capering on the swim platform, cheering squeakily and slapping one another with tiny high-fives. As I watched, one little figure dived off the platform, while another cannon-balled into the warm Bahamian water.

The trolls. One of them produced a basket of mini-tumblers and a tiny bottle of Norsk Aquavit. I heard a tiny clink of tiny glasses.

"To 'ell vit' the shnow!" cried one tiny figure. "Dis is de life! I vill shtay!" He tossed his tiny glass in a long silvery arc over the dark water and flung himself overboard. I heard a chorus of ecstatic squeaking, and then all the others leaped in behind the leader. I could see tiny Vs of water opening behind them as they swam toward the dark mouths of the sea-caves and disappeared.

The morning dawned bright and still, already warm. The wooded shores lay dark against the clear blue sky, the water crystal-green below the boat and turquoise in the distance. A couple of sleek dolphins browsed easily among the anchored boats, their foreheads rising as they breathed, their dorsal fins slicing the water, mammals like ourselves, symbols of elegant adaptation at the interface of sea and air. A light wind ruffled the water.

March 15, I noted in the log. I started the diesel. Marjorie dropped the mooring line, and the little blue motor-sailer moved gently over the shallow bar, back into the Sea of Abaco. We raised all the sails and cut the engine. Greg was at the wheel.

"What course do I steer?" asked Greg.

"The course," I said, "for the first time in eight months, is zero-zero-zero. Due north."

ABOUT MAGNUS

Magnus is a Viksund MS-33 motor-sailer, built in Norway in 1973. Her Viksund Goldfish 31 hull was also used as the platform for a fishing boat version.

Magnus is 33' overall and 31' on deck, with a beam of 10'6", a draft of 3'10", and a displacement of 14,000 lb. She's ketch-rigged and double-ended, with a large aft cabin and a sheltered centre cockpit. She is heavily constructed to Det Norske Veritas standards – the Scandinavian equivalent of Lloyd's of London. The hull is almost unsinkable, with watertight bulkheads forward and aft of the engine room. The cabin sole is also sealed, and provides a double bottom. And all the many storage compartments under the berths and seats are glassed right to the hull.

Magnus has berths for up to eight people, which is ridiculous. The main salon has 6'5" headroom, a convertible dinette, and an inside steering station with a suite of new Raymarine instruments – autopilot, GPS, radar, speed and depth indicators, and VHF radio. The galley includes a refrigerator and freezer. A roomy head compartment contains an Air Head composting toilet

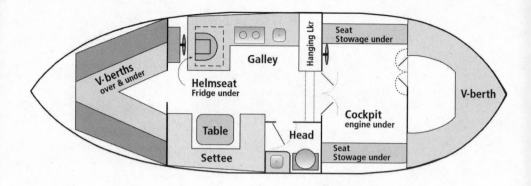

Magnus
Accommodations Plan
31' l.o.d. x 10'6" max. beam

and a sink with manual and pressure water, and a shower. Aft of the galley is a spacious hanging locker.

The front half of the huge cockpit sole lifts to reveal the 35-hp Yanmar diesel. The engine room also contains four deep-cycle house batteries, a separate starting battery, a battery combiner and smart-charger, a 1500W inverter, two electric bilge pumps and a manual one, plus the hot-water furnace that heats both cabins and also the domestic hot water. A good-sized "cargo hold" under the aft half of the cockpit holds spare parts, water hoses, extra anchors, folding bicycles, and other equipment.

The aft cabin – a guest room that also serves as an office – has two quarter berths that can be bridged to make another double.

Her sail plan includes a new full-battened, slab-reefing mainsail and mizzen, a stack-pack on the main, and a roller-furling jib. Half the standing rigging and much of the running rigging has been replaced. She has a Lofrans electric anchor windlass, a stainless platform on the bowsprit, with two bow rollers, and a stainless swim platform with integrated ladders at the stern.

For more detail on the boat, visit www.silverdonaldcameron.ca/magnus.html. *Magnus* absorbed a great deal of time and money before we left, but she proved to be exactly what we'd hoped for: a comfortable shoal-draft cruising vessel admirably suited to the Intracoastal Waterway and the Bahamas, and safe in the open sea.

VIKSUND BOATS

Established in 1966, Viksund Boats (in Norwegian, *Viksund Båt AS*) was among the first fibreglass boatbuilders in Scandinavia, and is still going strong. The company was founded by Erling Viksund (b. 1937), and is now managed by his son Rune. Viksund builds boats in Norway, Sweden, and Sri Lanka. It has produced more than six thousand boats, including boats for Asian and African fishermen, power yachts for European owners, and rescue vessels for the Greenland Coast Guard.